Southeast Asia
and the
Middle East

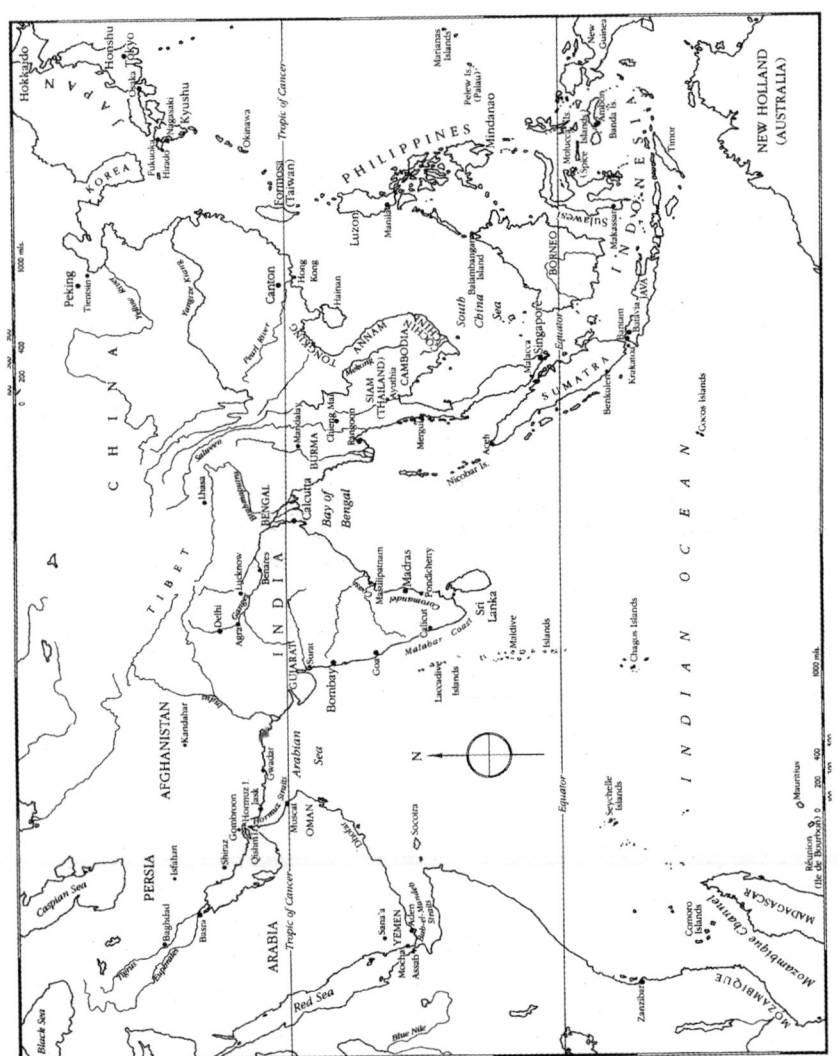

Southeast Asia and the Middle East: The Indian Ocean World

Southeast Asia and the Middle East

Islam, Movement, and the *Longue Durée*

Edited by
Eric Tagliacozzo

Stanford University Press
Stanford, California

© 2009 NUS Press

Stanford University Press
Stanford, California
Website: http://www.sup.org

ISBN:978-0-8047-6133-8 (pbk:alk.paper)

Published in the USA and CANADA by arrangement with National University of Singapore Press

NUS Press
National University of Singapore
AS3-01-02, 3 Arts Link
Singapore 117569
Website: http://www.nus.edu.sg/nuspress

All rights reserved. This book, or parts thereof, may not be reproduced in any form or by any means, electronic or mechanical, including photocopying, recording or any information storage and retrieval system now known or to be invented, without written permission from the Publisher.

This work is exclusively distributed and sold in the USA, its dependencies and Canada by Stanford University Press. Throughout the rest of the world, the work is exclusively distributed by National University of Singapore Press.

Stanford University Press Cataloging in Publication Data for this book is available at the Library of Congress.

Cover: Kuala Lumpur mosque with arabesque architecture
(Photograph Eric Tagliacozzo)

Printed in Singapore

Contents

Acknowledgments		vii
Orthographic Note		viii
1.	Southeast Asia and the Middle East: Charting Directions *Eric Tagliacozzo*	1

I. The Early Dimensions of Contact

2.	Finding Java: Muslim Nomenclature of Insular Southeast Asia from Śrîvijaya to Snouck Hurgronje *Michael Laffan*	17
3.	The Hajj, Islam, and Power among the Bugis in Early Colonial Riau *Timothy P. Barnard*	65
4.	The Origins and Contributions of Early Arabs in Malaya *Mohammad Redzuan Othman*	83

II. The Colonial Age

5.	The Middle East Connection and Reform and Revival Movements among the *Putihan* in 19th-century Java *M. C. Ricklefs*	111
6.	The Skeptic's Eye: Snouck Hurgronje and the Politics of Pilgrimage from the Indies *Eric Tagliacozzo*	135
7.	Challenging Inequality in a Modern Islamic Idiom: Social Ferment amongst Arabs in Early 20th-century Java *Sumit K. Mandal*	156

8. Southeast Asian Debates and Middle Eastern Inspiration: 176
European Dress in Minangkabau at the Beginning of the
20th Century
Nico J. G. Kaptein

III. The First Half of the 20th Century

9. Topics and Queries for a History of Arab Families and 199
Inheritance in Southeast Asia: Some Preliminary Thoughts
Michael Gilsenan

10. From Golden Youth in Arabia to Business Leaders in 235
Singapore: Instructions of a Hadrami Patriarch
Ulrike Freitag

11. M. Asad Shahab: A Portrait of an Indonesian Hadrami 250
Who Bridged the Two Worlds
Mona Abaza

IV. Into Modernity

12. Jihad and the Specter of Transnational Islam in 275
Contemporary Southeast Asia: A Comparative Historical
Perspective
John T. Sidel

13. Some Comparative Notes on Three Muslim Rebellion 319
Movements in Southeast Asia (Burma, Thailand, and the
Philippines)
Moshe Yegar

14. Political Islam in Post-Soeharto Indonesia: The Contest 349
between "Radical-Conservative Islam" and "Progressive-
Liberal Islam"
M. Syafi'i Anwar

Contributors 386

Index 388

Acknowledgments

This book took a long time to see the light of day and I am very grateful to a number of people and institutions for helping that process along. The idea started to germinate at the Asia Research Institute in Singapore in 2004, and I am grateful to that institution, and Tony Reid in particular as its former director, for funding a workshop that first explored some of the outlines of this topic. Several people who first presented papers at that meeting did not end up having their essays presented here, but I thank them nonetheless for their participation.

I am very grateful to Paul Kratoska, Muriel Bell, and Stacy Wagner for taking on the book. I am also very grateful to Sandy Lal and Joa Suorez for their patient editorial and organizational efforts, respectively, on behalf of the manuscript. I thank the anonymous reviewers, as well as, Michael Feener and Shawkat Toorawa, Associate Professors of Southeast Asian Islam and Arabic Literature at the National University of Singapore and Cornell University, respectively, who also contributed rigorous reads of the final accepted manuscript. I am very grateful to both of them. Finally, a number of scholars weighed in with suggestions and critiques over the years on how this book should ultimately look, and I wish to thank them for their input as well. Southeast Asia and the Middle East are often mentioned together in the news these days for reasons of violence, discord, and suspicion; in particularly bad months there seems to be little else connecting the two in the public domain of various media. This is a valid part of a larger story, but it is only a *part* of the story. I very much hope this book helps to complicate that narrative, and that the longer vantage — the *longue durée* of the book's sub-title — can be used to show this relationship in its fuller expression.

Eric Tagliacozzo
Ithaca, Autumn 2008

Orthographic Note

The huge geography and time period covered in this volume means that orthographic usages are mixed, and sometimes overlapping. I have endeavored to maintain some consistency where possible with a number of more common terms (for example, Hadrami, shaykh, Mecca, sharif, and sharifah), but this has not been possible in all cases due to the wide array of languages and nomenclatures in use from many different epochs and places. In allowing some leeway to individual contributors' orthographies I follow Louise Marlow's sensible approach to this problem in her recent edited volume, *Dreaming Across Boundaries: The Interpretation of Dreams in Islamic Lands* (Boston: ILEX and Cambridge, Mass.: Harvard University Press, 2008). Alongside Marlow, I also ask that any minor inconsistencies be indulged by the reader.

1

Southeast Asia and the Middle East: Charting Directions

ERIC TAGLIACOZZO

Introduction

Southeast Asia has enjoyed a long historical connection with the neighboring cultures of China and India. Many studies have investigated the nature of these contacts, showing us the long religious tendrils that brought Buddhism and Hinduism to classical Southeast Asia, as well as the vibrant commercial and diasporic avenues between China and the "lands beneath the winds." Any well-stocked university library will have dozens, if not scores, of titles on each of these oceanic connections.[1] Though the ties between Southeast Asia and the Middle East have also been extremely important in the past seven to eight centuries, there is a noticeable paucity of historiography on this particular trans-regional dialogue. This has become increasingly apparent in published studies of the historical period, but it is also true to a large degree in the contemporary world. Several good books exist on the Hadrami diaspora in the Indian Ocean.[2] There are also several extant works on education, religion, and trade connections between the Hejaz and Southeast Asia.[3] Nevertheless, we don't yet have a volume on what the parameters of this long-distance dialogue between civilizations have meant over the centuries. To address this lacuna, the present book explores the long-term nature of contact between Southeast Asia and the Middle East. The volume brings together a collection of scholars working on a broad spectrum of questions having to do with contact between these two arenas across the width of the Indian Ocean. The time frame for the study covers what the historian Fernand Braudel has called the temporal *longue durée*, which in this case is approximately 1,000 years.

Islam is one of the two primary foci of this book. Islam came to Southeast Asia no later than the end of the 13th century, as traders from the Indian subcontinent touched down in northern Sumatra and quickly spread into the rest of the Indonesian Archipelago.[4] By the early 16th century, almost a millennium after Muhammad spread his message across the Arabian Peninsula, parts of the coasts of insular Southeast Asia were professing various degrees of devotion to Islam. These adherents eventually spread up the Malay Peninsula, into the southern islands of the Philippines, and even onto limited stretches of territory on the Southeast Asian mainland. Yet how did Middle Eastern variants of Islam catch hold in Southeast Asia? Were the messages and forms that came identical to the ones that left the Hejaz, or did they undergo a process of transvaluation along the way? What are some of the useful ways of looking at transmission as a cultural, political, and religious phenomenon?

The second focus of the book is movement itself — the very act of travel between the Middle East and Southeast Asia over time. How were these two culture areas connected during the formative centuries of contact? How did the colonial age change these connections?[5] How are the two regions connected today? Have the means of civilizational dialogue changed, or are old forms still in operation? What are the mechanisms of communication between these two culture areas, and how have they evolved over time?

The present volume explores these questions and several interrelated sub-themes under the general rubric of Islam and movement, Southeast Asia and the Middle East. The idea of people in motion is one of these sub-themes, both for Hadramis (for instance) and for other actors who connected these two arenas. The bonds of religion itself are also important, both in their textual variants and as a matter of daily (or, in the case of the Hajj, seasonal) praxis. Education is also of great interest to the book, insofar as it was used as a linking tool between discrete geographical areas. Finally, culture and the Islamic public sphere are questioned, from the standpoint of both agency and transmission across trans-regional spaces. The volume investigates the long-term connections between Southeast Asia and the Middle East across all of these domains, both historically and in our own contemporary world.

The essays in this volume deal with the above questions through a variety of windows. The first quarter of the book explores the earliest dimensions of contact, predominantly before colonial control was achieved in the region. Michael Laffan starts off the discussion with an attempt at tracing the long-term meanings of two broad terms used in Arabic accounts for much of insular Southeast Asia. He argues that the first, *Zâbaj*, was connected to a world of the imagination, while the second, *Jâwa*, was very much bound up in notions of an expanding Muslim world. As such, his essay treats the two as separate, but related, parts of the *longue durée* of interactions between the Middle East and Southeast Asia. Laffan suggests four important points. First, he suggests that Arabic geographical knowledge as found in the cosmographies relied more on Greek sources and Malay toponyms than on any sustained communication with Indian sailors. Second, he argues that Jâwa only appears as a term in the 13th century by virtue of increased links binding China, Java, and West Asia. Third, he finds that the Arabic adjectival form for things Southeast Asian (Jâwî) was locally appropriated as meaning something Islamic. Finally, and somewhat tentatively, he suggests that there is a possibility that Malay conceptions of being "below the wind" may have helped the ancient term Zâbaj remain within cosmographies produced well into the modern period. This was the case even as Jâwîs took their places in Middle Eastern teaching circles in ever greater numbers over time.

The early period is also explored through places such as Riau, which had not yet borne the full brunt of European imperialism at the start of the 19th century. Timothy Barnard offers a second essay showing that prior to the advent of steam travel and the opening of the Suez Canal, very few Southeast Asians participated in the arduous journey to Mecca. In 1828, however, an important member of the Bugis elite of Riau, Raja Ahmad, participated in the Muslim pilgrimage. This marked the beginning not only of sustained numbers of Bugis pilgrimages, but also of an active recruiting of religious teachers from the Middle East who helped transform belief and understanding in Riau. The result, Barnard argues, was the construction of an elite who justified their presence through spiritual orthodoxy during a period in which their military and economic prowess was on the wane.

Mohammad Redzuan Othman continues this transnational thread by examining events on the (predominantly) precolonial Malay Peninsula. He posits that Arabs from the Middle East have exercised a great deal of influence in the Malay World, which started with their historical trading activities. Over time the customs and practices that they brought with them played a major role in converting the population of the Malay World to Islam. The Arabs who migrated and settled in Malaya, particularly from the middle of the 19th century, usually originated from the Hadramaut in Yemen. These Arabs often were successful entrepreneurs, and by using their wealth they played a significant role in spreading Middle Eastern understandings of Islam into Malay society. Islamization as a process undertaken by Arabs deepened the Malay bond with the Middle East, and ultimately it was felt in the important areas of both religion and education, opening a new chapter in their combined relationship. Othman states that since ancient times there had been an active Arab involvement with Southeast Asia, but after Islamization this became a two-way street, and increasingly Malays were making more journeys to the Middle East than Arabs did to the Malay World.

The second quarter of the book tackles the question of how an imposed milieu of European colonialism changed some of the context of the relationship between Southeast Asia and the Hejaz. M. C. Ricklefs is the first to bring the volume into the high colonial age. In 19th-century Java, he tells us, links between Java and the Middle East facilitated the spread of Islamic reform and revival movements, especially among the emerging Javanese middle class. Arabs and other international Muslim communities living on the *pasisir* were important in this development. Technology also played a role, particularly the spread of printing, the advent of steam shipping, and the opening of the Suez Canal in 1869, with all three phenomena encouraging an increase in pilgrimages from Java. The number of religious schools started to grow. Both Sufi *tarekats* and more *shari'a*-oriented approaches were represented among the reform movements. Messianism surrounding the turn of the 14th Islamic century (AH 1300/1882–83 CE) also played a role. The Middle East was clearly important in stimulating Islamic reform in Java. This was, however, only one part of the complex religious scene in 19th-century Java, as in some ways devout Javanese *putihan* were distancing themselves from others among their Javanese neighbors.

The high colonial age also offered unprecedented opportunities to travel between the opposite sides of the Indian Ocean, and this travel was facilitated by a sequence of influential imperial administrators. Tagliacozzo's essay suggests that the great Indies scholar/politician C. Snouck Hurgronje was an unusual yet important figure in this respect — a serious scholar of the Islamic world in all of its breadth, a patient listener for Southeast Asian Muslims themselves, but also a loyal agent of a coercive and increasingly paranoid Dutch colonial state. At the *fin de siècle* he acted as a facilitator for colonial subjugation and control, but at the same time he seemed to be ambivalent about his occupation and allegiances. Tagliacozzo's paper examines one important facet of Snouck

Hurgronje's dealings with Southeast Asia and the Middle East — the annual pilgrimage to Mecca of thousands of archipelago pilgrims. In order to fulfill this pillar of faith, a deepening stream of Hajjis and Hajjas transited across the Indian Ocean, and Snouck was deputized to chronicle and examine their voyages, both as part of this job and also as a component of his own education. Snouck wrote voluminously about the Southeast Asian Hajj, and his surviving missives on the subject — many of them personal in nature and not intended to be read by a large audience — often differ greatly from his official tracts on the topic. Tagliacozzo says that an examination of Snouck's Dutch-language correspondence elucidates much about how he conceptualized the pilgrimage as a transmission conduit of both Islam and extremism, the latter being something that the Netherlands Indies regime greatly feared. The author tells us that it is especially through these private letters that we can see Snouck's erudition, political leanings, and own moral sensibilities converging in the topic of pilgrimage, producing a useful glimpse into Dutch attitudes about the religion of their subject populations at the turn of the 20th century. Tagliacozzo critiques Snouck's own conceptions and the thoughts of his critics on the issue of the pilgrimage, and he asks how the Hajj can be utilized to understand crucial trends of coercion, control, and spiritual movement in a maturing colonial landscape.

If the Hajj encouraged travel, then people who self-identified as "Arab" could be found on both sides of the Indian Ocean, only partially as a result of such pilgrimages. Sumit K. Mandal focuses on the turn-of-the-century Dutch Indies and explores the religious and political engagement of the Arab community in colonial Java. He focuses specifically on the broadly defined struggles for justice and equality that characterized the years of the *pergerakan,* the years of "movement" in the early 20th century when anticolonial strivings were set in motion. At this time, Mandal tells us, the social hierarchy within Arab communities from the Hadramaut was affirmed by the hierarchical structure of colonial society. Ahmad Soerkati, a Mecca-trained scholar of Sudanese origin, articulated the first serious challenge to this hierarchy and inspired the rise of the organization Al-Irsjad in 1915. This organization's articulation and its critique of the entrenched social hierarchy of Arabs had much wider ramifications, as it generated dialogues between residents of colonial urban centers in Southeast Asia and Cairo, making an impact not only in Java but in the Hadramaut itself. To leaders of the *pergerakan,* the issues raised by the Irsjadis reflected a striving for democracy and equal rights. As such, the

Irsjadis' critique of authority was not only a democratic struggle against an antiquated social system transplanted from the Hadramaut (as one colonial observer believed), but also an attack on rank and privilege in colonial society itself.

The colonial rubric ends with an essay dealing with the controversy that arose in Minangkabau, West Sumatra, at the beginning of the 20th century between the Kaum Muda and Kaum Tua, two important social and religious groups. Nico Kaptein focuses in particular on the dispute over the permissibility of men wearing European dress items, such as trousers and neckties. These debates took place at a time when rapid changes in social and cultural circumstances were occurring and the traditional Islamic religious worldview was under severe threat. Interestingly, both camps invoked the authority of their kindred spirits in the Middle East. Kaptein shows in detail how these Middle Eastern ideas on dress were transmitted to and received in Southeast Asia. As an example, he illustrates how the Kaum Muda position, as voiced by Haji Abdullah Ahmad (1878–1933) of Padang, was derived from the Egyptian reformist journal *al-Manâr*; and how the Kaum Tua position, as voiced by Chatib Ali (1861–1936), originated from a great Meccan mufti of the era, ʿAbd Allâh ibn Muḥammad Ṣâliḥ al-Zawâwî (1850–1924). Amongst other things, the paper demonstrates that at the beginning of the 20th century the traditional hegemony of Mecca as the foremost intellectual center for Southeast Asian Islam was finally coming to an end. Other centers, such as Cairo, could now challenge this predominance.

The third section of the volume centers around families and specific personalities in the first half of the 20th century. The *fin de siècle* was an era of great flux, when individuals and clans could possess significant weight in quickly changing times. In this light, Michael Gilsenan analyzes the connections between family, law, property, and the state in the context of the Hadrami Arab migrations to colonial Southeast Asia in the early 20th century. The law in question in Gilsenan's case is both English and Islamic. Gilsenan finds that legal practices clashed, amalgamated, mutually influenced each other, and changed over time. The inheritance and transmission of goods and properties in the Hadrami diaspora presented particular problems and opportunities. Landed property, or *real* estate as we would now call it, became for elite groups the core of family fortunes in Singapore and Java, fortunes that equally affected the Hadramaut in Yemen. Wills and settlements quickly became grounds for dispute, with long-term implications over diasporic spaces. Such families were "legalized," and issues of gender from the beginning played a significant role in colonial courts, often deciding whether wills were "Mahomedan" or English. Drawing on two case reports, Gilsenan seeks to draw out some of the key issues that structured the constitution of family practices, narratives, and fortunes over space and time. He also highlights the analytical questions such materials pose to the researcher in trying to write about such questions in the first place.

The diaspora of clans and kin-affiliated groups had other important resonances besides those affecting law and property. Ulrike Freitag also focuses on the Hadrami community in Southeast Asia, and the questions she asks in her contribution are: how did people organize their journeys across the Indian Ocean before the advent of modern mass travel and communications? How did family businesses operate when branches of these same families were spread between the Arabian Peninsula and Southeast Asia, possibly with offshoots in East Africa, Egypt, and India at the same time? The document at the heart of Freitag's article is a letter of advice from the scion of a major Arab business family in Hadramaut to his younger relatives, the latter about to take over management of a Singapore-based firm. This single letter cannot answer all of the questions asked in the Introduction to this volume, but Freitag provides glimpses into the practicalities of long-distance travel and business management over a large diasporic space such as the Indian Ocean. At the same time, she searches for insights into the ideals of handling personal lives in these transnational situations.

Mona Abaza also focuses on the Yemeni diaspora by examining the biography of a Jakarta-born intellectual of Hadrami origin, Sayyid Mohammad Asad Allah bin Ali bin Ahmad bin Abdallah bin al-Hussayn bin Shahab al-Din (SMAS, born 1910). SMAS spent 18 years in Saudi Arabia and traveled widely in the Muslim world and Europe. By looking closely at the life of this "hybrid intellectual" who spent most of his days moving between the diverse geographic worlds of Islam, Abaza aims to make him an exemplar of the "intermediary," or the "go-between" among the different cultures of the Muslim world. Abaza analyzes three Arabic texts written by SMAS: one is the novel *Min samîm al-wâqi'* (*From the Innermost Reality: An Indonesian Novel*), subtitled "A Story Without Any Female Characters," which he published in Beirut. SMAS wrote that all of his novels were based on true stories, and that he tried to transform these into narratives; *Min samim al-waqe`* was the eighth novel that he wrote. Abaza contextualizes his writings within the global politics of the time and the shifting worlds of Islam. The two nonfiction books she discusses, *Pages from Contemporary Indonesian History* and *A Journey to the Interior of the Moro Islands*, address a wide Arabic public and inform the readers about the political situation in Southeast Asia at that particular time.

The last quarter of the book focuses on the movement of the Southeast Asia-Middle East relationship into the tenuous "modernity" of our own times. John Sidel starts off by offering a rejoinder to the literature on religious violence in Southeast Asia recently written by self-proclaimed "terrorism experts," who stress the role of Islamist networks closely linked to Al-Qaeda. In contrast, the paper stresses the breadth of transnational linkages between Southeast Asia and the Middle East, as well as the significance of other transnational forces promoting Christianity and secularization in the region. Against the terrorism experts' tendency to adopt a prosecutorial or "whodunit" mode of analysis, Sidel's essay pursues a less actor-centered, more structural analysis of the contexts in which violence in avowed defense or promotion of Islam has appeared in Southeast Asia over the past several years. At the outset, the paper poses a set of comparative questions as to the timing, location, targets, and forms of agency and mobilization associated with "jihad" in the popular sense of the term. The piece then traces and compares the diverging trajectories of the institutions and identities associated with Islam in the Philippines and Indonesia against a backdrop of national and international developments. Situated against this comparative historical and sociological backdrop, the violence perpetrated under the banner of Islam in Southeast Asia is shown to reflect not simply the machinations of Al-Qaeda and its local allies in the region, but a broader set of sociological and political changes in Southeast Asia and the Muslim world.

This concern with modern forms of Islamic transnationalism across the Indian Ocean continues in the remaining two essays of the book. Moshe Yegar argues that in recent decades, radical Islamic ideas have found their adherents in many Muslim (and other) countries, including those in Southeast Asia. He analyzes the relationship between the majority governments and three Muslim minority insurrection movements of Southeast Asia: the Muslim community of the southern Philippines (the Moros), the Malay-Muslim community of southern Thailand (the Patani Muslims), and the Rohingya Muslims of Arakan in western Burma. Yegar finds that the history of those three communities, as well as their motives for rebellion and their sources of inspiration, are different and distinct. Despite this, there are also distinguishable similarities. Yegar's essay compares these similarities as well as differences and indicates the options open to the "rebels" on the one hand, and to the three non-Muslim majority governments on the other. Yegar also queries to what extent the Muslim world at large, and Arab countries in particular, have shown any interest in those movements.

Syafi'i Anwar closes the collection by focusing on one of the most important developments of political Islam in post-Soeharto Indonesia: the contest between "radical-conservative Islam" (RCI) and "progressive-liberal Islam" (PLI). He argues that since the collapse of Soeharto's New Order regime, these two conflicting groups have been very active in promoting their ideas and gaining public support in Indonesia. Currently, the contest between these two groups not only creates controversial polemics and public debates, but also has serious political implications for Indonesian society as a whole. Interestingly, both the RCI and PLI camps have intellectual roots in and linkages with the Middle East. Anwar says that there is a clear process in the transmission of religio-political thought from the Middle East to Indonesia, which affects mind-sets and actions in both radical and liberal Islamic groups within Indonesian society. Anwar analyzes the contours of this contest between the RCI and PLI camps within contemporary Indonesian politics. He discusses how such transmission takes place, and the ways in which the two contesting groups disseminate their competing ideas. His paper also examines the ongoing tension between the two groups with regard to the future of Indonesian politics.

Though the present volume seeks to answer a number of important questions about the nature of contact between Southeast Asia and the Middle East, the book also points out a set of interrelated questions that still need to be problematized through further research. First among these, perhaps, is whether Islam is itself the central axis — the spine — of the *longue durée* relationship between the two culture areas. Is this true, or is there really no central spoke to speak of, with the history of secular contact between the desert and the tropics looming just as large as any religious connection between the two?[6] Ethnic markings also need to be deconstructed, as "Arabs," "Hadramis," and "Bumiputras" have all been self-categorized or categorized by the state as Muslim Southeast Asians, but in different ways and under different historical conditions. How flexible and how rigid have these categories been? Have they changed over geographic spaces, over time, and across various regional customs?[7] Finally, how much continuity and change has there been in Islamic ties generally between Southeast Asia and the Middle East, especially *vis-à-vis* important events such as the opening of the Suez Canal (in 1869), the end of World War I and the dissolution of the Ottoman Empire (in 1918 and after), the age of decolonization (1940s–60s), and even 11 September 2001? Were any of these Braudelian "epi-phenomena" crucial in changing Islam as it traveled in its many variants between Southeast Asia and the Middle East?

Two related questions concerning the movement of ideas, material, and people across the conduit of the Indian Ocean also loom as crucial in any discussion of the *longue durée* and Islam. The first of these involves directionality, and the tabulation of what exactly was moving either east or west across the vast maritime divide between Southeast Asia and the Middle East. It is clear that the westward channel was taken by Hajjis, workers, and students eager to study in the great centers of learning in the Middle East. Flowing in the opposite direction were *fatwas*, Hadramis, and waves of religious change, among many other objects, ideas, and human beings. Yet how did these flows change over time, from precolonial to colonial to postcolonial eras?[8] A second, somewhat related question involves the nature of national vs. transnational experience between Southeast Asia and the Middle East, as these designations have changed over the centuries. It may not always be appropriate to speak of "Malaysian" or "Singaporean" or "Indonesian" forms when these places were constituted differently at various points in time. Thus, it may be that some of the patterns of what are today Malaysian Penang and independent Singapore (both of which a century ago were amalgamated under the British Straits Settlements) may have had more in common in these questions than different, far-flung parts of what is today a united Malaysian state. These are the kinds of questions that this volume elicits and answers in particular times and places, though a more comprehensive explanation of these trends must be left to future research. It is hoped that these 14 essays will help point the way, however, toward an eventual unraveling of some of these questions.

One phenomenon that appears over and over again in many of the essays in this book is a palpable longing for the Middle East by Southeast Asians in a variety of temporal periods and locales. Was this a longing for a Middle Eastern style of life, replete with chadors, religious injunctions, and Wahhabi-inspired Islam? It certainly was not. But many, if not most, Muslim Southeast Asians seem to have a deep sense of the Middle East as being important to them in one way or another, as a site of sacredness, as a site of history, and as a site of the beginnings of their faith.[9] Millions of contemporary Muslim schoolchildren all over Southeast Asia study Arabic via the Qur'an, even as they are exposed to American movies, British football, French fashion, and Japanese scooters. In fact, it may not be out of place to suggest that the Middle East represents an "alternative modernity" to many Southeast Asians in some ways, to cultural paradigms long since presented by the colonial projects and postcolonial big capital of the West. This is an idea that the current volume explores as well — whether the Middle East should only be seen as a site, and as an idea, of the past to Southeast Asians, or whether it may indeed represent something modern and continually evolving at the same time.[10] The contributions in this book query these and many other characteristics of the centuries-long embrace between Southeast Asia and the Middle East, as people, products, and ideas have traveled the vast spaces of the Indian Ocean over the last 1,300 years.

Notes

1. There is a large industry of South Asian scholars, in particular, writing about these early contacts, with almost all of these books being published by Indian presses. Studies on the connections between China and Southeast Asia have had more eclectic provenances, including China, Southeast Asia, and the work of scholars from Japan and the West.
2. See, for example, Huub de Jonge and Nico Kaptein, eds., *Transcending Borders: Arabs, Politics, Trade, and Islam in Southeast Asia* (Leiden: KITLV Press, 2002); Natalie Mobini-Kesheh, *The Hadrami Awakening: Community and Identity in the Netherlands East Indies, 1900–1942* (Ithaca: SEAP, 1999); and Ulrike Freitag and William Clarence-Smith, eds., *Hadhrami Traders, Scholars, and Statesmen in the Indian Ocean, 1750s–1960s* (Leiden: Brill, 1997).
3. Important in these respects are Mona Abaza, *Indonesian Students in Cairo: Islamic Education, Perceptions, and Exchanges* (Paris: Cahier d'Archipel, 23, 1994); Michael Laffan, *Islamic Nationhood and Colonial Indonesia: The Umma below the Winds* (London: RoutledgeCurzon, 2003); David Parkin and Stephen Headley, eds., *Islamic Prayer across the Indian Ocean* (London: Curzon, 2000); and Patricia Risso, *Merchants and Faith: Muslim Commerce and Culture in the Indian Ocean* (Boulder, CO: Westview Press, 1995).
4. Books on the genesis of Islam in Southeast Asia are numerous; see Peter Riddel, *Islam and the Malay-Indonesian World: Transmission and Responses* (Honolulu: University of Hawai'i Press, 2001); Ahmad Ibrahim, Sharon Siddique, and Yasmin Hussain, eds., *Readings on Islam and Southeast Asia* (Singapore: ISEAS, 1985); Mohamad Taib Osman, ed., *Islamic Civilization*

in the Malay World (Kuala Lumpur: Dewan Bahasa dan Pustaka, 1997); and Taufik Abdullah, *Islam di Asia Tenggara* (Jakarta: LIPI, 1976).

5. This crucial question, which bridges the age of transmission and our own time period, has indeed received some attention. See Moshe Yegar, *Islam and Islamic Institutions in British Malaya: Policies and Implementation* (Jerusalem: Magnus Press, 1979); Deliar Noer, *The Modernist Muslim Movement in Indonesia, 1900–1942* (Singapore: Oxford University Press, 1973); Karel Steenbrink, *Dutch Colonialism and Indonesian Islam: Contacts and Conflicts, 1596–1950* (Amsterdam: Radopi, 1993); Karel Steenbrink, *Beberapa Aspek Tentang Islam di Indonesia Abad Ke-19* (Jakarta: Bulan Bintang, 1984); and C. Snouck Hurgronje, *Mekka in the Latter Part of the Nineteenth Century: Daily Life, Customs and Learning of the Moslims of the East Indian Archipelago* (Leiden: Brill, 1931).

6. It is indisputable, for example, that the Hajj — religious by definition as one of the five pillars of Islam — is the most active conveyor belt between Southeast Asia and the Middle East. Yet plenty of Southeast Asian Muslims also use the Hajj to visit friends, undertake business, and even engage in tourism as part of their time in the Middle East. This fact complicates this "wholly religious" practice considerably. See, for example, F.E. Peters, *The Muslim Pilgrimage to Mecca and the Holy Places* (Princeton: Princeton University Press, 1994); Michael Wolfe, *One Thousand Roads to Mecca: Ten Centuries of Travelers Writing About the Muslim Pilgrimage* (New York: Grove Press, 1997); William Roff, "The Meccan Pilgrimage: Its Meaning for Southeast Asian Islam," in Raphael Israeli and Anthony Johns, eds., *Islam in Asia* (II) (Boulder: Westview Press, 1984), 238–45; and Robert Bianchi, *Guests of God* (New York: Oxford University Press, 2004).

7. This question is particularly important among Southeast Asian Muslims who are not citizens of Muslim-majority states. For an overview, see Moshe Yegar, *Between Integration and Succession: The Muslim Communities of the Southern Philippines, Southern Thailand, and Western Burma/Myanmar* (Lanham, MD: Lexington Books, 2002); Raymond Scupin, "Thai Muslims in Bangkok: Islam and Modernization in a Buddhist Society," PhD dissertation, University of California Santa Barbara, 1978; Moshe Yegar, *The Muslims of Burma: A Study of a Minority Group* (Wiesbaden: Harrassowitz Verlag, 1972); and Peter Gowing, *Muslim Filipinos: Heritage and Horizon* (Quezon City: New Day Publishers, 1979). For a wider, theoretical lens, see Robert Hefner et al., *Islam in an Era of Nation-States* (Honolulu: University of Hawai'i Press, 1997), particularly the Introduction.

8. Understanding the nature of the exchanges was deemed to be of vital importance to colonial governments; the movement of so many people, after all, was seen to be potentially dangerous as part of pan-Islamic movements. For period views on this, see the articles by the great Indies scholar L. van den

Berg: "Het Pan-Islamisme," *Gids, De* 4 (1900): 228, and "Het Kruis Tegenover de Halve Maan," *Gids, De* 4 (1890): 68. For more modern historiography on this subject, see Tom van den Berge, "Indie, en de Panislamitische Pers (1897–1909)," *Jambatan* 5, 1 (1987): 15–24; D.H. Evans, "The Meanings of Pan-Islamism: The Growth of International Consciousness among the Muslims of Indonesia in the Late Nineteenth and Early Twentieth Centuries," *Itinerario* 9, 1 (1987); and Anthony Reid, "Nineteenth Century Pan-Islam in Indonesia and Malaysia," *JAS* 26, 2 (1967): 267–83.
9. For the idea of a Muslim centrality in global societies, see Marshall Hodgson, "The Role of Islam in World History," *International Journal of Middle Eastern Studies* 1, 2 (1970): 99–122.
10. The question of what the Middle East represents in a larger, civilizational context to world history has been taken up before. See, for example, David Gilmartin, "A Networked Civilization?", in *Muslim Networks from Hajj to Hip Hop*, ed. Miriam Cooke and Bruce Lawrence (Chapel Hill: University of North Carolina Press, 2005), pp. 51–68; and Edmund Burke, "Islamic History as World History," *International Journal of Middle Eastern Studies* 10, 2 (1979): 241–64.

I

The Early Dimensions of Contact

Traditional Apothecary, Sanaʿa, Yemen (Photograph E. Tagliacozzo)

2

Finding Java: Muslim Nomenclature of Insular Southeast Asia from Śrîvijaya to Snouck Hurgronje

MICHAEL LAFFAN

Introduction

In his account of Mecca as he saw it in 1885, Christiaan Snouck Hurgronje observed how the pilgrims and resident scholars from Southeast Asia were known to locals individually as Jâwî (or Jâwiyya for a woman), and collectively as the Jâwa or Jâwiyîn.[1] All these terms are related to the toponym that served in Arabic to define both Java the island and Southeast Asia the region, namely, Jâwa. But just as the boundaries of that toponym were unclear in the 1880s, so too were the parameters of these related ethnic ascriptions. Despite continuing encounters with Southeast Asian pilgrims, scholars, and guest workers in Saudi Arabia, or the regular sight of students of Cairo's famous al-Azhar University (greeted by local touts crying "Yâ Malayzî! Malayzî!"), the image of Southeast Asia and its peoples remains somewhat vague in the Middle East.

Of course, most outsiders to any region of the world are seldom able to distinguish the precise origins of the peoples they see, and thus group them in broadly similar, if not unitary, terms. This is not to say, however, that one should not perceive Southeast Asian unity at certain levels, particularly in terms of its underlying culture and history. One of the most influential advocates of Southeast Asia as an enduring fact has been Anthony Reid, who writes, "those who travel to Southeast Asia, from China, India, or anywhere else know at once that they are in a different place. In part this is a matter of environment."[2] Nevertheless, like Jâwa in the 19th century, the boundaries of this environment were always fuzzy.

Writing of the sea route to Siam in the late 17th century, one Persian, Muḥammad Rabîʿ b. Muḥammad Ibrâhîm, paused to note the following:

> ... there is not really a clear separation between the seas we crossed. An ordinary traveller would not be able to perceive where one sea ended and the next began. As for the various great gulfs, although they are usually designated by separate names, they are really all joined together. They flow from the same direction and merge in the Great Ocean. The scholars of travel and geography, confronted with many different place names, some near to each other and some separated by great distances, have wandered into the discords of choppy seas, doldrums and foul winds and they divide the great expanse of waters which lies along this path into seven distinct parts. They insist that each tract be defined as separate and distinct and have decided to ascribe a different name to every section.[3]

Even if the seas were all one, Muḥammad Rabîʿ still accepted that Siam, Java, Makassar, and Aceh were kingdoms distinct from mainland India and Sri Lanka and were treatable under the rubric "below the winds" (*Zîrbâdât*).[4] This conception has certainly captivated later writers, even if its boundaries — real and imagined — are always being tested.[5] Thus, it is worth casting an eye over the *longue durée* of interaction between Southeast and West Asia to find that while much of maritime Asia was often seen as a unitary zone, neither Jâwa nor Zîrbâdât have been as consistently placed as one might think.

The Classical Geographers, the Golden Khersonese, and Suvarṇadvîpa

The Islamic geographical tradition, with its occasional insistence on distinct seas and tracts of habitable earth, has its roots in both the Greek tradition and the tradition of India, whose imagined space of "al-Hind" could be problematic for these part-heirs of Claudius Ptolemy (ca. 87–ca. 150).[6] Before turning to what they made of the lands on the borders of China (al-Ṣîn), or yet attempting to use what they said to construct an argument about what may have happened there, it is worth examining what both earlier traditions may say about Southeast Asia in light of some of the recent research in the region itself.

The Greek and Indian geographical traditions were a by-product of oceanic trade. The prestige products of the archipelago — chiefly gold, resins, spices, and rare woods — have made their way to the courts and kitchens of India, Africa, China, and Europe since antiquity. For example, cloves, found solely on the remote island of Ternate, were known in Rome in the first century and had already been in use in China before then.[7] Another export, camphor, was known to Galen (129–ca. 216). Its Greek name (κάφουρα) probably derives from the Malay *kapur* via the Sanskrit *karpûra*. The modern English, on the other hand, comes from the Arabic *kâfûr*. There is even a Qur'ânic reference (76:5) to *kâfûr*-infused wine as a heavenly reward for the righteous, which is played against the punishments awaiting those who are ungrateful (*kafûr*^{an}) to God.

Pre-existing intra-regional exchange and the use of products such as cloves and camphor across Asia, however, do not necessarily imply that there was always a continuous and integrated network of maritime trade stretching between Rome and China. Present indications are that Southeast Asia was more a terminus for two global routes than the crossroads it was to become from the second century, and more especially once its courts adopted, by the late fourth century, forms of Buddhism or protected cults of Viśnu and Śiva, which Pierre-Yves Manguin has observed were manifested in a remarkably uniform aesthetic sense.[8]

Once a recognizably Indianized maritime Southeast Asia did become that crossroads, the stability of some of its component states could be subject to political developments at its market termini. Once the Sui dynasty (590–618) restored officially sanctioned Southeast Asia trade — traditionally designated under the guise of "tribute" — there were political repercussions along the coast of present-day Vietnam.[9] By the same token, later moments of instability in the southern Chinese ports, such as riots and the sacking of Guangzhou attributed to Arab and Persian pirates in 758,[10] or the famous massacre of Muslim merchants there during the Huang Chao rebellion 30 years later, may well have been a boon for insular Southeast Asia. Writing in the 12th century, al-Idrîsî (1100–65), of whom we shall hear much more, remarked that if ever China was convulsed by troubles, the (Muslim) merchants would descend to the harbors of a place they called Zâbaj.[11] It is these harbors that will concern us in much of what follows.

Even if cloves and camphor were to be found in the Mediterranean by the time of Galen at the latest, the imagined source of these goods did not then go beyond a fantastically wealthy region called the Golden Peninsula.[12] Such gilded images were probably transmitted into the Greek by Pharaonic and Indian sources, sources we now lack. Whatever the link, as maritime trade linking the Mediterranean to the Indian(ized) Ocean did expand, there would have been a parallel process of its scholarly unveiling until the time that Ptolemy, working in Alexandria, was able to assign names to several Southeast Asian ports.

Based on the sailors' itineraries he assembled and criticized, these included the tantalizing destinations of Iabadiû, Sabadibae, and Zábai.[13] Whereas scholars once placed the first two in insular Southeast Asia and the latter as mainland Champa,[14] or else argued for identifications within maritime Southeast Asia for each individually,[15] all three seem to be derived, by different linguistic paths, from the one identification echoing the Sanskrit Yavadvîpa, i.e., "the island of Yava" referred to in the Ramâyâna of Vâlmîki (see below). While its exact meaning is debatable, Waruno Mahdi has argued that this (first) Yava should not be confused with Java, but should instead be identified as pertaining to a Sumatran kingdom lying in the Batang Hari river basin, which appears to have arisen by the second century of the Common Era.[16] For our purposes, we should also note that he moreover suggests that it was influential on the Malay Peninsula, and that its name was most likely pronounced as Jaba by the sea peoples who facilitated its trade with the wider world.[17]

Before considering the ramifications of this argument, we should also keep another, perhaps overlapping, alternative in mind, and see Yava/Jaba as a yet larger regional complex that straddled the Sunda Straits, and to view the term as reflecting a broader ethnonym as a consequence. Indeed, if we consider the shared regional aesthetic noted by Manguin and the curious fact that later Javanese inscriptions (and inscriptions of their mainland contemporaries) group almost all Indonesian peoples under the rubric of Jâwa (compare the Khmer and Cham variant Jvâ),[18] one might well conclude that this term was long synonymous with a broader identity, and even that its sea-oriented peoples were the primary transmitters of Indianized culture into the region, including the Pallava script, from which the Malays, Javanese, and Khmers all derived their own writing systems.

Just as Ptolemaic knowledge of the region was a by-product of commerce, the preceding Indian knowledge of Southeast Asia would have been generated by expanded trade, with which this spread of Indic religion and scribal culture was integral. R.B. Sarkar once suggested that the wider dissemination of Buddhism during the reign of King Aśoka (r. 270–230 BCE) first altered the textual representation of Southeast Asia from a few vaguely defined lands to the south of Burma called Suvarṇabhûmi ("the land of gold") to Suvarṇadvîpa ("the isle of gold") as one of a series of entrepôt ports on the way to China.[19]

Then again, Sarkar did remark that around ca. 300 BCE there were already two major Southeast Asian landfalls seemingly known to Indian scholars. In the Râmâyana these are Suvarnarûpyakadvîpa and Yavadvîpa (which we have already encountered), but they seem to have been confused and conflated. Sarkar — anticipating Mahdi — argued that the name Yavadvîpa may well have been applied first to Sumatra and then, by extension, to its more easterly neighbor.[20] Such Indian confusions would also seem to presage the Ptolemaic duplications and, as we shall see, much later usage of Jâwa as an Islamic coverall voiced outside insular Southeast Asia. However, what concerns us here is no longer the location of "Java" per se, but an entity whose rulers inscribed a genealogical link to a place called Yava as a past model for emulation.

Śrîvijaya: Pretender to the Claims of "Yava"?

The multiethnic crews plying the routes from India and China always knew full well what islands they lay off. But as we are now bereft of their charts (if they ever used them) and most firsthand accounts of their kingdoms, we can only partially reconstruct the histories of their states from epigraphic data. The most enigmatic of these is perhaps Śrîvijaya (lit. "resplendent victory"), an entity that has left little in the way of major temples and monuments found in Cambodia, Champa, and Java.

Georges Coedès first suggested in 1918 that Śrîvijaya is identifiable with an entrepôt established at Palembang in the seventh century. Subsequent archeological finds have lent weight to this conclusion.[21] As a part of this, too, inscriptions placed as far afield as Chaiya, on the eastern side of the Isthmus of Kra, in 775, seemed to show that the same Śrîvijaya claimed influence over large parts of the Malay Peninsula in the eighth century — most likely by virtue of aspirations of monopolizing passing Indo-Chinese trade.

Such ideas, though, have been challenged of late. Michel Jacq-Hergoualc'h asserts that the China trade became important only after the Abbasid Revolution (and thus almost a century after the birth of Śrîvijaya).[22] Similarly, Mahdi's most recent work throws the longevity of Śrîvijayan paramountcy into serious doubt, and seems to point to earlier Sumatran claims over the peninsula being taken on from Java by the eighth century; though he is at pains to argue that the Śailendra Dynasty, best known for the commissioning of the Borobudur, had in fact come from Sumatra in the first place.[23]

Even if Coedès's notions of a long-lasting archipelagic empire are these days being recast in terms of it being more an occasional paragon state or a *primus inter pares*, Śrîvijaya sat in a Southeast Asian web of trade and competition. Sheldon Pollock furthermore suggests that it is reasonable to regard Śrîvijaya — like the subsequent kingdoms of Java and Angkor, which seem to have competed for influence over the Malay Peninsula — as participating in a wider ecumene that made use of Sanskrit for the declarative statements of its inscriptions and temples.[24] Pollock argues that this community was fragmented only in later centuries, when Sanskrit was abandoned by the courts — both in Southeast Asia and in India itself. This is perhaps true only in part, given that the majority of the surviving Śrîvijayan inscriptions were inscribed in Old Malay — albeit a Malay that invoked the authority of Sanskrit.

Indeed, while Palembang may well have claimed the role of suzerain over the straits from time to time, this would not have prevented rival cities from seeking alternate patrons, nor yet from sending occasional tribute of their own to China. One such rival was Malayu, sited at Jambi, which, according to one interpretation of the remarks of the monk Yijing, came under Śrîvijayan control only ca. 670 (see below).[25] Arguably, the Śrîvijaya encountered by outsiders was probably always a shifting zone of entrepôts that could coalesce for mutual interest, much like the estuarine polities that constituted Champa, or even Kra. This multicentered identity will prove of relevance when we turn to the Arab accounts.

Even with its various centers, Pollock is probably right to see Śrîvijaya as part of a wider Indianized world that involved Java.[26] On first inspection, this is seemingly made clear by an inscription at the Buddhist monastery of Nâlandâ, in Bihar (India), and datable to ca. 849 or 860. This records a sizeable endowment made by a ruler called Bâlaputra, the mahârâja of Suvarṇadvîpa.[27] It also outlines a dynastic link with a "land of Java" (Yavabhûmî), stating that Bâlaputra is the grandson of its former Śailendra king.[28] Such a linkage is also discernible from the older Chaiya inscription, whose two sides — the earlier perhaps Śrîvijayan and the later certainly Śailendran — are arguably related.[29]

Whereas Jordaan and Colless argue for an enduring Java at the heart of the archipelago, and one led by an Indian dynasty,[30] one might well conceive of an earlier Sumatran dynasty that extended its Malay hegemony into Java for a time. Certainly recent archeological finds in West Java seem to suggest that the earlier Śailendra "foreigners" may well have come from Sumatra.[31]

Yet their line could not last forever there either. Marijke Klokke, for one, has suggested that dynastic inscriptions in Java indicate that there was a "local" Śaivite interregnum in central Java between 803 (a year before the first known Javanese inscription) and 827. Coupled with this, it is hard to ignore the coincidence of Jayavarman II of Cambodia's inscription of 802, at which time he chose his moment to seek independence from (a presumably weakened) "Jvâ."[32]

The problem thus remains the identification of the Yava known to Śrîvijayans, Khmers, and Śailendrans alike, which will prove of wider relevance below. One Śrîvijayan inscription of 686, found on the island of Bangka, records both the incorporation of Kota Kapur ("Camphor Town") and preparations for an attack on "the land of Jâwa that is not submissive to Śrîvijaya."[33] This has often been identified as the west Javanese Taruma.[34] But, bearing in mind Mahdi's arguments, the unsubmissive land of Jâwa in the Kota Kapur inscription could indeed be understood as an erstwhile peninsular vassal of Malayu.

Ambiguity about Yava abounds on all sides of the South China Sea. Speaking of events some 90 years after the Kota Kapur inscription, the Vietnamese annals concerning the year 767 refer to (previous?) raids on the mainland stemming from a Java (Shepo) and the Southern Islands (Kunlun).[35] Even here, though, it is not certain that one is distinct from the other, or even that the "Java" mentioned (i.e., Shepo, once pronounced "Jaba") is Java, with which it can be safely identified by the late Tang and early Song periods (see more below).[36] Similarly, while a Cham inscription of 787 mentions repairs to a temple after an attack from Jvâ — also identified at one stage by Coedès as Java — this makes no obvious distinction between Javanese and Sumatrans.[37]

Even if the Java of the various eighth-century inscriptions is separate from Sumatra, the fragmentary evidence at hand could point to two (probably related) kingdoms that could have worked in concert at times — whether willingly, or with the weaker party serving the stronger with men and arms. And regardless of the definitive separation from central Java by the mid-ninth century, apparently Śrîvijayan claims to authority rooted in an ancient Jâwa pedigree continued to be made as late as the 11th century — strengthening, I believe, the idea that their Yava/Jâwa was an ancestral place imagined to have claimed authority over both islands and the peninsula, and thus over all passing trade.[38]

Despite the arguments about influence and territory alluded to above, the existence of Śrîvijaya need not be doubted. Neither should its engagement with local neighbors and the states of the Indian Ocean that could bring as much danger as recognition. According to Chinese sources, Shepo, now more likely Java proper, apparently attacked Śrîvijaya ca. 992 and was in turn attacked in 1016. Then, around 1025, Śrîvijaya suffered raids from the Cholas of southern India, with Malayu later assuming the mantle of its key entrepôt in missions to China sometime during the same century, perhaps in the years 1079–82.[39] Even so, the claimants to the authority (or perhaps just the reputation) of Śrîvijaya survived this blow, being finally felled by Java in the late 12th century.

Oliver Wolters once proposed that Śrîvijaya should be seen as the wellspring of Malay customs and traditions refined in 15th-century Melaka. However, this account relies on the Johorese record and plays down any contributions from the rival north Sumatran states of Pasai, and then Aceh, in forming what I shall suggest could just as readily be called Jâwî court culture. Whatever the case, after the Mongol interventions of the late 13th century, rulers of the western end of the island world who could now draw on the China trade directly would begin to replace both Sanskrit and their Indianized traditions with the script and religion of increasing numbers of the peoples of the Eastern Indian Ocean.[40] They included Tamils, Persians, and Arabs.[41] And what the northern Indian geographers had once called Suvarṇadvîpa, or perhaps Yavadvîpa too, the last of these traders seem to have called, or at least transcribed, Zâbaj.

Zâbaj and the Fabulous Isles of the Mahârâja

There seems to be evidence that Zâbaj was an established toponym when the Abbasid Caliph al-Ma'mûn (r. 813–33) commissioned a rectangular map of the world. What appears to be a 13th-century version of this map gives the name, but it places Zâbaj on the African coast below the orthographically similar Zanj.[42] Somewhat later statements concerning Zâbaj — or the variants Zabaj, Zabâj, and Rânaj — come in accounts compiled around the time the Nâlandâ inscription was made, and in a period of heightened sea contact between Southern China and the Abbasid port of Siraf in the Persian Gulf.[43] Like Ptolemy's work, these show evidence of being compiled from multiple sources that may well describe the same places with different names. Certainly some of their information intersects. The first, the *Akhbâr al-ṣîn wa-l-hind* (*Reports of China and India*), is attributed in part to the information of Sulaymân al-Tâjir ("Sulaymân the trader").[44] The second, the *Kitâb al-masâlik wa-l-mamâlik* (*The Book of*

Routes and Kingdoms), is ascribed to a Persian, Ibn Khurdâdhbih (or Ibn Khurradâdhbih).[45]

Zâbaj is mentioned only twice in the *Akhbâr* but may be located in the vicinity of Sumatra given that its description comes after Langabâlûs (the Andamans) and Râmnî (North Sumatra) — with its gold, cannibals, and groves (*fanṣûr*) of camphor.[46] Zâbaj itself is first mentioned as a kingdom (*mamlaka*) controlling Kalâh Bâr — where Bâr is explained as meaning both the kingdom and its coast. The latter is described as being "on the right side of India" (*mutayâmana 'an bilâd al-Hind*), that is, to the right of the continent when sailing to China.[47] This creates no small problem of identification, as the interpretation of Kalâh as being to the right of India proper, and thus on the wrong side of Arabic maps, is unlikely, even with the view that "Hind" ended only at the Cham-China border.

My proposal is that the meaning seems to indicate that the capital of Zâbaj was originally intended as being on the right, and not Kalâh. Either way, faced with a sea of possibilities, Tibbetts would not positively identify Kalâh. But, given the inscriptions at Chaiya discussed above, and Wade's reexamination of the Chinese sources, the low-lying land between Krabi in the west and Chaiya in the east is an obvious candidate for the principal land passage through a regional Kalâh Bâr.[48]

Equally problematically, the *Akhbâr* later notes that Zâbaj (which is never itself described) had in its vicinity a volcano that was called "the mountain of fire" (*jabal al-nâr*). The volcano was impossible to approach due to its constant emission of flame and smoke, and its lower slopes held all-important pools of freshwater.[49] While it is not clear from the passage who did the calling, the general context is that the mariners in need of water are both the source of the information and the namers of this landmark. And although Tibbetts was unwilling to nominate any mountain of fire not found on Java and Mahdi has made arguments for Sumatra's own Mt. Merapi (especially as the meaning in Malay is indeed related to the word "fire"), reference to what would have been a volcano reachable by ship would make Krakatoa a more likely candidate, and imply that greater Zâbaj exercised some control over the Sunda Straits, as it most likely did prior to the probable expulsion of the Śailendras from Java in the ninth century.

Ibn Khurdâdhbih sets out a similar relationship for Zâbaj as a kingdom that stretches north to Kra and (east) to the volcano. Further, he provides mention of Zâbaj and what seem to be its neighbors in a list of the sub-rulers of India (*mulûk al-hind*), though it is worth remembering that, perhaps in tribute to their ecumenical nature, Zâbaj and its compradors were often seen by outsiders as forming a zone *within* India, much as 19th-century scholars and Indian nationalist historiography imagined greater India beyond the Ganges.

The first sub-king listed in the *Kitâb al-masâlik* was perhaps called "the Jâba," and he was to be found in the vicinity of a ruler who sounds suspiciously like "king of the islands" (the text has *malik al-j.r.z.* rather than *malik al-juzur*), and another who could, by dint of another mistranscription, be a lord in charge of the monsoons, "the king of the typhoons" (*malik al-ṭâfin*).[50] In any case, the first of these kings was not yet called the Jâbat al-Hindî (i.e., "the Indian Jâba"). Rather, this expanded term is mentioned later in the text when the adjectival form is added to remind the reader of the Jâba's Indian context. I would be doubly cautious about accepting Tibbetts's assertion that this reference implied an Indian origin for the ruler concerned. The first mention of Jâba suggests that the extant manuscript may well be missing the word "king" (*malik*), which several of the other potentates have, and which would make the sentence syntactically more logical, giving "the king of Jâba."[51]

Most likely based on separate information, Ibn Khurdâdhbih mentions that the lord of Zâbaj had a distinct title. De Goeje's text gives *al-f.t.j.b* or *al-q.-.kh.t*, whereas Yusuf read *f.y.j.b.t*. Reflecting a Javacentric reading of early Indonesian history, Ferrand interpreted this as *punggawa*, and De Goeje and Kern read *Pati-Jaba*.[52]

Ibn Khurdâdhbih also lists another king who ruled "the isles of the eastern sea" (*jazâ'ir al-baḥr al-sharqî*) called "the Mah[â]râja." Thus, we apparently have at least three Southeast Asian sovereigns in the Arabic sources: (1) Jâba (or perhaps just the king of Jâba), (2) the ruler of Zâbaj (whose subsidiary title is indecipherable), and (3) the mahârâja of the Eastern Isles.[53] Like Ptolemy's three echoes, though, these could all stand for one dynasty that could claim the mantle of Yavadvîpa. Certainly the last title, that of mahârâja, was claimed by the ruler who had ordered the Chaiya stone to be erected.

The precise nature of political links within Southeast Asia is certainly not discernable in the account of Ibn Khurdâdhbih, who concentrated on trade and curiosities. After echoing the description of Langabâlûs supplied by Sulaymân al-Tâjir or his contemporaries, Ibn Khurdâdhbih described Râmî as a place where a small black people lived in the hills and a "white" sea people would paddle out to passing vessels to trade their ambergris for metal goods.[54]

After writing of giant snakes in the hills of Zâbaj, or enormous camphor trees, Ibn Khurdâdhbih notes that all the islands of this sea were "full of wonders."[55] Later, he speaks of the distances between Sri Lanka (Sarandîb), the Andamans, and Kra (written Kilah),[56] observing that the latter is part of the kingdom of Jâba al-Hindî, which again aligns with the (perhaps) Śrîvijayan and (certainly) Śailendran claims to authority. A Sumatran connection is all the more obvious, though, in the subsequent passages with their reference to gold, cannibals, and camphor. And when there is final mention of a Jâba in the *Kitâb al-masâlik*, it is clearly on Sumatra, being mentioned as but a short distance (overland?) from Barus.[57]

Ibn Khurdâdhbih's fusion of different sources — whether focused on Jâba as the name of the pre-eminent kingdom or on Zâbaj — is further complicated in another passage where he states that the king of Zâbaj *is* the mahârâja,[58] supporting the idea that Jâba, Zâbaj, and the isles of the mahârâja are all broadly identifiable with each other and with the memories of ancient Sabadibae, Iabadiû, and Zábai.

Speaking of this king, Ibn Khurdâdhbih records that each day the mahârâja received a measure of gold that was melted into an ingot and thrown into a pool of water. This tale was often repeated by subsequent compilers and may well have helped the Indian Abû Rayḥân al-Bîrûnî (973–1048) link Zâbaj to Sumatra, ca. 1030, when he stated that these isles were known to the Indians of his time as Suwarna Dîb (Suvarṇadvîpa).[59]

By comparison with these two early sources, and before al-Bîrûnî made this identification, it seems in the early tenth-century account of Abû Zayd of Siraf that Zâbaj is broadly identifiable with the fame of Śrîvijaya, especially given that the writer locates a primary toponym within it called Sribuza (*s.r.b.z.h.*).[60] And again the geography in Abû Zayd's account is consistent with the pan-archipelagic claims of its competing states, it being painted as a state with influence over 1,000 parasangs worth of "islands," including Kra and Râmî.

Whether Śrîvijaya (or even Śailendran Java) actually exerted control over the western archipelago consistently is moot, though there would appear to be some distant awareness of fluctuations of power in the region given the inconsistency of nomenclature and estimated size of various places. It is thus noteworthy that Abû Zayd deems the terrain of Sribuza proper to be half the size of neighboring Râmî, the primary source of camphor, while Kalah is sometimes described only as the midpoint between the lands of the Chinese and the Arabs rather than as the fiefdom of some other lord.[61] In any event, Zâbaj, though *not* impermanent Srîbuza, obviously served as an important linguistic coverall for the (primarily Malay) lands of India that lay before Cambodia (i.e., Qmâr, from the ethnonym Khmer) and Champa (Ṣanf). Furthermore, these Zâbaj lands as a whole are portrayed as an ancient rival of Qmâr when Abû Zayd recounts an allegedly old story of an attack by the former on the latter. Based on the once common interpretation of Jayavarman II's inscription of 802, Tibbetts adjudged this story to be an echo of eighth-century Javanese raids on Cambodia.[62] Then again, the story could be even older still. Manguin, for example, has suggested that the depredations of Śrîvijaya may have spelt an end to the old Funanese center of Oc Eo.[63]

Leaving aside the question of attacks and reputed imperium, it thus seems that Zâbaj takes on life in narrative Arabic sources on Southeast Asia only as a gloss for the space claimed by Śrîvijaya and Java alike. It may also have been that this term, pronounced by the Sinified Arabs engaged in the long-distance China Sea trade, inspired a shift in Chinese terminology, around 900, from the seemingly precise Shi-li-fo-qi to the more general San-fo-qi (as opposed to the literalist reading of "three Vijayas"), while the old Shepo drifted more and more to Java.[64]

Certainly the etymology of "Zâbaj" has often seemed far from clear. Ferrand once adduced from the researches of De Goeje that it is ultimately a corruption of the Pâli adjective "Jâwaka" via the Dravidian "Shâvaka."[65] However, this argument comprises a series of linguistic shifts taking place across the Indian Ocean (Pali > Tamil > Persian > Arabic) coupled with the peregrinations of the people themselves to the shores of the Persian Gulf after a putative colonization elsewhere in India. At one level, the argument conforms to the now discredited theories of the Indianization of Southeast Asia by migration. It also leads one to question why a people would have reharmonized their ethnonym at each step of their journey unless they had already lost their language, and thus their distinct identity as "Jâvaka people.

Intriguingly, though, one of Mahdi's sources for his reconstruction of Malayu as the heart of ancient Yava gives a very different possibility.[66] This is the oft-cited account of the Chinese monk Faxian, who called at a port en route to China in 414; the port is conventionally transcribed as Ye-po-ti. While scholars generally agree that Ye-po-ti is to be equated with Yavadvîpa — but disagree as to which Yava Faxian visited — it is noteworthy that the reconstruction of the contemporary Early Middle Chinese pronunciation is *jia-ba-dɛj*.[67] Just like the later Shepo, this, I would argue, is a very acceptable inspiration for — or, at the very least, good anticipation of — the Arabic Zâbaj that sits well with a fusion of the Greek Yavadvîpas: Zábai and Iabadiû. Indeed, first contact between the Islamizing West and all-important China was made at a time when the business of the caliphate was still handled by officials trained in Greek, or who continued to make reference to the Greek tradition that would so color early Muslim geography. As I will argue in the last part of this essay, however, the distant scholars may at times also have *misread* as much as misheard Zâbaj from reports of a different name altogether that corresponded to one of the believed domains of the mahârâja.

The Waning of Zâbaj and the Translocations of Qamar

Etymology aside, there is evidence in the Arabic accounts that Zâbaj begins to fade in relevance, or at least lose any precision, in the 11th century — even if some of the compilers continued to add the name next to what were the emerging toponyms of importance, and much as Sribuza had been accommodated by Abû Zayd within Zâbaj.

The first major change to the nomenclature of the region is signaled by al-Bîrûnî, who had equated Zâbaj with golden Suvarṇadvîpa. Hence Zâbaj was apparently still relevant as a term during his day, if in a general sense as the island of Sumatra. Still, al-Bîrûnî devoted little direct attention to Zâbaj as compared with a complex of islands that Sachau read as Dîbajât and which, due to their proximity to the "islands of Zanj," Tibbetts argued was a reference to the Maldives.[68] This would seem consistent given that al-Bîrûnî also made mention of an unusual variant of Qmâr, namely, Qmayr, placing it at the eastern terminus of "the islands of Zâbaj," described as an arc stretching across the Indian Ocean from the isles of Zanj in the west and passing through Dîbajât in the middle.[69]

By comparison, al-Bîrûnî's slightly later *Kitâb al-tafhîm*, ca. 1028, gives a different form for these medial isles, i.e., Dhabîḥât, which could be read as "the slaughtered ones" and might well hark back to the Tamil raids three years previously.[70] Further, it is this, perhaps more sanguine, form that is repeated by the most important fuser of the Ptolemaic and Arabic traditions, al-Idrîsî, who shifts both it, and a land he calls Qamar, farther into the space once occupied by Zâbaj.

Muḥammad bin Muḥammad al-Sharîf al-Idrîsî is famous for his fusion of all available geographical information at the behest of King Roger of Sicily in the 1150s. But while Tibbetts highlights al-Idrîsî's mention of Zâbaj, he ignores the fact that the scribes concerned were by no means agreed that there was such a place at all. Whereas Zâbaj was still a requisite toponym in the tenth century, it is totally absent from the firsthand accounts thereafter. None of the sources used for Cerulli's edition of al-Idrîsî's geography spell the term as we have.[71] Instead, we find that each scribe wrote, and often in internally consistent ways, that the Swahili Coast (Zanj) faced the islands of Zâlij, Zânij, Rânij, Râlij, Râ-ḫ, Râ-j, or yet Rânih.

The other problem with making al-Idrîsî's descriptions of places internally consistent is that, like his predecessors, he merged different accounts in quest of completeness as he swept back and forth in time and space across the isles between Africa and China. When al-Idrîsî first mentions what, for the sake of consistency, we will still call Zâbaj, it is to recount "an old story" that if ever there was trouble in China, the traders would come to that kingdom.[72] On the second occasion, it is in the context of being a general eastward destination for Zanjîs seeking to trade their metal.[73] Here the capital is named in the variant texts as something close to Abû Zayd's Sribuza, though none of the transcriptions (*s.t.r.h.* | *sh.r.n.w.h.* | *sh.r.n.d.h.* | *sh.r.b.w.t*) show that it was recognized directly. Then, when he returns to the poor and sparsely inhabited town of Sofala in Mozambique, al-Idrîsî notes that it was subjected to the raids of powerful kingdoms such as the islands of Zâbaj. But Zâbaj is only named as an example of a domineering neighbor, and the orthography of the various texts, where the letter *nûn* is the common element in three cases, shows that this should be read as Zanj.

When al-Idrîsî does shift more clearly to the eastern part of the Indian Ocean, he brings forward two toponyms: Anbûna and Qamar. The first is described as the "most powerful" island and a place in constant contact with the second, where a gold-bedecked queen wields power by popular consent. But if Anbûna may be an echo of the distant Ambon, al-Idrîsî's Qamar creates multiple problems of identification.

Coming beyond Dabîhât — described by al-Idrîsî as the first "island" beyond Sri Lanka, and as a coastal zone of traders and manufacturers — matriarchal Qamar gives several options, all related in some way to the morbid claims of Śrîvijaya. First is the notion of an ascendant Cambodia (the Qmâr of old) now stretching its influence over Kra, and which was indeed ruled in the late 11th century by a queen called Kambujarâjalakṣmî.[74]

The second option is the idea of a peninsular state, once a vassal of Śrîvijaya, that was claiming Cambodian territory. Jacq-Hergoualc'h has speculated that one such entity, Tambralinga, even challenged Cambodia in the early 11th century and has implied that the Cholas may have raided the region in response to an appeal for help from the Khmers.[75]

Still, while the Khmers may well have come to exercise greater influence over the Isthmus of Kra in the wake of the Tamil raids — and conceivably in partnership with the Cholas[76] — a third possibility is that matriarchal Qamar is a conflation of the name of a Sumatran port maintained by a recovering Malayu (perhaps Kampar) and the nearby Minangkabau highlands, famous for its gold and matrilineal social system.[77] An even firmer connection can be made when al-Idrîsî explicitly states that the ruler of Qamar (this time a male) lived in a capital called Malây[u], and that his rule was said by its people to stretch the length of the East and up to China in the north.

Even so, al-Idrîsî's Qamar could still fit several variants of an Indian Ocean world, whether conforming to a regionally active Tamil state, Cambodia in control of Kra, or just an echo of Śrîvijaya when it depicts a coastal entrepôt linking the wealth of East and West, its people dressed in the fine stuffs of China and Iraq, harbors with great ships, and emigrants living in the region who claimed to be descended from "Turks" (i.e., Chinese?).

After another long digression on Sri Lanka, which Wyatt once suggested became the protector of the court of Tambralinga in the late 12th century,[78] but which al-Idrîsî treats separately from Qamar, al-Idrîsî comes back to Sumatra a second time. This time, though, it is the Sumatra of Ibn Khurdâdhbih.[79] Another shift in time and place follows when al-Idrîsî has the waters of "the Cham Sea" (*al-baḥr al-ṣanfî*) lapping the shores of Sufâla.[80] Like all of the descriptions of Southeast Asia to date, this sea is imagined as part of the continuous ocean between China and Africa. Trade with the people of Qamar is mentioned here again, and, for the first time, the land of the mahârâja is mentioned — indicating yet another interpolation from an early text.

Despite Sufâla being in Africa, its description is just as relevant to the general history of religion around the eastern shores of the Indian Ocean. Trade is described as being in the hands of outside intermediaries who had come from all the surrounding islands. One manuscript even states that they came from "the lands of God Almighty and the isles as well."[81] Furthermore, these foreigners lived in segregation from the locals, with their veiled women remaining at home due to the overwhelming public nakedness — and just like the "Turks" along the Malay coast of Qamar?

In another pass over the region, al-Idrîsî jumps up to Kalah and repeats elements of Ibn Khurdâdhbih's account of the realm of the king he so confusingly calls Jâba al-Hindî. Apparently this was not a name understood by al-Idrîsî, who did not include the section on the names of the sub-rulers of greater India, or the later copyists, who usually recognized only the "Hind" part of the construct.[82] Next, he turns to the similarly dated Jâba, Salâht, and Hazlaj (i.e., Harlaj) but provides a fresh sketch of a ruler he accepts was called the Jâba, describing him as a lord who wears a gold crown, and a devout worshiper of the Buddha in a land dominated by temples and golden statues.[83]

At last we have a description, or at least a memory, that would seem to point to the Java of the long-displaced Śailendras rather than their Śaivite successors. However, this is more likely to be an old description of Śrîvijaya or its successors, who had sponsored Buddhist temples abroad, such as the one in the Chola domains before the raids of 1025, and another in Guangzhou in 1079.

So where is Java in al-Idrîsî's text? A hasty reading would suggest the island/port of Mâ'it, or perhaps Mâbit, where al-Idrîsî has traders thronged on the coast. It was also a place that faced the northward isle of Tiyûma (Tioman) and Qmâr and Şanf beyond — a designation that fits with Java's engagement with mainland peoples.[84]

This identification is unlikely, though, and Java and Borneo are not notable by their absence as they never really figured in the Arab accounts thus far, implying that the primary concern of Muslim shipping remained with the arterial China trade.[85] There is no identifiable mention of Arabs in any of the contemporary inscriptions from central and east Java. And it is only on al-Idrîsî's final pass through the region, and as he shifts back south from Champa, that he seems to be tracing a route that moves nearer to that island or Borneo.[86]

Meanwhile, Malây itself is described as a huge island stretching from east to west. There is, however, no mention of any peninsular territory, which seems to fit present knowledge of a much-reduced Sumatran entity, leaving the peninsula to be contested by the mainland powers such as Angkor, and the emerging threats of Sukotai and Pagan to the north. Even so, the Sumatran city is still described as an important entrepôt for Muslim-Chinese trade. It remains the abode of "the king of the islands," with his soldiers, ships, and great agricultural wealth, and an economy based on silver "Tartar dirhams."[87]

Regardless of the confusing and multilayered nature of al-Idrîsî's account, the identification of Qamar with Melayu-Jambi, and thus with what was still the most important part of the archipelago for the Arabs, was apparent on the maps resulting from it. This includes the circular model produced for Roger of Sicily in 1154.[88] Here Qamar looms large in the Indian Ocean even if it is very close to a deformed Africa, overshadowing neighboring Râmî and (defunct) Jâba.[89]

But just as it seems that Qamar could have been imagined as the domain of Melayu-Jambi, its etymology is as elusive as that of Zâbaj. Tibbetts was perhaps part way there with one argument that it was a conflation with mainland Qmâr, due to the older stories about Zâbaj's raid on the Khmers. Another possibility raised by him is that the appellation is tied up with the relationship between the African coast and Sumatra that is so prominent in al-Idrîsî's account. The word "Qamar" (i.e., "moon") was first used to describe the source of the Nile based on Ptolemy's "mountains of the moon." Later it was applied to Madagascar, though it was more commonly vocalized as Qumr, being ultimately applied to the Comoros, a one-time possession of the Chola kings.

Bearing this latter point in mind, this conforms to the longer history of an Indian Ocean filled with duplicated toponyms. Even so, the translocation of Qamar on the Arab charts, and to the detriment of Jâba and Zâbaj, reflects less an error of cartography than a recognition of shifts in political fortunes in the region. However, this recognition was concealed far from the Indian Ocean by the encyclopedic impulse for completeness. In the following section I will argue that it was only with the final demise of the successors of Zâbaj that Java, their conqueror, could appear. Ironically enough, this process of renaming was probably accelerated as peoples in some Sumatran ports converted to the religion of some of the mixed "Tartar" traders who had long been living among them, perhaps in deliberate distinction to the heirs of Zâbaj, their old rivals, or as the reins of the new Java slackened.

Jâba with a *wâw*, Islam Comes to Sumatra

Assembled by scholars in a mode that relied on the accumulated knowledge of the past, and lacking the personal experience of the region that their informants had, most general geographies, as opposed to the practical rutters, continued to focus on the products of the region, or on reporting (outdated) tales of the bizarre. It was in these accounts that Zâbaj would continue to figure as a wild place at the end of the known world.

Yet change was in the air on the eve of the 13th century, when the Mongols would devastate much of Asia and Muslim incursions in India would result in the sack of Nâlandâ in 1234. The Southern Song would turn to Southeast Asia afresh for income, and the rulers of Java would seek a place in the revived international trade at the expense of East Sumatra. It also seems that, apparently for the first time, Arab vessels were calling regularly at Javanese ports.[90]

It is, therefore, no coincidence to find the term "Jâwa" — rather than the old "Jâba" — now appearing in geographical treatises, the first of which is the *Mu'jam al-buldân*, compiled by Yâqût b. 'Abd Allâh (1179–1229).[91] It is worth adding, however, that Jâwa does not yet receive the distinct alphabetical listing that Zâbaj still merits. Instead, it appears within a much longer passage on the Indian Ocean, in which it is described as the first part of the lands of *China* (rather than India) reached by a perilous route, and takes its place beside Sri Lanka and Zâbaj:

> Then there are the lands of China. The first of these is Jâwa, to which the sailing is on a sea that is difficult to navigate and quick to destroy, before passing on to the clear [waters] of the lands of China. People have greatly exaggerated the description of this sea and its length and breadth, saying contradictory things detracting to the intelligence of their reporter. In it are great islands of number known to God alone. The largest and most famous of these are the islands of Sri Lanka (Saylân), which has many cities, and the island of Zânaj (*sic*).[92]

Another use of Jâwa as a regional term is found in the *Tarîkh al-mustabṣir* of Ibn al-Mujâwir (ca. 1228), where the writer describes the effects of lightning on a tree near the mosque of Mu'âdh b. Jabal in Yemen:

> In the same way mariners seek direction to the region of Java [*iqlîm al-jâwa*] simply by means of the frequent flashes of lightning, since in the season of travel to Java [*mûsim sifârat al-jâwa*] the rains are abundant, the sky completely overcast ... and the seas very rough.... Others have remarked that many Arar trees grow in these parts and if the resin runs from the tree, the sea appears to travellers like the flashing of lightning.[93]

Yet another spelling of the term (Jâwâ) appears in the Wüstenfeld edition of Yâqût. This comes in a poem by Abû Muḥammad al-Aswad composed for Ziyâda b. Bajdal al-Ṭarîfî al-Ṭâ'î. "Have you not seen the wind between Muwaysal and Jâwâ?" al-Aswad asks. We might, in turn, ask where Muwaysal and Jâwâ are. Even though he gives two terms for Sri Lanka in his *Mu'jam* (Sayalân and Sarandîb), Yâqût is unclear. And while this variant Jâwa passes without mention, Yâqût's explanation for Muwaysal is intriguing. As Yâqût has it, Muwaysal is a diminutive form for Mâsil, a waterway that channels torrents from the hinterland of the lands of the Ṭayyi', near Najd.[94] However, a separate listing for Mâsil within the *Muʿjam* describes it as being in the ancestral lands of the Banî ʿUqayl in Hadramaut, and one may well wonder if Muwaysal is actually a diminutive of the wadi linking their towns to the Indian Ocean.[95]

None of this necessarily entails that the peoples and politics of Jâwa were a widely known fact to "the Arabs" more generally in the early 13th century, although indications are that Java's harbors were at last coming to the attention of Arab shippers. In this process, notions of Qamar (now a more tangible Qumr) were being shifted back to Africa, as can be seen in Yâqût's account, which still maintained a space for a bizarre Zâbaj:

> Zâbaj: an island in the farthest lands of India beyond the Sea of Harkand [the Bay of Bengal] on the borders of China. It is said to be in the lands of Zanj and [inhabited by] a people that resemble humans except that their manners are most like those of monsters. There are *nasnâs* with wings like those of bats about which people in their books have recorded wonders.[96] There is to be found the muskrat, an animal resembling a cat from which a creamy emission is obtained. From what I have heard from travellers to those parts, the emission is the sweat exuded by a creature when it is hot, and which is then scraped off with a knife. God only knows.[97]

> Qumr is also an island in the middle of the Sea of Zanj. There is no greater island than it in that land. It has a few cities and kings, each one differing from the other. On its coasts are ambergris and *qmârî* leaf, which is a medicine that they call betel leaf (*waraq tânbul*), which it is not. It is also used to make candles.[98]

Despite the identification with a plant of Cambodia (i.e., *qmârî*), the reference to betel (from the Sanskrit *tâmbûla*, Arabic *tanbul*) shows that the effects of betel were known to these Qumr people even if they did not have the plant itself. Thus, the reference to *tânbul* is most likely to the Malagasy *tanbolo* (Buchnera leptostachya), a herb used for staining teeth.[99]

Certainly there is no question of Sumatra being Qamar when Marco Polo passed through the region ca. 1291–92. At this time, the Venetian emissary of Qubilai mentioned the existence of a major island that had eight separate kingdoms. Of these, he briefly described six: Ferlec (Perlak), Basma, Samara, Dagroian (Indragiri), Lambri (Lamreh), and Fansur. And although he did not mention the town of Samudra, perhaps ruled already by a Muslim king called al-Malik al-Ṣâliḥ (d. 1297), Marco Polo commented that Ferlec had been newly converted by the Muslim merchants who frequented the place.¹⁰⁰ These were more than likely al-Idrîsî's Indian Ocean middlemen, ever ready to serve under non-Muslim patrons, much as was observed on the Malabar Coast by Ibn Baṭṭūṭa (1304–77).¹⁰¹

However, what the distant al-Idrîsî had labeled Qamar, Marco Polo only knew as Java Minora. The difference is important, and Marco Polo's nomenclature arguably reflects the fact that he sailed with a Sino-Muslim crew conscious that Sumatra's fate was now more tightly bound to both Java and China. Certainly his description of Java Minora fits with what we now know from indigenous sources. According to Mpu Prapañca, composer of the *Deśawarṇana*, the Javanese king had ordered attacks on Malayû in 1275, and at the time of writing — in the 1360s — the Sumatran lands of Barat, Jambi, Palembang, Lampung, and (Muslim) Perlak were still loyal vassals that paid their taxes.

It is tempting to speculate from Prapañca's text that following the Javanese raids — which actually came from Singasari in 1263 — independent outsiders in Sumatra's eastern and northern ports were appointed to oversee the collection of tribute. To cite a later example in the hope that it might echo earlier practices, such a mode of governance was used in the 16th century when the sultan of Banten asserted control over Lampung and appointed Javanese, Malays, and Minangkabaus to ensure deliveries of pepper.¹⁰²

What, then, might have been the advantage offered to the agents of Singasari, and later Majapahit, beyond the usual stake in trade and tribute — especially in distant territories where a governor could easily become an independent ruler once the reins of authority were slackened? I suspect that a further motivation may also be found in the margins of Prapañca's *Deśawarṇana*. Much as he regarded only Bali as being in full conformity with Javanese cultural practice, he spoke of communities of evildoers on Java and of low-born traders and foreigners outside the Javanese social order. He also complained that Buddhist monks were not permitted to go west of Java.

From this, one might be tempted to see more Muslims both on Java and to the west of it, or even speculate that in exchange for continued tribute from Perlak and (probably) Samudra, and the rights to facilitate Sino-Javanese trade in the Indian Ocean, the Śaivite Javanese rulers were not to permit Buddhist missionaries to travel to some ports to reconvert the populations of ancient Zâbaj.¹⁰³

More problematically, though, Prapañca did not name Sumatra as Java — perhaps its ports were not to be accorded the honor. Still, even if Prapañca regarded only Bali as being in conformity with Javanese cultural practice, to outsiders writing on the western shores of the Indian Ocean there would be news of only one regional power, as we have seen from the *Tarîkh al-mustabṣir*, with its reference to "the region of Jâwa," or yet from Yâqût's Chinese-influenced Jâwa. This was once more a regional Jâwa, where the ancient echoes of the mahârâja would elide with the victories of Singasari and Majapahit, erasing Zâbaj and making all Southeast Asians Jâwa collectively. It might also explain why the Thais treated both Sumatra and Java as Chawa,[104] much like Cambodians of previous centuries, whose descendants were now using "Jvâ" interchangeably with "Melayu" to describe Muslims from the archipelago.[105]

It is thus no surprise that Jâwa was the collective noun used by Ibn Baṭṭûṭa ca. 1345 to describe the communities of Southeast Asians that he encountered in the Indian Ocean, first at Calicut on the Malabar Coast, and then at a westward point on the Malay Peninsula called Barahnakâr, where he claimed that the local Muslims consisted of a mixture of Jâwa and Bengalis.[106] And while much has been made of Ibn Baṭṭûṭa's arrival in Sumatra and his apparent ascription of the name Jâwa to that island, the nomenclature of his travelogue is not consistent nor necessarily limited to Jâwa as a single island. When Ibn Baṭṭûṭa first landed on Sumatra and identified it, correctly, as the source of the incense called *al-lubân al-jâwî*,[107] he actually stated that he had arrived at the *jazîrat al-jâwa*, which, given his previous reference to communities of Jâwa in the Indian Ocean and travels to the *bilâd al-jâwa*, is better read here as "the island of the Jâwa people."[108] It is only on the return journey from China — where the island world was now recognized as Javanese territory — that all the land below Qâqula, another old peninsular toponym, is referred to as Jâwa.[109]

Most interestingly, this sub-peninsular area included a widely spread pagan kingdom that was a superior source for all the spices of the archipelago, which Ibn Baṭṭûṭa called Mul Jâwa. But while Tibbetts nominated Java, we are most likely faced, yet again, with East Sumatra and the still-important port of Malayu-Jambi recognizing the suzerainty of Majapahit and thus being seen by outsiders as "Melayu Jawa." Or was it merely the memory of having been the "original" (*mula*) Jawa? Certainly the contention that Mul Jâwa is Java proper makes little sense for Ibn Baṭṭûṭa's itinerary. Rather, the logic of his purported journey, which followed the same path laid out by the geographers of old whom he may well have plagiarized, and his brief description of the kingdom — including the outdated claim that both Qmâra and Qâqula were subject to Mul Jâwa — fits instead with stories of Zâbaj.

Once they stepped ashore in Southeast Asia, outsiders such as Ibn Baṭṭūṭa were not insensible to the diversity within the Jâwî lands. Sumatra was still a site of multiethnic and multireligious trade, and it was by no means integrated within the Muslim world, even if some of its polities would start to look to that world for new orbits of allegiance and patronage.[110] And even if he may not personally have ventured there, the Moroccan seems at least aware that Muslims constituted a small minority of the Jâwa in the 14th century — though naturally he devoted most of his attention to that minority, then ensconced in the north Sumatran town of Samuṭra (Samudra-Pasai).

As Ibn Baṭṭūṭa describes it, Samuṭra consisted of a settlement four miles upriver surrounded by a wooden palisade with watchtowers.[111] It had a ruler who bore the name al-Malik al-Ẓâhir, a form that echoes that of his predecessor al-Malik al-Ṣâliḥ, who himself had most likely emulated the nomenclature of the Ayyubids of Yemen.[112] This sultan was said to be an avid follower of the Shâfiʿî school of law and an enthusiast for spreading the borders of Islam into neighboring territories.

There is also the suggestion of the involvement of Persians, or at least Farsi-literate Indians, in the process of Islamization within Samudra. Ibn Baṭṭūṭa gives the most eminent of the kingdom's jurists Persian names (al-Shirâzî and al-Iṣbahânî respectively). However, such names, and Shirâzî in particular, are also found in the parallel histories of the Islamization of the Swahili Coast and the Comoros (today's echo of Qumr) and do not definitively prove Persian involvement.[113] Either way, Ibn Baṭṭūṭa's intended link with India — where Farsi was the language of the courts — seems confirmed by his description of the Samudran council chamber being titled the *faradkhâna*. He also alludes to ongoing trade connections with the sultan of Delhi, in whose presence he had seen the use of the prized aloeswoods ʿûd jâwî and ʿûd qmârî.[114]

And while Zâbaj had probably faded from the more practical charts of the mariners who escorted Marco Polo and Ibn Baṭṭūṭa, who subsumed it within the regional Java recognized by China as the archipelagic power, it was not forgotten on the western edges of the Indian Ocean. Distant compilers such as Ibn Saʿîd (d. 1274), Dimashqî (d. 1327), and Ibn al-Wardî (d. 1457) had transposed, and would continue to transpose, variant spellings of Zâbaj in their overly comprehensive geographies, or else eased them into what Schrieke once called "the mists of parageography."[115]

Jâwîs in an Islamizing Ocean

Regardless of whether Ibn Baṭṭūṭa ventured east of India — given his account could just as easily have been drawn from descriptions of proud Sumatrans in Calicut — it was only natural that he applied a Persianate regal style to Samudra given that it still fitted into an Indian Ocean world. The Islamizing courts of Southeast Asia still imported teachers from India and beyond, much as their Indianized predecessors had welcomed multiethnic expertise to establish their entrepôts in earlier periods.[116] By the 15th century, rich Muslims of Pasai and of Gresik, on Java's north coast, could even afford to import grave-markers from Gujerat.[117] Equally, the Jâwî heirs of the Southeast Asians Ibn Baṭṭūṭa had met continued to be active along the oceanic trade routes. The 16th-century itinerary of Diogo Do Couto (1542–1616), for example, refers to the mixed presence of Malays and Javanese in Sri Lanka as "Jaõa."[118]

Certainly in the decades after their taking of the peninsular entrepôt of Malacca, Wolters's final claimant to the heritage of Śrîvijaya, the Portuguese still observed Southeast Asians — and Acehnese in particular — traveling on Gujerati ships bound for Jeddah, carrying precious loads of pepper for the markets of Cairo and, later, missives for the Sublime Porte.[119] The constant commerce of what they called the "Náos de Achem" also drew attention from the people of Hadramaut, whose shores they passed and whose own histories contain mention of Âshî, its vessels, and its religious debates. There is even mention of requests for *fatwa*s sent from that kingdom.[120]

Indications of such connections were revealed by Serjeant in his studies of Arabic manuscripts relating to the advent of the Portuguese in the Indian Ocean. In the oldest account presented by him, the *Târîkh Shanbal*, Serjeant was clearly perplexed by a passage relating to the events of the year AH 904 (1498–99). Serjeant renders this passage thus:

> [i]n this year the infidel Franks appeared off Mogadischo and Sabâdj. Their course ran under the wind, and he (the Frank) made for Kilwah where he built a fort.[121]

However, Serjeant admitted his inability to identify any "Sabâdj" in India, and also admitted to general confusion about the meaning of the phrase "below the wind" (*taḥt al-rîḥ*).[122] A rereading of the manuscript consulted by Serjeant may well show that the context is of the appearance of the Franks in the Indian Ocean, bounded by Somalia in the west and a dimly remembered Zâbaj in the east. However, the mention of "below the wind" presents us with a problem to which I shall return below.

Whatever those lands were, the shift from fabulous Zâbaj, the source of monsters and spices, to Jâwa, a recognizably Islamizing contact zone, would be confirmed only once Southeast Asians made their presence felt in the Middle East. This would have occurred as they participated in the Ḥajj or stayed on to study in such towns as Zabid in Yemen and Mecca itself. In fact, one of the earliest references to Jâwîs abroad is found in a 15th-century work of Yemeni biographical literature by a denizen of Zabid:[123]

> Abû 'Abd Allâh Mas'ûd b. Muḥammad al-Jâwî, [spelt] with a *jîm* and *kasr al-wâw*, was once known as a great and famous shaykh in the city of Aden and surrounding areas. He was one of the greats, a shaykh and jurist of the people of 'Uwâja. He was a colleague of the great jurist Ismâ'îl al-Ḥaḍramî, who benefited all and whose turban was a blessing to their souls. He was a master of character and upbringing, from whom a great many of the greats benefited, including the shaykh 'Abd Allâh b. As'ad al-Yâfi'î and others. Shaykh al-Yâfi'î noted him in his history [the *Mir'ât al-janân*] and praised him greatly, saying in recognition of him that the aforementioned shaykh was: 'The famous saint … the first to dress me in the tattered robe [of Sufism].'[124]

As Michael Feener points out, this named individual may or may not be Southeast Asian. But given his appellation, he must have had at least some connection with the region. The big surprise here is that not only is al-Jâwî described as a great teacher in Aden, but his famous contemporary and student were actually active at almost the very historical moment that Jâwa was being unveiled, and not so soon after the king of Samudra converted: Ismâ'îl al-Ḥaḍramî died in 1277, while al-Yâfi'î, the great compiler of saintly biographies, lived from 1298 to 1367.[125]

Aside from the Pasai tombstone of one al-Ṣaliḥ b. al-Malik al-Ashraf al-Jâwî, dated 1355, the next time the name "Jâwî" appears is when it is used by the mystical poet Ḥamza al-Fanṣûrî (d. 1527), who was perhaps the last Sufi of note to have visited the court of Samudra before the whole northern end of Sumatra was absorbed by Aceh in the 1520s. From his poems, we can ascertain that he came from Fansur, and that he joined a mystical brotherhood in Ayutthaya (known to the Persians as "the city of the boat"; *Shahr-i Nâv*) before venturing onward to Mecca and even Jerusalem. Otherwise, his poems — which are in Malay spiced with Arabic and Javanese words — make reference to Barus as the renowned source of camphor and the starting point of his journey, and Jâwî as his outward identity.

Hamzah Syahr Nawi zahirnya Jawi ... [126]	Outwardly Hamzah Syahr Nawi is Jawi ...
Hamzah Fansuri di dalam Mekkah	Hamzah Fansuri is in Mekkah
Mencari Tuhan di Bait al-Ka'bah	Seeking God in the house of the Ka'ba
Di Barus ke Kudus terlalu payah	Barus to Jerusalem is an arduous journey
Akhirnya dapat di dalam rumah	Yet finally He is found at home
...	...
Hamzah Fansuri di negeri Melayu	Hamzah Fansuri is in the land of Melayu
Tempatnya kapur di dalam kayu[127]	The place of camphor-laden trees

After the tombstone of al-Fanṣûrî, the next positive identification of Jâwîs in the study circles of Mecca and Medina comes in the 17th century, when new works were being addressed by Sufi masters, such as Ibrâhîm b. Ḥasan al-Kûrânî (1616–90), to an explicitly Jâwî audience following local interaction with their similarly named "friends" (aṣḥâbunâ al-jâwiyîn).[128] Indeed, al-Kûrânî sat in the teaching circles of Medina with perhaps the most famous of Ḥamza al-Fanṣûrî's successors, ʿAbd al-Raʿûf al-Sinkilî al-Jâwî (ca. 1615–ca. 1693), that is, ʿAbd al-Raʿûf, "the Jâwî from Singkel."[129] At this time, one must realize that Jâwî was still a term implying wider ethnic resonance for people from beyond the archipelago than those within it. Whether seen from Hadramaut or the Hejaz, such external and all-encompassing notions of identification seem reminiscent of the way that diverse peoples on the fringes of the Roman Empire could have a unitary culture ascribed to them.[130] Equally, if absorbed Barbarian populations could once have become Romanized — yet still distinct — by adherence to Roman law and participation in Roman culture, the Islamizing peoples of the western end of the Malay Archipelago most likely affirmed the designation "Jâwî" to describe a bond with Islamic culture, whether as

Jâwî Muslims or by their use of Malay and its distinct modified Arabic script, still known today as Jawi.

Al-Fanṣûrî made the ecumenical importance of Malay/Jâwî clear in the introduction to one of his works:

> The wretched Hamza Fansuri wishes to set forth the way to God and gnosis of Him in this book in the Jawi language. God Almighty willing, all God Almighty's servants unacquainted with Farsi and Arabic will be able to discuss the contents of this book.[131]

The concept of Jâwî being a hybrid cultural or linguistic ascription, rather than a purely ethnic one, is strengthened if we take on Reid's work on hybridity. Whereas in the 13th century Marco Polo seemed to refer to walled settlements of Chinese on the coast of Sumatra (al-Idrîsî's Tatars?),[132] between the 15th and 16th centuries assimilation of those communities on Java and Sumatra led to their identification by the Portuguese as Jaõas and Iauijs respectively.[133]

Whereas the former term might be tied to a perception of Javaneseness, the Malayo-Sumatran variant is both a tribute to the notion of connection to a Southeast Asian Islam and the very hybridity that it facilitated. Once Islam became the norm, rather than the exception, or else lacking the overwhelming presence of a non-Muslim other, notions of Jawiness would begin to lose their Malayo-Islamic salience, even if echoes remained. For example, Raffles, writing in 1818, treated Jawi as a term for hybridity, though it was still richly infused with notions of Islam and an attendant Arabness:

> Jahwí ... is the Malay term for anything mixed or crossed, as, when the language of one country is written in the character of another it is termed B'hása Jahwí, or mixed language; or, when a child is born of a Kilíng father and a Malay mother, it is called Anak Jahwí, a child of mixed race. Thus the Meláyu language, being written in the Arabic character, is termed B'hása Jahwí; the Malays, as a nation distinct from the fixed population of the eastern islands, not possessing any written character but what they borrow from the Arabs.[134]

Jâwîs Below the Wind

> Have you not seen the wind between Muwaysal and Jâwâ?
> As it settles upon you it heals. ...

I have suggested above that, more than being a term for the undoubted hybridity of the people of maritime Southeast Asian ports, Jâwî was both a pan-ethnic ascription used by Arabic-speaking outsiders cognizant of the importance of Java in the 13th and 14th centuries, and (increasingly) an Islamic cultural one for insiders. In the case of the former, the term is related to a geographical locus that places Jâwî peoples in necessarily Jâwî lands. For their own lands and seas, though, peoples of Austronesian background continued to refer to their own names, usually based on their estuarine capitals.

As Reid has also pointed out, many of the Southeast Asian polities described in his *Southeast Asia in the Age of Commerce* invoked the concept of being a community of lands "below the winds" (Malay: *bawah angin*).[135] Regardless of his decentering of Islam in his account, this framing, like that of Jâwî, is also connected with the indigenous flows of Islamization from the 14th century. Such flows were once more driven by Malay courts breaking free of Java, and came to take in some of the more easterly courts of the archipelago. And in time, too, their conception of a region below the winds would start to be accepted by some of the Muslim peoples of the Indian Ocean.

When I commenced this essay, I cited a Farsi echo of the phrase employed by a Persian in Siam in the 17th century. However, his "below winds" (Zîrbâdât) was a much-expanded version of a term used by his predecessor, 'Abd al-Razzâq Samarqandî, who, in an account of 1442, used the more limited "Zîrbâd" in a way that aligns with a Malay sense of region. In Hormuz, 'Abd al-Razzâq had noted the presence of the merchants of both Java (Châwa) and the "cities of Zîrbâd" (Zîrbâd Shaharhây), but in Calicut he wrote of those of Zîrbâd alone.[136]

Whereas scholars of Malay and Farsi have pointed in each other's direction when seeking the origins of *bawah angin* and *Zîrbâd*,[137] the widespread usage of the phrase in Malay texts suggests that the concept is of long standing and eastern Malay origin. And although no Malay text can be physically dated before the late 15th century, two of the oldest, describing matters in the 14th and 15th centuries — the *Hikayat Raja-raja Pasai* and the *Sulalat al-Salatin* — use *bawah angin* to describe maritime Southeast Asia as a community of (largely Malayo-Muslim) rulers stretching from Aceh to the Moluccas.[138]

The earliest direct evidence of local usage that I have seen so far is from the Moluccas, in a letter from Sultan Said of Ternate to the Dutch king in August 1599. This states that the letter was sent "from the land below the wind" (*dari tanah di-bawah angin*) and notes the arrival of W. Branderwijk, "a trader of land below the winds" (*saudagar dari tanah bawah angin*) who had just met "the king of Maluku, the possessor of the clove trees that were so famous in the land above the wind" (*telah sampailah kepada raja Maluku yang empunya pohon cengkeh yang terlalu masyhur di tanah atas angin*).[139]

A more famous example of a sub-aeolean designation comes three years later, in 1602, when the Acehnese ruler 'Ala' al-Din declared himself to be "the lord in power here below the winds who holds the throne of Aceh and Samudra and all the countries adjacent," in a trading permit to be used by the English in his territories.[140]

Then again, even if the indications are that *bawah angin* was recognized by Muslims within and beyond the region, it is not always found where one would expect it. In two Arabic letters to a Portuguese captain in 1520, Zayn al-Dîn, lord of "Shamûṭra," writes to the new rulers of Malacca in the hope that they might rein in one of their piratical captains, promising the benefits of trade in return, in the form of the goods of Barus or payment with the money of Bengal.[141] The only thing that Zayn al-Dîn claimed to be "under" was "the authority of the Lord of the universe" (*taht amr rabb al-'âlamîn*).

Whereas we do not have direct evidence that Malayo-Muslim rulers employed any equivalent of *bawah angin* in their letters to European rulers before ca. 1599, there are clear suggestions that this was the case with earlier correspondence with the Middle East. The first hint is admittedly tentative, but it is all the more logical given that it is bound up with the trade that linked Sumatra to the Indian Ocean. In the account of a Syrian physician of the late ninth century, as well as an attribution to a pharmacological text by Isḥâq al-Qayrawânî (d. 907), an explanation is given for why the camphor of Fansur was called *riyâḥî*. According to these authors, this was because this form of camphor was first discovered by a king of Fansur called Riyâḥ.[142] Riyâḥ is a known term in Islamic onomastics and is related to the Yemeni tribe of Tamîm — according to one of its members, Abû Sa'îd al-Tamîmî (d. 1166).[143] However, it is also the Arabic word for "winds."

Attention to the *rîyâḥî*-Fanṣûr link was first made by Dulaurier in 1846, though he did not attempt to tie it to "winds."[144] Based on his transcription of manuscripts of Avicenna (980–1037) and Ibn al-Bayṭâr (1197–1248), it seems that Rîyâḥ was later understood as a separate toponym, or at least as another source of camphor. Further, there is a suggestion in Ibn al-Bayṭâr's encyclopedia, quoting the *Murshid* of (the same?) al-Tamîmî, that an aromatic plant that smelt of camphor was additionally known as "the camphor of the Jews."[145]

One may wonder whether the origin of the story of a "King Riyâh" came from a letter brought to a commercial hub by a merchant charged to express the authority of a Malay ruler extending "below the winds." He might even have wanted himself called "the king of the winds" (*malik al-riyâh*). The subsidiary Jewish link could even be a function of the Fatimid attempt to take the Indian Ocean trade in spices away from the Abbasids in the tenth century.[146] Goitein's studies of the Geniza papyri have shown that a large part of this trade would be carried by Cairo-based Jewish merchants and their "Malay" partners based in Kra and Fansur.[147]

Once again we are faced with the orthographic and etymological problems of Zâbaj. Tibbetts argues that *riyâhî* is most likely an erroneous reading for *zabâjî*, based on the variant Zabâj.[148] But to my knowledge, this adjectival form never appears in the texts, nor is it a name recognized by al-Tamîmî in his dictionary of onomastics. Thus, I would suggest that both *riyâh* and the singular *rîh* could just as easily be an additional source of confusion over what the very *regional* and *Malay* sense that Zâbaj and its cognates entailed, but after being once again warped to conform to the Greek Zábai or harmonized with Chinese pronunciations of Jaba.

Wolters notes that the first seaborne Arab mission to China occurred in 724, implying that the ambassadors must have called at a Śrîvijayan port, from whence they most likely took the camphor as a gift they obviously regarded as precious.[149] Doubtless in the report of their return journey they would have relayed messages from the Śrîvijayan authorities — however their claims may have been expressed, whether as sons of Yavadvîpa or perhaps lords of the winds. But these could easily have been read by officials with a better knowledge of what Ptolemy had declared than what they heard or saw on paper.

Certainly, the handwritten "below the wind" is readily warped into any number of scribal possibilities, not least of which is "the throne of Zabaj" (*takht al-zabaj*). As Tibbetts observed, both the *alif* and the initial diacritical point were often left off manuscript renditions of Zâbaj, which led to variant readings such as Rânaj or confusion with the African Zanj; this was apparent in the ninth-century map seemingly commissioned by al-Ma'mûn, remembered as the great patron of the translation of Greek knowledge. Furthermore, as we have seen from al-Idrîsî's text, it is remarkable how few scribes recognized Zâbaj at all after the tenth century, even if it may have stuck in the parlance of the Muslim mariners for the Malay lands as a whole. There would also seem to have been some attempt to redress the long-term misunderstanding in later periods. For some reason, one scribe gave al-Idrîsî's Dabîḥât as *al-rîḥât*.[150]

Whatever the roots and potential confusions of "below the wind," much as Zâbaj became the accepted designation for the region from the ninth until the early 13th centuries, *bawah angin* ultimately found acceptance — but first in the Persian Zîrbâd. It also seems that such recognition could only be gained after Malay voices were being properly heard *as* Muslims — in the letters of their Qadis seeking *fatwa*s, from conversations with their merchants in the Indian Ocean harbors, or in councils with their students in the teaching circles of Aden, Zabid, and Medina.[151]

The first tangible hint of any Arabic acceptance of this nomenclature outside the archipelago, and one that aligns in any way with a sense of region, is found in a manuscript copy of the *Târîkh Shanbal* when a direction is assigned to the departing Portuguese in 1498. What makes this identification problematic at first sight is that after heading "below the winds," the Portuguese built a fort on the Swahili Coast. This need not be seen as incompatible if we consider that the designation "below the winds" could have been imagined as stretching across the southern swathe of the Indian Ocean, in which Austronesian shippers had long been active. The usage in the *Târikh Shanbal* thus may well reflect the same configurations that still linked Africa to Asia much as Zâbaj and Jâwa had floated together in the texts alongside Zanj, Sarandîb, and Qamar.

Setting aside such speculation on early usage, we are on firmer ground from the 16th century. 'Ala' al-Din Ri'ayat Shah of Aceh (r. 1540–67) must have wanted the Arabic version employed in letters to the Ottoman sultan, given that a reply sent from Constantinople in the 1560s refers to him as "the sultan ruling below the winds."[152] And we have also seen that the 1602 Acehnese document of free trade that mentioned "below the winds" was a translation of a concept intended for an Islamicate audience. Still, it was one that could incorporate the Europeans, much as the raja of Ternate could count a Dutch merchant as a trader of that shared world.[153]

Thus, indications are that in the expanding world of the 17th century, the notion of a region "below the winds" was also spreading beyond the Malay World. On the one hand, there is a clumsy Arabic letter written to James I in 1605 from the future Abu l-Mafakhir Mahmud Abd al-Qadir (r. 1624–51), in which the Bantenese ruler is styled, like his English counterpart, as a raja, and no mention is made of lands below the winds.¹⁵⁴ On the other, there is a fluent letter, dated 9 January 1665, from Sultan Abu l-Fattah (Ageng Tirtayasa)—whose court was in regular touch with Aceh and Mecca.¹⁵⁵ Here the Bantenese ruler acknowledges receipt of the cannon already requested from Charles II and refers to trade "below the wind" and the treachery of the Dutch toward "the people below the wind" (*ahl taḥt al-rîḥ*); the context implies the inclusion of the inhabitants of Java, named here as Jâwî land (*bilâd jâwî*).¹⁵⁶

With the conscious inclusion of Java into the lands below the winds — a process set in train with the rise of the north-coast Muslim state of Demak in the 15th century and the related sultanates of Cirebon and Banten — there would have increasingly been an awareness in the Middle East of new, non-Malay Jâwa. Perhaps for this reason, ʿAbd al-Raʾûf al-Sinkilî is more specific in his *Mirʾât al-ṭullâb* than his predecessors had been about the alignment of Malay and Jawi when he writes that he takes recourse to "the Sumatran (or perhaps 'Samudran') Jâwî tongue",¹⁵⁷ implying that there are other Jâwî languages in circulation in the Islamic ecumene.

We have also seen from Muḥammad Rabîʿ's usage, first mentioned at the very beginning of this essay, that the expanding notion of lands below the winds was reflected abroad in the 17th century, with the Farsi form changing from the Malay Zîrbâd to the Southeast Asian Zîrbâdât. Further, its adjectival form, Zîrbâdî, also mirrors the older Arabic Jâwî in terms of ethno-religious ascription, suggesting that Persians must have seen Zîrbâdîs in Burma and Siam much as Arabs would have recognized Jâwîs in the same places and similar faces. Echoes of this nomenclature were still to be found in the 19th century. Much as the mixed-race Muslims of Singapore were known as "Jawi Peranakan," in Burma the term "Zerbâdî" was used to describe both mixed-race Muslims and local converts to Islam.¹⁵⁸ Both communities nonetheless regarded themselves primarily as Southeast Asians by place of birth. However, it would appear that by the early years of the 20th century the designation Zîrbâdî had pejorative implications for Burmese nationalists, much as identifying oneself as part Arab came to carry a stain of disloyalty in Java in the 1930s.¹⁵⁹

Equally, to be identified as Jâwî was no longer viewed with enthusiasm by immigrant communities themselves, especially in the face of encouragement of racial classification by colonial regimes. With the advent of steam transportation, which was not subject to the whims of the winds that had defined an Islamizing region, greater numbers of Hadramis immigrated to a zone that would now be seared into their collective consciousness as Jâwa: the land of wealth, ease, and distraction.[160] As such, there was a market for genealogies for Jâwa-born Hadramis whose leaders began to establish schools to emphasize "their own" Arab language and ethnic identity within a Jâwî archipelago. Mandal argues that some Hadramis, forced into ethnic cantonments by Dutch colonial policies, also began to make use of a rhetoric in which they presented themselves as the "natural leaders" of their Jâwî coreligionists.[161] Some even began to speak of (and at times for) the Jâwa in the new forums of international Islam — newspapers and printed books — but that is another chapter in the ongoing story of the negotiation of cultural difference and affinity between the Middle East and Southeast Asia.[162]

Conclusion

In Ptolemaic and Han times, the western reaches of insular Southeast Asia, in which the entrepôt state of Jaba most likely sat, was a key transitional point for the India-China trade. The murmurs ultimately heard in the Mediterranean of a parallel sea of interrelated polities subsumed under variant understandings of its name, whether as Zábai, or the Indianized Sabadibae or Iabadiû, gave rise to the idea of the Javas. This was much what later European travelers, claimants to the heritage of Greece and Rome, expected to find when they came to the region. It was probably an identification confirmed as they sailed with Muslim pilots through their regional Jâwa.[163]

One of the great intervening stories bracketed by these different Javas is of the rise, submergence, and memory of Śrîvijaya — itself a claimant to the mantle of Yava — that occurred over the long period of trade between the Muslim West and China. In this period, the Yava of old was still vocalized by some visitors as Jâba but increasingly as Zâbaj, probably by agreement of the Chinese and Muslim mariners. Furthermore, the latter term was spelt in Arabic in a way that could elide with another, probably more localized, conceptualization of space in terms of the winds that brought the traders to their harbors.

With the loss of Kra, the Tamil raids of the 11th century, and enduring notions beyond the archipelago that mainland and maritime Southeast Asia were linked, the Śrîvijayan-inflected "Zâbaj" would be replaced by the more limited "Qamar" and "Melayu" before a Javanese ascendancy papered over 600 years of Straits history. This, in turn, would seed a new name in the Middle East for the Islamizing world of maritime Southeast Asia believed to be under the influence of the new claimant to the heritage of Yava. Even if Java had always been on the intra-insular routes, it was only now that it would feature properly on the charts from the West. Obviously this raises questions once more about how and when Islam came to Java, and should perhaps lead us to treat more seriously some of the texts that now seem on the margins of scholarly respectability.[164]

We should also continue to reread indigenous and exogenous sources in the light of developments in archeology. Whereas new international impulses have stimulated a need to know of the lands between India and China — whether with the globalization of Buddhism, the appearance of Southeast Asians in Arabia, or the later scourges of the Franks in the continuous Afro-Asian Ocean — Southeast Asian expressions of those international currents have usually been obscured in the transmission of information or the underlying assumptions of the region's visitors. The lands of Suvarṇadvîpa and Yava were a vague source of gold to the scholars before they became a recognized part of the Sanskritic ecumene, just as Zâbaj, and ultimately Jâwa, were first a source of exotic spices and tales of the bizarre. It seems today that the region is still trying to make its presence felt seriously as part of a "Muslim World" in a process well beyond the confusion of Zâbaj below the winds, and complicated instead by the politics of nation-states.

Notes

1. C. Snouck Hurgronje, *Mekka in the Latter Part of the 19th Century: Daily Life, Customs and Learning of the Moslems of the East-Indian-Archipelago*, trans. J. H. Monahan (Leiden: Brill, 1931), 215, n. 3.
2. Anthony Reid, "Introduction: A Time and a Place," in Anthony Reid, ed., *Southeast Asia in the Early Modern Era: Trade, Power, and Belief* (Ithaca, NY, and London: Cornell University Press, 1993), 3.
3. Muḥammad Rabî' b. Muḥammad Ibrâhîm, *The Ship of Sulaimân*, trans. J. O'Kane, Persian Heritage Series no.11 (London: Routledge and Kegan Paul, 1972), 160.
4. Unlike Reid, Ibrâhîm included Japan in that same zone, *Ship of Sulaimân*, 188–98.
5. Sanjay Subrahmanyam, "Writing History 'Backwards': Southeast Asian History (and the *Annales*) at the Crossroads," *Studies in History* 10, 1 (1994): 131–45, and "Notes on Circulation and Asymmetry in Two Mediterraneans, c. 1400–1800," in Claude Guillot, Denys Lombard, and Roderich Ptak, *From the Mediterranean to the China Sea: Miscellaneous Notes* (Wiesbaden:

Harrassowitz Verlag, 1998), 21–43. The overall debate is also addressed in Heather Sutherland, "Southeast Asia and the Mediterranean Analogy," *Journal of Southeast Asian Studies* 34, 1 (2003): 1–20.
6. For the Islamic geographical tradition, see S. Maqbul Ahmad, "Kharîta, khârita," in *Encyclopedia of Islam, New Edition* (hereafter *EI²*) 4: 1077–83. For a critical view of the phrasing of an Islamic South Asian world under the rubric of al-Hind, see Sunil Kumar, "Review of André Wink, *al-Hind: The Making of the Indo-Islamic World*," *Studies in History* 10, 1 (January–June 1994): 147–52.
7. Bérénice Bellina and Ian Glover, "Early Contact with India and the Mediterranean," in Ian Glover and Peter Bellwood, eds., *Southeast Asia: From Prehistory to History* (London: RoutledgeCurzon, 2004), 68–88, see p. 70.
8. Pierre-Yves Manguin, "Religious Networks, Merchant Networks: God and Mammon in Southeast Asian Indianization?", paper presented to the EUROSEAS conference, Paris, 1–4 September 2004.
9. William A. Southworth, "The Coastal States of Champa," in Glover and Bellwood, *Southeast Asia*, 209–33, see p. 223.
10. *Tzŭ-chih t'ung-chien*, 7062, as cited by Oliver Walters, *The Fall of Śrîvijaya in Malay History* (Ithaca: Cornell University Press, 1970), 39.
11. Al-Idrîsî, *Opus Geographicum*, ed. E. Cerulli *et al.*, 2 vols. (Rome: 1970), I, 62.
12. Paul Wheatley, *The Golden Khersonese: Studies in the Historical Geography of the Malay Peninsula before A.D. 1500* (Kuala Lumpur: University of Malaya Press, 1961), 123–59.
13. These names appear in the works of J. W. McCrindle, *Ancient India as Described by Ptolemy* (Calcutta: Thacker and Co., 1885); and G. F. Gerini, *Researches on Ptolemy's Geography of Eastern Asia* (London: Royal Asiatic Society, 1909). However, the first two terms are notable by their absence in the recent work of Berggren and Jones, for whom Zábai is the most important, but undefined, toponym to the east of Takôla: J. Lennart Berggren and Alexander Jones, *Ptolemy's Geography: An Annotated Translation of the Theoretical Chapters* (Princeton, NJ: Princeton University Press, 2000).
14. Henry Yule and Henri Cordier, *The Book of Ser Marco Polo*, 2 vols. (Amsterdam: Philo Press, 1975), II, 269.
15. One argument has Zábai as Jambi, Iabadiû as southwest Borneo, and Sabadibae as West Java: W. J. van der Meulen, "Suvarṇadvîpa and the Chrysê Chersonêsos," *Indonesia* 18 (October 1974): 1–40; and "Ptolemy's Geography of Mainland Southeast Asia and Borneo," *Indonesia* 19 (April 1975): 1–32. Van der Meulen (but not Ptolemy) may have been right regarding the general location of Zábai. Ptolemy criticized Marinos's placement of Zábai 20 days' sail from Kattigara along a southward-facing coast (the Malay Peninsula?). Cf. Berggren and Jones, *Ptolemy's Geography*, 156.

16. In several articles, Mahdi has argued that the literal Sanskrit meaning of "barley island" is acceptable by asserting that it refers to another cultigen possibly produced in Sumatra. For his most recent article, see "Yavadvipa and the Merapi Volcano in West Sumatra," *Archipel* 75 (2008): 111–43. On the other hand, Sergey Kullanda has attempted to link the term "Yava" to notions of being "beyond" or "below" the original homeland of Austronesian speakers, and claims that it first referred to Borneo. See Sergey Kullanda, "Nushāntara or Java? The Acquisition of the Name," *Indonesia and the Malay World* 34, 98 (March 2006): 91–7.
17. Waruno Mahdi, "Yavadvipa and the Merapi Volcano in West Sumatra," 114; and "Wie hießen die Malaien, bevor sie 'Malaien' hießen?" in A. Bormann, A. Graf, and M. Voss, eds., *Südostasien und Wir: Grundsatzdiskussion und Fachbeiträge* (Hamburg: Tagung des Arbeitskreises Südostasien und Ozeanien, 1993/5), 162–76.
18. I was first made aware of the nomenclature of the Javanese inscriptions by Jan van den Veerdonk, "Foreigners in Old Javanese Inscriptions," paper presented to the colloquium "Non-Javanese, Not Yet Javanese, and un-Javanese," Leiden, 25 March 2004.
19. H. B. Sarkar, "A Geographical Introduction to South-East Asia: The Indian Perspective," *Bijdragen tot de Taal-, Land- en Volkenkunde* 137–2/3 (1981): 293–323. For a view that continues, perhaps too literally, to differentiate Suvarṇabhûmi and Suvarṇadvîpa as mainland and insular Southeast Asia, see Pierre-Yves Manguin, "The Archaeology of Early Maritime Polities in Southeast Asia," in Glover and Bellwood, *Southeast Asia*, 282–313, see p. 293.
20. Sarkar, "A Geographical Introduction," 305. Vâlmîki's description of Yavadvîpa as a land of seven kings, an island with gold, silver, and gold mines is certainly more suggestive of Sumatra than Java. The relevant passage is repeated in Mahdi, "Wie hießen die Malaien," p. 165, who also suggests that Yavadvîpa may well have been a later inclusion in the text.
21. Georges Coedès, *The Indianized States of Southeast Asia* (Honolulu: East-West Center Press, 1968), 81–96 and passim. See also P-Y. Manguin, "Palembang and Sriwijaya: An Early Malay Harbour-City Rediscovered," *Journal of the Malaysian Branch of the Royal Asiatic Society* 66, 1 (1993): 23–46.
22. See Michel Jacq-Hergoualc'h, *The Malay Peninsula: Crossroads of the Maritime Silk Road (100 BC–1300 AD)*, trans. Victoria Hobson (Leiden: Brill, 2002).
23. See Mahdi's "Yavadvipa and the Merapi Volcano in West Sumatra."
24. Sheldon Pollock, "The Cosmopolitan Vernacular," *The Journal of Asian Studies* 57, 1 (1998): 6–37.

25. Jacq-Hergoualc'h, *Malay Peninsula*, 239. The reading of this passage is problematic, and Michael Vickery has proposed that the Chinese "Shi-li-fo-qi" cannot be an etymological match for "Śrîvijaya," implying in the process that Yijing was more likely observing a new attachment to Buddhism undertaken by the people of Jambi.
26. On Java's continuing integration in networks of Tantric Buddhism spanning India, Sri Lanka, China, and Japan, see Jeffrey Roger Sundberg, "The Wilderness Monks of the Abhayagiravihâra and the Origins of Sino-Javanese Esoteric Buddhism," *Bijdragen tot de Taal-, Land- en Volkenkunde* 160, 1 (2004): 95–123.
27. Clearly Sumatra mattered in the minds of the monks of Nâlandâ. After ordination there, the monk Atîśa (b. 982) was directed to Suvarṇadvîpa to perfect his knowledge of Mahâyâna Buddhism. He stayed there from 1011 to 1023. See Anil Kumar Sarkar, *The Mysteries of Vajrayana Buddhism: From Atisha to Dalai Lama* (New Delhi: South Asian Publishers, 1993). Jacq-Hergoualc'h also remarks that he was preceded in the eighth century by the putative introducer of Tantric Buddhism to China, Vajrabodhi. Jacq-Hergoualc'h, *Malay Peninsula*, 320. Similarly, from the time of Yijing, Chinese monks were advised to study in Suvarṇadvîpa. See Wolters, *Śrîvijaya*, 39.
28. Hirananda Shastri, "The Nalanda Copper-plate of Devapaladeva," *Epigraphia Indica* 17 (1924): 310–27. The inscription gives the name of the mother of Bâlaputra as Târâ, who was the daughter of King Dharmasêtu and consort to the mighty king who was the son of the ruler of Yavabhûmi. Cf. Jan Wisseman Christie, "Revisiting Early Mataram," in Marijke J. Klokke and Karel R. van Kooij, eds., *The Fruits of Inspiration: Studies in Honour of Prof. J. G. de Casparis* (Groningen: Egbert Forster, 2001), 25–55, see p. 30.
29. Jacq-Hergoualc'h, *Malay Peninsula*, 243–47, 270. Basing himself in part on the Chaiya inscription, Mahdi argues that the Java-based Śailendras were, in fact, the rulers of Yava/Melayu who had been displaced by the Śrîvijayans, returning to the peninsula in strength under Sanjaya in the eighth century; though the argument that Sanjaya was the nephew of the displaced King Sena of Yava would seem to stretch time a little too much. See Mahdi, "Yavadvipa and the Merapi Volcano in West Sumatra," 127–8.
30. The "myth" of Śrîvijaya will also be considered afresh by Roy Jordaan and Brian Colless, *The Mahârâjas of the Isles: The Śailendras and the problem of Sriwijaya* (Leiden: VTCZOAO, forthcoming).
31. M. Klokke, "The Sailendras: Javanese or Non-Javanese," paper presented to the colloquium "Non-Javanese, Not Yet Javanese, and Un-Javanese." The existence in Java of Old Malay stelae from the late eighth century (Christie, "Revisiting Mataram," 37) may suggest common Śrîvijayan cause with West Javanese Śailendras, or that they were already identical. It is interesting to note in this connection that the first inscription written in Old Javanese, as

opposed to Sanskrit (or Old Malay), appears in 804. Meanwhile, substantial finds, including Pali votive tablets, are continuing to be made in West Java that bear a similarity to material found in Sumatra.

32. Cf. Coedès, *Indianized States*, 100, 306.
33. See Mahdi, "Yavadvipa and the Merapi Volcano in West Sumatra," 119–20.
34. Cf. Manguin, "Archaeology," 304–5.
35. John N. Miksic, "The Classical Cultures of Indonesia," in Glover and Bellwood, *Southeast Asia*, 243. Whereas Miksic states that it was an attack from Java and the Southern Islands, Geoff Wade informs me that there is some ambiguity here. G. Wade, personal communication, 9 November 2004.
36. I am most grateful to Lewis Mayo for explaining the pronunciation and identification of Shepo.
37. Certainly Coedès was aware of the ambiguity of "Jvâ." See Coedès, 1929, cited in Jacq-Hergoualc'h, *Malay Peninsula*, 426.
38. A series of copperplates was inscribed during the reign of the Chola Râjarâja-Râjakêsarivarman (985–1013), announcing that a temple had been commissioned in his domains in 1005 by the same Yava-descended rulers of Śrîvijaya. See Shastri, "The Nalanda copper-plate," 312–3. From Menon's research, it appears that the Cholas accepted these claims regarding both Śrîvijaya and Śailendra, at times slightingly, as one and the same. A. G. Menon, "Copper Plates to Silver Plates: Cholas, Dutch and Buddhism," in Klokke and Van Kooi, *Fruits of Inspiration*, 291–317, infra. 296–7.
39. Cf. Wolters, *Śrîvijaya*, 42, 77ff. Wolters's arguments have not definitively established when Śrîvijaya fell, or which city did the falling. It is interesting to note, though, that after the Chola raids, the endowments of the Negapatam temple once supplied by the rulers of Sumatra were continued by the Chola king Râjendra I (r. 1012–44). Jacq-Hergoualc'h, *Malay Peninsula*, 274–5.
40. Even the 15th-century rulers of Ayutthaya would inscribe a major monument in four languages, including Arabic (or perhaps Persian) and Chinese, but excluding Sanskrit. David K. Wyatt, *Siam in Mind* (Chiang Mai: Silkworm Books, 2002), 26.
41. It would appear that Persians dominated the early Islamic trade with China, much as Sogdians and Bactrians are believed to have played a role in the preceding Vaiśnavite networks. Manguin, "Archaeology," 297. See also Jacq-Hergoualc'h, *Malay Peninsula*, 259, and the special issue of *Archipel* (No. 68, 2004) devoted to the subject of Persian involvement in Asian trade. It is further remarkable that while Persians may have been visitors to Java — perhaps listed under the North Indian rubric of Aryya — there is no evidence of any Arab contacts. Van den Veerdonk, "Foreigners."
42. Jeremy Johns and Emilie Savage-Smith, "The Book of Curiosities: A Newly Discovered Series of Islamic Maps," *Imago Mundi* 55 (2003): 7–24. Another indication of the early provenance, as far as Southeast Asia is concerned, is

shown by the fact that there is no mention of the islands that were known in the 13th century. Of the few Southeast Asian landfalls, only Samara (Samudra?) and Qadaḥ (Kedah?) seem recognizable.
43. The most commonly cited presentation of early Arabic texts is that of Tibbetts, which relies heavily on the work of Ferrand. See G. R. Tibbetts, *A Study of the Arabic Texts Containing Material on South-East Asia* (Leiden: Brill, 1979); and Gabriel Ferrand, *Relations de voyages et textes géographiques Arabes, Persans et Turks relatifs a L'extrême-Orient* (Paris: Ernest Laroux, 1913).
44. J. Sauvaget, *Relation de la Chine et de l'Inde* (Paris, 1948).
45. Tibbetts, *Arabic Texts*, 100–16 and passim. A later distillation is G. R. Tibbetts and Shawkat Toorawa, "Zâbadj, Zâbidj, Zâbag," *EI*[2] 11: 367–9. Tibbetts's reading of Ibn Khurdâdhbih is a 19th-century recension, *Kitâb al-masâlik*, ed. M. J. De Goeje (Leiden: 1892), 87–8, 132–3, 138.
46. Sauvaget, *Relation*, 4. Râmî or Râmnî is understood to be a reference to Lamreh. Tibbetts, *Arabic Texts*, 138–40; Edward McKinnon, "Beyond Serandib: A Note on Lambri at the Northern Tip of Aceh," *Indonesia* 46 (October 1988): 103–21.
47. Sauvaget, *Relation*, 8.
48. Geoff Wade, "From Chaiya to Pahang: The Eastern Seaboard of the Peninsula as Recorded in Classical Chinese Texts," in Daniel Perret, Amara Srisuchat, and Sumbun Thanasuk, eds., *Études sur l'histoire du sultanat de Patani, Études thématiques* (Paris: École française d'Extrême-Orient, 2004), 37–78. Tibbetts, who tended to believe distances above toponymic coincidence, objected to the equation of Kra with Kalâh, claiming that Arab sailors were not philologists (*Arabic Texts*, 125–6), and rejected the equation of Bâlûs and Barus for the same reason. Even so, there is a certain amount of consistency here, and given such a liquid shift, Kra would also seem a likely candidate for Ptolemy's Takôla. Cf. Berggren and Jones, *Ptolemy's Geography*, 172.
49. "They say that near to Zâbaj is a mountain, which they name 'the mountain of fire' and which cannot be approached. Smoke appears from it by day and tongues of fire by night. At its base are springs of cool and hot freshwater," Sauvaget, *Relation*, 10.
50. Ibn Khurdâdhbih, *Kitâb al-masâlik*, 16–7. I accept that this reading is very tenuous, as the more likely plural of typhoon (Ar. *ṭûfân*) should be *ṭawâfîn*.
51. Thus: *wa-min mulûk al-hind [malik] jâba wa-malik al-ṭâfin wa-malik al-juzur*.
52. Yusuf, on the other hand, favored the Sanskritized *vijayapati*. These readings are summarized in Tibbetts, *Arabic Texts*, 27, 108–9.
53. If a clearer text is located, readings of the name of Zâbaj's lord should, like so many of the toponyms and technical terms found in the Arab texts,

be taken in a Malay direction. For example, the word *bersila* was used in the *'Ajâ'ib al-hind*, attributed to al-Râmhurmuzî (ca. 1000), while Sauvaget (*Relation*, 38, n. 8) suggested that the Arabic term for the Straits, *Salâhṭ* (cf. Tibbetts: Salâhiṭ), is from the Malay *selat*.

54. Sauvaget, *Relation*, 8ff. There are parallels in the stories of dark and light peoples to the descriptions of the Swahili Coast. Freeman-Grenville once suggested that the "white" people might be understood to be foreign traders, perhaps Arabs and Persians. See G. S. P. Freeman-Grenville, *The Medieval History of the Coast of Tanganyika* (New York: Oxford University Press, 1962), 39. Then again, the relationship in Southeast Asia seems more akin to that between coastal "Malays" and the forest peoples responsible for the gathering of products sought after by the traders. See Barbara Watson Andaya and Leonard Andaya, *A History of Malaysia*, 2nd ed. (Houndmills: Palgrave, 2001), 12.

55. Ibn Khurdâdhbih, *Kitâb al-masâlik*, 65.

56. Ibn Khurdâdhbih, *Kitâb al-masâlik*, 66. Most texts appear to place variants of Langabalus in the Andaman archipelago, but Ibn Khurdâdhbih's islands would seem, phonetically at least, to have had some relationship to Barus, also described as a source of excellent camphor and (like much of Southeast Asia) home to cannibals.

57. Tibbetts, *Arabic Texts*, 28–9. On this location for Jâba, compare Ibn Khurdâdhbih, *Kitâb al-masâlik*, p. 66, who gives Harlaj or Hûlaj instead of the Salâhṭ or Harang of the *Akhbâr*. Barus, known from Ptolemy, is also to be identified with Fansur.

58. Ibn Khurdâdhbih, *Kitâb al-masâlik*, 68; Tibbetts, *Arabic Texts*, 28–9.

59. See Edward Sachau, ed., *Alberuni's India* (London: Trübner and Co., 1887), 103. Interestingly, Abû Zayd also writes of *both* Zâbaj and the land of gold, while al-Bîrûnî makes a double confusion, naming "the islands of Zanj" as the land of gold (p. 204) and then Suvarṇabhûmi (p. 157). It would also appear that Suwarna Dîb (*s.w.r.n.d.y.b*) may lie at the heart of another misunderstanding that has Sri Lanka in Arabic as Sarandîb (*s.r.n.d.y.b.*), predating European arguments about the identity of Ptolemy's Taprobane; Cf. Yule, *Marco Polo*, II, 295; Thomas Suárez, *Early Mapping of Southeast Asia* (Hong Kong: Periplus, 1999), 100–1. The Indian link with Suvarṇadvîpa was by no means a memory. Atîśa, for example, set out for Suvarṇadvîpa after his initiation at Nâlandâ.

60. The edition of Abû Zayd used by Ferrand was produced by M. Langlés (*Silsilat al-tawârîkh*, Paris, 1811) and translated by M. Reinaud: *Relation des voyages faits par les Arabes et les Persans dans l'Inde et à la Chine dans le IXe siècle de l'ère chrétienne*, 2 vols. (Paris: Imprimerie Royale, 1848). For the section on Zâbaj, see I, 92–135/II, 89–101.

61. Sauvaget, *Relation*, 90.

62. Tibbetts, *Arabic Texts*, 32–6, 112–3.
63. Manguin, "Archaeology," 300–1. Jacq-Hergoualc'h, basing himself in part on Singhalese accounts, identifies Tambralinga as a later assailant on the Khmers and writes that the Tambralingans could just as easily be classed as a Zâbaj people. Jacq-Hergoualc'h, *Malay Peninsula*, 425–6.
64. Coedès, *Indianized States*, 131. With thanks to Geoff Wade, who first informed me that the old Hokkien pronunciation of *shi-li fo-qi, si-li fut/but-se*, was a potentially acceptable rendering of Śrîvijaya, and that *san-fo-qi* (uttered *sna-fut/but-zue*) was "an acceptable rendering of Zabaj." Even so, he has also drawn my attention to the recent arguments of Michael Vickery undermining Coedès's etymological equation of the former with Śrîvijaya. Geoff Wade, personal communications, 22 September and 3 December 2004.
65. This was indirectly accepted by Tibbetts and Toorawa ("Zâba<u>dj</u>," 367) referring to Mahdi, "Wie hießen die Malaien," 171. I have pursued this with Pak Waruno, who indicated the original sources of the equation of Sayâbiga with Zâbaj. Interestingly, the *Encyclopedia of Islam* entry on the latter makes no cross-reference to Sayâbiga (s.v.), which itself is to be found as a revised version of the entry in the very first edition of the *Encyclopedia* by Ferrand: "Sayâbidja," *EI1* 4: 200–1. I am also informed by an editor of *EI²* that Shawkat Toorawa felt some discomfort in making this identification. Professor E. J. van Donzel, personal communication, 23 November 2004.
66. Mahdi, "Wie hießen die Malaien," 168, quoting Legge, 1886.
67. See Edwin G. Pulleyblank, *Lexicon of Reconstructed Pronunciation in Early Middle Chinese, Late Middle Chinese, and Early Mandarin* (Vancouver: UBC Press, 1991). For a brief discussion of early Chinese sources that point to *yaba or *jaba as cognates of Yava, see Mahdi, "Yavadvipa and the Merapi Volcano in West Sumatra," 114–6.
68. *Alberuni's India*, I, 253–4. Cf. Tibbetts, *Arabic Texts*, 50, n. 19.
69. *Alberuni's India*, I, 103.
70. See, for example, al-Bîrûnî's chart of the Indian Ocean, which distinguishes the *jazâ'ir al-dhabîḥât* from the *jazâ'ir al-zanj*. British Museum, Or. 8349, f. 58. For a copy of the map, see Ahmad, "<u>Kh</u>arîṭa."
71. See al-Idrîsî, *Opus*, I, 62, 67–86. Cf. Tibbetts, *Arabic Texts*, 51–4.
72. By comparison, the *Mukhtaṣar al-'ajâ'ib* referred to such events leading to Chinese pillaging of the islands of Zâbaj. See Tibbetts, *Arabic Texts*, 49.
73. Al-Idrîsî and others were aware of the long history of trade between Africa and the archipelago, and they claimed that dealings between the Zanj and sailors from Zâbaj were made easier by their languages being mutually intelligible. Whereas this might be a northward mapping of the links between Malay and Malagasy, Swahili does have numerous Malay borrowings and the Zang were also known to Indonesians. Javanese inscriptions from the tenth

to the 14th centuries, for example, refer to the presence of *Jenggi*. Van den Veerdonk, "Foreigners."
74. On the older tradition of Khmer queenship and mention of Kambujarâjalakṣmî, thought to have been a consort of Harṣavarman III (r. 1066–80), see Trudy Jacobsen, "Autonomous Queenship in Cambodia, 1st–9th century," *Journal of the Royal Asiatic Society*, series 3, no. 13, part 3 (2003): 357–75, see pp. 364–5.
75. Jacq-Hergoualc'h, *Malay Peninsula*, 355–6.
76. It has been suggested that the Cholas maintained a presence in North Sumatra and Kedah until ca. 1100. Miksic, "Classical Cultures," 247.
77. Yet another possibility is the port of Kampé (Aru), which had independent relations with southern India in the 13th century. See Andaya and Andaya, *A History of Malaysia*, 31. Even so, Kampar remains a stronger contender for what could have been considered one of two Qamars, of which there are 16th-century echoes. Ramusio's chart of 1554 shows a "Caimparr" at the site of present-day Kampar and a "Campar" on the mainland between Cambodia and Champa, a juxtaposition that, like the map's southward orientation, seems to pay tribute to a much earlier Arab original. Cf. Suárez, *Early Mapping*, 55–7, 134–5. Incidentally, Suárez's examples are contemporaries. The Idrîsid is from 1553 and the Spanish from 1554.
78. Wyatt, as summarized by Jacq-Hergoualc'h, *The Malay Peninsula*, 399–401.
79. Again we have Râmî, in which al-Idrîsî locates a small black forest people. They are also said to have little boats that run in good wind, sell amber in exchange for iron, and have camphor and pearls. Next comes Barus, where naked women are in charge of sales of goods to passing ships.
80. This sea was also associated by al-Mas'ûdî with the dominion of the mahârâja of Zâbaj. See Tibbetts, *Arabic Texts*, 38. Regarding the Cham connection, Geoff Wade has reminded me of the linguistic connections between Cham and Acehnese, Wiliam Southworth has spoken to me of the likelihood that many of the mainland coastal terms are Chamic, and Jacq-Hergoualc'h (*Malay Peninsula*, 269) notes the remarkably Chamic features of ninth-century sculptures found in the vicinity of Chaiya and beyond.
81. Al-Idrîsî, *Opus*, I, 79–80.
82. Variants given were Ḥabâbat al-Hindî, Ḥanâbat al-Hindî, Ḥadabat al-Hind, and Jâbat al-Hind.
83. Al-Idrîsî, *Opus*, I, 81.
84. Indeed, Khmers, Chams, and Mons outnumber many of the foreign groups in the east Javanese inscriptions. Van den Veerdonk, "Foreigners."
85. The same pattern is borne out by an examination of the China-Cham networks. Wade, "Champa in the *Song hui-yao ji-gao*."
86. Al-Idrîsî, *Opus*, I, 85.
87. Again this would exclude Java, as that island's economy shifted to the use of Chinese coins only ca. 1300 — and perhaps as part of a strategy to finally

wrest trade from what would by then be the Sumatran vassal of Majapahit. See Miksic, "Classical Cultures," 246, 251.
88. Konrad Miller, ed., *Weltcarte des Idrisi von Jahr 1154 n. Chr.* (Stuttgart: 1929); cf. Tibbetts, *Arabic Texts*, 53, 85, fig. 3. Among the sources used was a Bodleian Library manuscript (ms. Poc. 375), whose Southeast Asian pages are reproduced in Suárez, *Early Mapping*, 134–5.
89. One Idrîsid map of the 13th century also copies the form of Râmî, but it does not assign it a name. Johns and Savage-Smith, "Book of Curiosities," plate 2; Suárez, *Early Mapping*, 134–5.
90. Under the Southern Song, Chinese vessels had already begun to "winter" in Lamuri in the late 12th century, while Java began to receive official visits in 1225. See Wolters, *Śrîvijaya*, 42.
91. Tibbetts, *Arabic Texts*, 114. For the passages relating to the *Mu'jam al-buldân*, Tibbetts uses F. Wüstenfeld, ed., *Jacut's geographisches Wörterbuch*, 6 vols. (Leipzig: 1866–73).
92. *Jacut's Wörterbuch*, I, 506. Wüstenfeld (V, 58) notes that Zâbaj is intended.
93. Translation from G. R. Smith, "Ibn al-Mujawir's 7th/13th Century Arabia — The Wondrous and the Humorous," in A. K. Irvine, R. B. Serjeant, and G. Rex Smith, eds., *Miscellany of Middle Eastern Articles in Memoriam Thomas Muir Johnstone 1924–83* (Harlow, Essex: Longman, 1988), 111–24, see p. 113. Arabic in parentheses from Abû l-Faḍl Yûsuf b. Ya'qûb b. al-Mujâwir, *Ṣifat bilâd al-Yaman wa-Makka wa-ba'ḍ al-Ḥijâz al-musammât târîkh al-mustabṣir*, ed. O. Löfgren (Leiden: Brill, 1951), 81.
94. *Jacut's Wörterbuch*, IV, 691.
95. A modern poem linking the 'Aqîl clan of Hadramaut with Jâwa would not sound unusual. One of its most famous descendants who made his fortune in Jâwa in the 19th century was Sayyid 'Uthmân (1822–1914). His atlas of Hadramaut shows how the region consists of many torrents that eventually flow into one *sayl* and out into the Indian Ocean. 'Uthmân b. 'Abd Allâh b. 'Aqîl al-'Alawî, *Aṭlas 'arabî* (Leiden: 1886 [reprint]).
96. Such wonders figured heavily in the 13th-century *'Ajâ'ib al-makhlûqât* of al-Qazwînî. One Farsi version dating from the 16th century provides images of the *nasnâs* in the form of winged maidens. See L. Or. 8907, ff. 52–9. A century later Muḥammad Ibrâhîm described the *nasnâs* as ape-like bipeds that emitted loud shrieks like women. *Ship of Sulaimân*, 166.
97. *Jacut's Wörterbuch*, II, 901. A copy of the *Mu'jam* made in 1784 perfunctorily lists Zâbaj as "the lands of India on the borders of China" (*bilâd al-hind fî ḥudûd al-ṣîn*). L. Or. 295 f. 153 verso.
98. *Jacut's Wörterbuch*, IV, 174; Cf. L. Or. 295: "Qumr is also an island in the middle of the Sea of Zanj. There is no greater island than it in that land. It has a few cities."

99. See J. Richardson, *A New Malagasy-English Dictionary* (Antananarivo: London Missionary Society, 1885).
100. Yule, *Marco Polo*, II, 284. Polo's Samara may be Samudra, as the Malay *hikayat* refer to this state as having been converted from Perlak.
101. Ibn Baṭṭūṭa, *Riḥlat Ibn Baṭṭūṭa al-musammâh tuḥfat al-nuẓẓâr fî gharâ'ib al-amṣâr*, ed. Ṭalâl Ḥarb (Bayrût: Dâr al-Kutub al-'Ilmiyya), 572.
102. Ota Atsushi, *Changes of Regime and Social Dynamics in West Java: Society, State, and the Outer World of Banten, 1750–1830* (Leiden and Boston: Brill, 2006).
103. On Prapañca's complaints and mention of outsiders, see Mpu Prapañca, *Deśawarṇana (Nâgarakṛtâgama)*, ed. Stuart Robson (Leiden: KITLV Press, 1995), 35, 82, 84.
104. *The Royal Chronicles of Ayutthaya*, trans. Richard D. Cushman, ed. D. K. Wyatt (Bangkok: The Siam Society, 2000), 9–10.
105. Carool Kersten, "A Sultan on the Throne of the Dhammaraja: Cambodian and Dutch Sources on the Conversion of Ramadhipati I (1642–1658)," unpublished paper. It is also curious to note that *Cha Va* in Vietnamese denotes foreign traders, but that the meaning expanded to include traders of any nationality, even Indians and Africans. Geoff Wade, personal communication, 13 October 2004.
106. *Riḥlat Ibn Baṭṭūṭa*, 572, 577, 618. In the case of the first mention, Ibn Baṭṭūṭa lists the Jâwa as the second of the main groups of people that flocked to Calicut (after the Chinese), which he painted as the best-attended port in South India. The second mention of Jâwa comes when he entrusts his concubines and servants to their leader there.
107. That is, benzoin, a word that derives from *[lu]bân jâwî > benjoin*. The 1553 Turkish translation of a navigational treatise by Sulaymân b. Aḥmad al-Mahrî (ca. 1511) mistakenly makes reference to the Sumatran incense at the commencement of the section on Java. Tibbetts, *Arabic Texts*, 216, n. 111.
108. *Riḥlat Ibn Baṭṭūṭa*, 617, 619. This also has the same implications for the *iqlîm al-jâwa* in the *Târikh al-mustabṣir*: "the region of the Jâwa people."
109. *Riḥlat Ibn Baṭṭūṭa*, 649.
110. Marco Polo alleged that the townspeople of Basma, Samara, Dagroian, Lambri, and Fansur — not yet Muslim in his eyes — claimed such a relationship to the Great Khan (of China, or China via Java?), but he made no such statement for Muslim Ferlec. Yule, *Marco Polo*, II, 284–99.
111. *Riḥlat Ibn Baṭṭūṭa*, 619–22. For translations of the passages on Southeast Asia, and mention of Mul Jâwa with its infidel king, see H. A. R. Gibb and C. F. Beckingham, trans. and annot., *The Travels of Ibn Baṭṭūṭa A.D. 1325–1354*, vol. IV (London: Hakluyt Society, 1994), 874–87.
112. That al-Malik al-Ẓâhir was a real person seems confirmed by the existence of a tombstone of his daughter, datable to either 1380 or 1389. M. C. Ricklefs,

A *History of Modern Indonesia Since c. 1300* (Basingstoke: Macmillan, 1993), 4.

113. *Shîrâzî* may well have been a generic term for "trader." See Freeman-Grenville, *Medieval History of Tanganyika*, 32–42, 74–7. By comparison, the Shirazis of the 16th century were instrumental in the conversion of the Comoros. See G. Rotter, "Ḳumr," *EI*^{2} 5: 379–81.
114. *Riḥlat Ibn Baṭṭūṭa*, 470. Al-Idrîsî had already commented on the qualities of *'ûd qmâri*, remarking that the aloeswood of Ṣanf was superior. Al-Idrîsî, *Opus* I: 81.
115. B. J. O. Schrieke, *Indonesian Sociological Studies: Ruler and Realm in Early Java* (The Hague: van Hoeve, 1957), 267. According to Schrieke (p. 263), Ibn Baṭṭūṭa noted that the sultan of Samudra was the maharaja of Zâbaj, although no such reference exists in the Arabic edition I consulted nor the translation made by Gibb.
116. Two, somewhat dated, articles that highlight the role of Indian visitors in the process of Islamization are G. W. J. Drewes, "New Light on the Coming of Islam to Indonesia?" *Bijdragen tot de Taal-, Land- en Volkenkunde* 124 (1968): 433–59; and Stuart Robson, "Java at the Crossroads," *Bijdragen tot de Taal-, Land- en Volkenkunde* 137, 2/3 (1981): 259–92. From van den Veerdonk's analysis it is also clear that Sinhalese and Indians — particularly Dravidians and Tamils — were regular visitors. Van den Veerdonk, "Foreigners."
117. Elizabeth Lambourn, "From Cambay to Samudera-Pasai and Gresik: The Export of Gujerati Grave Memorials to Sumatra and Java in the Fifteenth Century C.E.," *Indonesia and the Malay World* 31, 90 (July 2003): 221–89.
118. Cecilia Ayala, personal communication, September 1999. Such local identification seems to have confused later colonial governments that used the island as a dumping ground for their Southeast Asian exiles. What the Dutch referred to as Sri Lanka's Javanese community became the nucleus of a Malay one under the English. Adrian Vickers, "'Malay Identity': Modernity, Invented Tradition, and Forms of Knowledge," *Review of Indonesian and Malaysian Affairs* 31–1 (1997): 173–212, see pp. 188–9.
119. Charles Boxer, "A Note on Portuguese Reactions to the Revival of the Red Sea Spice Trade and the Rise of Atjeh, 1540–1600," *Journal of Southeast Asian History* 10, 3 (1969): 415–28; Anthony Reid, "Sixteenth Century Turkish Influence in Western Indonesia," *Journal of Southeast Asian History* 10, 3 (1969): 395–414. The precise nature of the Acehnese missives and the question of a faux Acehnese ambassador to the Sublime Porte have been treated recently by Giancarlo Casale, "The Ottoman Age of Exploration: Spices, Maps and Conquest in the Sixteenth-Century Indian Ocean," PhD dissertation (Harvard University).
120. Serjeant notes how frequently Aceh appears in Hadrami works of the 16th century. See R. B. Serjeant, *The Portuguese off the South Arabian*

Coast: *Ḥaḍramī Chronicles* (Oxford, 1963), 110, n. 3, for reference to the ships, and 168 in regard to *fatwa*s being requested of the Qadi of Shihr by Acehnese in AH 943 (1536/7) or perhaps AH 954 (1547).
121. Serjeant, *Portuguese off the Arabian Coast*, 41. The (now missing) text, ascribed to Sharîf Aḥmad Shanbal 'Abd Allâh b. 'Alawî (d. 1514), was acquired in the 1940s from the Qadi of Hurayda, 'Alî b. Sâlim Âl al-'Aṭṭâs. It is described in R. B. Serjeant, "Materials for South Arabian History: Notes on New MSS from Ḥaḍramawt," *Bulletin of the School for Oriental and African Studies* 13 (1949–50): 281–307, 581–60, see pp. 291–3.
122. Serjeant, *Portuguese off the Arabian Coast*, 41, 169.
123. This information was brought to light by Michael Feener, "Tracings of Southeast Asian History in Texts of *Tabaqât* Literature," paper presented to the 2004 meeting of the Association for Asian Studies, San Diego.
124. Abû l-'Abbâs Aḥmad b. Aḥmad b. 'Abd al-Laṭîf al-Sharjî al-Zabîdî, *Ṭabaqât al-khawâṣṣ: Ahl al-ṣidqa wa-l-ikhlâṣ* (Bayrût: al-Dâr al-Yamaniyya, 1987), 341.
125. Michael Feener and Michael F. Laffan, "Sufi Scents across the Indian Ocean: Yemeni Hagiography and the Earliest History of Southeast Asian Islam," *Archipel* 70 (2005): 185–208.
126. Abdul Hadi W. M., *Hamzah Fansuri: Risalah tasawuf dan puisi-puisinya* (Bandung: Mizan, 1995), 109
127. Hadi, *Hamzah Fansuri*, 126, 128. Elsewhere, al-Fanṣûrî takes pride in the camphor trees of his homeland, stating that even the chairs within the Heavenly equivalent of the Ka'ba were "all of camphor from the trees of Fansur," Hadi, *Hamzah Fansuri*, 25.
128. Azyumardi Azra, *The Origins of Islamic Reformism in Southeast Asia: Networks of Malay-Indonesian and Middle Eastern 'Ulamâ' in the Seventeenth and Eighteenth Centuries* (Honolulu: University of Hawai'i Press, 2003), 41. On another occasion a request for a *fatwa* placed before al-Kûrânî is described as emanating from "some of the isles of Jâwah" or from "some of the people of Jâwah." See L. Or. 5660, f. 12 verso.
129. P. G. Riddell, *Transferring a Tradition: 'Abd al-Ra'ûf al-Singkilî's Rendering into Malay of the Jalâlayn Commentary* (Berkeley: University of California Press, 1990).
130. Patrick J. Geary, *The Myth of Nations: The Medieval Origins of Europe* (Princeton: Princeton University Press, 2002).
131. Hadi, *Hamzah Fansuri*, 59. Similarly, in 1601, Shams al-Dîn al-Samaṭrâ'î announced that he had written his *Mir'ât al-mu'min* "in the Jawi language" in order to render words of the religious sciences "for those people who do not understand Arabic or Farsi." Quoted in George Henrik Werndly, *Maleische spraakkunst: Uit de eige schriften der Maleiers opgemaakt* (Amsterdam: Wetstein, 1736), ii.

132. Miksic, "Classical Cultures," 248.
133. Anthony Reid, "Hybrid Identities in the Fifteenth Century Straits," in Geoff Wade and Sun Laichen, eds., *Southeast Asia in the Fifteenth Century: The Ming Factor* (Singapore: NUS Press, forthcoming).
134. T. S. Raffles, "On the Meláyu Nation, With a Translation of Its Maritime Institutions," *Asiatick Researches* 12 (1818): 102–58, see pp. 127–8.
135. Anthony Reid, *Southeast Asia in the Age of Commerce: The Lands below the Winds* (New Haven: Yale University Press, 1988).
136. My attention was first drawn to the term *Zîrbâd(ât)* and its implications by Sanjay Subrahmanyam, "Notes on Circulation," 22. Thus far, I have found no occurrence of Zîrbâd in the accounts of previous Islamic navigators. Steingass's *Persian-English Dictionary* simply notes that Zîrbâd is "the name of a country," while the Leiden manuscript of Yâqût's *Muʿjam* gives Zîrbâd as "an island in the vicinity of Fars." L. Or. 295, f. 159 verso. The Wüstenfeld edition appends the history of some other kingdom not identifiable with Southeast Asia: *Jacut's Wörterbuch*, II, 966. For an English translation of the travel account of ʿAbd al-Razzâq, based on the edition of Quatramère (1843), see "Abd er-Razzâk," in R. H. Major, *India in the Fifteenth Century* (London: Hakluyt, 1857).
137. Compare the entry "angin" in Wilkinson, *A Malay-English Dictionary* (wherein the Persian "up" and "down" are confused) with "Zirbad" in Henry Yule and Arthur Coke Burnell, *Hobson-Jobson: Being a Glossary of Anglo-Indian Colloquial Words and Phrases, and of Kindred Terms, Etymological, Historical, Geographical and Discursive* (London: John Murray, 1886).
138. See the Malay Manuscript Pages maintained by Ian Proudfoot <http://www.mcp.anu.edu>.
139. Letter held in the Dutch Royal Archives, KHA 13 XII-B-2. A copy of this letter, accompanied by a faulty translation, is found in Rita Wassing-Visser, *Royal Gifts from Indonesia: Historical Bonds with the House of Orange-Nassau (1600–1938)* (Zwolle: Waanders, 1995), 26.
140. *Aku raja yang kuasa di-bawah angin ini yang memegang takhta kerajaan negeri Aceh dan negeri Sammudara dan segala negeri yang ta'alluq ke negeri itu.* Bodleian Library, MS Laud Or. e.5. This letter, which commences with the announcement that it is "the Jawi version," is reproduced and discussed by W. G. Shellabear, "An Account of Some of the Oldest Malay MSS. Now Extant," *Journal of the Straits Branch of the Royal Asiatic Society* 31 (1898): 107–51.
141. I base my reading here on the transcriptions of G. F. Pijper (1893–1988), who seems to have examined two letters in the Portuguese archives. Leiden University Library, OLG, Pijper Collectie. An amicable deal seems to have been concluded, and the Portuguese had a small garrison in Pasai to protect their factory until their expulsion by Aceh in 1524. Ricklefs, *History*, 33.

142. Ferrand, *Relations*, 112–3.
143. See Abû Sa'îd 'Abd al-Karîm b. Muḥammad b. Manṣûr al-Tamîmî al-Sam'ânî, *al-Ansâb*, 5 vols. (Beirut: Dâr al-Jinân, 1988), III, 111.
144. M. Dulaurier, "Études sur l'ouvrage initulé: Relation des voyages ... dans le IXe siècle de l'ère chrétienne," *Journal Asiatique* (August–September 1848): 217–9.
145. Cited in Ferrand, *Relations*, 274–5. Cf. Dulaurier, "Études sur l'ouvrage initulé," 218–9. The potential link with a Tamîmî of Yemen is additionally interesting. We know from the Geniza documents that Yemen, and Aden in particular, figured in the spice networks. By the 13th century, a fortress within the walls of Zabid was known as *Kâfûrî*. See G. R. Smith, *The Ayyûbids and Early Rasûlids in the Yemen*, 2 vols. (London: Gibb Memorial Trust, 1974–78), II, 169.
146. Bernard Lewis, "The Fatimids and the Route to India," *Revue de la Faculté des Sciences Economiques de l'Université d'Istanbul* XI (1949–50): 355–360.
147. On the Jewish role in this trade, see S. D. Goitein, *A Mediterranean Society: Economic Foundations* (Berkeley: University of California Press, 1967), 153–5, 315. References to the spices of Southeast Asia being imported to Cairo and Alexandria are documented in the Geniza papyri. The deaths of two Jewish merchants in Kra and Fansur were recorded in letters from the 13th century. See S. D. Goitein, *Letters of Medieval Jewish Traders* (Princeton: Princeton University Press, 1973), 227–9.
148. Tibbetts, *Arabic Texts*, 100, n. 2.
149. Wolters, *Śrîvijaya*, 26, 39. Wolters also notes that camphor had already been introduced to China from Southeast Asia after 441 and was thus not regarded so highly by its recipients.
150. Al-Idrîsî, *Opus*, I, 69–70.
151. Although Azra's syntax suggests that the notion was also found in the prelude to a *fatwa* requested by 'Abd al-Ra'ûf from Ibrâhîm al-Kûrânî, ca. 1675, there is no reference to "above the winds" in the manuscript he cites. Compare Azra, *Origins of Reformism*, 64–5, and L. Or. 5660, fols. 12 recto–12 verso.
152. *Taḥt al-rîḥ ḥâkimî sulṭân*. Giancarlo Casale, personal communication, 18 March 2004.
153. In a letter of 1669, the sultan of Jambi refers to the governor-general as the ruler "who governs all the Dutchmen above the winds and below the winds." See Shellabear, "An Account," 135–9.
154. PRO SP 102/4/8. See also Annabel Teh Gallop, "Seventeenth Century Indonesian Letters in the Public Record Office," *Indonesia and the Malay World* 31, 91 (November 2003): 412–39. Abu l-Mafakhir would gain the title of sultan only after sending a mission to the sharif of Mecca in 1638.
155. PRO Ext 8/2, folio 126. The letter in question has the Islamic date of 16 Jumada II 1075, but the English dated it as 20 or 26 December 1664.

156. The original request for weapons in Arabic is Ext 8/2, folio 45.
157. L.Or. 1633, 4–5.
158. The etymology of "Zerbadi" and its relevance in Burma is discussed in Moshe Yegar, *The Muslims of Burma: A Study of a Minority Group* (Wiesbaden: Harrassowitz, 1972), 33ff.
159. Amitav Ghosh, *The Glass Palace* (London: Flamingo, 2000), 240; Natalie Mobini-Kesheh, *The Hadrami Awakening: Community and Identity in the Netherlands East Indies, 1900–1942* (Ithaca: SEAP, 1999).
160. Engseng Ho, "Hadhramis Abroad in Hadhramaut: The *muwalladîn*," in Ulrike Freitag and William G. Clarence-Smith, eds., *Hadhrami Traders, Scholars and Statesmen in the Indian Ocean, 1750s–1960s* (Leiden, New York, and Köln: Brill, 1997), 131–46, see pp. 134, 143.
161. Sumit K. Mandal, "Natural Leaders of Native Muslims: Arab Ethnicity and Politics in Java under Dutch Rule," in Freitag and Clarence-Smith, *Hadhrami Traders*, 185–98.
162. See M. F. Laffan, "Another Andalusia: Images of Colonial Southeast Asia in Arabic Newspapers," *Journal of Asian Studies* 66, 3 (2007): 689–722
163. Tomé Pires, using "Moorish charts," called the eastern islands of Indonesia "the Javas," Armando Cortesão, trans. and ed., *The Suma Oriental of Tomé Pires* (London: Hakluyt Society, 1944), lxxxi. Later, ca. 1591, the Englishman Ralph Fitch used the same term for the entire archipelago. See Schrieke, *Indonesian Sociological Studies*, 259.
164. H. J. de Graaf and T. G. T. Pigeaud, *Chinese Muslims in Java in the 15th and 16th Centuries: The Malay Annals of Semarang and Cerbon*, ed. M. C. Ricklefs (Clayton, VIC: Monash University, 1984).

3

The Hajj, Islam, and Power among the Bugis in Early Colonial Riau

TIMOTHY P. BARNARD

It is the obligation of every Muslim who is not prevented from doing so by economic or legal circumstances to undertake a pilgrimage to Mecca at least once in their lifetime. This pilgrimage, known as the Hajj, is an important spiritual event in the life of all Muslims and instills returning pilgrims with honor and respect in their communities. In areas far from the Hejaz, such as Southeast Asia, the Hajj can be a very expensive and time-consuming experience. This was particularly true before the advent of steam travel and the opening of the Suez Canal in 1869. While more than 5,000 Southeast Asians traveled to the Holy Land annually around 1890, only about 2,000 people went every year during the mid-1800s.[1] The pilgrims who made the arduous journey returned to Southeast Asia with elevated status, which gave the Hajj even greater importance in relation to power and standing in the community at the time. While Michael Laffan has brought new attention to the role of networks and power that the Hajj created in Southeast Asia in the late 19th century, many of these connections were beginning to appear much earlier in the century.[2]

Among the Southeast Asians making the difficult journey in the early 19th century were members of the Riau elite who were the descendants of Bugis mercenaries who had attained preeminence in the region in the early 18th century. The journey was of such importance it was recorded in a traditional history of the Bugis in Riau, the *Tuhfat al-Nafis*, which presents the Hajj within the context of the growing Islamic orthodoxy that became prevalent among the Riau Bugis in the 19th century.[3] The Hajj, by creating an elite highly knowledgeable in Islamic beliefs, thought, and government, was vital to the Bugis attempt to maintain power in their society. By wrapping themselves in a cloak of Islamic respectability, the Bugis were able to maintain control over the Malay sultans and give themselves legitimacy in comparison with the Dutch, long after Bugis economic and military power had dissipated.

This paper will focus on descriptions of the Hajj conducted by a member of the Riau elite, Raja Ahmad, who traveled to Mecca in 1828, as well as the context for his travel. In order to appreciate the significance of this Hajj, however, it is important to understand the role of Islam in the traditional Malay polity and how the Bugis came to power in Riau through their military strength. While the Hajj was an important spiritual journey, Raja Ahmad's pilgrimage was undertaken during a period in which the residents of Riau, and their rulers, were facing new challenges, the greatest of which was spreading European imperialism. Following defeats by the Dutch in the late 18th century, the Bugis had to search for new methods to maintain their position of leadership over society. These new methods involved Islam, and it is during this period that the first of the Riau elites went on the Hajj. The second section of this paper will contain a description of the pilgrimage of Raja Ahmad from the *Tuhfat al-Nafis*. This will then be juxtaposed with the description of Meccan life that Christiaan Snouck Hurgronje, the Dutch Islamicist, recorded in the 1880s, as well as the writings of Abdullah Munshi, who participated in the Hajj some two decades after Raja Ahmad.[4] The third section will conclude with an analysis of how this pilgrimage fits into the context of the Bugis and the role of Islam in Riau.

The Bugis and the Role of Islam in Riau Society

The Riau-Lingga Archipelago is the series of islands located directly south of Singapore. During the 18th century, Bugis warriors rose in power to rule this region along with the distant Natuna and Anambas Archipelagoes.[5] The Malay sultans of Johor previously had ruled Riau with the *daulat*, or sovereignty, of the ancient polities of Srivijaya and Melaka, having moved to the region following the Portuguese capture of Melaka in 1511. For the next 200 years the Malay rulers of Johor operated within an environment of increasing tension and competition with both European and Southeast Asian rivals, but they were able to survive and even prosper.

The traditional Malay polity focused entirely around the king, or raja.[6] Among the factors linking the community to the ruler was the intimate association between the ruler and religion. Anthony Milner has postulated that the reason for the conversion of Malay rulers to Islam was not only to further promote trade with Arab and Indian Muslims, but also the possibility of tapping into more modern spiritual doctrines and techniques that would appeal to the rulers' followers and further enhance their own status.[7] Once a ruler decided to embrace Islam, he quickly commanded his subjects to do the same. This relationship between the Malay ruler and Islamic belief in the community can be seen in the *Sejarah Melayu*, the court chronicle of Melaka, when following the conversion of Sultan Muhammad Shah, the first Muslim ruler of Melaka, "every citizen of Malaka, whether of high or low degree, was commanded by the Raja to do likewise."[8] Although Malay rulers during the early modern period viewed their polities as part of the medieval Muslim world, it was mainly in the context of trade, commerce, and technology.[9] More orthodox Islamic beliefs did arise at times, but they were often seen in contrast to the traditional power of the Malay ruler since they offered a new center of spiritual power far from the Malay World. This inherent opposition can be seen in the statement of Sultan Mahmud of Melaka when he supposedly announced that the Hajj was unnecessary as "Malacca was to be made into Mecca."[10] The Malay polity, therefore, focused both politically and spiritually around the ruler. Although Malays were Muslim, their form of Islam focused entirely on the ruler and his polity, rather than the distant Hejaz.

The traditional relationship between Malay rulers and their subjects continued in Johor until 1699. By that time, the inability of another Sultan Mahmud to maintain the prosperity of his predecessors, in combination with his sadistic tendencies, led his chief advisers to murder him in order to stop his destructive practices. The *bendahara*, or prime minister, assumed the sultanate, but deep divisions remained among the elite. Raja Kecik, a Minangkabau claiming to be the son of Sultan Mahmud, sought to exploit these divisions but was defeated in a series of battles against Bugis mercenaries who represented the Malay leaders.[11] The descendents of the *bendahara* sultan thus were able to retain his position as the Malay ruler of the Riau-Lingga Archipelago. To compensate these Bugis mercenaries for their assistance, the sultan granted the position of Yang Dipertuan Muda (viceroy), together with all real political control of the Riau-Lingga Archipelago, to the leader of the Bugis community and his descendants.[12]

Following the installation of the Bugis in a position of power within the Malay community, the role of the Malay sultan grew increasingly irrelevant. Control over the all-important trade port fell into the hands of the descendants of the original leaders of the Bugis mercenaries. The strategic position of the Riau-Lingga Archipelago allowed the Bugis leaders to maintain power for the first 50 years of their rule while their military prowess reinforced it.[13] As the polity began to return to its former prominence in the region, a confrontation with the Dutch in Melaka became increasingly likely. This became a reality in 1783–84, when a long series of battles between Riau and Dutch forces occurred, resulting in the death of the fourth Yang Dipertuan Muda, Raja Haji Fisabilillah.[14] The death of Raja Haji brought an end to much of the Bugis military presence in Riau. The decline in their martial prowess was further emphasized when the fifth Yang Dipertuan Muda, Raja Ali, fled to Borneo in November 1784 to escape a Dutch military offensive against Riau. The role of Yang Dipertuan Muda fell into disuse for the next 16 years due to the destruction of any legitimacy the Bugis may have had in a military sense.

The nadir of Bugis rule in the Riau Archipelago ended around 1800, when Sultan Mahmud III invited Raja Ali back to Riau and reinstalled him as the Yang Dipertuan Muda.[15] The marriage of Sultan Mahmud III to Raja Hamidah, the daughter of Raja Haji, in 1804 cemented this new alliance between the Bugis and the Malay sultan. The small island of Penyengat, situated off Bintan and opposite the strategically important Riau River, was given to Raja Hamidah and the descendants of Raja Haji as a wedding present by the sultan. This event symbolized the formal split of the kingdom into two distinct halves.[16] The Bugis would rule Riau from Penyengat, while the Malay elite would rule Lingga from the island of the same name. As seen in this division, the political situation in Riau had changed radically during this period. Fighting within the Malay faction and decreased Bugis military strength led to compromises with the European powers in the region. These compromises led to the British presence in Singapore and the establishment of a separate state in Johor for another class of Malay nobility, the temenggong. Prior to the agreement between the temenggong and the British, the Malays and Bugis in Riau-Lingga had also signed a treaty with the Dutch in 1818; that treaty gave the Dutch veto power over the choice of who would be the new sultan, allowed them to bring their warships into Riau, and allowed them to place a resident in Tanjung Pinang.[17] This agreement, coupled with the Treaty of London in 1824, created further splits in the formerly powerful Riau-Lingga polity that crippled any political or economic power it had once had.

A new phase had begun with the return of the Bugis to a limited position of authority after 1804. Although this elite had been intermarrying with the Malay elite for several generations, and no longer had any ties to Sulawesi, they often maintained their status as "Bugis" due to its correlation to power in the community.[18] Since the military justification for their presence would clearly not be plausible following decades of military defeats, the Bugis Yang Dipertuan Mudas turned to a new reason for their presence in this Malay polity. Vivienne Wee has suggested that this new reason was religion, which would have worked as a counter to the traditional power of the Malay sultan.[19] Although the Malay sultan was identified with Islam, it was a belief that reinforced the ruler's special status in society and not necessarily one of a universally spiritual brotherhood. The Bugis, in contrast, began promoting Penyengat as a center of more orthodox Islamic studies and piety, which also corresponded with growing orthodoxy in Mecca once the Wahhabi took control of the holy city in 1803. The growth of this religious role directly influenced the growing intensity of orthodox Islamic belief throughout the Malay World in the 19th century, which manifested itself in several forms.[20] One of these forms was participation in the Hajj, and it is during this period that the first Riau Bugis went on the pilgrimage. Because the Hajj played an important role in this development, the next section will analyze the experience of the first Riau-Bugis Hajji to understand how it fits within the context of local religious developments in Riau and the general experiences of Southeast Asian pilgrims in Mecca.

An Account of the First Hajji: Raja Ahmad

The first Hajji among the Riau Bugis was Raja Ahmad, and the *Tuhfat al-Nafis*, the seminal indigenous history of Bugis rule in Riau, describes the journey with details that represent its importance to the community. The text is court based and legitimates the role of the Bugis in the newly organized Johor polity; it was written by Raja Ahmad and subsequently edited and expanded by his son Raja Ali Haji, who accompanied him on the journey in 1828.[21] It is a transitional work in Malay historiography, and this can be attributed to the deep pride of the authors in their Islamic and Bugis heritage, which would not let them blindly accept the mythic elements in traditional Malay histories.[22] As Bugis military and economic power began to diminish, the justification for the Bugis' presence in this historical text shifted to their role as protectors of Islam. The Hajj played a prominent role in this legitimation. By focusing on the account of the pilgrimage of Raja Ahmad, therefore, a better understanding of its importance to the Bugis community in Riau can be obtained.

In this section of the paper, the account of Raja Ahmad will be compared with another description of the journey, written by a prominent Malay author who also undertook the pilgrimage when Southeast Asia was on the cusp of high imperialism. This author is Abdullah Munshi, who was a well-known scribe for the British and one of the early chroniclers of the founding of Singapore. Abdullah was an Indian-Malay, thus also an "outsider" much like the Bugis of Riau, who — in his writings — embraced the role that Europeans, or more specifically the British, could play in the development of the region. Abdullah was hostile toward Malay sultans, which put him in contrast with the authors of the *Tuhfat al-Nafis*, who were trying to justify their traditional rule in the region. Abdullah made the journey in 1854 and died while still in the Hejaz. His account is valuable not only for the details he provides about the journey, but also because it reflects the spiritual importance of the pilgrimage, particularly when he writes poetry about the awakening it created in him.[23]

In addition, this section will occasionally use the work of Snouck Hurgronje, who wrote a description of Jawi, or Southeast Asian Muslims, in Mecca in the late 19th century. A fascinating figure in the annals of Dutch scholarship, Snouck Hurgronje worked as the Dutch consul in Jeddah in the mid-1880s; he even studied surreptitiously in Mecca for six months in 1884. He later collected his observations and in 1888–89 published one of the best-known accounts on Meccan life. The first volume was a survey of the geography and history of Mecca and has yet to be translated into English. The second volume, however, describes "the social and family life, marriage and funeral customs, and the learning of the Meccans and their foreign guests, and has a final chapter on the Jawah."[24] Although his observations were made more than 50 years after the pilgrimage of Raja Ahmad, Snouck Hurgronje provides rich details of the pilgrimage experience of Southeast Asian Muslims. By combining these accounts with an understanding of Snouck Hurgronje's distinctively negative approach to Meccan life, an enhanced understanding of the pilgrimage experience of Raja Ahmad, and its importance in Riau, may be obtained.

In the 1820s Raja Ahmad was an important figure among the Bugis elite of Riau. He acted as an adviser to the rulers, both Bugis and Malay, in the Riau-Lingga Archipelago and often represented them in foreign courts. According to the *Tuhfat al-Nafis*, Raja Ahmad returned from visits to other courts on Java, whereupon he traveled to Lingga, the seat of the Malay sultan, and asked for permission from the sultan to take the pilgrimage. According to the *Tuhfat al-Nafis*, "this was granted, because Raja Ahmad wanted to fulfill a vow and a religious obligation."[25] Raja Ahmad returned to Riau, where he made preparations for the journey. After obtaining 14,000 dollars to cover the expenses for the journey, Raja Ahmad went to Singapore and then Penang to wait for a ship that could take him to the Hejaz. During this period, Raja Ahmad was greeted and entertained by other prominent Malays. Raja Ahmad did not need to stay long in Penang before he hired approximately half the space below decks on a Turkish felucca and set sail.

While Raja Ahmad sought the approval of the Malay sultan, and rented out most of a ship for his journey to Jeddah, Abdullah Munshi did not explain the need for his journey in 1854. He simply left during Chinese New Year from Singapore and slowly made his way as a passenger on various vessels that sailed from Singapore to Melaka and on to Penang. Eventually he made his way to India and then Jeddah, after stops in Aceh and other ports. Abdullah was a lone passenger, not part of a larger entourage, experiencing the slow movements of sails from port to port and visiting various dignitaries and praying at mosques along the way.[26]

After a short voyage Raja Ahmad reached Jeddah, on 18 Syaban, in the hijra year 1243.[27] Upon arrival ...

> Raja Ahmad went ashore and all the Sheikhs came to greet him formally, because they knew he wanted to go on the pilgrimage that year. Among those who came were Sheikh Ismail, Sheikh Ahmad Musyafi, and a messenger from Sheikh Daud. Each Sheikh wanted to take Raja Ahmad to his own house, but in the meantime Raja Ahmad had taken a liking to Sheikh Ahmad Musyafi because the latter had once been a retainer and because he was a locally born Bugis descended from the Forty. Wearing the pilgrim garb, Raja Ahmad traveled to *Mecca the Exalted*, with Sheikh Ahmad Musyafi.[28]

The shaykhs who met Raja Ahmad in Jeddah were known as *mutawwif* and acted as guides for the pilgrims while they were in the Hejaz. They not only acted as escorts but also helped pilgrims with renting of accommodations, interpreting, and anything else they might need. By the 1880s the number of Jawi traveling to the Hejaz warranted the existence of 180 shaykhs. Earlier in the century, however, when travel from Southeast Asia was less frequent, the number was certainly less.

But, with the growing trend of pilgrimage and orthodoxy, the presence of Riau-Bugis in Jeddah acting as shaykhs should not be surprising. Each of these shaykhs had the rights to any pilgrim from a specific area or ethnic group in Southeast Asia. The shaykh was often from that area, as was Shaykh Ahmad Musyafi for Raja Ahmad, "whose language he speaks and with whose peculiarities he is familiar."[29] While Snouck Hurgronje saw the shaykhs' role as exploitative at best later in the century, Raja Ahmad felt that he was simply being treated with the proper respect due a member of the Bugis elite.

The arrival of Raja Ahmad and his entourage in Jeddah, and their reception by the shaykhs, was also apparently a common occurrence in Mecca in the 19th century. In 1854 Abdullah was first inspected by a Turkish official while on board the boat, made to wait a night, taken to the dock where he paid customs taxes amidst a chaotic mix of coolies and baggage, and finally met his shaykh.[30] Snouck Hurgronje describes such a scene when he writes that if a shaykh obtains information that a well-to-do pilgrim is approaching by ship, "he goes himself to Jeddah, or sends his son there to supervise the reception."[31] Although Raja Ahmad was the first of the Riau-Bugis to take the pilgrimage, the community soon became well known in Mecca. According to Snouck Hurgronje, pilgrims from the region were "much better known than other really much more important [provinces, because of the] personal importance of the Jawah coming from thence on pilgrimage."[32] By the 1880s the Bugis of Riau had become established as an important element of the Jawi population in Mecca. The arrival of Raja Ahmad in 1828, however, would have led to competition among the shaykhs for his patronage. The statement "all the Sheikhs came to greet him formally," therefore, may not simply be an example of the *Tuhfat al-Nafis* attempting to exaggerate the importance of Raja Ahmad, as proposed by Matheson and Milner, but stresses that there had not been many representatives of the Riau elite who had participated in the Hajj previously, as was true when Snouck Hurgronje wrote his account, or there was knowledge of the financial capabilities of the group.[33] The shaykhs, therefore, might have been trying to obtain the right to act as the guide of Raja Ahmad and his entourage while in the Hejaz, which subsequently could be parlayed into acting as the guide for future pilgrims from the region.

Upon arrival, the prospective pilgrims were transported from their larger seagoing vessels to smaller boats that took them to shore, where they were greeted by the shaykhs or their representatives. After dispensing of gifts, the guides "are able quickly to take measure of their customers, to find out what accommodation they need and for how long."[34] By camel, the journey to Mecca from Jeddah took two days.

The typical arrival of Jawah in Mecca is described by Snouck Hurgronje as follows:

> When a caravan of Jawah pilgrims draws into Mekka, one often hears the street youngsters, and mule-drivers shouting out, with scornful gestures: *manshuri* (*pentjuri*, Malay: thief) or *tiwan* (*tuwan*, Lord). These *canaille* persecute all the few fashionable foreigners with their ill-will, and the Jawah, until they have become accustomed to the conditions, behave in a peculiarly helpless fashion.[35]

Despite the contempt Snouck Hurgronje openly displays here for the ability of Southeast Asian pilgrims to protect themselves in Mecca, none of this "ill-will" is described or perceived by Raja Ahmad or Abdullah in their accounts, although Abdullah does describe Jeddah as being "busy" (*terlalu ramai*).[36] At the time of his pilgrimage, however, there were not large numbers of Jawi in the Hejaz. Although this would change by the 1870s, when the Dutch opened a consular office in Jeddah, it is doubtful that Raja Ahmad encountered the same reception as other Southeast Asians did later in the century.

As is true with most pilgrims upon arrival in the Hejaz, Raja Ahmad participated in an *umrah*, or minor pilgrimage. The arrival in the city was a moving experience, the culmination of a long and spiritual journey. The experience moved Abdullah to write a *syair*:

> I go within the noble city
> I am oblivious of the joys and pleasures of this world
> As if already possessed of heaven and all it holds
> I give thanks a thousand times to the most noble God
> I am oblivious of the troubles and torments of the journey
> The months of torments brought about by the passion, the longing, for the house of Allah.[37]

Participation in an *umrah* was a common practice at the time, since transportation to the Hejaz was not a scheduled and orderly trip, as it became following the introduction of steamships and more dependable schedules based on European travel networks. The period of time that a pilgrim waited to participate in the Hajj could be weeks or months. Although the *umrah* does not carry the same prestige as the Hajj, it may be taken at any time of year. This is in contrast to the Hajj, which occurs at a specific time. According to Snouck Hurgronje, during this waiting period, "be this interval long or short, the Mekkans allow the patients not a moment's peace and literally storm them on all sides with their divine wares."[38]

While in Mecca, Raja Ahmad "stayed with Sheikh Ahmad Musyafi and all the Mecca Sheikhs came to visit him there." Snouck Hurgronje adds that a pilgrim in Mecca would be visited by many prominent people of the Meccan community, although much would depend on the wealth of the traveler. On occasion, well-to-do pilgrims would stay at the house of their shaykh (Snouck Hurgronje 1931: 226, 254). As for Raja Ahmad:

> When he had finished meeting everyone, he stayed in *Mecca the Exalted* waiting to leave for *Medina the Illustrious* to visit the grave of Allah's Prophet (may Allah bless him and grant him peace). He was only filling in time until the end of Ramadan.[39]

The trip to Medina was dangerous, however, due to the presence of thousands of Bedouins who were attacking travelers. This was occurring because of a political dispute between a "prince" of Mecca and the sultan of the Ottoman Empire, which also involved a murder. Eventually, Raja Ahmad and his entourage, accompanied by Shaykh Ahmad Musyafi, were able to make the journey to Medina in a heavily armed caravan. This problem apparently continued to plague the area until the late 19th century, since travel to Medina at that time was restricted without "an escort of Turkish soldiers as soon as the road had been pronounced safe by the Government authorities."[40]

Upon arrival in Medina:

> Raja Ahmad then visited the grave of Allah's Prophet (*may Allah bless him and grant him peace*). Following this he went to Baki'a, to the grave of the Companions. He then traveled to Mount Uhud to the grave of the uncle of the Prophet (*may Allah bless him and grant him peace*) who was called Our Lord Hamzah and who was martyred on Mount Uhud. Raja Ahmad made pilgrimages to all the places people visit, and when this was done he bought land for a hostel for the descendants of Sheikh Saman.[41]

The visiting of holy sites was common among the Jawi in the Hejaz. Snouck Hurgronje, in his own cynical manner, describes this as a method by which the "sheep are shorn by various shearers,"[42] since the pilgrims were assessed additional charges for these trips. He, however, does not take into account the perceived importance that the Southeast Asian Muslim would place on visiting such sites. In Southeast Asia, the visiting of *keramat* graves and other holy places was common practice in the past and still persists today, and Abdullah mentions that visits to the graves of Adam and Eve on Fridays were part of "Arab adat" at the time.[43]

The *Tuhfat al-Nafis* then reports that Raja Ahmad returned to Mecca and bought two houses, which he gave to shaykhs. These homes were considered to be *waqf*-houses, which could be used as dormitories and learning centers. By donating houses or land for religious purposes, Raja Ahmad was both gaining spiritual prestige for himself and laying a foundation for future pilgrimages among the Riau elite. In addition, following his Hajj, Raja Ahmad purchased a *waqf*-house for Shaykh Ahmad Musafyi, the Bugis guide he used.[44] Later in the 19th century, there were numerous *waqf*-houses in Mecca, each belonging to a different Southeast Asian ethnic group. "Such foundations are partly founded by a great gentleman whilst making the Hajj and later supported at his cost and managed by someone whom he appointed."[45] These homes were the most tangible legacy of Raja Ahmad's pilgrimage.

Following his trip to Medina, Raja Ahmad was able to participate in the Hajj. His account of the pilgrimage is similar to other accounts of the time, and actually takes up only a small portion of the text. It is described as follows:

> After this it was time to make the pilgrimage, and Raja Ahmad visited the shrines and then joined with the Hajjis, Muslims from all over the world, who had come to halt on the plain of Arafat. He circumambulated the Ka'ba, and ran seven times between the hillocks Safa and Marwa. After throwing stones at Mina, he returned to Mecca and recited the beginning of the creed, wearing a turban. Raja Ahmad afterwards bought a piece of enclosed land at Mina on which he asked Sheikh Ahmad Musyafi to build a hostel. When all this was done, Raja Ahmad began the return trip to the Jawi lands, escorted by the Mecca elders as far as Jedda. He then boarded a Turkish berik whose captain was Sayid Muhammad Ali. He again rented half the space below decks and they set sail.
>
> According to the story, Raja Ahmad was the first prince from Riau and Lingga to make the pilgrimage. No one before him had done so. It could be said that he opened the way for other Riau princes to make the pilgrimage to *Mecca the Exalted*.[46]

Thus, Raja Ahmad completed his pilgrimage. Upon his return, a new era in the Bugis presence in Riau had begun, and the Hajj would play an important role in it.

The Hajj and Its Importance in Riau

The pilgrimage of Raja Ahmad fits within an atmosphere of growing Islamicism among the Riau elite and all of Southeast Asia. Part of this revitalization of Islam in Southeast Asia may be related to the increasing number of Hajj pilgrims whose journey was to be facilitated by the advent of the steamship and increased traffic between Southeast Asia and Europe following the opening of the Suez Canal in 1869. By 1900 almost all of the Bugis elite in Riau had taken the pilgrimage.[47] Although Raja Ahmad participated in the Hajj long before the appearance of steamships on international trade routes that were linked to the Hejaz, he is typical of the growing focus of Southeast Asian Muslims toward the Middle East.[48]

Southeast Asian pilgrims would often stay in the Hejaz for several years of religious study following the pilgrimage, and some of the most famous Malay scholars in Mecca were from Riau. The attitudes that were acquired while studying in the Hejaz were of contempt toward the religious practices of the highly syncretic culture of the Malay World. According to Snouck Hurgronje, "they start by regarding their own home as a dunghill in comparison with pure, holy Mekka, because the outer forms of life here (in Mekka) bring to mind the Moslim faith; there often the heathen past."[49] This contempt, coupled with a revitalization of religious knowledge, was the primary ingredient that the returning pilgrim/scholar Hajji brought to his community.

The pilgrimage, however, worked both ways. Just as Southeast Asians were going to Mecca to fulfill their religious obligations, many Arabs from the Hadramaut — who made up 95 per cent of the Arabs in Southeast Asia — were coming to the Malay World.[50] This, however, was not a new phenomenon in the region. Arabs had been coming to the area and settling for centuries. These immigrants usually worked as traders, small businessmen, or, more importantly, religious teachers throughout the region. The island of Penyengat, with the morally pious Bugis, had been and continued to be a magnet for these religious teachers since the mid-18th century. These teachers would often stay for several years.[51] A dormitory was constructed for their use, and the Bugis elite were anxious to study under such learned men. The strict beliefs these Arabs taught conveyed the same messages that the Hajjis were receiving on their pilgrimages.

One of the manifestations of this trend was the adherence of the Riau elite to the Sufi order of Nakshabandiyya, which promoted purity of Islamic ritual.[52] Nakshabandiyya first became prominent on Penyengat in

1857 with the visit of Shaykh Ismail, who is credited with introducing the order to Riau.[53] Following a proliferation of its ideals in Riau, a stricter Islamic atmosphere began to permeate Penyengat society to the point that the recitation of traditional Malay *pantun*s and lute playing were proscribed, because "they led to loose behavior between men and women."[54] Although Riau had become a backwater on Southeast Asian trade routes by the mid-19th century, with the harbor becoming "death-like,"[55] it began to fill a new niche in Malay society by promoting a religiously pious and literate elite who could guide the community to a new prosperity based on Islamic principles.

The most notable aspect of the growing Islamic legitimation of Bugis rule in Riau-Lingga was in the area of literature. During the mid-19th century, many members of the Bugis community on Penyengat began to express themselves through a wide range of Malay forms of literature.[56] While traditional pastimes and entertainment, such as composing animal and bird *syair*, continued, this new literary output also included local histories, Malay grammars and dictionaries, as well as translations of Islamic religious texts. The works reflected the growing intensity of religious belief in the community and attitudes toward the type of relationship that ideally existed between a good ruler with pious beliefs and his subjects.

The writings of Raja Ali Haji ibn Raja Ahmad, one of the authors of the *Tuhfat al-Nafis*, were the epitome of this renaissance in Malay literature. The grandson of Raja Haji, Raja Ali, was a leading adviser to the Yang Dipertuan Mudas for more than 40 years and had accompanied his father on the pilgrimage in 1828. Raja Ali Haji combined the two roles of literary figure and adviser in many of his works, which ranged from political tracts and history to poetry and Malay dictionaries.[57] The goal of much of his work was the preservation of the unique status of the Bugis in Riau. While he is most famous today for his histories, *Tuhfat al-Nafis* and *Silsilah Melayu dan Bugis*, Raja Ali Haji was better known in the mid-19th century as an adviser whose writings and knowledge provided the basis for Bugis political rule. The tone of his works reinforced the belief that the Bugis had been placed in Riau as moral guides to the community. The best example of this type of work is *Thamarat al-Mahammah*, or *The Benefits of Official Duties*, a manual describing the correct procedures for appointing a new ruler, the conduct of a ruler, and the establishment of a legal system.[58] These works emphasized that the most important duty of a ruler was to provide a climate conducive to the practice of religion, unlike the writings of Abdullah Munshi, who believed that rulers were a hindrance to the development of their subjects; he advocated an abolition of the sultanates. Raja Ali Haji, however, believed that the community could prosper if a ruler developed the proper religious atmosphere where spiritual rituals and obligations could be performed. The ruler of such a society had the additional duty to provide a good example for his people and set the moral standards for the community. The political consequences of this belief were realized in October 1857, when the Bugis supported the Dutch decision to depose the Malay Sultan Mahmud IV on the grounds that he was an un-Islamic playboy.[59] The Bugis, thus, had returned as the most powerful political faction within the Riau-Lingga polity through their role as Islamic "policemen," not as martial warriors as had been the case in the 18th century.

The changing role of the Bugis in Riau society thus seems to have evolved from a military justification to one based on religion. The clearest expression of this role is seen in the renaissance in literature that occurred in 19th-century Riau. Another aspect of this trend can be related to the first Hajj. It is this pilgrimage that opened the door for the subsequent development of other aspects of the Islamic religion in Riau. Although the Bugis had returned to their role as rulers in the chaotic Riau-Lingga polity during this period, the growing power of the Dutch and British, and the expansion of their grip on the economic and political power in the region, also gave an impetus to the focus on Islam among the Riau elite. Of these two northern European colonizers, however, the Dutch, who controlled the Riau area, were perceived as the more antagonistic toward Islam. This was due to restrictions the Dutch placed on pilgrims in the territories they controlled.[60] This antagonism was exacerbated by the presence of a Dutch resident in Tanjung Pinang—opposite Pulau Penyengat—since 1818, which was a constant reminder to the Bugis elite of their diminished power. The growth of Islamic beliefs in Riau-Lingga, therefore, was part of the justification for the Bugis presence in the region in relation to both the traditional Malay rulers and the encroaching Dutch.

Conclusion

The Bugis had come to prominence in the Johor-Riau area in the early 18th century due to their military capabilities. By the end of that century, their ability to maintain power in the region was crippled following a series of naval battles with the Dutch. In order to justify their return to a position of power in a non-Bugis area, they turned to religion, and the Hajj played a prominent role in this justification. By participating in the pilgrimage prior to the advent of steam travel, and with increasingly easy access to Mecca, the Riau-Bugis elite gained status in the community and were able to insert themselves into a growing network of Islamic belief, particularly in the context of the Wahhabi takeover of Mecca in 1804 and increasing European power in Southeast Asia. These various worldwide events also allowed the Bugis elite of Riau to link their beliefs with a more orthodox form of Islam that was in great contrast to the traditional relationship of the Malay sultan to Islam.

In addition, "the Hajj serves indirectly as a channel through which currents of intensive Moslim life find their way to the Jawah lands."[61] The Hajj exposed the Riau elite to Islamic philosophy, literature, and political theory, which they subsequently adapted to their own culture to create a "Bugis renaissance," the most lasting legacy of their presence in the 19th century. It also tied them into a larger context of change among Southeast Asian Muslims in the 19th century, and allowed them to take a leading role in the future development of Islamic thought in the region. By examining the pilgrimage of one of the members of this Riau elite, the initial phase of a transformation that Michael Laffan has ably described can be seen. Only by examining other primary sources, and using any other available sources to further expand upon these early accounts, can a better understanding of the development of Southeast Asian Islam and the role of the pilgrimage prior to high imperialism be obtained.

Notes

1. Jacob Vredenbregt, "The Haddj: Some of Its Features and Functions in Indonesia," *Bijdragan voor Taal-, Land-, en Volkenkunde* 118, 1 (1962): 93, 148.
2. Michael Laffan, *Islamic Nationhood and Colonial Indonesia: The Umma below the Winds* (London: RoutledgeCurzon, 2003).
3. Raja Ali Haji ibn Ahmad, *The Precious Gift (Tuhfat al-Nafis)*, trans. Barbara Watson Andaya and Virginia Matheson (Kuala Lumpur: Oxford University Press, 1982).
4. C. Snouck Hurgronje, *Mekka in the Latter Part of the 19th Century*, trans. J. H. Monahan (Leiden: E. J. Brill, 1931); Abdullah Munshi, *Kisah Pelayaran Abdullah ke Kelantan dan ke Judah* (Kuala Lumpur: Fajar Bakti, 1981).
5. Leonard Andaya, *The Kingdom of Johor 1641–1728* (Kuala Lumpur: Oxford University Press, 1975), 279–323; Timothy P. Barnard, *Multiple Centres of Authority: Environment and Society in Siak and Eastern Sumatra, 1674–1827* (Leiden: KITLV, 2003).

6. A. C. Milner, *Kerajaan: Malay Political Culture on the Eve of Colonial Rule* (Tucson: University of Arizona Press, 1982).
7. A. C. Milner, "Islam and Malay Kingship," *Journal of the Royal Asiatic Society* 1 (1981): 46–70.
8. C. C. Brown, transl., *Sejarah Melayu or Malay Annals* (Kuala Lumpur: Oxford University Press, 1970), 44.
9. Virginia Matheson and A. C. Milner, *Perceptions of the Haj: Five Malay Texts* (Singapore: Institute for Southeast Asian Studies, 1984), 11.
10. This quote is taken from Milner, "Islam and Malay Kingship." In addition, there is only one mention of a Hajj in the traditional Malay histories prior to the account of Raja Ahmad's pilgrimage. This is in the *Hikayat Hang Tuah*. An English translation can be found in Matheson and Milner, *Perceptions of the Haj*, 4–14.
11. Barnard, *Multiple Centres of Authority*, 55–78; Samad Ahmad, *Kerajaan Johor-Riau* (Kuala Lumpur: Dewan Bahasa dan Pustaka, 1985), 1–8.
12. Andaya, *Kingdom of Johor*, 295–6.
13. An example of their increasing power was their ability to replace the Malay sultan at their own will. This was done in 1762 with the installation of the infant Sultan Mahmud against the wishes of the Malay elite. See Raja Ali Haji ibn Ahmad, *The Precious Gift*, 123–7.
14. See Raja Ali Haji ibn Ahmad, *The Precious Gift*, 167–76. The descendants of the five legendary Bugis brothers are always referred to as "Raja," whether male or female. Despite his name, Raja Haji Fisabilillah never participated in the Hajj.
15. Carl A. Trocki, *Prince of Pirates: The Temenggongs and the Development of Johor and Singapore 1784–1885* (Singapore: Singapore University Press, 1979), 27–35; Vivienne Wee, "Melayu: Hierarchies of Being in Riau," unpublished PhD thesis, Australian National University, 1985, 262–3.
16. Virginia Matheson, "Pulau Penyengat: Nineteenth Century Islamic Centre of Riau," *Archipel* 37 (1989): 156; Wee, *Melayu*, 203.
17. Muchtar Lufti, *Rusydiah Club* (Pekanbaru: Universitas Riau, 1975), 7.
18. Jan van der Putten, "A Malay of Bugis Ancestry: Haji Ibrahim's Strategies of Survival," in Timothy P. Barnard, ed., *Contesting Malayness: Malay Identity across Boundaries* (Singapore: Singapore University Press, 2004), 121–34.
19. Wee, *Melayu*, 263–5.
20. Christine Dobbin, *Islamic Revivalism in a Changing Peasant Economy: Central Sumatra 1784–1847* (London and Malmo: Scandinavian Institute of Asian Studies, 1983); Barbara Watson Andaya, "Gender, Islam and the Bugis Diaspora in Nineteenth- and Twentieth-Century Riau," *SARI* 21 (2003): 83–5.
21. Barbara Watson Andaya and Virginia Matheson, "Islamic Thought and Malay Tradition: The Writings of Raja Ali Haji of Riau (ca. 1809–ca. 1870)," in Anthony Reid and David Marr, eds., *Perceptions of the Past in Southeast Asia* (Singapore: Heinemann, 1982), 108–28.

22. J. Noorduyn, "Some Aspects of Bugis Historiography," in D. G. E. Hall, ed., *Historians of South East Asia* (London: Oxford University Press, 1961).
23. Abdullah Munshi, *Hikayat Abdullah* (Kuala Lumpur: Oxford University Press, 1970); Abdullah Munshi, *Kisah Pelayaran Abdullah ke Kelantan dan ke Judah* (Kuala Lumpur: Fajar Bakti, 1981).
24. Snouck Hurgronje, *Mekka in the Latter Part of the 19th Century*, v.
25. Raja Ali Haji ibn Ahmad, *The Precious Gift*, 247.
26. Abdullah Munshi, *Kisah Pelayaran Abdullah ke Kelantan dan ke Judah*, 92–114.
27. The date corresponds to 5 March 1828.
28. Raja Ali Haji ibn Ahmad, *The Precious Gift*, 249. "The Forty" refers to the original 40 Bugis who assisted the sultan of Johor in defeating Raja Kecil in the 1720s.
29. Snouck Hurgronje, *Mekka in the Latter Part of the 19th Century*, 24.
30. Abdullah Munshi, *Kisah Pelayaran Abdullah ke Kelantan dan ke Judah*, 115–7.
31. Snouck Hurgronje, *Mekka in the Latter Part of the 19th Century*, 24.
32. Ibid., 231.
33. Matheson and Milner, *Perceptions of the Haj*, 20.
34. Snouck Hurgronje, *Mekka in the Latter Part of the 19th Century*, 24–5.
35. Ibid., 223.
36. Abdullah Munshi, *Kisah Pelayaran Abdullah ke Kelantan dan ke Judah*, 117.
37. Matheson and Milner, *Perceptions of the Haj*, 23.
38. Snouck Hurgronje, *Mekka in the Latter Part of the 19th Century*, 228.
39. Raja Ali Haji ibn Ahmad, *The Precious Gift*, 249–50.
40. Snouck Hurgronje, *Mekka in the Latter Part of the 19th Century*, 48.
41. Raja Ali Haji ibn Ahmad, *The Precious Gift*, 249–50.
42. Snouck Hurgronje, *Mekka in the Latter Part of the 19th Century*, 233.
43. See Abdullah Munshi, *Kisah Pelayaran Abdullah ke Kelantan dan ke Judah*, 117. An example of a visit to a *keramat* grave site in the past would be the importance placed on the visit of Hang Tuah, a Malay cultural hero, to Eve's grave outside of Medina in the *Hikayat Hang Tuah*. For an easily accessible account, see Matheson and Milner, *Perceptions of the Haj*, 4. For a contemporary account of *keramat* graves in Riau, see Wee, *Melayu*. Wahhabi followers eventually destroyed many of these sites since they construed such worship as being in contrast to their strictly monotheistic beliefs. This type of orthodoxy quickly spread to Riau. See Watson Andaya, "Gender, Islam and the Bugis Diaspora in Nineteenth- and Twentieth-Century Riau," 84–5; and John Lewis Burckhardt, *Notes on the Bedouins and Wahabys Collected during his Travels in the East* (London: Henry Colburn and Richard Bentley, 1831).
44. Raja Ali Haji ibn Ahmad, *The Precious Gift*, 251.

45. Snouck Hurgronje, *Mekka in the Latter Part of the 19th Century*, 255.
46. Raja Ali Haji ibn Ahmad, *The Precious Gift*, 251.
47. Jacob Vredenbregt, "The Haddj," 148; Raja Ali Haji ibn Ahmad, *The Precious Gift*, 248–51.
48. Anthony Reid, *An Indonesian Frontier: Acehnese and Other Histories of Sumatra* (Singapore: Singapore University Press, 2005), 226–48.
49. Snouck Hurgronje, *Mekka in the Latter Part of the 19th Century*, 233.
50. W. H. Lee-Warner, "Notes on the Hadhramaut," *Geographical Journal* 77 (1931): 220.
51. Raja Ali Haji ibn Ahmad, *The Precious Gift*, 283–5.
52. All of the Penyengat Bugis were members of this order; see Raja Ali Haji ibn Ahmad, *The Precious Gift*, 285. The Nakshabandiyya order had become popular in India in the 15th century and was introduced into Sumatra by the 17th century; see John Voll, "Linking Groups in the Networks of Eighteenth-Century Revivalist Scholars," in Nehemia Levtzion and John O. Voll, eds., *Eighteenth-Century Renewal in Islam* (Syracuse, N.Y.: Syracuse University Press, 1987), 84–5.
53. Abu Hassan Sham, "Tariqat Naqsyabandiah dan Perannya dalam Kerajaan Melayu Riau Sehingga Awal Abad Kedua Puluh," in *Tamudan di Malaysia* (Kuala Lumpur: Pesatuan Sejerah Malaysia, 1980), 80.
54. Raja Ali Haji ibn Ahmad, *The Precious Gift*, 283–4.
55. J. T. Thompson, "A Glance at Rio," *Journal of the Indian Archipelago* 1 (1847): 69.
56. Virginia Matheson, "Questions Arising From a Nineteenth Century Riau Syair," *Review of Indonesian and Malaysian Affairs* 17 (1983): 3–7.
57. U. U. Hamidy, *Riau Sebagai Pusat Bahasa dan Kebudayaan Melayu* (Pekanbaru: Bumi Pustaka, 1983), 93–8; Jan van der Putten and Al Azhar, eds., *Di Dalam Berkekalan Persahabatan: 'In everlasting friendship': Letters from Raja Ali Haji* (Leiden: Department of Language and Cultures of Southeast Asia and Oceania, 1995), 1–25.
58. Barbara Watson Andaya and Virginia Matheson, "Islamic Thought and Malay Tradition: The Writings of Raja Ali Haji of Riau (ca. 1809–ca. 1870)," in Reid and Marr, *Perceptions of the Past in Southeast Asia*, 115–6.
59. Virginia Matheson, "Mahmud, Sultan of Riau and Lingga (1823–1864)," *Indonesia* 13 (1972): 119–146.
60. Vredenbregt, "The Haddj," 90–154; Anthony Reid, *An Indonesian Frontier: Acehnese and Other Histories of Sumatra* (Singapore: Singapore University Press, 2005), 226–48.
61. Snouck Hurgronje, *Mekka in the Latter Part of the 19th Century*, 262.

4

The Origins and Contributions of Early Arabs in Malaya

MOHAMMAD REDZUAN OTHMAN

Introduction

For centuries, Arabs from the Middle East have exercised a great deal of influence in the Malay World. It started with trading activities, when Arab sailing ships ventured to the Far East in search of prosperity. The advent of Islam transformed the Arab presence into a mission that helped convert the population of the Malay World to Islam. Arabs spent a considerable time, sometimes the greater part of their lives, in the Malay World propagating Islam by peaceful means. Beginning from the middle of the 19th century, the Arabs who migrated and settled in the Malay World, including Malaya, originated from Hadramaut, a piece of land situated at the southern extremity of the Arabian Peninsula. Like their predecessors, the Arabs of Hadramaut, or the Hadramis, were entrepreneurs and played a significant role in spreading the understanding of Islam in Malay society.

The Arabs' Trade with the Malay World

The Arabs' intercourse with the Malay World is reported in several accounts, some of which predate the beginning of the Christian era, handed down by Greek and Roman writers.[1] It started with their trading activities in the Indian Ocean, from where Arab traders extended their trading ventures to China. According to G. R. Tibbetts, who cites a Muslim historian, their presence may well have dated from as early as the fifth century.[2] Since the Malay World and other parts of Southeast Asia are situated approximately in the middle of the route between India and China, Arab traders probably reached this region a little earlier than they did China.[3] Despite these early contacts, their apparent presence in the region was recorded only in AH 55/CE 674 by the Chinese, who mentioned the existence of a Muslim settlement in East Sumatra, headed by an Arab chief.[4]

Constant contacts with the Malay World inspired some of these Arabs to write accounts of their trading expeditions, which have provided this region with a wealth of historical literature.[5] This information, which includes accounts of the Malay Peninsula in ancient times, has been one of the main sources to which Malays have been indebted when writing their early history.[6] Among the Arabs who wrote about the Malay World between the second half of the ninth and the first half of the tenth centuries were Yaqubi (CE 875–80), Ibn al-Faqih (CE 902), Ibn Rustah (CE 903), Ishaq ibn Imran (circa 907), and Muhammad ibn Zakariyya al-Razi (d. 923 or 932).[7] After the advent of Islam in the Middle East, a greater body of evidence was unearthed which further showed the presence of Arabs in the Malay World, such as the discovery in Kedah of two silver coins of the Abbasid Dynasty from the reign of al-Mutawakkil (CE 847–861). The finding of these coins, one dated CE 848, at least shows the existence of a trade link between Kedah and the Arab World during the ninth century.[8]

Even though Arab traders were long acquainted with the Malay World, products from this region did not constitute the bulk of their trading items in the early days; the Arabs' main trade relationship was with China.[9] Until the tenth century, relatively limited amounts of spices were traded by Arab traders; the bulk of trade goods brought from the East to Baghdad, which was one of the most important market centers in the Middle East, consisted of luxury items.[10] Similar goods were also traded in Cairo and Alexandria, and although there was mention of spices (mainly cloves, and occasionally nutmeg and mace) in the commercial records, these trade items were extremely rare and expensive.[11] In was only in the 11th and 12th centuries that the spice trade began to increase in importance, together with textiles and dyes. The importance of spices as trading goods emerged when a mixture of pepper, ginger, cinnamon, sugar, cloves, and nutmeg came into demand in Europe to cure all sorts of ailments. Spices were also found to be useful as flavoring for meat and became increasingly popular in the European diet.[12]

The increasing importance of the Malay World to Arab traders was clearly demonstrated when the traders discovered that many of the commodities that were demanded by China, India, the Arab World, and (via the latter) Europe could be found in this area of Southeast Asia.[13] By the 13th century, when bulk commodities began to enter the East-West trade, three trading centers were established to facilitate long-distance trade — India, Melaka, and China. This led to the discontinuation of the traditional voyages of Arab dhows to China, and trade became organized into three sectors, divided by the intermediate emporium on the Straits of Melaka.[14] The 13th century also saw two premier Southeast Asian emporia, Srivijaya and Fo-lo-an, which Paul Wheatley believed to be Kuala Brang in Trengganu, being regularly frequented by Arab traders.[15]

By the 15th century, the segmented trading pattern was fully taken advantage of by East-West traders, and only a few junks from China still reached India. Most of them instead stopped at Melaka, while Indian-owned ships covered the section between Melaka and the Indian coast and Arab-owned ships dominated the Arabian Sea.[16] Due to increased Arab intercourse with the various islands of the Malay-Indonesian Archipelago, Melaka, which was founded in the early years of the 15th century, had by this time come into prominence as a successor to Kalah.[17] Its strategic location in the Straits of Melaka and the conversion of its rulers to Islam encouraged an increasing number of Arab ships to make its city-port their main trading center in the East. It has been found that in the 15th and early 16th centuries, apart from Arabs from southern Arabia, there were also considerable numbers of Arabs from Egypt who traveled to Melaka. These Arabs formed, along with others, the foreigners who made up a relatively large colony of merchants in the city-port.[18] By the latter half of the 15th century Melaka had become an essential terminus of the Indian Ocean trade; it had a population of some 40,000 to 50,000, with foreign merchants forming a large colony.[19]

Despite Arabs continuing to be actively involved in the Eastern trade, from the 13th century onward trade in the Middle East had begun to show signs of decline. This gradually had a significant effect on Arab trade in the Far East. The decline of Middle Eastern trade was attributed to a number of factors. The internal factors were the diminishing supply of products due to devastating wars, a drop in the region's capacity to export agricultural produce, a decline in the production of its handicrafts, and a decrease in its population. In addition to these circumstances, there were external factors instrumental in its decline. Former customers of Middle Eastern traders in Europe were able to produce their own commodities; and they also had the capacity to buy exotic products from the East directly from the producing areas. They had also gained expertise in producing more competitive goods, which greatly undermined the products of the Middle East.[20]

Beginning from the closing years of the 15th century, Arab trade in the Far East suffered another crucial blow. Following the success of the Christian conquistadors in the Iberian Peninsula, the Portuguese waged a campaign to eliminate Muslims elsewhere in the world. For the century and a half that followed, the Portuguese managed to control maritime trade in the Indian Ocean. This significantly affected the previous Arab monopoly over regional trade, which had never been seriously challenged before.[21] The fall of Melaka to the Portuguese in 1511 was an important turning point that contributed to the diminishing role played by Muslim traders, particularly Arab traders from the Middle East, in the waters of the Malay World. Although trade relations between the Arabs and the Malay World were greatly reduced, contact continued to flourish through Islam. Arab trade with the Malay World re-emerged only in the middle of the 19th century, with the leading role now played by Arabs from Hadramaut.

The Arabs and the Islamization of Malays

The advent of Islam (CE 622) significantly motivated the Arabs to be more venturesome, spurred by the motive of spreading the new faith in addition to trading activities. By CE 651, the Muslim Arabs had already established their first embassy in China.[22] The rise of two powerful dynasties, the Umayyad Caliphate in West Asia (CE 660–749) and the Tang Dynasty in the East (CE 618–907), also encouraged sea trade between the eastern and western parts of Asia and enabled the Arab trade to flourish.[23] Despite these trading activities, the earliest known record of probable Muslim settlement in the region is a Chinese report of the existence of an Arab settlement in east Sumatra headed by an Arab chief in AH 55/CE 674. Large-scale Muslim emigration to this region, mainly by traders who had settled in Khanfu (Canton), was reported by al-Mas'udi in AH 265/CE 877. These traders fled Canton following an abortive revolt in CE 878 against the Tang emperor.[24]

As a result of the turmoil, a large number of Muslim traders, including Arabs, Persians, and probably Chinese Muslims, emigrated to the Malay World and brought about a rapid spread of Islam.[25] These emigrants took refuge in Kalah, on the west coast of the Malay Peninsula, which some historians believe is the present-day Kedah (Merbok estuary).[26] The conclusion that the Muslims took refuge in Kedah, however, is inconclusive, due to conflicting accounts given by various Arab geographers as to the site. Recent historical and archeological research has come up with new suggestions concerning its most likely location, which indicate it may have been Kelang, in the Malay Peninsula, or Takuapa, in present-day Southern Thailand.[27] Despite the confusion that shrouds its location, what is certain is that Arab trading ships had fully penetrated the seas of Southeast Asia by the seventh century and continued to frequent those waters for almost the next 1,000 years.[28]

Even though the Arabs were the most probable early preachers who converted the Malays to Islam, most Orientalists who have studied the spread of Islam to the Malay World have arrived at the conclusion that Islam was brought to the region by the Indians, not the Arabs.[29] The theory that the religion was brought from the Indian subcontinent was first mooted by the Dutch scholar Jan Pijnappel, the first professor of Malay studies at the University of Leiden. Pijnappel asserted that Islam was brought to this region by Arabs who had not come directly from Arabia, but rather from Gujerat and Malabar, in India.[30] This theory was further enhanced by a study in 1912 by J. P. Moquette, who found that the style of gravestones in Pasai dated 1428 (17 Dhul Hijjah AH 831) was identical to the style of the stone found at the grave of Maulana Malik Ibrahim (d. 1419) in Grisik. Following this discovery, it was established that the gravestones in both Pasai and Grisik were similar to those found in Cambay and Gujerat, in India.[31] Taking this as evidence, later scholars of the Islamization of Malays, such as R. A. Kern, B. Schrieke, G. H. Bousquet, B. H. M. Vlekke, J. Gonda, T. W. Arnold, R. O. Winstedt, Brian Harrison, and others, also conclude that Islam was introduced to this region from the Indian subcontinent.[32] Their assertion is further supported by the fact that the Gujerati ports were major ship-building centers and by the 15th century Gujerati merchants were familiar traders at Malay ports.[33]

Pijnappel's theory of the Indian origin of Islam in the Malay World prompted other Orientalists, including Christiaan Snouck Hurgronje,[34] to embrace the same contention. Hurgronje, however, went even farther by arguing that the Islam that came to this region was introduced specifically from southern India.[35] G. E. Morrison, who made a study of the introduction of Islam to Samudra-Pasai, the Muslim kingdom where Islam is believed to have first been introduced, also concluded that the Islam that was introduced to this region came from southern India. He based his argument on the long-standing trade relation that had existed since pre-Islamic times between the two regions and his study of *Hikayat Raja-Raja Pasai*, which he concluded to be wholly colored by a southern Indian background.[36] Similarly, Kenneth Hall, a historian who made a "re-assessment" of the study of the introduction of Islam to the Malay World, came up with the parallel conclusion that Islam was introduced to this region from southern India.[37]

However, another historian, A. H. Hill, though he subscribed to the theory that Islam came to the Malay World from India and not directly from Arabia, believed that both the southern and northern Indian Muslims played their role in the Islamization of the Malays.[38] R. O. Winstedt, who had researched extensively on Malay culture, was not convinced that the Arabs had had much influence on the Islamization of Malays.[39] Interestingly, to prove his point, Winstedt cited several examples quoted from the traditional Malay literary work *Sejarah Melayu*, which showed that some Malays had not been so receptive to the teaching of Islam and that the Arabs had faced difficulties in teaching them the religion. One was the case of Maulana Sadar Jahan, an Arab religious teacher from Jeddah who expressed his displeasure over a man named Sri Rama who was intoxicated. In front of Bendahara Sri Maharaja, the infuriated Sri Rama responded by questioning the sincerity of the Arab preacher and accusing him of using religion for material gains.[40] Winstedt strongly believed that the available evidence for the Islamization of the Malays pointed to India, that the significant role played by the Arabs in enhancing the process emerged only after the invention of steamships, and that these Arabs were from Hadramaut.[41]

Despite the theories proposed by these Orientalists, there were several scholars who put forward the theory of the "Arab factor" in the introduction of Islam in the Malay World. One of the first to come up with this theory was Professor Keyzer of Delft Academy, who was one of the earliest scholars of Muslim law in Holland. He linked the propagation of Islam in the Malay World with Egypt, where the Shafii school has long occupied an important place. Niemann and De Hollander, other Dutch scholars who studied the Islamization of the Malays, also pointed out the role played by Arabs, as did John Crawfurd, William Marsden, the Portuguese historian Diego de Couto, and other scholars.[42] T. W. Arnold, who studied the propagation of the Muslim faith to various parts of the world, was of the opinion that although the religion was introduced by missionaries from southern India, proselytizing efforts were also actively undertaken by Arabs.[43]

The study of the Islamization of the Malays *vis-à-vis* the prominent role played by Arabs from the Middle East is far from complete if local traditions are not taken into account as being equally important to archeological finds and cultural factors. Various native reports from the region, in the form of both written records and oral traditions, constitute a valuable source of knowledge about the past. Although they are sometimes mixed with fictional elements, they do indeed record the history of this region.[44] The inclusion of local traditions in the study of the introduction of Islam to the Malay World, however, has been rejected by most Orientalists and Western scholars.[45] They view the narratives, preserved by local traditions, that Islam was introduced to this region from Arabia as having no historical basis, and categorically believe that all the evidence points to India as the source from where Malays received knowledge of their faith.[46]

Looking at Malay traditions, it is evident that the early Muslim missionaries who converted their forefathers to Islam were Arabs who came directly from Arabia. Most of them married native women after converting them to the faith, and the role of preaching the new religion was then continued by their descendants. Some of them converted native rulers and married into their families, later inheriting from them and becoming sultans or rulers of their own states; still others held religious offices such as *qadi*s (judges), *mufti*s (the highest authorities in Islam in the Malay states), and religious teachers.[47] According to tradition, the Muslim kingdom of Perlak, founded in the early 12th century, was established by Sayyid Abdul Aziz (who ruled 1161–88), an Arab who came from the Quraish tribe. His descendants are also said to have exercised a strong leadership influence in the kingdom until it was taken over by the descendants of the local princes.[48] The presence of Arabs who exerted a strong influence in the northern part of Sumatra was reported by Marco Polo and Ibn Battuta, who stopped over there awaiting the change of monsoons on their world journeys.[49]

Traditional Malay literary works are more explicit in their accounts of the influential role played by Arabs in the early history of the Malay kingdoms. In *Hikayat Raja-Raja Pasai*, Merah Silu, the founder of the kingdom of Pasai, is said to have seen in a dream the Prophet Muhammad and the arrival of Shaykh Ismail at the port of Pasai, sent by the ruler of Mecca to teach Islam to the people of the kingdom.[50] In *Sejarah Melayu*, there is an account of an Arab, Shaykh Ismail from Mecca, who came to Samudra to spread the religion of Islam.[51] In another account an Arab from Jeddah, Sayyid Abdul Aziz, is said to have converted to Islam the Sultan of Melaka, later known as Raja Muhammad.[52] *Sejarah Melayu* also mentions the visit to Melaka of a Sufi master from Mecca by the name of Maulana Abu Bakar, who brought with him the book *Kitab Dur al-Mazlum* (*Durr al-Manzum*).[53] According to the annals, the book was written by Abu Ishaq al-Shirazi in Medinah. After the book was completed, the author requested one of his students, Maulana Abu Bakar, to take it to Melaka so that its teachings could be disseminated there. In Melaka the arrival of the book was greeted with high regard, and even Sultan Mansor Shah learned its contents, taught by Maulana Abu Bakar himself. Realizing the importance of the book, the Sultan ordered it to be sent to Pasai to be translated into Malay.[54]

In another Malay literary work, *Hikayat Merong Mahawangsa*, the Arab missionary Shaykh Abdullah al-Yamani is said to have come directly from Arabia and converted to Islam the ruler of Kedah, who was subsequently known as Sultan Muzaffar Shah.[55] Early descriptions of the role of an Arab missionary are also found in Acehnese traditional literary works. There are reports that Islam was introduced into the northern tip of Sumatra sometime around 1112 by an Arab preacher named Shaykh Abdullah Arif. One of his disciples, Shaykh Burhanuddin, later continued Shaykh Arif's Islamic missionary works as far away as Priaman, on the west coast of Sumatra.[56]

According to Syed Muhammad Naguib al-Attas, the Islamization of the Malays introduced the Arabs' intellectual culture, which the Malays associated with a higher civilization, to replace the mental stagnation of the earlier Hindu-Buddha period.[57] One aspect of the culture introduced to and adopted by Malays following this process was the use of the Arabic script known as *Jawi*, which for many years, perhaps centuries, may have been developed and refined by Arabs who had learned the Malay language.[58] The process of Islamization also led to a massive borrowing from the Arabic language, from which almost every Malay word related to religious worship was obtained.[59] The extensive use of *Jawi* and the borrowing of Arabic fostered Malays' intellectual progress and the broadening of their worldview, in addition to providing a conducive environment for the deepening of their knowledge using the script as a medium.

Early Arabs who came to the Malay World were committed in their efforts to spread Islam. Arab religious scholars, especially the first few generations, were a prominent feature in Malay life, as were Arab entrepreneurs. Abdullah Munshi, who wrote around 1807, demonstrated an interesting example of the prominent role played by Arab religious scholars in Melaka and the Malays' high expectations of them. Following the death of his Qur'an teacher, a successor had to be found. It was at this juncture that an Arab shaykh from Yemen, a certain Mu'alim Muhyil-Din domiciled in Aceh, came to Melaka and astounded everyone with his skill in reciting from the Qur'an. To support his presence there, 40 or 50 students each agreed to pay him $5 a year. Apparently he was an effective teacher, ensuring that his students understood the basic principles of recitation. Abdullah also mentions that after a year Mu'alim Muhyil-Din returned to Aceh and was replaced by Shaykh Alawi Ba Fakih of Yemen, who showed an extraordinary knowledge of Arabic and knew Malay. Melakan elders arranged his stay, and 50 or 60 students signed up and paid $5 each. Shaykh Alawi Ba Fakih first lectured on the *Umm al-Barahin*, then on various other works of *fiqh*, with special reference to ritualistic matters governing prayer and related aspects.[60]

Since many of the Arabs were relatively well off, they used their influence and wealth to establish mosques, along with which came religious activities. They taught religion in the mosques, gave Qu'ran-reading instruction, delivered sermons and lectures, led the Muslims in congregational prayers, and sat on mosque committees. It is significant that it was the Arab religious teachers who made the mosque not only a place of worship but also a center of learning.[61] Through the efforts of these teachers, the early 20th century also saw several religious schools being built in Malaya. The Arabs' wealth helped establish endowments from whose income these schools were maintained and the teachers were paid. This practice, whereby the income from *waqf* properties was used to maintain religious schools, was a tradition widely practiced in the Middle East for the running of religious institutions, which the Arabs emulated to run the schools they established in the Malay World.[62]

One Arab who played a significant role in establishing a number of Arabic schools in Malaya was Habib (Sayyid) Hassan al-Attas.[63] In 1914 he founded Madrasah al-Attas in Johor Bahru, and in 1923 he founded Madrasah al-Attas Ketapang in Pekan, Pahang. The latter was the first Arabic religious school in Pahang. In Singapore a wealthy Arab, Sayyid Omar al-Sagoff (1850–1927), established Madrasah al-Sagoff in March 1913.[64] Apart from these Arabic schools, other religious schools established by the Arabs were the al-Mashhor in Penang and al-Junayd in Singapore. The establishment in Malaya of such schools — also known as Arabic schools or *madrasa* — by wealthy Arabs was part of the latters' desire to establish the Arab tradition in the land as well as to produce more efficient teachers educated in the Arabic medium. From these schools the students obtained a proficiency in Arabic, which enabled them to understand the Arabic text well, thereby becoming better "authorities" in religious matters and extending a better understanding of Islam to fellow Malays.[65]

The wealthy Arabs who set up these schools not only established endowments for their maintenance, but also provided them with high-quality teachers brought from Arabia. One of the outstanding *madrasa*s established and endowed by Arabs was Madrasah al-Mashhor. The *madrasa* was established in 1916, initially as a school teaching Qur'an and other basic Islamic knowledge. It was set up through the efforts of several Arabs, among them Sayyid Mahzar Aidid, Sayyid Ali Bawazir, Sayyid Umar al-Sagoff, Sayyid Umar Mahzar, and Sayyid Hassan al-Baghdadi. It was named Madrasah al-Mashhor in honor of a respected Sayyid on the island, Sayyid Ahmad al-Mashhor.[66] At the *madrasa*, the majority of the teaching staff were Arabs. This enabled it to maintain a high standard of Arabic being taught; in fact, it was about the best in Southeast Asia. The high reputation attained by Madrasah al-Mashhor led to a rapid increase in its enrolment, with students coming from all over Malaya, Laos, Cambodia, Thailand, Brunei, the Philippines, Indonesia, and even India. This distinction enabled the school to emerge as a leading center for Arabic and Islamic education in Southeast Asia before World War II.[67]

In addition to having the majority of its teachers imported from Arabia, Madrasah al-Mashhor also maintained, from the time of its establishment, a tradition of appointing Arabs as *mudir* (head teacher). After its earliest *mudir*, Sayyid Shaykh al-Hadi, left the *madrasa* in 1919, his place was taken by another Arab, Shaykh Abdullah al-Maghribi. In 1923 the post of *mudir* was filled by Shaykh Abu Bakar al-Rafi', whose tenure in office in the 1920s and 1930s was generally regarded as the period of the school's highest reputation.[68] During this period many graduates of the *madrasa* were sent to Cairo for further studies.[69] While in office, Shaykh Abu Bakar also brought about several improvements in the school's infrastructure and introduced new approaches in its teaching. As a progressive *alim* (religious scholar), Shaykh Abu Bakar also contributed to the molding of the religious and political thoughts of his students, and his reformist ideas were prevalent to a high degree among the students of the *madrasa*.[70]

Beginning from the late 1930s, although the role of Arabs in religious affairs and the propagation of Islam still persisted, the Malays gradually became increasingly prominent; a greater number of their students returned to Malaya after acquiring knowledge of Arabic and Islam in Mecca and Cairo. Despite this, the respect for Arabs continued to prevail in Malay society, due to the formers' hard work, sincerity and commitment to bringing about social change in the community, and capability to adapt well to society.[71]

The Arabs' Migration and Integration

In all probability, it was the Arabs of the southern coast of the Arabian Peninsula who were the first navigators of the Indian Ocean and who discovered the Far East.[72] Evidence of their being great mariners may be found in their old lexicons, pre-Islamic poetry, and the religious writings of the pagan Arabs.[73] The strategic location of the Malay Peninsula, which was situated on the ancient international maritime route, enabled it to emerge as a vital stopping place for foreign merchants; and since pre-Islamic times it was also a regular shipping route for Arab traders.[74] By the middle of the ninth century the Malay Peninsula was increasingly frequented by the enterprising southern Arabian Arabs, since it was the obligatory passage between West and East for any ship bound for China. Evidence of Arab trading activity in China during this period is provided by two independent accounts of the route at that time, Ibn Khurdadhbih's *Kitab al-Masalik wa al-Mamalik* and Sulayman's *Akhbar al-Sin wa al-Hind*.[75]

The southern Arabian Arabs' active involvement in inland trade as well as maritime trade in the adjacent seas and beyond, to the vast expanse of the Indian Ocean, as a source of livelihood was encouraged by a number of factors. The contributing internal factor was the aridity and barrenness of their homeland (with the exception of a few coastal areas), which was not suitable for agricultural activities.[76] Another important factor that led these Arabs to turn to trade for a living was the stagnation, sometimes decline, of the economy of their area and the increase in the population, which could not be accommodated any more by the cities of Hadramaut.[77]

The prominence of the southern Arabian Arabs in trading ventures was also assisted tremendously by the advantage of their location, which enabled them to function, centuries before the advent of Islam, as intermediaries between Europe and the East. Their trading activities in the Indian Ocean were also greatly facilitated by favorable geographical conditions related to the monsoons. The monsoon winds, which blow steadily across the Indian Ocean in one direction and then in the reverse direction for several months at a time, allowed the passage of sea transport from Southwest Asia and ports farther East.[78] Taking full advantage of the monsoons, Arab traders were able to calculate with great accuracy the time it would take for them to reach their destination and for the return journey.[79]

For these southern Arabian Arabs, however, it was more than just their enviable strategic position, the monsoons, the aridity of the region, and their entrepreneurial skills that motivated them to become traders.

Their active involvement in trading activities, particularly in the Indian Ocean, was encouraged also by the existence farther north of a fairly high form of organized society living in conditions of prosperity. This society provided an important market for their merchandise from the East, including, above all, luxury goods. History has shown the presence of a nearly continuous period of human civilization in the Middle East or Southern Europe from the time of the Sumerians onward. This continuous period of civilized society is believed to have created an almost permanent demand for Eastern products, although it varied in intensity depending on how well-developed the civilization was at a given time.[80]

Most Arabs who came to the Malay World traveled from the main city-port of Aden. The emergence of Aden as an important city-port dated back to the fall of Baghdad in 1258, when some Arab trading activities were shifted there. Its importance as a trading center was recorded by Marco Polo (1294) and later by Ibn Battuta (1325–55), who visited it and mentioned it as a prosperous city-port. A century later, in 1443, when the Venetian Nicolo Conti visited the port, he described it as "an opulent city remarkable for its buildings."[81] The land in which the city-port was situated was also recorded in the Malay literary work *Hikayat Hang Tuah*. On his journey to Rum, the Malay legendary hero Hang Tuah mentioned passing through it before entering the Red Sea.[82] Aden continued to function as an important trading port in the following centuries and was also an important gateway for the Arabs of Hadramaut who began to migrate to the Malay World, including Malaya, before the arrival of the Dutch in the 17th century.[83]

Most of the southern Arabs settled in Malaysia today trace their roots to Hadramaut.[84] However, Arabs of any origin, at least until recently, were perceived by Malays as descendants of the Prophet, a genealogical link that elevated them to a noble ancestry, with supernatural powers and an inherited missionary role.[85] With the title of "Sayyid" or "Shaykh" appended to their names, the Arabs reaffirmed their distinguished status, which gained them special respect as direct inheritors of the wisdom of Islam and possessors of an unexampled piety and religious merit.[86] This respect, which the Arabs enjoyed in the eyes of Malays, was supplemented by the belief that the former possessed special powers. The Malays were thus careful and fearful in their dealings with the Arabs.[87] Cleverly using the Malays' perception of their genealogical link with the Prophet, the Arabs gained acceptance and access into many Muslim ruling houses in the Malay World. Under these circumstances, the Arabs were generally accepted as being from a noble or royal background and were treated with deference.[88]

The Arabs of Hadramaut, or the Hadramis, originally belonged to the leading Kathiri tribe, of southern Arabian stock. Toward the close of the 15th century, disputes erupted among members of the ruling family. As a result of these struggles, the Hadramis were left with only the eastern portion of Hadramaut, with its chief towns of Tarim and 'Say'un' under their control. The western part, with the ports of Shihr and Mukalla, was controlled by the Hadramis' rival, the Qu'aiti Sultanate.[89] Tarim and Saiwun were identified as major centers of intellectual activity, while al-Mukalla and Shihr were largely mercantile.[90] Since pre-Islamic times the Hadramis have often been described as the most sophisticated and enterprising people in southern Arabia, even though the area has had a long history of tension and disaster. The Hadramis have also had a long history of migration to neighboring Arab countries as well as to India and other distant countries in East Africa and the Far East. In 1938 it was estimated that at least half as many Hadramis lived outside Hadramaut as did in it.[91]

It is difficult to ascertain when exactly the Hadramis decided to migrate in large numbers to the Malay World, but there are several explanations for the phenomenon. The geopolitical and economic situation of Hadramaut itself was an important factor in encouraging migration. The arid lands, which frequently suffered from long periods of drought followed by floods, resulted in food shortages in Hadramaut. Over the previous centuries, revenues obtained from transit commerce had also ceased to flow, due to the decline in trade with the Far East. The difficulties faced in earning a living ultimately stimulated emigration as a way out in search of a decent livelihood.[92] Since the early days the Hadramis were tempted to go overseas — not only to seek a living for themselves but also to carry on the tradition of remitting home annually such monies as would enable them and their families to purchase the necessities (and often the luxuries) of life that could not be produced locally.[93]

Another reason for the migration of the Hadramis was the prolonged conflicts among the tribes in the area and also the devastating war with the Wahhabis. The Wahhabis tried to eliminate what they considered to be incorrect practices of Islam, including those of the Hadramis. As a result, many of the Hadramis' books were destroyed and mausoleums of their saints were demolished. The desire to avoid persecution and bitter ideological conflicts forced many Hadramis to emigrate.[94] Against the hostile and unfavorable conditions in their homeland, the environment overseas was particularly welcoming. In the early 20th century there was an increasing demand for religious teachers in various places, including Malaya, following the opening of several Arabic religious schools. Hadramaut, which has a long history as an important center of learning, was never short of a supply of *ulama* (religious scholars) whose influence and reputation extended overseas and provided a source of teachers for these schools.[95] Despite all these reasons, undoubtedly the overriding factor that led these Arabs to emigrate was their search for a happier livelihood than was possible in their own infertile and impoverished homeland.[96]

Even though there was a steady trickle of Hadramis to Malaya prior to the British intervention, significant numbers of Hadramis migrated only in the early 19th century. When Singapore came under British administration in 1819, the Arabs were among its pioneering settlers. A substantial Arab migration to the region, however, was most noticeable from the mid-19th century to the early 20th. The opening of the Suez Canal in 1869 partly explained the increase in migration, since the port of Aden was situated in the middle of the shipping route. Aden, which re-emerged as an important port between Europe and the Far East following the opening of the canal, enabled the Hadramis to travel to and from the region with ease. The rapid economic growth experienced by the Malay states and especially Singapore under the British administration also attracted many Arab entrepreneurs who wished to try their fortune there.

Despite their relatively large-scale migration, the exact number of Arab migrants after the arrival of the British is unknown, except for the Straits Settlements, where some records are available. However, their numbers here and also in the Malay states, as with other communities, cannot be taken for granted since there is no way of checking the reliability of the records. According to Omar Farouk Shaeik Ahmad, who referred to the Straits Settlement Census, the Arabs in Penang numbered 322 in 1871 and 449 in 1891.[97] Their numbers increased gradually during the following years, registering 473 in 1901, 702 in 1911, and 520 in 1921.[98] In the Malay states, however, no record of the Arabs' early population is available, even though they were widely distributed and formed a very distinctive demographic minority group in the village communities. The earliest census of their population was made in 1891, with 51 members being recorded for the state of Perak, 27 for Selangor, and 20 for Negeri Sembilan.[99] Even though their numbers were relatively small, these Arabs domiciled in the Malay states were not only active as entrepreneurs and propagators of Islam, but were also involved in politics and administration.[100]

Available records, however, show that the early Arab population was concentrated mostly in Singapore. In early January 1830 the Arabs numbered 28, all male, out of a total population on the island of 20,243; their number continued to increase steadily in the following decades.[101] In 1884, according to Van den Berg, who referred to the Straits Settlements Census, 835 of the 1,637 Arabs found in the Straits Settlements lived in Singapore.[102] On the island, the early Arab population was concentrated in the area that used to be known as Middle Road, in a "quarter" bounded by Arab, Baghdad, Basrah, and Jeddah streets.[103]

The Hadrami Arab migrants were males who regularly sent remittances (*mawasalat*) to support their wives at home.[104] These Arabs who migrated to Malaya and elsewhere were generally divided into two groups. The first were the Sayyid group, who claimed that they were descendants of the Prophet and traced their genealogy through the line of Isa al-Muhajir. His great grandson, Ali bin Alawi, institutionalized the Alawiyyah Sayyids in Hadramaut in the early 12th century.[105] These Arab Sayyids regarded themselves as having the most noted descent and most notable religious status in society.[106] Most of the Arabs who migrated to Malaya claimed to belong to the Sayyid Alawiyyah or Sayyid group.[107] As part of their family tradition, the Sayyid group traced their genealogy through the patrilineal line, whereby those who were born to an Arab father were considered to be Arab even if the mother was not. Based on this criterion, the Sayyid group could be divided into those of "pure Arab" descent, where both parents were Arabs, and "born Arabs," whose mothers were non-Arab. According to the 1921 census, the "pure Arabs" numbered 370 out of 1,858 in the Straits Settlements, 107 out of 656 in the Federated Malay States, and 238 out of 1,802 in the Unfederated Malay States. Since the number of Arab women who migrated was small and intermarriage with Malay women was common, the "born Arab" Sayyids were much greater in number.[108]

During the period soon after their arrival, the Arabs of the close-knit Sayyid group tried as far as possible to preserve their identity. To keep their family genealogy intact and their place of origin identified, they were recognized by their family names. In Kedah, for example, as elsewhere, where many of the migrant Hadramis of this group settled, they were identified by their family names, the most prominent including al-Baraqabah, al-Shahabuddin, al-Junayd, al-Aidid, al-Sagoff, Ba Faqih, al-Kaff, al-Mahdali, al-Jamalullail, al-Qadri, al-Attas, al-Mihdar, al-Jufri, Al bin Yahaya, and al-Idrus.[109] Apart from the Sayyid group, another group of Hadramis who also migrated, but were much fewer in number, consisted of scholars and holy men (*mashayikh*, plural of *shaykh*), tribesmen (*qaba'il*, plural of *qabila*), and the poor (*masakin*, plural of *miskin*).[110] These Arabs normally used the title "Shaykh," which implied that they were not descendants of the Prophet, while there were others who preferred not to use any title.

Before World War II, even though the Arabs who migrated to Malaya and elsewhere tended to foster a close and lasting relationship with their countries of domicile, they seldom broke the bonds with their homeland. This bond was clearly evident in Kathiri state, which was where many of the Arabs in Malaya originated. Extensive social and commercial ties bound together these two widely divided regions, and the economies of Kathiri state and Malaya became almost wholly dependent on funds remitted to Saiwun and Tarim from the extensive Far East business holdings of several great Kathiri families. Their contribution to the prosperity of the state was observed by the Dutch explorer D. van der Meulen, who visited Hadramaut in May and June 1931. He recorded that when he and his entourage reached Horeida, the tribal village of the family of al-Attas, they saw many beautiful houses and mosques that had been built from the wealth accumulated in Java and Singapore. In the village they also found a large number of Dutch subjects, many of whom spoke Malay; and the Malay language was even frequently heard being spoken on the streets.[111] Van der Meulen also noticed that these Arabs preserved strong emotional and spiritual ties with Hadramaut, which were manifested in their dress, language, and intensity of religious life. They returned to their homeland to visit families, to make the pilgrimage, and often, ultimately, to die.[112] Those who finally decided to return and settle down in their homeland after long years of absence brought into existence in Hadramaut a society of retired businessmen who had became almost more used to speaking Malay than their native tongue and who had on their walls pictures of Singapore, Penang, or Batavia.[113]

Even though the Hadramis' migration has long ceased, their presence can still be felt in Malaya, in the form of their descendants. Most of them still maintain their family names, and they enter into mixed marriage with members of other Muslim communities. The new generation of Arabs in Malaysia were born locally, and they have taken advantage of their *bumiputra* (sons of the soil) status and privileges to fill many professions in the country. Today they constitute an important component of the Muslim population of Malaysia and are increasingly closely becoming identified and accepted as part of the Malay community.

Conclusion

From contacts that were initially based on trading activities, the Malays converted to Islam. The Islamization of the Malays elevated their bond with the Middle East, which no longer rested on a merely commercial basis but now encompassed the important areas of religion and education. This opened a new chapter in their relationship. In ancient times there was active Arab involvement with the East, but after Islamization this became a two-way interaction, with the Malays making increasingly more journeys to the Middle East than did the Arabs to the Malay lands. Although the Arabs' earlier predominance was confronted by colonial powers that arrived in Malayan waters from the beginning of the 16th century, the Malays' attachment to the Middle East and the Arabs persisted. This stemmed from the feeling of indebtedness to the community that had contributed to and influenced the development of their civilization, through the process of Islamization.

Notes

1. G. R. Tibbetts, "Pre-Islamic Arabia and South-East Asia," *JMBRAS* 29, 3 (1956): 182; see also Alauddin Ismail Samarrai, "The Muslims in the South Seas and the Beginning of the Portuguese Challenge," *The Islamic Review* 45, 12 (December 1957): 27.
2. Tibbetts, "Pre-Islamic Arabia and South-East Asia," 207.
3. Ibid.
4. Syed Naguib al-Attas, *Preliminary Statement on a General Theory of the Islamization of the Malay-Indonesian Archipelago* (Kuala Lumpur: Dewan Bahasa dan Pustaka, 1969), 11.
5. Paul Wheatley, "Arabo-Persian Sources for the History of the Malay Peninsula in Ancient Times," in K. G. Tregonning, ed., *Malaysian Historical Sources* (Singapore: Department of History, University of Singapore, 1965), 10.
6. For works by these Arab writers and others, and their contributions as a source of the early history of the Malay Peninsula, see G. R. Tibbetts, "The Malay Peninsula as Known to the Arab Geographers," *Malayan Journal of Tropical Geography* 8 (1956): 21–60; G. R. Tibbetts, *Arab Navigation in the Indian Ocean Before the Coming of the Portuguese* (London: The Royal Asiatic Society of Great Britain and Ireland, 1971); Wheatley, "Arabo-Persian Sources," 10–9; Abdul Azim Hashemi Nik, "The Background of Acquaintance With Malay Societies: Evidence Found in Existing Islamic Geographical Texts," paper presented at the Second Conference on Malay Civilisation, 15–20 August 1989, Ministry of Culture and Tourism of

Malaysia, Kuala Lumpur, 1–42. For a brief account of several leading Arab travelers and writers on oceanography and allied subjects, see Abdul Ali, "The Arabs as Seafarers," *Islamic Culture* 54, 4 (October 1980): 218–9; and Affan Seljuq, "Some Muslim Geographers on South-East Asia," *Journal of the Pakistan Historical Society* 37, 2 (April 1989): 125–32, an extract from accounts by two Arab geographers, Ibn Khurdadhbih, *al-Masalik Wa al-Mamalik*, and Ibn Rustah, *Kitab Al-Alaq al-Nafisah*.
7. Rita Rose Di Meglio, "Arab Trade with Indonesia and the Malay Peninsula from the 8th to the 16th Century," in D. S. Richards, ed., *Islam and the Trade of Asia: A Colloquium* (Pennsylvania: University of Pennsylvania Press, 1970), 110.
8. H. G. Quaritch Wales, "Archeological Researches on Ancient Indian Colonisation in Malaya," *JMBRAS* 18, 1 (1940): 32.
9. Ibid., 108.
10. Andre Wink, "'Al-Hind': India and Indonesia in the Islamic World-Economy, c. 700–1800 A.D.," *Itinerario* 12, 1 (1988): 44.
11. Anthony Reid, "An 'Age of Commerce' in Southeast Asian History," *Modern Asian Studies* 24, 1 (February 1990): 12
12. Kenneth R. Hall, "Trade and Statecraft in the Western Archipelago at the Dawn of the European Age," *JMBRAS* 54, 1 (1981): 22.
13. Rose Di Meglio, "Arab Trade with Indonesia and the Malay Peninsula," 108.
14. Wink, "'Al-Hind,'" 44.
15. Paul Wheatley, "Desultory Remarks on the Ancient History of the Malay Peninsula," in John Bastin and R. Roolvink, eds., *Malayan and Indonesian Studies* (Oxford: Clarendon Press, 1964), 60–1.
16. W. H. Moreland, "The Ships of the Arabian Seas about A.D. 1500," *Journal of the Royal Asiatic Society* (January 1939): 64.
17. S. M. Yusuf, "The Route of Arab Mariners Through al-Zabaj (Further India)," in S. M. Yusuf, *Studies in Islamic History and Culture* (Delhi: Adam Publishers and Distributors, 1989), chapter IV, 167.
18. Archibald Lewis, "Maritime Skills in the Indian Ocean 1368–1500," *Journal of the Economic and Social History of the Orient* 16, 2–3 (1973): 245.
19. Ibid., 262–3.
20. See Charles Issawi, "The Decline of Middle Eastern Trade 1100–1850," in Richards, *Islam and the Trade of Asia*, 245–66.
21. Caesar Adib Majul, "Theories on the Introduction and Expansion of Islam in Malaysia," *Siliman Journal* (1964): 338. It is an irony that the early Portuguese voyagers in the Indian Ocean had to rely upon the assistance and guidance of Arab navigators. See Abdul Ali, "Struggle Between the Portuguese and the Arabs of Oman for Supremacy in the Persian Coast and the Indian Ocean," *Hamdard Islamicus* 9, 4 (1986): 75–7.

22. See J. V. Mills, "Arab and Chinese Navigators in Malaysian Waters in about A.D. 1500," *JMBRAS* 47, 2 (1974): 7.
23. Uka Tjandrasasmita, "The Sea Trade of the Moslems to the Eastern Countries and the Rise of Islam in Indonesia," in *Studies in Asian History*, proceedings of the Asian History Congress 1961 (New York: Asia Publishing House, 1969), 93.
24. Syed Naguib Al-Attas, *Preliminary Statement*, 11.
25. See S. M. Imamuddin, "Arab Mariners and Islam in China," *Journal of the Pakistan Historical Society* 33, 3 (July 1984): 177.
26. George Fadlo Hourani, *Arab Seafaring in the Indian Ocean in Ancient and Early Medieval Times* (Princeton, N.J.: Princeton University Press, 1951), 71, 78; Yusuf, *Studies in Islamic History and Culture*, p. 139. For a discussion of the accounts of Arab geographers about the location of Kalah, see Tibbetts, "The Malay Peninsula as Known to Arab Geographers," 24–33.
27. For an enlightening discussion of the candidature of Kelang as the possible location of Kalah, see S. Q. Fatimi, "In Quest of Kalah," *Journal of Southeast Asian History* 1, 2 (September 1960): 62–101. See also Fatimi's article "Peace, Unity and Universality," *Intisari* 1, 1 (n.d.): 28; and Brian E. Colless, "The Traders of the Pearl. The Mercantile and Missionary Activities of Persian and Armenian Christians in South-East Asia," *Abr-Nahraian* IX (1969/70): 24. Paul Wheatley, who also tried to identify the exact site of Kalah, however, arrived at the conclusion that none of these places fitted all the accounts given by various Arab geographers. He concluded that Kalah could be any place along the coast from the Mergui Archipelago to the west coast of the Malay Peninsula. See Wheatley, "Desultory Remarks," note F, 68–70; for a discussion of the archeological evidence, as opposed to literary findings, for the candidature of Pengkalan Bujang in Kedah and Kakhao Island near Takuapa in Southern Thailand, see Alastair Lamb, "A Visit to Siraf. An Ancient Port on the Persian Gulf," *JMBRAS* 37, 1 (July 1964): 1–19; for the candidature of Kakhao Island, see also Lamb's article "Takuapa: The Probable Site of Pre-Malaccan Entrepot in the Malay Peninsula," in John Bastin and R. Roovink, eds., *Malayan and Indonesian Studies* (Oxford: Clarendon Press, 1964), 76–86.
28. Wheatley, "Arabo-Persian Sources," 10.
29. Ismail Hamid, "A Survey of Theories on the Introduction of Islam in the Malay Archipelago," *Islamic Studies* 21, 3 (1982): 89.
30. G. W. J. Drewes, "New Light on the Coming of Islam to Indonesia?" *Bijdragen Tot de Taal, Land- en Volkenkunde* 124 (1968): 440.
31. Ibid., 443–4.
32. See S. Q. Fatimi, *Islam Comes to Malaysia* (Singapore: Malaysian Sociological Research Institute Ltd., 1963), 5–6.

33. S. Arasaratnam, *Islamic Merchant Communities of the Indian Subcontinent in Southeast Asia* (Kuala Lumpur: University of Malaya Press, 1989), 5.
34. Drewes, "New Light," 440–1; C. C. Berg, "The Islamization of Java," *Studia Islamica* 4 (1955): 111.
35. Drewes, "New Light," 440–1.
36. See G. E. Morrison, "The Coming of Islam to the East Indies," *JMBRAS* 24 (1951): 28–37.
37. Kenneth R. Hall, "The Coming of Islam to the Archipelago: A Re-assessment," in Karl L. Hutterer, ed., *Economic Change and Social Interaction in Southeast Asia: Prehistory, History, and Ethnography* (The University of Michigan: Center for South and Southeast Asian Studies, 1977), 221.
38. See A. H. Hill, "The Coming of Islam to North Sumatra," *Journal of Southeast Asian History* 4, 1 (1963): 16–7.
39. R. O. Winstedt, "The Advent of Muhammadanism in the Malay Peninsula and Archipelago," *JSBRAS* (December 1917): 171.
40. Ibid., 172.
41. R. O. Winstedt, "The Early Muhammadan Missionaries," *JSBRAS* (March 1920): 5–6.
42. Hamid, "A Survey of Theories," 93.
43. See T. W. Arnold, *The Preaching of Islam: A History of the Propagation of the Muslim Faith* (Lahore: Sh. Muhammad Ashraf, 1979), 368–9.
44. Hamid, "A Survey of Theories," 94–5.
45. One of them was J. C. Bottom, who leveled the most extreme criticism against Malay histories. He wrote, "History to the Malays has not until recently been either a science or an art, but an entertainment. Accuracy, completeness, organised exposition were not the vital principles; what best pleased were legend, fantasy and pleasant hotch-potch of Court and port gossip." See J. C. Bottom, "Malay Historical Works," in Tregonning, *Malaysian Historical Sources*, 38.
46. Arnold, *The Preaching of Islam*, 370.
47. Hamid, "A Survey of Theories," 94–5.
48. Slamet Muljana, *Runtuhnya Keradjaan Hindu-Djawa dan Timbulnya Negara2 Islam Di Nusantara* (Jakarta: Penerbit Bhratara, 1968), 132.
49. J. A. E. Morley, "The Arabs and the Eastern Trade," *JMBRAS* 22, 1 (March 1949): 354.
50. Drewes, "New Light," 437–8; see also W. G. Shellabear, *Sejarah Melayu* (Petaling Jaya: Penerbit Fajar Bakti Sdn. Bhd., 1984), 41–2.
51. See Shellabear, *Sejarah Melayu*, 40–2.
52. Ibid., 54–6.
53. Ibid., 114–5.
54. See Yahya Abu Bakar, "*Melaka Sebagai Pusat Islam Abad ke XV Masihi*," *Sari* 1, 1 (January 1983): 37–8.

55. Hamid, "A Survey of Theories," p. 95.
56. Syed Naguib Al-Attas, *Preliminary Statement*, p. 11.
57. The explanation given by Syed Naguib al-Attas of mental stagnation during the Hindu-Buddha period is particularly enlightening. His argument rejects the views advocated by several Western orientalists who placed special significance on the period in the Malay-Indonesian Archipelago before the introduction of Islam. See Syed Muhammad Naguib al-Attas, *Islam Dalam Sejarah Dan Kebudayaan Melayu* (Kuala Lumpur: Penerbit Universiti Kebangsaan Malaysia, 1984), 12-9.
58. W. G. Shellabear, "The Evolution of Malay Spelling," *JSBRAS* (July 1901): 77.
59. W. A. O'Sullivan, "The Relation Between Southern India and the Straits Settlements," *JSBRAS* (July 1901): 67.
60. See Anthony H. Johns, "Islam in the Malay World, an Exploratory Survey with Some Reference to Quranic Exegesis," in Raphael Israeli and Anthony H. Johns, eds., *Islam in Asia*, vol. II (Jerusalem: The Magnes Press, 1984), 129; Yusof A. Talib, "Munshi Abdullah's Arab Teachers," *JMBRAS* 63, 2 (1990): 27-9.
61. Omar Farouk Shaeik Ahmad, "The Arabs in Penang," *Malaysia in History* 21, 2 (December 1978): 6.
62. See A. L. Tibawi, "Origin and Character of *Al-Madrasah*," *The Bulletin of the School of Oriental and African Studies* 25 (1962): 232.
63. In addition to being addressed as Sayyid, the al-Attas family is also addressed as Habib, which means "the beloved" or "the honored." See Abdallah al-Bujra, *The Politics of Stratification. A Study of Political Change in a South Arabian Town* (Oxford: Clarendon Press, 1971), 15. Habib (Sayyid) Hassan was born in 1832, a son of Sayyid Ahmad bin Sayyid Hassan al-Attas, a trader who arrived in Pahang in the early 19th century from Hadramaut. Habib Hassan received part of his education at al-Azhar University, in Cairo, and lived in Egypt for 12 years. After that he returned to Singapore, where he taught at Madrasah al-Sagoff for two years before moving to Garoet, in the Praeanger Residency, to teach at a school there. Like his father, Sayyid Hassan was an influential figure in Pahang and managed to accumulate wealth through his entrepreneurial skill and his close relationship with Pahang royalty. Sayyid Hassan was a generous man who used his wealth to finance religious education, built many mosques, and donated lands for Muslim burial grounds in Pahang, Johore, and Hadramaut. He died on 21 March 1932. For an account of his life and contributions to Islamic life in Malay society, see *Almarhum Sayyid Hassan Ahmad al-Attas. Seorang Mujahid dan Pembangun Ummah* (Johor Bahru: Wakaf Almarhum Syed Hassan bin Ahmad Alattas, 1984), 11-32; Mahayuddin Haji Yahaya, *Sejarah Orang Syed di Pahang* (Kuala Lumpur: Dewan Bahasa dan Pustaka, 1984),

90–1. See also CO 537/931, Marriot (Governor's Deputy) to Amery, 1 April 1925; enclosure *The Malayan Bulletin of Political Intelligence*, no. 28, April 1925.

64. See *Neracha* 3, 75 (5 March 1913): 1; *Tunas Melayu* 2, 2 (12 March 1912).
65. M. A. Rauf, "Islamic Education," *Intisari* 2, 1 (n.d.): 22–3.
66. See Rahim Osman, "Madrasah Al-Masyhur al-Islamiyyah," in Khoo Kay Kim *et al.*, *Islam di Malaysia* (Kuala Lumpur: Persatuan Sejarah Malaysia, 1980), 76–7.
67. Omar Farouk Shaeik Ahmad, "The Arabs in Penang," 8.
68. Rahim bin Osman, "Madrasah al-Masyhur al-Islamiyyah," 78–9.
69. One of the students of the *madrasah* who was provided with a scholarship through the initiative of Shaykh Abu Bakar al-Rafi' to further his studies in Cairo was Abu Bakar Ashaari. See *Ar-Rajaa* 2, 2 (1 August 1928): 14.
70. Saliha Haji Hassan, "Dr. Burhanuddin al Helmi 1911–1969," *Jebat*, no. 14 (1986): 158.
71. Ismail Hamid gave an interesting example of an Arab woman in his village in Perlis before and during World War II who adapted herself well to the community and gained great admiration from fellow villagers. She was the only literate woman in the community, taught religious knowledge, and provided a form of entertainment by narrating Islamic histories. See the account of her in Ismail Hamid, *Arabic and Islamic Literary Tradition. With Reference to Malay Islamic Literature* (Kuala Lumpur: Utusan Publication & Distributors Sdn. Bhd., 1982), v–vi.
72. Caesar Adib Majul, "Theories on the Introduction and Expansion of Islam in Malaya," 236.
73. S. M. Imamuddin, "Islam in Malaysia. Impact of Bengal, the Deccan, Gujerat and Persia in the Early Middle Ages," *Journal of the Pakistan Historical Society* 29, 4 (October 1981): 260.
74. See Kenneth R. Hall, "Trade in the Malay World. An Historical Perspective," in Mohd. Amin Hassan and Nik Hassan Shuhaimi Nik Abdul Rahman, eds., *The Eighth Conference of the International Association of Historians of Asia. Selected Papers* (Bangi: History Department UKM, 1988), 207–10.
75. See George Fadlo Hourani, *Arab Seafaring*, 66.
76. Peter Boxhall, "Arabian Seafarers in the Indian Ocean," *Asian Affairs* 20 (Old Series vol. 76), 3 (October 1989): 287.
77. Caesar Adib Majul, "Theories on the Introduction and Expansion of Islam in Malaya," 338–9.
78. Tibbetts, "Pre-Islamic Arabia and South-East Asia," 217.
79. S. M. Imamuddin, "Arab Mariners and Islam in China," *Journal of Pakistan Historical Society* 32, 3 (July 1984): 159.
80. See Tibbetts, "Pre-Islamic Arabia and South-East Asia," p. 183.

81. Morley, "The Arabs and the Eastern Trade," p. 153.
82. Kassim Ahmad (ed. with new intro.), *Hikayat Hang Tuah* (Kuala Lumpur: Dewan Bahasa dan Pustaka, 1993), 533. After ten days' sailing from Acheh Darul Salam, Hang Tuah is said to have reached Bab Mokha with the state of Abyssinia situated to its left.
83. R. B. Serjeant, "The Sayyids of Hadramawt," in *Studies in Arabian History and Civilisation* (London: Variorum Reprints, 1981), p. 25, chapter VII.
84. Before 1968 the term "Hadramaut" was applied chiefly to the south Arabian states of the Kathiri and Qu'aiti Sultanates. Since 1968, however, the term has been applied to the governorates of Shabwa and Hadramaut of the Republic of South Yemen. The latter state united with North Yemen in 1990, and the area became part of the unified state of Yemen.
85. Bujra, *The Politics of Stratification*, 23. Even though most Arabs who came to Malaya traced their origin to Hadramaut, a small number of them came from Hijaz and elsewhere. In Malaya these non-Hadrami Arabs played a significant role as religious teachers and in the propagation of Islam among the Malays.
86. William R. Roff, *The Origins of Malay Nationalism* (Kuala Lumpur: Penerbit Universiti Malaya, 1980), 41; W. H. Lee Warner, "Notes on the Hadhramaut," *The Geographical Journal* 77, 3 (March 1931): 220.
87. This belief seems to have been universally accepted throughout the Malay World; a similar notion was also found in 19th century Aceh. See C. Snouck Hurgronje (trans. by A. W. S. O'Sullivan), *The Achehnese*, vol. 1 (Leiden: E. J. Brill, 1906), 155–6. The supernatural power believed to have been possessed led to the graves of some pious Arabs being highly revered by Malays. Among these graves recorded by Winstedt were those of Shaykh Muhammad and Shaykh Ahmad at Bukit Gedong, Melaka; Shaykh Muhammad Ali at Simpang Lima, Kelang; and Sayyid Makbuli at Taiping. See R. O. Winstedt, "*Keramat*: Sacred Places and Persons in Malaya," *JMBRAS* 2, 3 (December 1924): 275–6.
88. Omar Farouk Bajunid, "The Arabs in Southeast Asia: A Preliminary Overview," *Hiroshima Journal of International Studies* 2 (1996): 22.
89. R. A. Cochrane, "An Air Reconnaissance of the Hadhramaut," *The Geographical Journal* 77, 3 (March 1931): 210. For a discussion of the rise of the Kathiri and the Qu'aiti states, see W. H. Ingrams, *Aden Protectorate. A Report on the Social, Economic and Political Condition of the Hadhramaut* (London: H. M. Stationery Office, 1937; reprinted 1939), 27–35.
90. R. B. Serjeant, "Historians and Historiography of Hadhramaut," *Bulletin of the School of Oriental and African Studies* 25 (1962): 239.
91. Bujra, *The Politics of Stratification*, 4.
92. Joseph Kostiner, "The Impact of the Hadrami Emigrants in the East Indies on Islamic Modernism and Social Change in the Hadramawt During the

20th Century," in Raphael Israeli and Anthony H. Johns, eds., *Islam in Asia*, vol. II (Jerusalem: The Magnes Press, 1984), 208.
93. Lee Warner, "Notes on the Hadhramaut," 219.
94. Mahayuddin Haji Yahaya, "*Latarbelakang Sejarah Keturunan Sayid Di Malaysia*," in Khoo Kay Kim *et al.*, *Tamadun Islam Di Malaysia* (Kuala Lumpur: Persatuan Sejarah Malaysia, 1980), 73; Kostiner, "The Impact of the Hadrami Emigrants," 209.
95. Bujra, *The Politics of Stratification*, p. 4.
96. R. H. Smith, "Notes on the Kathiri State of Hadhramaut," *The Middle East Journal* 7, 4 (1953): 503.
97. According to the Straits Settlement Census, the total population of Penang in 1871 was 61,797; and in 1881 it was 123,886. See Omar Farouk Shaeik Ahmad, "The Arabs in Penang," p. 5.
98. Ibid.
99. Morley, "The Arabs and the Eastern Trade," Appendix C, p. 175.
100. For a discussion on the Arabs' active involvement in the politics and administration of the Malay states during the period, see Mohammad Redzuan Othman, "Hadramis in the Politics and Administration of the Malay States in the Late Eighteenth and Nineteenth Centuries," in Ulrike Freitag and William G. Clarence-Smith, *Hadrami Traders, Scholars, and Statesmen in the Indian Ocean, 1750s–1960s* (Leiden: Brill, 1997), 82–93.
101. See *Singapore Chronicle*, no. 165 (Thursday, 15 July 1830). The Singapore Census shows the number of each class of inhabitant recorded on 1 January 1830.
102. Roff, *The Origins of Malay Nationalism*, 40. Van den Berg, however, considered that the given figure of 445 adult males in Singapore was "much too high." He believed that there were "at the most 200 adult (male) Arabs actually settled at Singapore." He attributed the alleged excess to the number of Arabs in transit to the Netherlands Indies. His own figure of 580 male and female Arabs in Singapore includes children above the age of ten years.
103. Morley, "The Arabs and the Eastern Trade," 167.
104. Peter Riddle, "Religious Links Between Hadhramaut and the Malay-Indonesia World, c. 1859 to c. 1950," in Ulrike Freitag and William G. Clarence-Smith, *Hadrami Traders, Scholars, and Statesmen in the Indian Ocean, 1750s–1960s* (Leiden: Brill, 1997), 221.
105. Mahayuddin Haji Yahaya, "*Latarbelakang Sejarah Keturunan Sayid*," 13–4.
106. Bujra, *The Politics of Stratification*, p. 13.
107. Mahayuddin Haji Yahaya, *Sejarah Orang Syed Di Pahang* (Kuala Lumpur: Dewan Bahasa dan Pustaka, 1984), p. 26. Although most Hadramis who migrated to this region claimed to belong to the status group, Roff believes that most of them were actually common folk from the towns with a primary interest in small-scale trade. See William R. Roff, "South-East Asian Islam

in the Nineteenth Century," in Ann K. S. Lambton and Bernard Lewis, eds., *The Cambridge History of Islam*, vol. 2 (Cambridge: Cambridge University Press, 1970), 170.

108. See J. E. Nathan, *The 1921 Census of British Malaya* (London: Waterloo & Sons Ltd., 1922), 91.
109. Faridah Romly, "*Orang Arab di Kedah*," BA thesis, Universiti Kebangsaan Malaysia, 1983–84, 63–4.
110. The division of Arabs into two social groups is discussed in Safie Ibrahim, "Islamic Religious Thought in Malaya," PhD dissertation, Columbia University, 1987, 145–6. See also W. H. Ingrams, *Aden Protectorate*, 36–41.
111. See D. van der Meulen, "A Journey in Hadhramaut," *The Moslem World* 22, 3 (July 1932): 387.
112. Roff, *The Origins of Malay Nationalism*, 42.
113. Morley, "The Arabs and the Eastern Trade," 144–5.

II

The Colonial Age

Learning the Qur'an, Aceh, Indonesia (Photograph E. Tagliacozzo)

5

The Middle East Connection and Reform and Revival Movements among the *Putihan* in 19th-century Java

M. C. RICKLEFS[1]

In the 1840s there were significant numbers of professionally religious people in Javanese society — mosque officials, religious teachers, guardians of holy sites, students at *pěsantrens* (religious schools) — who were known collectively as *kaum* (the religious folk) or *putihan* (the white ones). On the north coast, evidently this group was sometimes also called *santri* (students of religion), foreshadowing a usage that would become common in the mid-20th century. The Dutch called them *geestelijken*: clerics or religious people. There is no evidence, however, that they yet formed a force for puritanism, fundamentalism, or revivalism.[2]

Arabs

The *pasisir* (north coast of Java) was a place where attitudes were becoming different from those deeper in Java's interior, one major element in this difference being the presence there of Arab and other international Muslim communities. Arabs had a particular social standing, because they were commonly members of the commercial elite and were from the heartlands of Islam and, in the case of *sayyids*, because they claimed direct descent from the Prophet. Their family and business connections with the Middle East exposed them to events there more directly than was true of most Javanese. The Wahhabi conquest of Mecca in 1803 was one of many dramatic Middle Eastern events in the first half of the 19th century, for it threatened the integrity of the Ottoman Empire and unleashed an iconoclastic puritan movement within the holiest city of Islam. The Wahhabis were expelled from Mecca in 1818 by Ottoman forces. But by this time they may already have contributed to inspiring the violently reformist Padri movement in West Sumatra — the first such movement of the modern era in Indonesia — which precipitated Dutch intervention and the subsequent Padri War (1821–38).[3] The impact of Middle Eastern political and intellectual ferment in the 19th century[4] was thus already felt in West Sumatra before the time that this study of the Javanese commences. From about the 1850s, ongoing developments in the Middle East began to have significant impacts in Java as well, and the Arabs seem to have been a major conduit for those impacts amongst Javanese society. In the early 1880s, the Dutch scholar L. W. C. van den Berg wrote that there were particularly large numbers of Arabs in the *pasisir* towns, notably in Cirĕbon, Pĕkalongan, Sĕmarang, and Grĕsik, where even Javanese notables were exposed to their "Mohammedan or rather Arabic" influence.[5]

The missionary J. E. Jellesma found Surabaya in the 1850s to be less congenial than some of his colleagues had found the interior, in part because of the Arab presence, it seems. "The Mohammedans here are hostile, and still more uninterested, about Christianity," he wrote. "Those who live nearest to me are under the authority of the Pangeran (prince), the landowner, a half Arab."[6] But it was not only Arabs whom Jellesma thought hostile. In 1853 he warned the governors of the Netherlands Missionary Society that there were also Javanese who were hostile to Christianity. He spoke of "the fanaticism of the Mohammedan priests" and "the opposition of the heads."[7] A decade later, his colleague H. Smeding similarly regarded the head of Blitar to be a "so-to-say full-blooded Mohammedan, many say indeed a fanatic, a man strict in formalities who in the eyes of the world holds firmly to the prescriptions of Islam." He was, claimed Smeding, a false, low character feared by his subjects and loved by none.[8] Yet it seems clear that it was the *pasisir*, with its Arab communities, that played a leading role in early Islamic reform movements and in opposing the first fitful European efforts at Christian missionizing among Javanese.

One report from 1848 suggests that the number of Arabs and other foreign Muslims in the coastal areas was small in terms of the total population, but large enough to have a significant impact. In that year, Tĕgal reportedly had a total population of 317,446, of whom 98 per cent were Javanese. There were 3,025 Chinese and 2,275 Arabs, Bengalis, Malays, and other Asian Muslims (Moors). Europeans numbered only 286.[9] In considering missionary strategies, in 1846 Jellesma wrote that it was better to begin in the interior than on the coast, "where most of the Mohammedan priests and Arabs are found." Yet even in the interior, he said — employing a military metaphor that occurs more than once in missionary sources — the stronghold of Javanese Islam was firm, "for the number of priests is nevertheless great and *Hajjis* and Arabs continuously arrive."[10] G. Brückner—one of the first, most experienced, and most frustrated of missionaries in Java, who had arrived in 1814 — said that in Sĕmarang in 1850 there was strong devotion to Islam among the populace, particularly among the more eminent citizens, "because of the great number of priests and Arabs who live or travel from here and who have a remarkable influence on the people."[11] Hoezoo, too, saw Sĕmarang as a hostile place for missionizing. This was partly because irreligious Europeans there gave a bad impression of what sorts of people Christians were, he thought. But it was more because of the influence of the many Arabs,

> who avidly profit from the indifference of the [European] Christians to instill in the Javanese an aversion to the 'already obsolete' religion of the Prophet Jesus, who openly call us *kafirs* (unbelievers) and teach the pious Muslims to pray for the destruction of our faith, who in all sorts of ways pave the way to superstition and promote a fanaticism that can only nourish hatred for anyone who is not a follower of the honoured Prophet. ... Not to mention the known scoundrels and fanatics who are banished here from the interior and entrusted to the watchful oversight of the police.[12]

Kudus on the *pasisir* was a place of piety, too. It is the only city in Java to have permanently acquired the name of a Middle Eastern Islamic holy site, for it is named after al-Quds (Jerusalem). There, many Javanese revealed "a certain zeal for Islam."[13] The people of Kudus were known as great traders as well as pious Muslims, for there were many *kaum*, Hajjis, and *santris*. But not everybody was pious — there were also 80 dancing girls (i.e., prostitutes) there, for whom the colonial government provided a clinic and a Javanese medical officer.[14]

The Pilgrimage

Technological changes were enhancing communication between the Middle East and Java in the mid-19th century and were supportive of religious reform efforts. The spread of printing was important. A Javanese translation of the Qur'an was printed for the first time in Batavia in 1858.[15] Later in the century, the Hadrami Arab Sayid Uthman bin Aqil bin Yahya al-Alawi (1822–1913)[16] became a major voice for reformist Islam. He remained based in Batavia, and his many publications — more than 100 titles — were all originally published in Arabic or Malay. But some were also published in Javanese translations,[17] and undoubtedly his works were also influential with Arabs living among the Javanese.

The advent of steam shipping made the pilgrimage from Java to Mecca easier, a matter of serious concern to the Dutch. The colonial regime in Java was suspicious of the influence of religious, whether Christian or Muslim, and disliked the interference of Christian missionaries almost as much as it feared the influence of Arabs and *Hajjis*. But there were far more Arabs and *Hajjis* than there were Dutch Protestant missionaries, so more vigorous efforts were needed with regard to the former. The latter, in any case, always had a potential to call on allies in the Netherlands, which the Arabs and *Hajjis* could hardly do. So while Dutch records reflect irritation with Christian missionaries, they more clearly reflect a *Hajji*-phobia throughout most of the nineteenth century.

In 1825 Batavia established regulations and procedures for the Hajj that required fl. 110 to be paid for a special passport to travel to Mecca — that being a large sum at the time — and *bupatis* were asked to discourage Javanese from undertaking the Hajj as much as possible. But this attempt to restrict the pilgrimage met with limited success. Pilgrims bypassed the regulation by traveling via Sumatra or Singapore. So in 1852 these rules were abandoned. A Hajji still needed a passport, but the financial burdens were thrown out. Then in 1859, new regulations were introduced. Now it was necessary for *bupatis* to certify that aspirant Hajjis had sufficient means to undertake the pilgrimage and to support families left behind. The pilgrims had to report to the Dutch consul in Jeddah when they arrived in the Middle East. On their return, they were examined by Javanese officials to verify that they had really gone to Mecca — as opposed to spending time in a place such as Singapore and claiming on their return to have completed the Hajj — before they could adopt the title and dress of a Hajji. This policy remained in place until the beginning of the 20th century.[18]

It was not only the reduction in the cost of the Hajj that encouraged greater numbers of Javanese to go, but also the advent of steam shipping.[19] In 1869 an entrepreneur — an Arab to judge from his name, given as Sayid Muhammad Aidit — announced that he had bought a steamship specifically for the transport of Hajjis from Batavia to Mecca. Previously, he said, pilgrims who had gone by sail had had to endure cramped conditions and many had become ill. But now they would travel in comfort in Muhammad Aidit's steamship for only Rp. 150.[20] Over the years, improvements in technology — greatly enhanced by the opening of the Suez Canal in 1869 — contributed to a major increase in Hajj traffic from Java.

The numbers of Hajjis traveling from Java (or from Java and Madura, which were amalgamated administratively and thus appear together in many Dutch records) vary slightly in different sources. Sometimes they include ethnic Sundanese from West Java as well as the Madurese. Thus, for much of the 19th century it is not always possible to isolate ethnic Javanese from Central Java and East Java within these statistics. Fortunately, we can do so for the period 1850–58 with regard to both departures and returns. The two figures often differ significantly, because some Javanese stayed in Mecca or elsewhere in the Middle East for a time — a few of them for many years — before returning home, while not a few died before completing their journey, particularly from cholera and smallpox. Ignoring all of these complexities and accepting that the statistics did not capture all of the Hajjis from Java, for there were still those traveling via Sumatra and Singapore, it is nevertheless obvious that there was a major increase in the number of Hajjis from Java during the 1850s, as shown in Table 1.

TABLE 1

Hajj Departures and Returns from Javanese-speaking Residencies, 1850–58[21]

Year	Departures	Returns
1850	48	190
1851	23	83
1852[22]	238	403
1853	610	235
1854	995	235
1855	1137	546
1856	1739	546
1857	1715	976
1858	2283	848

This increase continued. Figures for all of the Netherlands Indies (of which, at this time, Java and Madura represented the core) reported the departure of 2,212 aspirant Hajjis in 1866 and 3,258 in 1870.[23] By

1867, shortly before the opening of the Suez Canal, the total number of Hajjis recorded as living in Java had grown to 73,658; and by 1868 the figure was 96,670.[24] Thereafter, with much of the Indonesia-Europe steam navigation going via the Suez Canal, and thus past Mecca's doorstep, numbers grew still further. The 1872–73 Hajj season saw peak figures. This was a year of a "Hajj akbar," when the day of Arafat fell on a Friday. Popular belief had it that a Hajj performed in such a year carried seven times the merit of another.[25] The Dutch consul in Jeddah reported that some 150,000 pilgrims came to Mecca during that season, about one-third from outside Arabia. From Java there were 3,554. This figure may be compared with the total from all of British India of 5,620, or from nearby Egypt and Turkey of 11,170. The Javanese — who had a greater distance to traverse than almost any Hajjis — were, in other words, a significant element among the overseas pilgrims in Mecca. In general, pilgrims from the Dutch territories in Indonesia were also regarded there as being among the more prosperous.[26]

C. Th. van Deventer commented at the end of the century as follows:

> ... by undertaking the pilgrimage to Mecca, [*Hajjis*] have already shown that they have more energy and also rather more capital than their fellow village-dwellers and, upon their return, moreover regard themselves as a good deal more elevated in esteem than ordinary natives.... Their status as *hajis* elevates their social significance.[27]

The procedure by which the *bupati*s and other officials examined anyone claiming to be a returned Hajji was meant to prevent the fraudulent use of that title and its attendant advantages. People were asked about their experience in Mecca and were required to have the stamps of the Netherlands consulate in Jeddah in their passport. Only after successfully passing the examination process were they given authorization to call themselves a Hajji and to wear the associated Arab-style clothing. This was part of a general responsibility laid upon *bupatis* to oversee the professionally religious people and their establishments in their areas. The implementation of this policy was not, however, always satisfactory. Records were not always kept accurately, so readers must accept that figures given for religious professionals in the sources are not to be regarded as entirely reliable.[28]

Some Europeans did not share the prevalent Hajji-phobia, believing that the social influence of Hajjis would diminish as their numbers grew. Others thought this folly:

When their number in relation to the population is big enough, then [their influence] will plunge to nil, so people hope. Fortunately they've not experimented with this, for the number of *Hajjis* could have rapidly become so great that the dangers associated with that would have come into being before the desired number was reached.[29]

Yet this view was not necessarily entirely false. While the growth in the number of Hajjis was an important part of the story of Islamic revivalism, reformist Islam also distanced itself progressively from much of Javanese society. The Javanese newspaper *Bramartani* reflected something of that declining social influence when, in 1873, it reported on the implementation of the post-1859 procedures for testing the validity of pilgrimage claims in the Panaraga (Madiun) area, the site of the famous *pĕsantrens* of Banjarsari and Tĕgalsari and other schools. Previously, a Hajji returning from Mecca was met with a carriage by learned scholars and *priyayi* (aristocratic and bureaucratic elite) and was grandly received. But with the changed regulations, now a returning Hajji was tested by an official about his understanding of texts, then examined by the *bupati* and his most senior official about religion, then tested by an assistant for knowledge of the holy places in Mecca and Medina and of the seas crossed during the trip, being required to point these out on a map. As a result of this, in Panaraga many who claimed to be Hajjis failed when they were examined, *Bramartani* reported.[30]

The number of Hajjis and consequently of the professionally religious *putihan* as a group continued to grow in Java. It was reported that an increasing number of people whom the Dutch regarded as notables (*aanzienlijken*) were going on the pilgrimage: up to 242 in 1872, which, as noted above, was the year of a Hajj akbar.[31] Figures for the number of Hajjis present in Java in 1874 fortunately allow us to distinguish Javanese-speaking Residencies, as shown in Table 2.

These figures reflect the significant numbers of Hajjis found especially on the *pasisir*, and particularly in the major commercial cities of Sĕmarang and Surabaya. In the interior, only the court city of Surakarta had numbers of Hajjis comparable to those found in the larger towns of the coast. The link between trade and piety that so often arises in the history of Islam was also discernible here. Poensen observed in 1881 that "insofar as the native trade is of significance, it is mainly in the hands of Hajjis and of *santris* who follow their example. Even the peddling trade of the markets is in their hands to a considerable extent."[32]

TABLE 2

Hajjis in Javanese Residencies, 1874[33]

Pasisir Residencies	Hajjis Present
Cirĕbon	1,463
Tĕgal	1,158
Pĕkalongan	972
Sĕmarang	4,998
Jĕpara	2,059
Rĕmbang	651
Surabaya	3,110
Pasuruan	746
Prabalingga	117
Bĕsuki	149
Banyuwangi	143
Interior Residencies and Principalities	
Kĕdiri	502
Madiun	843
Surakarta	1,312
Yogyakarta	836
Kĕdu	923
Bagĕlen	798
Banyumas	467

The numbers continued to grow. The Hajj akbar years of 1880, 1885, and 1888 produced particularly large numbers from across the Dutch-ruled Indonesian territories, but the figures that are readily available do not enable us to separate out the Javanese-speaking territories. We can, however, give such figures for Central Java, East Java, Madura, Surakarta, and Yogyakarta for some years later in the 19th and at the beginning of the 20th centuries, which show a steady flow of significant numbers on the Hajj, as shown in Table 3.

Fed by the rising numbers of Hajjis, the number of religious professionals and their schools grew significantly in the later years of the century. There are problems with getting comparable definitions so that statistics can tell a meaningful story, but nevertheless the general trend is clear enough, as can be seen in the Table 4.

TABLE 3

Hajj Departures from Javanese-speaking Areas and Madura, Selected Years, 1884–1911[34]

Year	Hajjis
1884	2,568
1885	2,501
1898	5,322
1899	N/A
1900	2,274
1901	1,546
1902	1,232
1903	1,172
1904	N/A
1905	2,543
1906	2,940
1907	1,128
1908	4,630
1909	3,243
1910	3,602
1911	7,614

TABLE 4

Religious Professionals (*geestelijken*) and Religious Students in Java, 1863–74[35]

Year	Religious Professionals	Students
1863	64,980	93,680
1864	65,103	97, 384
1865	72,440	103,699
1866	73,832	110,315
1867	73,658	109,242
1868	95,670	121,590
1869	78,816	129,575
1870	N/A	142,178
1871	138,775	189,955
1872	90,023	162,474

Thus, the number of religious professionals and religious students roughly doubled in the years 1863–71. Table 5 shows the breakdown of these figures among the Javanese-speaking Residencies in 1872.

As was true of the figures about Hajjis given in Table 2 above, in Table 5 we again see the prominence of the *pasisir*, and particularly of Sěmarang and Surabaya. Among interior areas, only the court city of Surakarta had numbers of religious teachers like those of the larger towns of the coast, although its total number of *santris* (students) was lower than for the major coastal towns. Nevertheless, the numbers of religious professionals in the interior were significant. In 1884, the unhappy missionary H. C. Kruyt wrote to the head of his mission society in Rotterdam as follows:

TABLE 5

Religious Professionals (*geestelijken*) and Religious Students in Javanese-speaking Residencies, 1872[36]

Pasisir Residencies	Religious Professionals (*geestelijken*)	Students
Cirěbon	5,983	6,590
Těgal	2,478	4,832
Pěkalongan	2,592	3,202
Sěmarang	7,978	15,911
Jěpara	4,151	11,750
Rěmbang	3,422	6,370
Surabaya	7,409	13,740
Pasuruan	2,782	7,211
Prabalingga	752	4,937
Běsuki	3,797	6,382
Banyuwangi	291	3,772
Interior Residencies and Principalities		
Kědiri	3,338	4,859
Madiun	2,821	6,526
Surakarta	7,367	3,386
Yogyakarta	2,446	4,361
Kědu	4,537	9,636
Bagělen	6,766	4,338
Banyumas	2,704	2,010

The Middle East Connection and Reform and Revival Movements 121

> The diligence of the Mohammedans appears above all in Sukabumi,[37] because the *patih* [the senior Javanese administrator] is a great zealot. The prayer-times are observed faithfully and punctually. Those who don't know the usual formulae are taught daily in the mosque. That building is chock-full on Fridays. Sukabumi is swarming with *Hajjis*.[38]

It would not, however, be consistent with the evidence to see these developments as a single religious phenomenon — simply as pious people enhancing the observance of their faith across Javanese society — for this growth in religious life seems to have fed diverging trends. Sharp-eyed readers will already have noted something odd between Tables 2 and 5. One might imagine that, in this context of increasing religiosity, where there were more religious teachers and other professionally religious *putihan*, there would also be more Hajjis. That is, that a generally high level of religious activity and a high level of Hajjis would go together. But it was not so. Table 6 compares those two tables, setting the number of religious professionals (*geestelijken*) in Javanese-speaking Residencies in 1872 (Table 5) against the number of Hajjis in Javanese Residencies in 1874 (Table 2).

The statistical variations here tell us that high numbers of religious professionals in a population did not produce comparably high levels of pilgrims; or if they did, the returning Hajjis did not always go back to their places of origin. Both Hajjis and religious professionals tended to be found in high numbers on the central *pasisir*, the categories relating to each other in the range of 1.6–2.6 religious professionals:Hajjis in most places. Along the coast to the southeast of Surabaya, however, the numbers of religious professionals were not reflected in those of Hajjis. In that region—an area of significant Madurese immigration — except in remote Banyuwangi, where numbers in both categories were too small to be significant, the ratio was in the range from 3.7 to a remarkable 25.48 religious professionals per Hajji. In the interior of the island, the ratio of religious professionals to Hajjis was in the range 3.4–8.5, except for Yogyakarta, where the ratio was closer; but the number of both was low when compared to its peer court city of Surakarta. Sartono Kartodirdjo provides figures for religious teachers and Hajjis in 1887, which show a similar pattern. In Javanese-speaking Residencies, where there were higher numbers of religious teachers (called *kyai* in Javanese), there tended to be lower figures of Hajjis, and vice versa.[39]

This suggests that there were at least two statistically evident categories of religious leaders in Java during this time and they tended to

TABLE 6

Ratio of Religious Professionals (*geestelijken*) in 1872 to Number of Hajjis in 1874, in Javanese-speaking Residencies

Pasisir Residencies	Religious Professionals (1872): Hajjis (1874)
Cirĕbon	4.09:1
Tĕgal	2.14:1
Pĕkalongan	2.67:1
Sĕmarang	1.60:1
Jĕpara	2.02:1
Rĕmbang	5.26:1
Surabaya	2.38:1
Pasuruan	3.73:1
Prabalingga	6.43:1
Bĕsuki	25.48:1
Banyuwangi	2.03:1
Interior Residencies and Principalities	
Kĕdiri	6.65:1
Madiun	3.35:1
Surakarta	5.62:1
Yogyakarta	2.93:1
Kĕdu	4.92:1
Bagĕlen	8.48:1
Banyumas	5.79:1

stay out of each other's way. Not all Hajjis came back from Mecca with revivalist ideas that they tried to spread among their compatriots, of course, but many did; and they were, it seems, concentrating in areas where there were fewer established religious professionals. There were certainly *kyais* who were also Hajjis, but there were many who were not and who, we may guess, found the newfangled ideas coming out of the Middle Eastern experience of Hajjis to be inconsistent with their understanding of true Islam. So where the Islam of the *kyais* was strong — the teachings of pious men whose faith, in many cases, was close to the mystic synthesis of the aristocratic elite — the new ideas of Hajjis may have found a less cordial reception than elsewhere. That is not to suggest that *kyais* or the aristocratic elite were actually opposed to the pilgrimage. In 1879, for example, Sultan Hamĕngkubuwana VII of Yogyakarta sent four emissaries on the Hajj with orders to construct accommodation in Mecca on his behalf so that pilgrims could stay at no cost.[40] But the statistics suggest that there was a contest of ideas developing in Islamic circles, in which *kyais* and Hajjis tended to play separate roles. Similar circumstances were noted by the colonial government's adviser for Islamic and indigenous affairs, E. Gobée, in 1928. He drew a distinction between the leaders of Sufi brotherhoods — who would have been *kyais* — on the one hand, and the teachers of *kitab* — the less mystically inclined, more *shari'a*-oriented figures — on the other. "In many areas conflict is prevalent between the *tarekat* gurus and the *kitab* gurus," he said.[41]

While some schools maintained older Javanese traditions, others embraced a reformist, *shari'a*-oriented orthodoxy, including, it seems, the most famous *pĕsantren*, that at Sidasrĕma in Surabaya. The Yogyakarta aristocrat R. Natarata (also known as Sasrawijaya) set out to seek mystical wisdom by traveling from teacher to teacher around 1870–71. At Sidasrĕma he found more than 3,000 *santris*. But he discovered that the *kyai* there would not teach him Sufism, for he was a defender of *shari'a*-oriented orthodoxy. The *kyai* reportedly said the following:

> As for Sufism (*'ilmu tarekat*), I have declared it truly forbidden (*kula haramakĕn*). In this life, a person should do no more than carry out the obligations of the five pillars of Islam: ... the confession of faith, the prayer, paying the religious tax, fasting in the month of Ramadan and the fifth, if you are able, to go on the *hajj*. ... Oh, my son, do not persist in searching for secret knowledge and then cast off the *shari'a* of God's Emissary.

In the wake of this rejection, Natarata went to an Arab in Surabaya who eventually — after Natarata had undertaken further travels — was willing to teach him Sufism.[42]

This *shari'a*-oriented orthodoxy occasionally even crept into the correspondence pages of the Javanese newspaper *Bramartani* (at that stage titled *Jurumartani)*, which was generally an unsympathetic venue for such ideas. One correspondent objected to the Javanese practice of having a lavish communal meal (the *sidhĕkah malĕman*) on certain nights of the fasting month, on the grounds that this had no Islamic origin.[43] Another, who called himself "the mendicant" (*tiyang pĕkir*), wrote of the increasing number of people who were praying, attending the mosque, and reading the *Qur'an*. But there were still many young people dedicated to pleasures that were improper for one committed to religion, he said: raising dogs, playing cards, and watching dancing girls. All this must be stopped.[44] At the same time, the missionary-scholar Carel Poensen noted how the "orthodox Muslims" rejected the various mystical sciences (*ngelmus*) of Javanese religious tradition.⁴⁵ A rather bitter exchange took place in *Jurumartani* in 1868. A correspondent who was impressed (as were most) with the scientific advances of the modern world wrote critically of religious folk (*kaum*) who could only read out the contents of Islamic books and traditions but could not set out all the human discoveries that were being published in newspapers. A *kyai* from Cirěbon wrote in reply that these *kaum* could not set out the deeper meaning of things in *Jurumartani* because it was not a suitable place for religious teachings.⁴⁶

Bramartani received a reformist correspondent's letter in 1879 that represented iconoclastic Islamic orthodoxy. The author, who signed himself only with the initial "D," complained of the many superstitions of village folk — which received condemnation from many of the newspaper's correspondents — and of searching for worldly benefits through veneration of spiritually sacred places, holy graves, and hidden powers. This diminished the worship of God, D wrote, echoing the orthodox rejection of *shirk* (polytheism, the ascribing of partners to God or the worship of other than God). Did "my people the Javanese" think that a Hajji who had died could rise again from the grave and dispense medicine, hand out money, or guarantee a long life? Should not humankind instead concentrate on the Lord Allah, who is all-powerful, and be thankful to Him? But if one prayed to God, one must observe preconditions: If one wanted to be cured of illness, one must take medicine; if one wanted to be rich, one must engage in trade. There were no spirits (*setan*): many Europeans had entered caves and other places never before visited by humans and had never seen a spirit, D said, curiously acknowledging an implicit epistemological superiority of European observation. *Bramartani*'s Javanese editor reacted to this final touch by adding the comment that in Europe there were still people who believed in superstition, but there were far more in Java. "My people the Javanese," he wrote, were reluctant to free themselves of everything handed down from their ancestors, but nowadays there were many of the elite who were capable of wisdom and they would be an example to the common folk.⁴⁷ Between the near-Wahhabism of D and the faith in science of *Bramartani*'s editor yawned a chasm of contending visions of reform.

As the *shari'a*-oriented reformers progressed, so also, we may presume, did a sense of distance from the European colonizers of Java — a distancing that contributed also to the gap between reforming

Muslims and the *priyayi* elite, with its taste for things Western. Among the many Islamic legal opinions (*fatwa*) available to Javanese Hajjis in the later 19th century were those in an 1892 collection compiled in Mecca specifically for Indonesian pilgrims, among whom a large proportion were Javanese. One question dealt with there was whether a Muslim could wear clothes of the kind worn by Christians. On the authority of Ahmad ibn Zaini Dahlan (1817–86), the head of the Shafi'i school of law in Mecca — the school adhered to by Indonesian Muslims — the *fatwa* declared that Muslims must reject clothing worn by *kafirs* (infidels).[48] In societies such as 19th-century Java, clothing had long been a way of expressing who individuals were and who they were not. For pious Muslims under Christian colonial rule, the latter may have been growing even more important than the former. And it was not just that they were not European Christians. They were also demonstrating that they were not peasants, *priyayi*, or indeed, in some senses, Javanese. As the famous Javanese poem *Wedhatama* put it, "Oddly enough they deny their Javaneseness, and at all costs bend their steps to Mecca in search of knowledge."[49] Similarly, from the vantage point of Kědiri in East Java, Poensen observed that when a returned pilgrim donned his Arab-style dress, "He feels himself to be a *Hajji*; he has ceased to be Javanese — he is a *Hajji*. By means of the pilgrimage, Islam has turned him into a citizen of the world."[50]

Sufism

In addition to the continuing defenders of the Javanese mystic synthesis and the *shari'a*-oriented reformers, Sufi *tarekats* also played an important role in 19th-century Java. What Hajjis brought back from Mecca and what found a receptive soil in Java was not only the law but also Islamic mysticism. While much of what went on in Sufi circles is obscure, it is clear that the Naqshabandiyya order was of particular significance. There were two Sufi orders that represented the Naqshabandiyya in Java in the 19th century. The first was the Naqshabandiyya proper of the Khalidiyya branch, introduced to the Indonesian Archipelago by the Sumatran Shaikh Isma'il Minangkabawi, who returned there from Mecca in the 1850s. He based himself mainly in Riau and Singapore but had considerable influence throughout the archipelago. Among his students and followers were many Javanese.[51] The second was a new Sufi order that combined Naqshabandiyya and Qadiriyya techniques and was thus called

Qadiriyya wa Naqshabandiyya. This was the creation of Shaikh Ahmad Khatib (d. c. 1875 in Mecca)[52] of Sambas, West Kalimantan. It also spread throughout the archipelago and is still a major force today.

Both Naqshabandiyya and Qadiriyya wa Naqshabandiyya gave greater emphasis to observing the five pillars of Islamic orthodoxy than was true of the previously dominant order, the Shattariyya. Consequently, conflicts between them and the Shattariyya were not uncommon. Leaders of these orders were also more anti-Christian and, to varying degrees, thus more opposed to Dutch colonial rule. Nevertheless, the Shattariyya could also produce anticolonial movements, as happened in at least one minor case in Madiun in 1886.[53] In the late 1880s, it was reported that in Banyumas and Bagĕlen, Shattariyya was still the larger order, but Naqshabandiyya was next in size of following. Its foremost leader there was one Muhammad Ilyas, who had a personal following of 1,000 adherents. His sole purpose was reportedly "to stimulate better fulfillment of the Islamic religious obligations" and the practice of *dhikr* (recitation of pious formulae as a mystic exercise). The Shattariyya, by contrast, was said to be "not of such a mystical character as Naqshabandiyya" and "not so strict in its demands as the other sect."[54]

Both the Naqshabandiyya and the Qadiriyya wa Naqshabandiyya should thus be seen as part of the Islamic reformist movements of the 19th century. The principal difference in their social impact was that the Naqshabandiyya tended to gain adherents among the elite of Javanese society, while the Qadiriyya wa Naqshabandiyya found more supporters among the common people. While mystical in orientation, they sought greater observance of the obligations of the faith, as those obligations were set out in Islamic sources, known in Mecca and increasingly being emphasized in Java. Sufi *tarekats* had long been known in Java, but in the precolonial era they had evidently coexisted comfortably with the dominant mystic synthesis of Javanese Islam. The Naqshabandiyya and Qadiriyya wa Naqshabandiyya of the 19th century were no longer, it seems, prepared to make such compromises. There was no room for the Goddess of the Southern Ocean in their spiritual life.

Because both *tarekats* initially spread among Javanese in a way that was invisible to the Dutch, it is not clear when they first became a significant force. When the colonial regime became worried about the anticolonial potential of these *tarekats* in the 1880s, they gathered reports; these reports indicated that in most places in Java, Naqshabandiyya had been introduced c. 1850–60.[55]

The role of Arabs is less clear in the case of Sufi *tarekats* in Java than in the case of the *shari'a*-oriented reform movements. But there can be no doubt that there were Sufis among Arabs in Java, just as was true anywhere else in the Islamic world. For example, when an Arab named Sayid Abdullah and an Indian companion named Syekh Yusup visited Pasuruan in 1873, some 500 locals flocked to them for blessing and healing. The visitors asked for no money, neither slept nor ate (so *Bramartani* reported), and spent their entire time in Sufi *dhikr*, asking only to be fed.[56]

The most prominent Javanese *shaykh* of the Naqshabandiyya Khalidiyya in the 1880s was H. Abdul Kadir of Sĕmarang. He was initiated into the Naqshabandiyya in Mecca by the head of the order, Sulaiman al-Zuhdi. He returned to Sĕmarang and attempted to promote the Naqshabandiyya there, but found that most people still preferred the Shattariyya order. In 1881 he was said to have promoted "a serious movement in the religious field" in the interior of Java. The elderly *pangulu* (head of the mosque) in the Yogyakarta subsidiary principality of the Pakualaman fell under Naqshabandiyya influence. Behind closed doors at night, Naqshabandiyya *dhikr* was being taught in the Pakualaman mosque. This *dhikr* was so exhausting, with its large number of repetitions of the confession of faith that there is no God but God (*La ilaha illa 'llah*), that two devotees in Surakarta and one in Kota Gĕde had perished of exhaustion, the Dutch were told.[57] The growth of followers in Yogyakarta proceeded so secretly that neither Prince Pakualam V (r. 1878–1900) nor Sultan Hamĕngkubuwana VII (r. 1877–1921) knew of this until told by the Resident of Yogyakarta, or at least so the Dutch claimed. The old *pangulu* of the Pakualaman was consequently dismissed, and Abdul Kadir's pupils who were promoting his teachings were expelled from Yogyakarta. The chief *pangulu* of the sultan's mosque in Yogyakarta condemned the new teachings. Abdul Kadir also visited Surakarta and there gained influence over three princes who were sons of Susuhunan Pakubuwana IX (r. 1861–93) and — more ominously — over the prince who was the commander of the Mangkunagaran Legion. These four were admonished to mend their ways, and Abdul Kadir was prohibited from entering the city. His movement also won a significant following — this time among commoners — in Kĕdu. All of this seemed too much of a threat to the established order, both of the Dutch and of the Javanese monarchs in Surakarta and Yogyakarta. So H. Abdul Kadir was arrested and exiled from Java.[58] This provoked at least one angry protest, from one Purwasastra, who wrote to the Resident of Sĕmarang demanding to know on what grounds Abdul Kadir had been arrested, Muslims engaged in *dhikr* had been expelled from the mosque of Surakarta upon the orders of the Resident, and Naqshabandiyya teachings had been denounced.[59] The colonial regime was, of course, unmoved.

In Banten, in West Java, Qadiriyya wa Naqshabandiyya became a powerful social and political as well as religious force. Its leaders gained widespread influence and by the 1880s had begun to plot a rebellion against the Dutch colonial regime and its local representatives, both indigenous and European. In July 1888 a significant insurrection broke out in Cilĕgon under the leadership of these Sufis. Both European and indigenous people were killed and wounded before the rebellion was put down.[60] Similarly, a major rebellion of Muslim Sasaks against their Hindu Balinese overlords on the island of Lombok in 1891–94 was led by a local Naqshabandiyya leader. This precipitated Dutch military intervention there.[61] Nothing comparable occurred in the Javanese heartlands of Central Java and East Java, but the Cilĕgon and Lombok uprisings made the Dutch all the more nervous of the influence of *tarekat* leaders throughout their Indonesian territories.

At the turn of the century, Ky. H. M. Muhammad Shaleh bin Haji 'Umar al-Samarani (c. 1820–1903), or Ky. Shaleh Darat as he was known,[62] played a leading role in communicating orthodox Sufi teachings of the kind associated with al-Ghazali to Javanese audiences. His greatest work — among the 13 or more he wrote — was the first Javanese-language interpretation of the Qur'an done from a Sufi perspective, *Tafsir faidl al-rahman fi tarjamah tafsir kalam malik al-dayyan*. Ky. Shaleh Darat had studied with various teachers in Java, including a grandson of H. Amad Mutamakin, a controversial Islamic teacher of the earlier 18th century.[63] He went on to study Qur'anic interpretation in Mecca and, upon his return to Sĕmarang, set up a *pĕsantren* where he taught Sufism within the context of Islamic reform, that is, mysticism in harmony with observation of the *shari'a*. Among those who are said to have studied with Ky. Shaleh Darat were several major figures of the early 20th century, including K. H. Hasyim Asy'ari (one of the founders of Nahdlatul Ulama), K. H. Ahmad Dahlan (the founder of Muhammadiyah), and R. A. Kartini (the famous young Javanese woman who aspired to emulate what she thought of as the liberated women of Europe). Ky. Shaleh Darat's writings were published in Javanese using Arabic script by lithograph presses in Bombay, Singapore, and Cirĕbon, and they can still be found in bookshops and *pĕsantrens*.[64]

Islamic Messianism for the New Islamic Century

In the 1880s, there was messianism abroad in the Islamic world. This was fed by the impending turn of the Islamic century. AH 1300 began in November 1882. Many Muslims expected a renewer of the faith, or indeed a messiah, to arrive with the new century. In this *fin-de-siècle* atmosphere, Dutch colonial authorities in Indonesia were particularly concerned about two developments far from Indonesia's shores. The first was an alleged anti-Christian plot in Mecca in 1881 under the famously anti-Christian Sharif of Mecca 'Abd al-Muttalib (d. 1886), a plot that supposedly involved Javanese.[65] The second was the progress of the Mahdi movement in Sudan. In 1881 Muhammad Ahmad b. Abd Allah declared himself to be the Mahdi — the Islamic messiah — in Sudan, and in 1883 he defeated the Egyptian army there. Although the Mahdi died in 1885, it was not until Kitchener's defeat of the Mahdi's army at Omdurman in 1898 that the Mahdist movement was finally crushed. In the mid-1880s the affairs of the Mahdi were discussed in the archipelago among both Arabs and local people. On the part of some people, there was reportedly a tendency to exaggerate the significance of Mahdism's achievements and a refusal to believe that the Mahdi had died.[66]

Such developments may have encouraged the spread of millennial and messianic ideas within pious Islamic circles in Java. Messianic ideas, inspired as much by the turning of the Javanese (AJ) century in 1871, were found in Akhmad Ngisa's messianic Ratu Adil movement in Banyumas in 1871 and in the Akmaliyah ideas taught by Ky. Hasan Maulani, M. Malangyuda, and Ky. Nurhakim from the 1840s to the 1880s. There was a more orthodox Islamic variant of such ideas as well.

Conclusion

This paper looks at only a part of the complex religious scene in 19th-century Java. Many developments had local, indigenous roots and were little influenced by developments in the Middle East. There were many Javanese who rejected the calls of reformers and began to distance themselves from Islamic orthopraxy. There were others who held firm to the prior mystical interpretations of Islam, with local supernatural forces playing a role. By the 1870s, there was even an explicitly anti-Islamic fashion among at least some of the elite. The 19th century also saw the first conversions of Javanese to Christianity. These complexities are explored in my book *Polarising Javanese Society: Islamic and Other Visions c. 1830–1930* (Singapore: NUS Press; Leiden: KITLV Press; Honolulu: University of Hawaii Press, 2007), from which this paper is taken. Within all of this complexity, however, there can be no doubt that the 19th-century Islamic reform and revival movements of the Middle East played a decisive role in stimulating change in religious circles on Java.

Abbreviations:

ARZ   Archief Raad voor de Zending, held in the Utrecht city archives (het Utrechts Archief)

BKI   *Bijdragen tot de Taal-, Land- en Volkenkunde*

BM   *Bramartani* (in the period 1864–11 August 1870, titled *Jurumartani*)

MNZG   Mededeelingen van wege het Nederlandsche Zendelinggenootschap

MR   Mail Report, Netherlands National Archives, The Hague

SI   *Studia Islamika*

TNI   *Tijdschrift voor Nederlandsch Indië*

Notes

1. Part of this chapter is taken from my book *Polarising Javanese Society: Islamic and Other Visions c. 1830–1930*.
2. L. W. C. van den Berg, "De Mohammedaansche geestelijkheid en de geestelijke goederen op Java en Madoera," *TBG* 27 (1882): 8–9. See also P. Bleeker, "Hoofdstuk II: Pasoeroean," *TNI*, pt. 2 (1849): 26–7; Anon., "Algemeen overzigt van den toestand van N.I., gedurende het jaar 1846," *TNI* (n.s.) 1, 1 (1848): 371; Martin van Bruinessen, "*Pesantren* and *kitab kuning*: Continuity and Change in a Tradition of Religious Learning," *Ethnologica Bernensia* 4/1994: *Texts from the Islands* (Bern: Insitut für Ethnologie, 1994), 132–3.
3. The extent to which the Wahhabis directly inspired the Padris is disputed. Christine Dobbin sees direct inspiration at work, but Werner Kraus is inclined to see the Padris more as part of a wider reformist atmosphere within the Islamic world at that time. See Christine Dobbin, *Islamic Revivalism in a Changing Peasant Economy: Central Sumatra, 1784–1847* (London and Malmö: Curzon Press, 1983), 128; Werner Kraus, *Zwischen Reform und Rebellion: Über die Entwicklung des Islams in Minangkabau (Westsumatra) zwischen*

den beiden Reformbewegungen der Padri (1837) und der Modernisten (1908): Ein Beitrag zur Geschichte der Islamisierung Indonesiens (Wiesbaden: Franz Steiner Verlag, 1984), 15–6.
4. See Albert Hourani, *Arabic Thought in the Liberal Age, 1798–1939* (London: Oxford University Press, 1970).
5. Van den Berg, "Geestelijkheid," 35–7.
6. J. E. Jellesma, Dagverhaal August 1849–15 January 1850, dd. Surabaya, 1 February 1850, in ARZ 509.
7. J. E. Jellesma, Majawarna, to Bestuurders NZG, Rotterdam, 15 August 1853, in ARZ 509.
8. H. Smeding, Rotterdam, to Bestuurders NZG, Rotterdam, 21 March 1862, in ARZ 206. Note that Smeding had by this time returned to the Netherlands for health reasons; S. Coolsma, *De zendingseeuw voor Nederlandsch Oost-Indië* (Utrecht: C. H. E. Breijer, 1901), 266.
9. Anon., "Algemeen overzigt 1846," 99.
10. J. E. Jellesma, Surabaya, to Bestuurders NZG, Rotterdam, 31 December 1846, in ARZ 509.
11. G. Brückner, Sĕmarang, to Bestuurders NZG, Rotterdam, 12 January 1850, in ARZ 511.
12. W. Hoezoo, Sĕmarang, to Bestuurders NZG, Rotterdam, 20 February 1854, in ARZ 210.
13. W. Hoezoo, Sĕmarang, to Bestuurders NZG, Rotterdam, 5 December 1855, in ARZ 210.
14. Purwalĕlana [pseudonym for Condranagara V], *Cariyos bab lampah-lampahipun Raden Mas Arya Purwalĕlana* (2 vols.; Batavia: Landsdrukkerij, 1865–66), vol. I, 200–2. See also Marcel Bonneff (transl.), *Pérégrinations javanaises: Les voyages de R.M.A. Purwa Lelana: Une vision de Java au XIXe siècle (c. 1860–1875)* (Paris: Editions de la Maison des sciences de l'homme, 1986), 191–2.
15. Poersoewignja and Wirawangsa, *Javaansche bibliographie gegrond op de boekwerken in die taal, aanwezig in de boekerij van het Bataviaasch Genootschap van Kunsten en Wetenschappen/Pratélan kawontenaning boekoe-boekoe Basa Djawi (tjiṭakan) ingkang kasimpen wonten ing geḍong boekoe (Museum) ing pasimpenan (bibliothek) XXXIII* (Batavia: Bataviaasch Genootschap, 1920), vol. I, 181.
16. Azyumardi Azra, "Hadrâmî Scholars in the Malay-Indonesian Diaspora: A Preliminary Study of Sayyid 'Uthmân," *SI* 2, 2 (1995): 1–33; Karel A. Steenbrink, *Beberapa aspek tentang Islam di Indonesia abad ke-19* (Jakarta: Bulan Bintang, 1984), 134–7.
17. Poerwa Soewignja and Wirawangsa, *Pratélan*, vol. II, 121.
18. S. Keijzer, *Onze tijd in Indië, beschreven in bundles* ('s-Gravenhage: H. C. Susan, C. Hzoon, 1860), 9, 56–7; Jacob Vredenbregt, "The Haddj: Some of Its Features and Functions in Indonesia," *BKI* 118, 1 (1964): 98–100.

19. G. M. van der Linden, "Wat zijn hadjie's en welke is hun invloed op het volksleven der Javanen," *Indisch Genootschap: Algemeene vergadering op 21 Maart 1859*, 1–3.
20. *BM*, 19 August 1869.
21. Calculated from F. G. P. Jaquet, "Mutiny en hadji-ordonnantie: Ervaringen met 19e eeuwse bronnen," *BKI* 136, 2–3: 310–1. Jaquet also comments on the limited reliability of such figures. Cf. Keijzer, *Onze tijd*, 186, 188–91, which gives similar results covering all of Java and Madura, 1849–58.
22. This was the year payments for the passport ceased.
23. Johan Eisenberger, *Indië en de bedevaart naar Mekka* (Leiden: Boekhandel M. Dubbeldeman, 1928), 204.
24. [C. E. van Keesteren] v.K., "De Koran en de driekleur," *Stemmen uit Indië*, no. 1 (1870): 34.
25. This idea was common at the time and is specifically reported in *BM*, 19 August 1880, another Hajj akbar year, but is often rejected now. E.g., see <http://www.islamicity.com/dialogue/Q431.HTM>.
26. Anon., "De Indische bedevaartgangers," *TNI* (n.s.) 3 (1874): 60–1.
27. Van Deventer, *Overzicht van den economische toestand der inlandse bevolking van Java en Madoera (*Koloniaal-economische bijdragen I; 's-Gravenhage: Martinus Nijhoff, 1904), 99.
28. Van den Berg, "Geestelijkheid," 2; L. Th. Mayer, *Een blik in het Javaansche volksleven* (2 vols.; Leiden: E. J. Brill, 1897), vol. I, 209–10.
29. Keijzer, *Onze tijd*, 181.
30. *BM*, 10 July 1873.
31. E. de Waal, *Onze Indische financien: nieuwe reeks aanteekeningen* (9 vols.; 's-Gravenhage: M. Nijhoff, 1876–1907), vol. I, 245.
32. C. Poensen, "Naar en op de pasar," Kĕdiri, May 1881, in ARZ 261; also in *MNZG* 26 (1882): 1 et seq.
33. Ibid., 246–7. See also the figures for departing and returning Hajjis broken down by Residencies in Java in anon., "De regeering van Nederlandsch Indie tegenover den Islam," *TNI* (n.s.) 7 (1878): 208–9.
34. Vredenbregt, "Haddj," 140–2.
35. De Waal, *Indische financien*, vol. 1, 251–2.
36. Ibid., 253.
37. There are several Sukabumis. I presume that Kruyt, who was writing from East Java (see the following note), meant Sukabumi in Prabalingga Residency, East Java.
38. H. C. Kruyt, Majawarna, 20 October 1884, in ARZ 145.
39. Sartono Kartodirdjo, "The Peasants' Revolt of Banten in 1888: Its Conditions, Course and Sequel; A Case Study of Social Movements in Indonesia," *VKI* 50 (1966): 332 ('s-Gravenhage: Martinus Nijhoff).

40. *BM*, 28 August 1879. It is worth noting, however, that no sultan of Yogyakarta or susuhunan of Surakarta himself undertook the Hajj — nor would the Dutch probably have allowed one to do so — until the following century, after Indonesian independence.
41. E. Gobée to Resident of Kědiri M. H. Doornik, 8 May 1928, in Arsip Nasional Republik Indonesia, *Laporan-laporan tentang gerakan protes di Jawa pada abad-XX* (Jakarta: Arsip Nasional Republik Indonesia, 1981), 217.
42. Tanaya, *Sang Pinudyasma R. Natarata iya R. Sasrawijaya sarta jasané kang arupa kasusastran 'ilmu luhung* ([Surakarta:] Para kadang mitra tresna budaya, 1977 [mimeo]), 1–8.
43. *BM*, 25 February 1869.
44. *BM*, 7 October 1869.
45. C. Poensen, "Bijdragen tot de kennis …," Kědiri June 1869, in ARZ 261.
46. *BM*, 2 January and 16 January 1868.
47. *BM*, 17 April 1879. I am uncertain of the editor's name at this stage. He referred to the Javanese as *bongsa kula tiyang Jawi*, so he was clearly Javanese, but he signed himself on this occasion as *Juru ngarang* (the writer).
48. Nico Kaptein, ed., *The Muhimmât al-Nafâis: A Bilingual Meccan Fatwa Collection for Indonesian Muslims from the End of the Nineteenth Century* (Seri INIS 32; Jakarta: INIS, 1997), 3, 161, 199.
49. Stuart Robson, ed. and transl., *The Wedhatama: An English Translation* (KITLV working papers 4; Leiden: KITLV Press, 1990), 36–7 (with minor variation from Robson's translation).
50. C. Poensen, *Brieven over den Islām uit de binnenlanden van Java* (Leiden: E. J. Brill, 1886), 68.
51. Consul-General G. Lavino, Singapore, to GG, 6 December 1889, in MR 1889, no. 866/18 December; Martin van Bruinessen, "The Origins and Development of the Naqshabandi Order in Indonesia," *Der Islam* 67, 1 (1990): 161–4, 169–73; idem., *Tarekat Naqsyabandiyah di Indonesia: Survei historis, geografis, dan sosiologis* (Bandung: Penerbit Mizan, 1992), 98–101.
52. I am grateful for the advice of Dr. Werner Kraus concerning the year of Ahmad Khatib's death.
53. MR 1886, nos. 759/1 December and 812/24 December. The leader was one Ky. Ngali Muhammad, who reportedly emphasized the importance of the five daily prayers and *dhikr* of the Shattariyya order. He was arrested and given 20 days hard labor.
54. MR 1889, no. 41/26 January. See also van Bruinessen, *Naqsyabandiyah*, 163–4.
55. Pelzer, Resident of Priangan, to GG, Bandung 29 September 1885, in MR 1885, no. 642a/9 October. L. W. C. van den Berg, "Over de devotie der Naqsjibendîjah in den Indischen archipel," *TBG* 28 (1883): 163; N. D. Schuurmans, "De tariqah Naqsjibendijjah op Java," *Nederlandsch Zendingstijjdschrift* 2 (1890): 265.

56. *BM*, 17 April 1873. Most Arab Sufis would presumably have been associated with the 'Alawiyya *tarekat* rather than the *tarekats* that Javanese joined.
57. On Naqshabandiyya *dhikr*, see van Bruinessen, *Naqsyabandiyah*, 80–1.
58. MR 1881, nos. 981/31 October, 1007/4 November, 1041/9 November, 1102/28 November; van den Berg, "Naqsjibendîjah," 162–5; Michael F. Laffan, "'A Watchful Eye': The Meccan Plot of 1881 and Changing Dutch Perceptions of Islam in Indonesia," *Archipel*, no. 63 (2002): 101–5 (note that Laffan refers to Abdul Kadir as Abdul Karim, a name that appears in Dutch archival sources).
59. Poerwosastro to Resident Sĕmarang, 20 October 1881, in MR 1881, no. 1041/9 November; Laffan, "Watchful Eye," 105.
60. Kartodirdjo, *"Peasants' Revolt"*, chs. 5–8. Note that Kartodirdjo refers to the Qadiriyya wa Naqshabandiyya *tarekat* simply as "Kadiriah."
61. Van Bruinessen, *Naqsyabandiyah*, 28.
62. After his home in Kampung Mĕlayu Darat, Sĕmarang.
63. M. C. Ricklefs, *The Seen and Unseen Worlds in Java, 1726–49: History, Literature and Islam in the Court of Pakubuwana II* (Honolulu: Asian Studies Association of Australia in association with Allen & Unwin and University of Hawai'i Press, 1998), ch. 4.
64. M. Muchoyyar, ed. and transl., *Tafsîr Faidl al-Raḥmân fî tarjamah tafsîr kalâm mâlik al-dayyân, karya K.H.M. Shaleh al-Samârani (suntingan teks, terjemahan dan analisis metodologi)*, PhD thesis (Yogyakarta: IAIN Sunan Kalijaga, 2002), xv–xxiii, 1–17, 71, 78–9. It is not clear into which *tarekat* or *tarekats* Shaleh Darat had been initiated.
65. Laffan, "Watchful Eye," 85–101.
66. B., "De godsdienstige beweging op Java," *Indische Gids* 2 (1884): 741; G. Lavino, consul-general, Singapore, to GG, 25 September 1885, in MR 1885, no. 638/13 November.

6

The Skeptic's Eye: Snouck Hurgronje and the Politics of Pilgrimage from the Indies

Eric Tagliacozzo

Introduction

Christiaan Snouck Hurgronje (b. 1857, d. 1936), professor of Arabic at Leiden University and political/military adviser to the Dutch Indies government for several decades, was an anomaly. He was a keen scholar of Islam in its many manifestations, a sympathetic ear for Southeast Asian Muslims, but also a willing servant of a repressive and increasingly anxiety-filled Indies colonial state. In the late 19th and early 20th centuries, he oiled the Netherlands' apparatus of domination and control but seemed (on occasion) unsure and unhappy with this role at the same time. This article examines Snouck Hurgronje's dealings with the annual Southeast Asian pilgrimage to Mecca. As thousands of indigenous inhabitants from the Indies made the trip to Arabia each year in order to fulfill this pillar of faith, Snouck Hurgronje was charged with surveilling their passage, both as an occupation and as a matter of his own intellectual interest. He wrote copiously about the pilgrimage to Mecca in letters and other correspondence, though these writings — private and not to be seen by the public at large — sometimes differed greatly from his published works on the subject.[1] An analysis of Snouck Hurgronje's writings tells us much about what he thought of the Hajj as a transmission vehicle of religion and of militancy, the latter being something that the Dutch colonial state feared greatly. Yet it is especially through his letters that we see how his politics, intellect, and own moral convictions merged in the issue of the Hajj, forming a window into colonial mentalities about Islam and movement at the *fin de siècle*. This essay examines Snouck Hurgronje's own thoughts and the thoughts of his critics on the matter of the Hajj, and asks how pilgrimage can be used to discern important patterns of politics, classification, and religion in a high colonial state.

Snouck had in-depth experience on the ground in Arabia that colored his writings on the Hajj to a great degree. He entered Mecca in February of 1885 and stayed there for six months studying Islam and the Netherlands Indies (or "Jâwa") community in particular.[2] While he was in residence in the holy city, he was able to meet and interact with prominent personalities from the Malay-Indonesian Archipelago, including members of the Acehnese war party who still were engaged in a vigorous project of resistance against their Dutch colonial overlords.[3] The time he spent in the Hejaz became an important part of his personality, one historian of his life has argued, shaping his views on Islam and also adding to his self-belief that he had put in the time and energy to understand cultural and religious patterns in this part of the world better than almost all of his contemporaries.[4] Snouck also converted to Islam (although the sincerity of this conversion has been hotly debated by many), and he married two Indies women, the first from Aceh and the second from Sunda, West Java, fathering five children in all between his two wives.[5] It was this combination of personal, family, and intellectual experience with both the Middle East and Southeast Asia that gave Snouck great influence in Dutch colonial policy-making circles. Indeed, as many contemporary scholars (most of them Dutch) have shown, it was from this foundation that Snouck went on to become arguably Holland's greatest Orientalist and interpreter of Islam, a moniker Snouck might have agreed with himself.[6]

The respect and borderline adulation that Snouck received from many Dutchmen was not accorded, in most cases, by Indonesians. One Indonesian historian has traced what he calls Snouck's campaign against Indonesians of Arab descent.[7] Another has tried to show how the burgeoning nationalism of the early 20th-century Indies was actually a front erected by Snouck and other prominent Dutch planners, all in an effort to distract archipelago indigenes away from the callings of Islam in the Indies.[8] Exclamations of his rabid objections to anything he saw as "pan-Islamic" have also been registered in contemporary Indonesian historiography.[9] It is difficult to reconcile these often-angry accusations with the alternate image of Snouck as scholar, chronicler, and traveler to the Middle East, let alone with his professed conversion to Islam and his extended Muslim family. Yet it is true that a map he commissioned by one of his Gayo servants ended up being sent to the Dutch military to help in their pacification of the Gayo lands in North Sumatra.[10] It is also true that Snouck wrote prolifically on Aceh, and that these writings often were used to help the Europeans in their effort to win the long guerrilla war there that dragged on for decades around the turn of the 20th century.[11] An Acehnese man I met recently taught me my first word of that language: when the name of Snouck came up, he told me that the Acehnese have a special term for him, which roughly translates to a "dead, rotting dog" that is left in the street.[12] These kinds of designations — "learned Orientalist" and "rotting dog" — give an indication of the paradoxes of Snouck's life and of his legacy. This article examines some of this duality through the lens of Snouck and his views on the Southeast Asian Hajj.

Policy and the Making of the Netherlands Indies Hajj

One of the reasons that Snouck is so interesting and paradoxical as a colonial civil servant has to do with his attitudes toward the administrative regulation of the Hajj. From the beginning, it seems, Snouck was against most forms of Dutch interference in the pilgrimage, and he was constantly advising his countrymen not to meddle in affairs that were better left alone. At the very end of the 19th century, he was called upon to explain why so many archipelago pilgrims, once registered as intending Hajjis in the Indies, were not coming home to Southeast Asia after they had completed their religious obligations. This matter was of some concern to many Dutch officials in various parts of the Indies. Snouck answered that the issue of non-return should not be used as a political tool to interfere with the pilgrimage, as a certain number of Hajjis were indeed dying during the voyage, and some even went with this ultimate goal in mind.[13] Snouck also militated against the dreaded requirement of return-passage tickets for Hajjis, which was enforced for some time, warning that many archipelago pilgrims would do anything to avoid the stipulations. The reason for this was a lack of funds: many Hajjis could not hope to raise enough money at one time for both legs of the voyage to and from Arabia, and went with the idea that they would work in the Hejaz or elsewhere to earn enough money for the return passage home. From a practical standpoint, however, this meant that Indies Hajjis were sailing outside of Dutch surveillance channels, including from Singapore to the tiny Red Sea principality of Djibouti.[14] Snouck felt that passes were indeed necessary for Dutch maintenance of the Hajj as an institution, but that this was as far as most colonial supervision should go on what was ultimately a journey of faith and religious conviction.[15]

If Snouck was against making the Hajj more difficult for Netherlands Indies subjects as a matter of principle, he was even more against day-to-day manifestations of attempted colonial controls. Interestingly, one issue that absorbed him in this regard was clothing, and whether the Dutch Indies state should be regulating the kinds of clothing its subjects wore on returning from the Hajj. There had been motions in this direction by some in high policy-making circles, because it was thought by this lobby that distinctions based on the Hajj should be lessened as a matter of governance, so that Hajjis would not have so much influence when they returned home to the Indies. Snouck thought this was daft — he advised the director of education, religion, and industry in the Indies that this would be extremely difficult to enforce, that it was purposeless and ultimately, he wrote, dangerous to attempt.[16] Archipelago Hajjis had enjoyed the distinctions of their pilgrimage — sartorial and otherwise — for hundreds of years, and it would be folly, Snouck thought, to try to change this. He related a story to his superiors that a Pontianak Hajji had smiled and told the Dutch consul in Jeddah that "your government is afraid of our turbans;" Snouck felt that this was a kind of scorn the colonial authorities could do without.[17] Nevertheless, he felt some outward forms of Dutch governance were worth continuing, such as fingerprinting, despite the protests against it by many pilgrims. The utility in this case of open maintenance of the Hajj was worth the difficulties, Snouck felt, because of the useful information the colonial authorities gleaned from this practice.[18]

There were those in Dutch policy circles who continued to agitate for tighter and tighter controls on the Hajj, however, so that Snouck found himself in the position of defending the continuance of the pilgrimage as a religious act of devotion. Some of these complaints had to do with security: in the mid-1890s, for example, the consuls of France, Britain, Russia, and Portugal were attacked by Bedouins in Jeddah, causing fear for the safety of European legations in the doorway city to Mecca. Snouck pointed out that the grand sharif of Mecca and the governor of the Hejaz were both well aware of the situation, that they knew exactly who the culprits were, and that they were bringing them to justice even as Snouck was writing.[19] But the complaints also had to do with other matters, such as disease and the spread of disease though water in the Holy Cities. Snouck, ever the logical civil servant, brought a sample of holy Zam-zam water from Mecca back to Holland and had it analyzed by chemists. It was not the water,

Snouck cautioned his superiors, that was spreading disease, but simply the overwhelming numbers of pilgrims all congregating in one place and at one time.[20] He also pointed out that disease was often spread by the mismanagement of Europeans themselves, as in the case of the *Gelderland*, en route from Jeddah to Batavia in 1890. The ship, with 700 souls on board, reported cholera along the voyage, but there was no doctor on board to help treat it, and British ship-crews in the Red Sea threatened to strike if any of the afflicted Hajjis were allowed to disembark and join up with their own fleet.[21] Snouck was constantly trying to correct what he saw as misrepresentations in the colonial apparatus, therefore; misrepresentations that were allowed to stand unchallenged would affect Dutch policy in malevolent ways.

Snouck blamed much of this situation on the colonial system of governance in Asia itself. In an important memo to the Netherlands Indies administration in 1890, he pointedly told his superiors that there were official statistics on the Hajj, and then there were the real numbers — with the two sets of figures not necessarily meeting anywhere in the same neighborhood.[22] Part of the problem, according to him, was that Dutch officials both in the Hejaz and in Southeast Asia were often unprepared for the kinds of reporting duties that were expected of them. Very few spoke or read Arabic, and this was of concern not only in Jeddah and in the Holy Cities, but also in the Straits Settlements and in the Dutch Indies ports, where such abilities could be utilized in helpful ways.[23] Snouck felt that language — or a lack of appropriate languages — was only part of the problem, however. Also important, in his eyes, was the fact that Dutch civil servants in the Hejaz had little notion of the history and/or culture of the region, something that could be picked up only with years of experience. It was precisely this long experience that was lacking in Netherlands officialdom in Arabia, Snouck said.[24] This naiveté led to exaggerations of dangers and misinterpretations of real problems, both of which hampered the Dutch cause in trying to understand and manage a yearly event of such enormous proportions as the Hajj.

If policy problems could not be solved in the Hejaz in relation to the Hajj, many Dutch planners felt that it would be wise to issue warnings to the Indies pilgrims about the dangers that they might face there. Snouck was resolutely against this idea. He told the minister for the colonies in 1922 that he had been against this notion for more than 30 years and still stood firm in his stance — he felt warnings would do more harm than good. A certain percentage of the Indies population (and more people in the Middle East) would see this as colonial Christian attempts to stem the tide of pilgrimage, the linking of province and center in the maintenance of the Muslim faith. Snouck saw this as problematic, but he was adamant in insisting that "pilgrims can only with difficulty be protected against their own ignorance," and that they would be attacked on the roads between Mecca and Medina whether they were warned or not.[25] In a much earlier missive to the Indies government, Snouck had in fact stressed that warning the pilgrims had absolutely no effect and might indeed be counterproductive. Archipelago sojourners were warned against Snouck's will in 1890 (because of troubles the previous year in the Hejaz), and that year — despite the warnings — the numbers of Hajjis from the Indies outstripped the numbers from the previous eight seasons.[26]

The policy problem of dealing with adverse perceptions in the Middle East with regard to Holland's organization and conduct of the Hajj on behalf of its subjects was one that took up much of Snouck's time. The Dutch, like other European colonial powers, felt they had to be seen as protectors of their respective colonial pilgrimages rather than as custodians (or worse, religious policemen). Yet the news was rarely good on this front, and Snouck spilled much ink on trying to deal with negative perceptions of Dutch policy in Arabia. The prime culprits, in his eyes, were the pan-Islamic press, who constantly beat the drum of "religious brothers" having to perform one of their five sacred duties under the yoke of repressive (and Christian) powers.[27] Snouck identified the inflammatory writings as coming from both Arabic and Turkish semi-official newspapers, and though the Turkish government had made some surface attempts to stop the "rantings," there was no end yet in sight.[28] Matters had become unsafe enough in the Hejaz in 1915 (with the onset of World War I) that Snouck was finally overruled by his compatriots and official warnings did go out to Indies pilgrims, a move that occasioned an immediate protest by the Ottoman government.[29] Snouck, and indeed many European policy-makers, were united in one sense, though: they did not want to see the Ottomans emerging as the "official voice" of Muslims worldwide.[30] Many disagreements could be smoothed over when it came to this one, very basic premise of pan-colonial accord regarding the Hajj.

Yet it was indeed the instability and chaos caused by World War I that led to a hardening of many Dutch policies toward the conduct of the pilgrimage, and toward movement between Southeast Asia and the Middle East generally. Beacons and lights along the Red Sea routes were washed away and not maintained, and navigation became dangerous in much of the Middle East because of a lack of personnel to care for the maritime channels. Many of the big shipping companies also did not give over vessels for the Hajj in the early days of the war, and prices rose, so that it became less and less practical to go.[31] The Dutch issued a warning (again against Snouck's wishes) and finally temporarily banned the Hajj in 1915.[32] The ban stranded many archipelago peoples in the Hejaz, whether or not they were there in order to perform their pilgrimage. Snouck knew from his own experiences in Mecca that there were many Indies subjects in fact living and studying or working in Arabia, and that these people were affected by the draconian enforcement of the Dutch ban as well.[33] He tried to make policy-makers in The Hague see that a ban on the Hajj was causing problems for a broad spectrum of Dutch subjects, only some of them involved in the Hajj itself; but his pleas fell on deaf ears. Snouck finally had to content himself with a forlorn letter to the minister for the colonies in 1916, where he observed that Indies Hajjis must be told as soon as possible that their pilgrimage would not be interfered with again, once all had returned to normal. Not to do so, Snouck added, would only give more impetus to those in the Hejaz and elsewhere already beating the drums of pan-Islam.[34]

Snouck and the Problems of the Pilgrimage

Snouck spent much of his energy as a Dutch civil servant analyzing and enacting policies having to do with the Netherlands' interests in the Middle East, including the conduct of the Hajj. Yet he also was keenly interested in the problems archipelago pilgrims faced in the Hejaz, and he wrote copiously in his correspondence about the trials and tribulations ordinary pilgrims encountered in the Holy Cities. Snouck explicitly stated that the majority of Indies Hajjis had little idea of what they were in for in Arabia; they were prepared for hardships, he argued, and this was exactly what their experiences had taught them in the deserts of the Hejaz.[35] It was well known, Snouck told the governor-general of the Indies, that archipelago pilgrims were attacked more frequently than other Hajjis, partially because an entire array of interests on the ground knew that by necessity they had to carry large sums of cash to make their long journeys from so far away. Snouck argued that Indies subjects should be reminded before they left home that the Hajj was compulsory only for adults who could perform it without burdening their families, a warning that he hoped might stem at least a small amount of the enthusiasm for this journey that was so important — yet also so dangerous — to many.[36]

Yet there was also a certain amount of resignation in Snouck's dealing with the dangers of the Hajj, a kind of recognition that he as a civil servant (and anyone else like him) had only limited powers to change long-existing dynamics. He acknowledged that plundering of the Mecca/Medina caravans was a way of life in the desert.[37] He also acknowledged that demands for compensation because of these attacks were likely to continue well into the future, until local governments and foreign consuls in the Hejaz could guarantee some kind of safety for the camel-trains that crossed the Arabian wastes.[38] But he did not think that this state of affairs would be changing anytime soon. Late in his career, he wrote that such plundering of pilgrim caravans had been a part of this experience for 40 years in the Hejaz, and that it likely had been part of the "pilgrim experience for one thousand years before this."[39] But there were limitations on what foreign governments could do. Mecca and Medina were open to Muslims only, he intoned to the governor-general in Batavia, the open spaces of the desert were lawless for everyone, and any attempt by Europeans to travel there was an invitation to "purchase death."[40]

One problem concerning the Hajj that Snouck devoted even more attention to than the safety of the Indies caravans was the role of health and sanitation in the experience of archipelago pilgrims. Snouck felt that cholera was more or less endemic to the Holy Cities.[41] The situation was helped along, he wrote to the governor-general in Batavia, by Indies pilgrims sailing both across the Indian Ocean and locally in Red Sea waters secretly, and outside of the surveillance (sanitary and otherwise) of the European powers.[42] The quarantine station at Kamarin island (close to Jeddah) was not really equipped to stop an epidemic of cholera should the disease break out during the time of the Hajj.[43] Snouck pointed out that archipelago pilgrims both drank and bathed in the limited supplies of water available in the Hejaz, making effective sanitary control extremely difficult. Certain basic behavioral practices would have to change, he said, before anything approaching an integrated system of health management could be expected while thousands upon thousands of pilgrims were on Hajj.[44]

Yet if Snouck saw problems with the behavioral practices of pilgrims, he also found fault with those charged with keeping them safe and healthy while they performed their religious duties. He termed the international sanitary office in the Red Sea region "a comedy and a means toward making money," an accusation that may not have been far from the truth.[45] A suggestion by the Dutch consul in Jeddah to appoint a health inspector for the region, however, did not sit well with Snouck; he had little faith, he confided in the minister for the colonies, that this would help matters at all.[46] The reason, he said, was that the system, and the administrator, would eventually be co-opted by the Turkish government. In the Turks, he saw no real friendship or caring for the flood of Hajjis — their main concern was making money off the health regulations, he stated bitterly in a missive to the minister for the colonies.[47] If relief was going to come to those who traveled far from their own countries in order to sojourn to Mecca as part of their faith, it would have to come from sources other than the guardians of the Holy Cities.

The problem was where this help could be found. Here again, as with the attacks on caravans, Snouck demonstrated a keen critical eye for identifying problems but offered little by way of solutions for helping the Hajjis, whom he held both in contempt and close to his heart. Snouck correctly identified the graft of low-level officials in the architecture of the Red Sea sanitation controls as the main impediment to progress. These men merely lined their pockets under the existing system, he wrote, fleecing pilgrims out of their savings while offering little in return by way of any real benefits.[48] He told the minister for the colonies that so long as the Turkish government continued to appoint the inspectors, doctors, and officials populating the system, current rates of disease and mortality could be expected to continue.[49] Graft, he said, was simply endemic to the system as it was presently conducted.[50] Yet Snouck, perspicacious as always, was at a loss to ever effect change in the system he so despised. He had vitriol for everyone in terms of the problems facing Hajjis (including Hajjis themselves), but he had little to put forward to ease their often difficult lot.

Snouck and the Everyday Life of the Hajj

If Snouck was interested in the safety of the Hajj caravans and in the health of pilgrims, both problems that plagued the conduct of this huge transnational movement for many years, then he was also a keen observer of everyday life on the Hajj. He commented voluminously on the work contracts that many Hajjis signed in order to finance their passage to the Holy Land, and which often landed them in deep debt, sometimes stranding them in the Hejaz for many years.[51] Archipelago pilgrims were particularly susceptible to this problem, as they often did not take enough money with them from Malaya or the Indies, sometimes lost funds along the way, were robbed, and also had credit problems (including having to pay high interest to financiers) on their initial travel loans to Arabia.[52] Certain high-profile facilitators of the Hajj in Southeast Asia, Snouck wrote, such as the al-Sagoff family in Singapore, also helped them along into debt by overcharging them for their passages.[53] Yet curiously, Snouck was skeptical — and probably wrongly so — about reports of slavery in the Hejaz involving archipelago pilgrims, even going so far as to say that because this was so forbidden by Islam, it could not be happening on a wide scale as a part of the Hajj.[54] Snouck here seems to have taken the canonical dictates of Islam — which he knew better than almost anyone else at this time — more seriously than the lived realities of many pilgrims, who found their travels choked with difficulties that also were a part of this longest of journeys.

Snouck also invested a lot of his time in learning the ins and outs of how pilgrim-guides (or *shaykhs*) worked in the conduct of the Hajj. *Shaykhs* were crucial to the entire system of the pilgrimage: they ferried hopeful Hajjis to and from their own countries, took care of them in the Arabian Peninsula, and generally were responsible for their welfare in a myriad ways. Hajjis had stamps on their passports explicating clearly which *shaykhs* they "belonged to," and these same *shaykhs* (especially those from Southeast Asia) paid very large sums of money in order to obtain their licenses.[55] Because the business was so profitable, many Dutch policy-planners wondered if the numbers of these *shaykhs* wasn't increasing immensely, though Snouck responded to this concern by supplying figures that Netherlands Indies *shaykhs* were remaining more or less constant in number toward the end of the 19th century.[56] He described some of these *shaykhs* in a letter to the general secretariat in Batavia in 1896, focusing on one *shaykh* in particular who was well-known in Mecca for supplying pilgrims from Banyuwangi in Java (these Hajjis were much desired in the Holy Cities because they were considered to be rich and brought considerable quantities of cash to spend on goods while they were in the Hejaz).[57] But Snouck also focused on shipping companies in this process, who by the 1890s were transporting Hajjis from all over Southeast Asia, including Batavia, and were even hiring men to work for them to find pilgrims to fill the berths. These men were paid fl. 2.50 per head if they were able to convince potential Hajjis to buy a ticket, and fl. 5 per head for those who bought tickets directly from them as agents.[58]

The pilgrim-guides were not just a matter of academic interest for Snouck. He saw them as abusive and basically parasitic on the Hajji community. In another long letter to the general secretariat, Snouck explained that pilgrims could do almost nothing without the help of their *shaykhs*: every step they took in the Holy Land, all of their purchases, and all matters concerning both spiritual and worldly concerns were to be answered and taken up by their *shaykhs* as official intercessors for the Hajjis.[59] This was a shame, Snouck stated, because many *shaykhs* were completely crooked, men who barely looked after their charges and were sometimes not above stealing their worldly possessions if any of their pilgrims should die in the Hejaz (which, in fact, happened with some frequency).[60] The system was riddled with corruption, Snouck wrote, and it was well known that the *shaykhs* were often as predatory on the Jâwa communities of sojourners as many of the Bedouins and Arabs of the desert.[61] Foremost among these, Snouck told the governor-general, was the grand sharif himself, the hereditary emir of Mecca. The *shaykhs* were next in line after the emir, yet they had even more influence than he did on their day-to-day lives in Arabia. This was all the more the pity, Snouck wrote, because many Hajjis did not want to complain about the vile treatment they received — they thought that doing so would tarnish the memory of their spiritual quest in the Hejaz.[62]

Though Snouck was extremely critical of the *shaykhs* as exploiters of Hajjis, he had a nuanced opinion about many religious men who did want to return to the Indies, sometimes even as *shaykhs*, in order to recruit new Hajjis. One man in particular, a famed religious teacher in Mecca originally from Lampung in South Sumatra, excited Snouck's attention in 1894. The man, known as "Ahmad Lampung," wanted to return to the Indies that year in order to ferry new pilgrims back to the Hejaz. Snouck was worried that he would not be given permission to re-enter the Dutch possessions in Southeast Asia because of Batavia's deepening policies of conservatism *vis-à-vis Vreemde Oosterlingen* (Foreign Asians); there was a good chance his plea for repatriation would not be accepted. Snouck argued against this, pointing out that the man was a famed teacher, who wanted to return under totally peaceful and acceptable terms to his homeland after a lifetime of learning in the Holy Cities.[63] The plight of a second man, this time a religious teacher from Madura named Ahmad Sarkawi, also prompted Snouck to write to his superiors six years later. Like Ahmad Lampung, Ahmad Sarkawi wanted to return to Madura, partially to lecture in the mosques on his home island, partially to see family, and partially to encourage a flow of new pilgrims to Arabia. Snouck argued strongly that this should be allowed.⁶⁴ It was this intensity of feeling — sometimes directed against the Muslim community (such as the *shaykhs*, or even many Hajjis as "ignorant" and "troublesome"), and sometimes directed against his own government — that made Snouck such a paradoxical figure.

Snouck was also keenly interested in the mechanics of pilgrim transport, in addition to his copious writings on *shaykhs* and Hajji work contracts. Part of his interest in this subject came from the massive internal policy arguments that were occurring in Dutch administrative circles at the time, concerning the best procedures to use for passes, tickets, and compulsory practices to enforce a smooth (and, from the Dutch standpoint, obedient) Hajj.⁶⁵ Snouck correctly pointed out to his superiors in 1895 that many current and former government practices *vis-à-vis* pilgrim transport engendered open hatred and distrust of Europeans in the hearts and minds of Hajjis themselves.⁶⁶ By the early 20th century, almost all of the pilgrim traffic from the Indies was in the hands of three large companies, and prices had risen to the highest levels ever recorded for the trip across the Indian Ocean.⁶⁷ Snouck cautioned the minister for the colonies that somehow the situation would have to be stabilized or there would be dire consequences, and he made a plea for some kind of "honorable understanding" between shipping companies, agents, and the Hajjis themselves so that the dynamics of the journey would be fair to everyone concerned.⁶⁸

What was clear, however, was that this "honorable understanding" about the difficulties of pilgrim transport was nowhere in sight. Many Hajjis in the Hejaz waited years in order to be able to return to the Indies after their initial sojourns; these were many of the *blijvers* ("those who stayed"), archipelago subjects who had completed their Hajj but had decided to stay on in the Arabian Peninsula in order to work or further their religious study. The shipping companies had few provisions for these people, because they had not purchased the round-trip tickets the companies desired; and they also were sometimes classified by the Dutch colonial state as *Vreemde Oosterlingen* if they had stayed away from the Indies for too long.⁶⁹ There were a host of other complicated problems affecting Hajj transport: passengers on outbound ships who were found to be destitute, or in debt or partial debt to agents or the shipping companies, and even some who had had their belongings (and savings) plundered in the Hejaz and now had no way to pay their fares home.⁷⁰ The problems again, said Snouck, led inexorably back to the *shaykhs* — everyone had to trust them (caravan drivers, shipping companies, lodgers, and victualizers) to get the Hajjis back and forth between the Indies and Arabia. But again, Snouck reminded his superiors, these were men who could not frequently be trusted.[71]

Yet if Snouck was hard on the *shaykhs* and their role in the transport regime across the Indian Ocean, he was equally accusatory of the European shipping companies themselves as being complicit in the miseries of many pilgrims. He saw the existing international accords as useless, ultimately as a collection of rules and regulations put into place in order to further line the pockets of many who made money on the passage of so much paperwork. This venom was reserved for officialdom.[72] Yet the majority of his bile was saved for the shipping companies themselves, whom he accused of agitating for 40 years to enforce the system of return tickets, first "in the interests of the Hajjis," then "in the interests of the government," but really only in their own self-interest, he advised the minister for the colonies.[73] The compulsory return passage did not help most Hajjis, because it put the initial cost of the journey outside the realm of possibility for many, and limited their freedoms to stay in the Hejaz to work or learn as they saw fit for themselves.[74] When the aforementioned three giant shipping companies won the legal right to enforce round-trip passages as a condition of applying for Hajj in 1922–23, Snouck saw this as a defeat in a legislative battle that he had waged for decades.[75] In this, as in many other matters, Snouck showed the complexity of his position as both warden and protector of the Southeast Asian pilgrim.

Conclusion

It would be a mistake to judge Snouck Hurgronje or any other colonial servant of the *fin de siècle* period under a contemporary code of ethics or values. Snouck Hurgronje was a man of his times, and this meant that he generally saw colonialism as something helpful and potentially salutary for the peoples he helped rule. Nevertheless, there is something achingly modern about Snouck Hurgronje as well, an almost ethnographic desire to get as close as possible to his subject, to understand it, and then to take his information and tales home for the benefit of his own audience (and for himself).

Snouck was an administrator, and much of his understanding and his perspective on the Hajj was seen through this prism, one of governance and administration of a huge and unwieldy trans-regional phenomenon.

Yet he was also interested in the problems faced by archipelago pilgrims, as they wound their way across the Indian Ocean and into the deserts of the Hejaz to perform their religious duties. Caravan attacks and cholera were the substance of Snouck's problem-solving, a never-ending cycle of difficulties that presented themselves as fodder for his well-trained mind to solve. Snouck resolved few of these dangers and annoyances. There is a persistent resignation, in fact, in much of his writings about the Hajj, as he realized it was too large an event for any one man to fully master or control, despite his formidable abilities. It is perhaps through his writings on the everyday conduct of the Hajj that Snouck served posterity best: he left a record, a gloriously detailed and informed record, of the passage of millions from the tropics to the desert over four decades of sojourning. For this, if nothing else, he should be thanked, whatever his faults.

Snouck loved the Middle East, and he particularly loved to study the connections between the Hejaz and "his own" Netherlands Indies, the place where he got his start as an administrator, a civil servant, and, to some extent, a scholar. He was capable of writing about these connections in very lucid, and sometimes very moving, terms. He knew that archipelago pilgrims dearly wanted to "kiss the black stone, drink from the Holy well at Zemzem, … and throw stones in the dale of Mina."[76] He spoke of the Hajj as the last of the five pillars of the Muslim faith, but he knew that it was not least in the hearts of the faith's practitioners, as they spent huge amounts of money and time to make the lengthy journey. And he saw in the great radials of the pilgrimage the seeds of fraternity and knowledge and equality, as when he said that "in the mosques of Mecca men can see during seminars students and professors of all shades and colors: coal-black, green (which is what Arabs call those of a lighter complexion), brown, yellow, and white, all brothers, and the same differences are seen in the denizens of the Holy City, even sometimes in the members of a single Meccan family."[77] Mecca, during the Hajj, was perhaps a form of paradise to Snouck: a place where learning and scholarship came before all other worldly pursuits and divisions. Indeed, he took it as part of his intellectual program to explain that which he loved and found so fascinating to a wider public, scholarly and otherwise, in a series of writings that spanned nearly a half-century of elucidation.[78]

Yet as many contemporary scholars have begun to show, his role was much more complex than as a mere interpreter of Islam for the uninitiated in the Western world. He was captivated by the Hajj, and was moved by it, but he also saw the seeds of danger in the passage of so many men and ideas across the vast spaces of the Indian Ocean separating the Hejaz and the "Netherlands' own Indies." Snouck reported regularly on Hadramis passing back and forth between Arabia and Southeast Asia, and his notations were duly cataloged (and his recommendations for surveillance acted upon) by an anxious Batavia regime.[79] Snouck also made sure to weave a tight but ever-expanding web of informants and information-gatherers while he was in Mecca, men whom he could count upon to supply him with intelligence — scholarly, religious, and other — while he sat in the mosques and pursued his studies.[80] Finally, he was completely immersed in the ongoing conflict in Aceh, so much so that it is extremely difficult to see where his ethnographic and scholastic interests ended and his role as a conduit for useful information to the colonial government began.[81] Snouck was a complex man, and he lived in complex times. His individuality, life experiences, and penchant for self-belief (accompanied often by a denigration of other scholars' and officials' opinions) led him to have enormous influence in Dutch policy circles. Yet it is perhaps through his writings on the Hajj that these paradoxical aspects of his personality and of his lived experience are seen best, as they reveal him for what he was — sagacious, competent, and politically implicated in morally complex ways — all at once. In some senses he was a harbinger of the model "scholar-official" who became prevalent in colonial projects worldwide in the first half of the 20th century, though this might be viewed as an ambiguous legacy at best.

Notes

1. His two most famous published works in this vein were *Het Mekkaansche Feest*, his 1880 doctoral dissertation from Leiden, and his masterpiece *Mekka in the Latter Part of the 19th Century: Daily Life, Customs and Learning, the Moslims of the East-Indian Archipelago* (Leiden: E. J. Brill, 1931).
2. P. Sj. van Koningsveld, "Orientalistik Sebagai Ilmu-Bantu Kolonial: 'Masuk' Islamnya Snouck Hurgronje," in P. Sj. van Koningsveld, *Snouck Hurgronje dan Islam: delapan karangan tentang hidup dan karya seorang orientalis zaman kolonial* (Jakarta: Girimukti Pasaka, 1989), 95.
3. P. Sj. van Koningsveld, "Izharu 'l-Islam Snouck Hurgronje: Segi Sejarah Kolonial yang Diabaikan," in Koningsveld, *Snouck Hurgronje dan Islam*, 172.
4. A. J. P. Moereels, *Chr. Snouck Hurgronje* (Rijswijk: V. A. Kramers, 1938).
5. P. Sj. van Koningsveld, "Raden Jusuf di Bandung Mengakhiri Kebungkamannya Sekitar Pernikahan-Pernikahan Islam Ayahnya, Christiaan Snouck Hurgronje,"

in Koningsveld, *Snouck Hurgronje dan Islam,* 164–5; and Snouck Hurgronje to Th. Noldeke, 28 April 1924, in P. Sj. van Koningsveld, *Orientalism and Islam: The Letters of C. Snouck Hurgronje to Th. Noldeke from the Tubingen University Library* (hereafter OI) (Leiden: Leiden University Press, 1985), 324.

6. Snouck Hurgronje always had his critics as well, in his own time as in the present; see Harry Benda, "Christiaan Snouck Hurgronje and the Foundations of Dutch Islamic Policy in Indonesia," in Ahmad Ibrahim *et al.*, eds., *Readings on Islam in Southeast Asia* (Singapore: ISEAS, 1985), 61–9; P. Sj. van Koningsveld, "Snouck Hurgronje Zoals Hij Was," *De Gids* 9/10 (1980): 763–84; F. Schroeder, "Orientalistische Retoriek: Van Konongsveld over de Vuile Handen van Snouck Hurgronje," *De Gids* 9/10 (1980): 785–806; L. I. Graf, "Christiaan Snouck Hurgronje en Zijn Critici," *De Gids* 9/10 (1980): 807–30; and Fred Lanzing, "Snouck Hurgronje, Schrijver," *Indische Letteren* 16, 4 (2001): 154–69.

7. Hamid Algadri, "Snouck Hurgronje Menentang Asimilasi Keturunan Arab," in Hamid Algadri, *C. Snouck Hurgronje, Politik Belanda Terhadap Islam dan Keturunan Arab* (Jakarta: Penerbit Sinar Harapan, 1984), 85–94.

8. Tengku Hasan M. de Tiro, "Indonesian Nationalism: A Western Invention to Contain Islam in the Dutch East Indies," in M. Ghayasuddin, ed., *The Impact of Nationalism on the Muslim Word* (London: Muslim Institute, 1986), 61–73.

9. Hamid Algadri, "Prof. Snouck Hurgronje Menentang Gerakan Pan-Islam," in Algadri, *C. Snouck Hurgronje, Politik Belanda Terhadap Islam dan Keturunan Arab,* 117–52.

10. P. Sj. van Koningsveld, "Penulisan Sejarah Suatu Perang Ekspansi Kolonial. Lima Puluh Tahun Setelah Kematian Snouck Hurgronje," in Koningsveld, *Snouck Hurgronje dan Islam,* 261.

11. Snouck Hurgronje, *Het Gajoland en Zijne Bewoners* (Batavia: Landsdrukkerij, 1903), 314–5; K. van der Maaten, *Snouck Hurgronje en de Atjeh Ooorlog,* vol. I (Rotterdam: Oostersch Instituut te Leiden, 1948), 38–41.

12. Interview with "Achmed" (not his real name), Universitas Islam Antarabangsa, Gombak (Kuala Lumpur), 18 June 2004.

13. Snouck Hurgronje to the Director of Education, Religion, and Industry, 28 September 1897, in E. Gobee and C. Adriaanse, eds., *Ambtelijke Adviezen van C. Snouck Hurgronje* (Hague: Martinus Nijhoff, 1959) [multi-volume, hereafter AASH], 2, 32: 1324. Many Hajjis did indeed die on the voyage, or while in the Hejaz, but this was not considered to be a "problem" by many pilgrims, who saw the added blessings of such a death if a Hajji passed away while performing the fifth pillar of the faith.

14. Snouck Hurgronje to Governor-General, NEI, 19 May 1904, in AASH, 2, 32: 1330.

15. Snouck Hurgronje to Governor-General, NEI, 7 September 1900, in AASH 2, 32: 1326. See also Snouck Hurgronje, "Hadji Politiek?" *Java-Bode*, 6–8 March 1899: 353–68.
16. Snouck Hurgronje to Director of Education, Religion, and Industry, 25 December 1900, in AASH, 2, 32: 1326.
17. Snouck Hurgronje to the General Secretariat, 26 March 1890, in AASH, 2, 32: 1322.
18. Snouck Hurgronje to Minister for the Colonies, 5 September 1910, in AASH, 2, 32: 1506. See also Snouck Hurgronje, "De Hadji-Politiek der Indische Regeering," *Onze Eeuw*, 1909: 331–60.
19. Snouck Hurgronje to Government Secretary, 3 December 1895, in AASH, 2, 32: 1346.
20. Snouck Hurgronje to Director of Education, Religion, and Industry, 8 January 1901, in AASH, 2, 32: 1338.
21. Snouck Hurgronje to Director of Education, Religion, and Industry, 12 January 1891, in AASH, 2, 32: 1335.
22. Consideratieen en advies naar aanleiding van het verslag van den Consul te Djeddah over te gevaren, waaraan de hadji's van het volgend jaar zullen zijn blootgesteld, 21 November 1890, in AASH, 2, 32: 1332.
23. Snouck Hurgronje to Director of Education, Religion, and Industry, 25 May 1889, in AASH, 2, 32: 1466.
24. Snouck Hurgronje to the First Government Secretary, 26 October 1895, in AASH, 2, 32: 1343.
25. Snouck Hurgronje to Minister for the Colonies, 20 April 1922, and Snouck Hurgronje to Minister for the Colonies, 9 December 1923, both in AASH, 2, 32: 1348–9.
26. Snouck Hurgronje to Director of Education, Religion, and Industry, 30 May 1891, in AASH, 2, 32: 1336.
27. Snouck Hurgronje to Minister for the Colonies, 25 September 1915, in AASH, 2, 32: 1353. See also G. S. van Krieken, *Snouck Hurgronje en het Panislamisme* (Leiden: Brill, 1985), and Snouck Hurgronje to Th. Noldeke, 15 August 1912, in OI, 169.
28. Snouck Hurgronje to Minister for the Colonies, 2 October 1915, in AASH, 2, 32: 1355.
29. Minister for the Colonies to Adviser for Indies and Arabian Matters, 28 September 1915, enclosed in Snouck Hurgronje to Minister for the Colonies, 2 October 1915, in AASH, 2, 32: 1356.
30. Snouck Hurgronje to Minister for the Colonies, 26 August 1916, in AASH, 2, 32: 1364.
31. "Waarschuwing van de Algemeene Secretaris" (1915), enclosed in Snouck Hurgronje to Minister for the Colonies, 2 October 1915, in AASH, 2, 32: 1357.

32. Snouck Hurgronje to Minister for the Colonies, 23 October 1915, in AASH, 2, 32: 1359. See also Snouck Hurgronje, "De Mekkagangers en de Oorlog," *Nieuwe Rotterdamsche Courant*, 24–25 November 1915: 299–310.
33. Snouck Hurgronje to Minister for the Colonies, 24 August 1916, in AASH, 2, 32: 1361.
34. Snouck Hurgronje to Minister for the Colonies, 10 September 1916, in AASH, 2, 32: 1366.
35. Snouck Hurgronje to Minister for the Colonies, 8 January 1910, in AASH, 2, 32: 1313.
36. Snouck Hurgronje to Governor-General, NEI, 20 June 1889, and Snouck Hurgronje to Governor-General 30 January 1906, both in AASH, 2, 32: 1307 and 1310.
37. Snouck Hurgronje to Minister for the Colonies, 18 September 1922, in AASH, 2, 32: 1316.
38. Snouck Hurgronje to Governor-General, NEI, 30 January 1906, in AASH, 2, 32: 1311.
39. Snouck Hurgronje to Minister for the Colonies, 13 June 1923, in AASH, 2, 32: 1317.
40. Snouck Hurgronje to the General Secretariat, 30 December 1893, in AASH, 2, 32: 1472.
41. Snouck Hurgronje to Governor-General, NEI, 6 June 1903, in AASH, 2, 32: 1455.
42. Snouck Hurgronje to Governor-General, NEI, 23 May 1905, in AASH, 2, 32: 1455.
43. Snouck Hurgronje to Minister for the Colonies, December 1931, in AASH, 2, 32: 1463.
44. Snouck Hurgronje to the Resident of Batavia, 23 December 1905, and Snouck Hurgronje to Governor-General, NEI, both in AASH, 2, 32: 1462 and 1474.
45. Snouck Hurgronje to Minister for the Colonies, 23 December 1908, in AASH, 2, 32: 1458.
46. Snouck Hurgronje to Governor-General, NEI, 24 April 1903, in AASH, 2, 32: 1453–4.
47. Snouck Hurgronje to Minister for the Colonies, 14 December 1908, in AASH, 2, 32: 1457.
48. Snouck Hurgronje to Director of Education, Religion, and Industry, 30 May 1894, in AASH, 2, 32: 1451.
49. Snouck Hurgronje to Minister for the Colonies, 2 April 1909, in AASH, 2, 32: 1460.
50. Snouck Hurgronje to Minister for the Colonies, 2 July 1910, in AASH, 2, 32: 1461.
51. Snouck Hurgronje to Director of Education, Religion, and Industry, 3 January 1891, in AASH, 2, 32: 1440. See also Georg Stauth, "Slave Trade, Multi-

culturalism and Islam in Colonial Singapore: A Sociological Note on Christiaan Snouck Hurgronje's 1891 Article on Slave Trade in Singapore," *Southeast Asian Journal of Social Science* 20, 1 (1992): 67–79.
52. Snouck Hurgronje to the General Secretariat, 26 August 1896, in AASH, 2, 32: 1445.
53. Snouck Hurgronje to Director of Education, Religion, and Industry, 15 October 1895, in AASH, 2, 32: 1443.
54. Snouck Hurgronje to Governor-General, NEI, 16 August 1898, and Snouck Hurgronje to Director of Education, Religion, and Industry, 15 October 1895, both in AASH, 2, 32: 1449 and 1444.
55. Snouck Hurgronje to Director of Education, Religion, and Industry, 19 July 1892, in AASH, 2, 32: 1377.
56. Snouck Hurgronje to Director of Education, Religion, and Industry, 4 July 1898, in AASH, 2, 32: 1379. Hurgronje stated that in 1884 there were 180 Indies shaykhs in Mecca, while in 1898, according to the Dutch consul in Jeddah, there were 186. The numbers of shaykhs, however, were increasing in number generally from the late 19th into the early 20th centuries.
57. Snouck Hurgronje to General Secretariat, 24 September 1896, in AASH, 2, 32: 1391.
58. Snouck Hurgronje to Director of Justice, 17 March 1893, in AASH, 2, 32: 1381.
59. Snouck Hurgronje to General Secretariat, 7 October 1893, in AASH, 2, 32: 1383.
60. Snouck Hurgronje to Director of Education, Religion, and Industry, 10 March 1891, in AASH, 2, 32: 1371.
61. Snouck Hurgronje to Governor-General, 20 January 1905, and Snouck Hurgronje to Governor-General, 13 January 1905, both in AASH, 2, 32: 1400 and 1396.
62. Snouck Hurgronje to Governor-General, 22 October 1904, in AASH, 2, 32: 1478.
63. Snouck Hurgronje to Resident, Lampung Districts, 24 September 1894, in AASH, 2, 32: 1386.
64. Snouck Hurgronje to Governor-General, 1 March 1900, in AASH, 2, 32: 1387. See also Snouck Hurgronje, *De Islam in Nederlandsch-Indie* (Baarn: Hollandia, 1913), 24.
65. Snouck Hurgronje to Director of Education, Religion, and Industry, 23 August 1893, in AASH, 2, 32: 1402. For more on this issue, see P. Sj. van Koningsveld, "Snouck Hurgronje alias Abdul-Ghaffar. Beberapa Catatan-Pinggir Kritik Sejarah," in Koningsveld, *Snouck Hurgronje dan Islam*; P. Sj. van Koningsveld, "Sisa-sisa Kolonial Dalam Kebijaksanaan Negeri Belanda Dewasa ini Mengenai Islam," in Koningsveld, *Snouck Hurgronje dan Islam,* 275; and Jan Willem Naarding, *Het conflict Snouck Hurgronje-van Heutsz-van*

Daalen: een onderzoek naar de verantwoordelijkheid (Utrecht: A. Oosthoek, 1938), 1–116.
66. Snouck Hurgronje to Director of Education, Religion, and Industry, 19 July 1895, in AASH, 2, 32: 1405.
67. Snouck Hurgronje to Governor-General, 16 October 1903, in AASH, 2, 32: 1421.
68. Snouck Hurgronje to Minister for the Colonies, 4 March 1910, in AASH, 2, 32: 1427.
69. Snouck Hurgronje to Minister for the Colonies, 21 July 1907, in AASH, 2, 32: 1426.
70. Snouck Hurgronje to Minister for the Colonies, 29 July 1906, in AASH, 2, 32: 1436.
71. Snouck Hurgronje to Governor-General, NEI, 22 October 1904, in AASH, 2, 32: 1478.
72. Snouck Hurgronje to Minister for the Colonies, 16 August 1923, in AASH, 2, 32: 1429.
73. Snouck Hurgronje to Minister for the Colonies, 23 March 1923, in AASH, 2, 32: 1428.
74. Snouck Hurgronje to Director of Education, Religion, and Industry, 2 May 1900, in AASH, 2, 32: 1419.
75. Snouck Hurgronje to Minister for the Colonies, 5 June 1932, in AASH, 2, 32: 1439.
76. Snouck Hurgronje, *De beteekenis van den Islam voor zijne belijders in Ost-Indië* (Leiden: E. J. Brill, 1883), 14.
77. Snouck Hurgronje, *De Islam en het Rassenprobleem* (Leiden: E. J. Brill, 1922), 19–20.
78. For just a sampling of these writings, see Snouck Hurgronje, "De Islam," *De Gids* 2: 239–73, 454–98; 3: 90–134; "Nieuwe Bijdragen tot de Kennis van de Islam," *BTLV* 4, 6 (1882): 357–421; "Le Droit Musulman," *Revue de l'Histoire des Religions* 19, 37 (1898): 1–22, 174–203; "De Beteekenis van den Islam voor jijne Belijders in Oost-Indie," in *Wetenschappelijke Voordrachten Gehouden te Amsterdam in 1883, ter Gelegenheid der Koloniale Tentoonstelling* (Leiden: E. J. Brill, 1894), 93–122; "Het Mohammedanisme," in H. Colijn, *Neerlands Indie* (Amsterdam, 1911), I: 243–65; "Politique Musulmane de la Hollande," in *Collection de la Revue du Monde Musulman* #14 (Paris, 1911); "Notes sur le Mouvement du Pelerinage de la Mecque aux Indies Neerlandaises," in *Collection de la Revue du Monde Musulman* #15 (Paris, 1911): 397–413; "De Islam in Nederlandsch-Indie," in *Groote Godsdiensten* (Baarn: Hollandia-Drukkerij, 1913), II, #9; "Vergeten Jubile's," *De Gids* 87, 7 (1923): 61–81.
79. See Huub de Jonge, "Contradictory and Against the Grain: Snouck Hurgronje on the Hadramis in the Dutch East Indies, 1889–1936," in Huub de Jonge and

Nico Kaptein, eds., *Transcending Borders: Arabs, Politics, Trade, and Islam in Southeast Asia* (Leiden: KITLV Press, 2002): 219–34.

80. See Michael Laffan, "Raden Aboe Bakar: An Introductory Note Concerning Snouck Hurgronje's Informant in Jeddah, 1884–1912," *BTLV* 155, 4 (1999): 517–42.

81. W. F. Wertheim, "Counter-Insurgency Research at the Turn of the Century — Snouck Hurgronje and the Aceh War," in W. F. Wertheim, *Dawning of an Asian Dream: Selected Articles on Modernization and Emancipation* (Amsterdam: University of Amsterdam Press, 1973), 136–48, and Snouck Hurgronje to Th. Noldeke, 25 June 1898, in OI, 65.

7

Challenging Inequality in a Modern Islamic Idiom: Social Ferment amongst Arabs in Early 20th-century Java*

SUMIT K. MANDAL

Reflecting a modern dilemma, a news story in 1914 related a potential challenge to the high status of *sayyid*, a social group whose prestige rested on the claim of descent from the lineage of the Prophet Muhammad. Reverence of sayyid, recognizable from their family names, accoutrements, endogamous practices, and so forth, had become traditional in many enclaves of Muslim Java. The news report, however, brought out the fragility of their claim when it described an attempt to impersonate a sayyid and thus highlighted the possibility of interlopers publicly performing as sayyid. If sayyid could be replicated like the manufactured goods of the modern era — already available to the masses of the Dutch colony — it could only signal the eventual demise of their privileged position. The report proclaimed: "It is the strangeness of these times, not only is money counterfeited but there are also fake Sayid."[1] The story unfolds as follows:

> Recently, a Sayid accompanied by a Chinese had been in and out of the villages in the district of Karangjati, Blora[.] The Sayid claimed to be Syekh Mohamad Oemar bin Sayid Jahja from Mecca and the Chinese was Ong Swie I, a very capable *doekoen* [indigenous healer].
>
> The sayid, who [also] came in the capacity of a doekoen, drew the unwavering faith of fanatic villagers and easily obtained money from them[.] It is known with certainty by the police that 5 people gave up to 17 guilders, the majority of them were haji as they are indeed rich[.] Others gave no less than one guilder [each].
>
> Unfortunately for the Sayid, as soon as he struck the *abangan* [syncretist Muslims], he was reported to the police and apprehended.

... it appears that he is a [wicked] person named Kasan from the village of Cepu (Panolan) ...

Beware, O my brothers, one has to be cautious in the age of *kemajuan* [progress], many tablet pills [sic] are scattered about.

The previous year in Solo, Ahmad Soerkati issued a *fatwa* (Islamic legal pronouncement) that questioned *kafa'ah* (equivalence), the doctrinal cornerstone of sayyid claims to a privileged place among Muslims, and launched a formative moment in the history of Arabs in Java.

To speak of Arabs as I do in this chapter is to grossly oversimplify in the interest of conciseness. Michael Gilsenan's elaboration of the dynamic relations of blood, property, and movement will stand as a necessary corrective to the stasis I inevitably attribute to Arabness as a result of oversimplification. Almost all those regarded as Arab by the state and society in Indonesia, Malaysia, and Singapore in the modern era have their origins in the Hadramaut, the narrow coastal valley along the southern coast of the Arabian Peninsula, which faces the Indian Ocean. Over the millennium, Hadrami — as they are called — traveled to the farthest reaches of this seascape to constitute a creole diaspora with a specific character. As Engseng Ho has shown through his studies of Hadrami genealogies, communities in the diaspora could appeal to a transoceanic cultural space and memory, indeed even to a timelessness, when we consider the spiritual descent of the Prophet carried by sayyid.[2] At the same time, they were intimately tied to the societies in which they settled.

Sayyid were part of the social world of Java. Their place in the Arab-Muslim urban milieus of Java was strong — fortified by wealth, the blessings of the Dutch overlords at times, and the cultivation of a tradition of leadership over fellow Arabs and Muslims.[3] And, as reported in the preceding news story, they were often regarded with unqualified respect in certain quarters, namely, the *kaum putihan* (orthoprax Muslims), who are here referred to disapprovingly as "fanatic" — not unlike prevailing Dutch opinion of the time.[4]

It is significant that Kasan's ploy was undone by abangan, thus bringing to our attention a group that is inadequately considered in discussions of Arabs and Islam. When Arabs have been ascribed a powerful influence *vis-à-vis* Javanese Muslims, they mostly refer to kaum putihan milieus. As the locus of this influence is not always so specified, it is often presumed to include all Javanese. Although the position of *ashraf* — the more general Arabic term for the descendants of the Prophet in Islam — has been enshrined in the doctrine and social relations of numerous

Muslim societies, their place in Java was secondary to the ruler and his appendages.[5] Thus, this Islamic institution was Javanized in the manner of others, such as the use of *Khalifah* (Caliph) in the titles of Javanese rulers even though it contravened Islamic orthodoxy.[6] On the whole, while the authority of sayyid found a place within the variegated cosmologies of Muslims in Java, it was not restricted to or defined by the Hadrami social hierarchy. This hierarchy was remade in Java, and sayyid authority was variously translated within the island's cosmologies.

Ironically, the admonition at the end of the above news report to seek the genuine in an uncertain age — to seek genuine sayyid, in this instance — was asserted at the very moment sayyid claims to superiority were under challenge. This challenge came from Soerkati's critique of sayyid authority based on the principle that all Muslims were equal. In 1913, while he was teaching at the Djamiat Cheir School in Batavia, Soerkati visited Solo. He spoke at a gathering of Arabs at the home of their captain, Awad bin Soenkar. He suggested that the unwelcome cohabitation of a *sharifah* (female descendant of the Prophet) with a Chinese gentleman could be resolved by pooling funds for her to leave her partner. As this met with no response, he proclaimed that an alternative solution would be for a Muslim to step forward and take her hand in marriage. Sayyid protested on the basis of kafa'ah that no Muslim other than a sayyid could marry a *sharifah*, but Soerkati re-affirmed that the marriage of any Muslim with the said sharifah would be lawful as long as her father gave her hand away in accordance with Islamic prescriptions. News of this *fatwa* was cabled to Soerkati's sayyid employers in Batavia, who greeted him rather coolly upon his return. Soon afterward, in 1914, he left Djamiat Cheir.[7]

Soerkati's *fatwa* created a furor among sayyid circles that brought to light a strong concern among them for the preservation of their hereditary social standing; enough sayyid members of Djamiat Cheir were disconcerted that it led to the departure of their "highly valued head teacher."[8] At the turn of the century, Djamiat Cheir shared with the Chinese the desire for *kemajuan* (progress) and established a pioneering modern organization that included among its members Arabs, native elites, and, at its Surabayan associate Alcheiriah, Indians. Although these organizations, their schools, and the readers of Arab-based publications such as *Al-Bashir*, *Tjermin Islam*, *Oeotoesan Hindia*, and *Oetoesan Islam* belonged to milieus that were united under the banner of kemajuan, it would appear that they shared an unquestioned presumption of sayyid leadership. Kafa'ah had become tacitly upheld, and respect for sayyid had become tradition.[9]

The social hierarchy within Arab communities was affirmed by the hierarchical structure of colonial society. By the end of the 19th century, urban centers in Java were far more racialized than would have been the case 100 years or so earlier. The Dutch crown had taken over control of the island as well as other territories from the Dutch East India Company in 1800 and gradually established a modern imperial state. In the eyes of this state — the Netherlands Indies — the social composition of the colony consisted of three political and legal strata: Europeans, foreign Orientals (Chinese, Arabs, and others), and natives. Although the claims of the state were not totalizing in power, novel and fairly rigid social divisions based on "race" were well established as the 20th century unfolded.

Soerkati articulated the first serious challenge to sayyid authority in Java that inspired the rise in 1915 of the organization Al-Irsjad, sometimes referred to as Al-Irshad. This chapter explores Arabs' engagement in an Islamic idiom with the broadly defined struggles for justice and equality that characterized the years of *pergerakan*, the years of "movement" in the early 20th century when anticolonial strivings were set in motion.[10]

Hadrami Social Hierarchy Remade in Java

A rather important precedent for Soerkati's call for equality was set in Singapore in 1905, when a sharifah married an Indian Muslim with the consent of her father and created a scandal among sayyid for defying kafa'ah. An Arab subsequently wrote to *al-Manâr* and asked whether such a marriage was lawful in Islam. When the Arab received an affirmative reply, a debate ensued between sayyid and Muhammad Rashid Rida, the renowned editor of this Cairo-based modernist Islamic journal. The Singapore-based scholar Sayyid Umar al-Attas proclaimed the marriage unlawful by claiming descent as the most important criterion of kafa'ah, while Rida, in his rejoinder, argued against descent and in favor of religious compatibility, freedom (from slavery), character, wealth, and parental consent.[11] Singapore was a mainly sayyid colony in which the sayyid's position as politico-religious leaders was firmly entrenched by their wealth, largely in landholdings, and the mutually beneficial relationship established with the British rulers.

Conditions in Java differed considerably. While sayyid were a dominant face of Arabness, there were a variety of Hadrami social classes represented. Importantly, fissures between these classes intensified in Java not only with Soerkati's critique but because of great political changes wrought with the decline of the Ottoman Empire. In July 1916, a cable was sent to the Sarekat Islam (SI, Islamic Association — a key organization of the pergerakan era) in Batavia, bringing news of Sharif Husain's victory over the Ottomans in the Hejaz. The Arab Revolt that began on 5 June 1916, with the promise of support from the British, had concluded with the momentous defeat of the Ottomans.[12] With Mecca and Medina firmly within his grasp, Sharif Husain laid claim to the caliphate on the basis that the institution should be restored to its rightful heirs, the ashraf. Under siege in Java, a strong contingent of sayyid who had formed no previous alliance with the sharif now rallied behind his cause as the claim to the caliphate by fellow ashraf accorded well with their own interests in preserving a position of power in Java.

While sayyid in Java did enjoy better treatment from the Dutch on the whole, and certainly some — such as the scholar Sayyid Oesman — had cultivated very close ties with the government, their economic and political position was not so firmly entrenched as in Singapore. Here, *shaykh* and others even lower in the hierarchy had risen up the colonial social ladder by taking advantage of commercial opportunities unavailable to them in the Hadramaut, and by appointment to the position of headman — frequently with administrative authority over sayyid. Such inversions in the political economic hierarchy shaped an Arab Javanese world that seemed to little resemble their forefathers' distant land of origin.

These inversions did not mean that the temporal and spiritual authority of the sayyid was eliminated in Java. Sayyid still possessed the most significant economic networks up to the end of World War I, and in certain respects there did not appear to be any other Arab social classes in the public life of Java. While this was clearly not actually the case, it does suggest that the kind of self-identification critical to the making of Arabs as a "race" within the racialized colony seemed to have been based on the community's leadership and hence strongly sayyid in character. Altered from the Hadramaut context in a number of significant ways, the sayyid in Java were still the elite, in financial and cultural terms. Being "Arab" meant being sayyid, firmly founded upon a position of leadership in political, economic, and religious terms. Van den Berg believed that elites such as the sayyid were more likely to remain unchanged and more like their kin in the Hadramaut:

> [T]he institutions and norms of the Hadramaut in the Arab colonies of the Netherlands Indies had experienced certain modifications. Naturally, this occurred most strongly in the small settlements of Arabs, and

among the families that did not occupy a high social position in the Hadramaut.[13]

Alongside the prominent participation of sayyid in the early years of the SI, and the major role they played in funding and shaping a key organization that arose in 1918,[14] two rather important ways in which sayyid were entrenched in Java need to be raised.

First, it should be noted that in a way that brings together Dutch power, Arabs, and natives, the figure of Sayyid Oesman influenced the course of life in Java well after his death in 1914. None other than Christiaan Snouck Hurgronje, the subject of Eric Tagliacozzo's chapter, played a role in giving prominence in public life and political security to this sayyid and his work. Sayyid Oesman's *Kitab al-Qawanin as-sjarijjah* [sic.] (Book of the Administration of Islamic Law) was expressly written in Malay in Arabic script in order to fulfill a need he believed was long overdue for a practical handbook on the principal points of Islamic law for native Muslim officials. First published in 1881, it sold out speedily, and in 1894 Sayyid Oesman published a revised and expanded edition.

The significance of this book is twofold: It was widely used by the officials of the *raad agama* (religious council, adjudicating matters concerning family and inheritance in Islamic law) that was instituted by the Dutch throughout Java;[15] and its rulings about Arabs are critical to our understanding of their politico-religious position in the colony. In Chapter 19 of the work, Sayyid Oesman lists a number of characteristics of birth, profession, and other factors by which spouses were ranked in Islamic law. Here, Arabs were ranked higher than non-Arabs, the Quraish tribe in particular were distinguished from other Arabs, and within this group the descendants of Muhammad were a higher class.[16]

Noting that little support was found in legal texts against the marriage of a sharifah with a non-sayyid, Snouck Hurgronje added that Sayyid Oesman nonetheless saw "a marriage of a woman from a sayyid line with a native of Indonesia as an example of unrivalled moral decay."[17] This "inconsistency," he suggested further, was forgivable because Sayyid Oesman did not feel, given his assumption of a "noblesse oblige" of sorts, that he should preach to members of his lineage and give vent to their vexation over the immoral and dishonest practices of many of them in this region. Snouck Hurgronje made the interesting point that when many Hadrami had lived in a land with entirely different social relations, and a sayyid from the Hadramaut allowed his daughter to marry an "ordinary" Arab, Javanese, or Malay, he became an enemy of his foremost co-descendants. Indeed, Sayyid Oesman once issued a vehement denouncement of the *panghulu* (religious head) of Sumenep who did not recognize any special inviolable birthrights of the daughters of sayyid.[18]

Besides the rather significant institutionalization of the special place of sayyid through the widespread use of *Kitab al-Qawanin as-sjarijjah* (sold also by the famous pergerakan press Setija Oesaha), a second manner in which sayyid authority had become entrenched was through such practices as the kissing of hands and feet that had become customary among Arabs and natives in Java.[19] A Javanese wrote to *Oetoesan Islam* regarding the untoward presence at a Surabaya mosque of Chinese whose feet he had planned to kiss when he mistakenly believed them to be sayyid.[20] The practices and beliefs that constituted the veneration of sayyid tradition were described by D. A. Rinkes, then adviser at the *Kantoor voor Inlandsche and Arabische Zaken* (Office of Native and Arab Affairs), as a "usurped custom" (*geusurpeerde adat*) that was not rooted in Islam.[21] Aside from the *fatwa* dismissing kafa'ah, then, predictably Soerkati found all manner of veneration of sayyid indefensible on theological grounds.

Around the time that Soerkati issued the notorious *fatwa*, Syekh Oemar bin Joesoef Manggoesj, the captain of Arabs in Batavia, refused to kiss the hand of a certain Sayyid al-Attas.[22] The dispute that arose inspired a *fatwa* from Sayyid Oesman in which he declared that the kissing of the hand of sayyid was not obligatory. Such departures from the abovementioned noblesse oblige made Sayyid Oesman unpopular among those sayyid who guarded these customs more closely. The latter rested assured, nevertheless, that at a little over 90 years old, he remained firmly opposed to the modernist Muslim thinking of the time.[23] While Sayyid Oesman's *fatwa* was in accordance with Soerkati in this instance, the latter's position on kafa'ah was grounded in Muhammad Rashid Rida's "insistence on the rights of reason in interpreting the Quran and *hadith* [the utterances and deeds of the Prophet]."[24] Soerkati founded Al-Irsjad upon this modernist perspective with the financial backing of Manggoesj as well as other sympathizers following his departure from Djamiat Cheir in 1914.

Al-Irsjad and the Drive for Social Equality

The Djamyat Alislahwalersjat Al Arabia Di Batavia [sic.] (The Arab Reform and Guidance Association in Batavia, commonly abbreviated to Al-

Irsjad) was legally incorporated on 20 August 1915. Its statutes consisted of ten articles. Housekeeping regulations were appended to the statutes in 1919 and both parts published in Arabic alongside a complete Malay and partial Dutch translation.[25] The variations in meaning between the Arabic and Malay renditions of Article 2 — the goals of the organization — are significant enough to warrant detailed consideration. In Arabic, it states that Al-Irsjad was established to collect and maintain funds to defray the costs of a number of projects (the first of the three descriptive sections that follow is pertinent to the present discussion):

> (A) The promotion of Arab customs in accordance with the religion of Islam and the teaching of writing and reading in Arabic to people [*al-ummah*], and the advancement of the Arabic language, Dutch and other necessary languages.[26]

The same section in Malay translation is as follows:

> (A) Carrying out of the customs and traditions of Arab people following the prescriptions of the Islamic religion and the advancement of Arabic, Dutch and other languages.[27]

The Arabic version more strongly advocated the promotion of those aspects of the Arab tradition that fell within the bounds prescribed by Islam, and its meaning can be properly understood only within the context of the social world of Arabs in Java. Following the recent challenges to sayyid authority from Soerkati's *fatwa* and Manggoesj's act of defiance, it can be surmised that the article, in its remaking of "Arab" and "Islam," advocated the exclusion of customs that propagated the veneration of sayyid in Java. In this regard, it should be noted that members of Al-Irsjad did not see this veneration as confined to the Arab community. Article 5 stated the functions and selection of the *bestuur* (executive) and expressly excluded sayyid from it. In a report approving the organization's legal incorporation, Rinkes noted that Article 5 acted as a counterweight to the practically exclusive control of sayyid over pre-existing organizations.[28]

The organization's housekeeping regulations strongly indicate its members' desire for institutionalizing the equal treatment of their fellow members and students. While the impetus for the establishment of the organization was the fight against sayyid privilege, it appears that its members stood for broader concerns. Forty-one members gathered in Batavia in February 1919 for a general meeting in which officials were elected and the statutes of the organization were discussed and approved. Following this, housekeeping regulations in 22 sections were introduced.

The third article of the section in these regulations concerned the intake of students:

> Article 3: At no time is a member of the executive or a head of a school or a teacher permitted to treat one student differently from another, in whatsoever a manner, whether that child resides in the boarding house (in the care of the school[)] or outside, is rich or poor[.] It is incumbent upon them to treat equally all these students in all matters which take place within the school.[29]

The above was carefully worded to ensure that the school organization did not replicate the social hierarchies of either the colonial order or its Arab communities. Given the entrenchment of these hierarchies, this article may well have been to encourage and guide administrators and teachers in the ways of equal treatment and perhaps even protect them in the event that such treatment gave offense to any party. A similar self-consciousness about ensuring equality in a racialized setting informs the final section of the regulations, which govern the conduct and motives of members. The second article of this section is as follows:

> Article 2: It is mandatory upon the executive of the organization and its members to respect the views of their colleagues, in addition to ensuring good behaviour in their deliberations, and implementing fair regulations and equality among themselves, without heed to the person's wealth or poor circumstances, rank or race, age or profession.[30]

Natalie Mobini-Kesheh has shown how Al-Irsjad began "as an informal grouping of like-minded individuals whose immediate aim was to raise funds to support Soerkati's school."[31] She makes an important observation of the financial practices of the organization, revealing how the organization sustained the establishment of schools from 1915 onward. She notes, "Al-Irshad was established as a fund-raising body, and effective management of the association's finances was a constant concern of the central executive [and pithily expressed] in the oft-repeated aphorism *al-mal ruh al-'amal*: money is the spirit of action." Instructively, she adds that the "almost obsessive concern with financial matters reflects al-Irshad's origins as an association of successful Hadrami traders."[32]

Much like earlier endeavors by Arabs, often modeled after Chinese efforts, the establishment of schools underscored Al-Irsjad's establishment and mission. Djamiat Cheir pioneered the earliest waves of schools, beginning in the early 1900s.[33] As we have seen, this organization hired Soerkati, along with other highly qualified Sudanese and Arab teachers, in order to improve the standard of the modernist Islamic education it provided. Soerkati's departure and subsequent establishment of his own school set in motion a radically new phase in which not only a modernist Islamic education but with it notions of social equality were introduced. It was in schools, then, that Al-Irsjad's notions of equality were tested and contested. Schools could reproduce either the unquestioned — tacit — presumption of sayyid authority[34] or, as in the case of Al-Irsjad schools, an entirely new basis for Arab communities in Java. According to Joseph Kostiner, the fundamental premise of the Al-Irsjad's drive for education was to be rid of what was felt to be superstition and spiritual stagnation from the centuries of sayyid domination of education.[35] It was believed that this was the only way in which the class differences, conflict, and economic backwardness of Hadrami society could be overcome.

Al-Irsjad Schools

Generous contributions from numerous wealthy Arabs, including sympathetic sayyid, allowed for the establishment of the first Al-Irsjad school in Batavia.[36] Founded in March 1915, the Madrasah Al-Irsjad Al-Islamiah (Al-Irsjad Islamic School) — "the efforts of part of the Arab community at advancing the education of Muslim children" — offered seven classes in its program, beginning in classes A and B, to teach children of about seven years old classical Arabic, "civics" (*prihal keadaban*), counting with words, and games and pictures for play; B differed only in that the memorization of parts of the Qur'an was introduced.[37] While the basics introduced in the first two years were expanded after class 1, mathematics, behavior, and the five obligations in Islam were introduced. After class 2, theological subjects were taught as well as writing in the roman alphabet; and in the final year, class 5, Malay and Dutch were taught besides the various subjects already noted. The program was designed around a firm grasp of Arabic and a gradual transition from memorization to a strong emphasis on reading and comprehending the Qur'an, *tarikh* (history), and so on. The school provided a hostel in which students were obligated to study Arabic or Dutch in the nighttime in addition to their regularly scheduled lessons, and they prayed five times a day alongside their teachers. Its procedures, codes of conduct, holidays, and so on reflected a strong emphasis on discipline and, as Mobini-Kesheh has noted, the management of financial matters.

In 1917, the Al-Irsjad school in Batavia advertised 150 students, of whom about 80 were native and some 70 Arab. It offered day and boarding school facilities and claimed in the latter instance to provide "good care and teaching through the night and day by teachers knowledgeable in Islamic religion and other secular disciplines."[38] With the enthusiastic support of its benefactors, Al-Irsjad soon overshadowed Djamiat Cheir in its zeal for the establishment of educational facilities throughout the archipelago.[39]

With the Batavia school as their model, numerous other schools were started by the growing numbers of Al-Irsjad branches in the region. Notably, in 1920 Al-Irsjad opened a school in Surabaya, the largest and probably wealthiest Arab community in Java, based on the model of its Batavia school. Al-Irsjad schools taught a varied curriculum that, in the course of time, adopted Muhammad Abduh's stress on instruction in *tauhid* (unity of God), *fiqh* (jurisprudence), and *tarikh*.[40] As cooperation between Al-Irsjad and such organizations as the modernist Muslim Moehammadijah increased, more native students were admitted into these schools.

The superior training in Arabic language, literature, and Islamic subjects at Al-Irsjad schools meant that it was the logical course for their graduates to continue their education in Cairo or at another center of scholarship in the Arabic-speaking world. Mobini-Kesheh notes an important contradiction built into the high-quality Arabic-language education of these schools: That "al-Irshad education fed ultimately into an overseas education system, rather than one in the Indies, suggests a further means by which al-Irshad schools inculcated a sense of separateness from the indigenous population."[41]

Al-Irsjad in the Overall Drive for Education

Besides Al-Irsjad, other organizations emerged with a modern educational mission. Often they named themselves *madrasa* to distinguish themselves from *pesantren* (traditional Islamic schools) as well as European-style institutions. They were set up often in the interest of Muslims as a whole, whatever their class background. For example, in 1916 such a school was established in Pekalongan, the town on the north coast of Java famed for its Arab batik traders. The school was said to have been set up by Djama'ah Samail Hoeda (Association of Supreme Guidance) in an advertisement that appeared in 1918 in the pages of the Surabaya-based and Arab-run publication *Oetoesan Islam*.[42] Headed by Syekh Ali Soengkar, this school, like other modernist Islamic institutions in its mold, claimed to teach knowledge that brought benefits in this world and the next. The Qur'an, Arabic language, jurisprudence, mathematics, and behavior formed the subjects of the first year; and subsequently, in a five-year course of study, Malay and Dutch were introduced in addition to theology.[43] The school placed an advertisement in the publication *Sinar Islam* indicating that it had chosen to lighten the burden of payment so that "everyone could enroll their children."[44]

Although eclipsed by Al-Irsjad, Djamiat Cheir continued in its mission as the pioneer Arab educational organization. Sayyid Moehamad bin Hashim, headmaster of the school and an editor of the Indies publication *Pertimbangan*, wrote a description in 1917 of the educational efforts of Djamiat Cheir. He provided a weekly schedule of classes for each level of its program. Organized soundly around an Islamic education, its foundation year in a five-year course was heavily focused on the Arabic language, *fiqh*, reading the Qur'an, mathematics, and in some measure *tajwid* (the art of Koran recitation) and *Elmoe Perangi* (martial arts);[45] the second year was not much different, with grammar as the only addition. In the third to fifth years, besides a number of other subjects, Malay in the roman alphabet was taught, and *tauhid* was introduced.[46] An education here was clearly founded upon first the mastery of the Arabic language, then the gradual introduction to theology.

Education was hotly contested between the various organizations, and the lines of dispute were not necessarily shaped or dominated by sayyid-Irsjadi differences only. The Al-Attas School is a good example. The school was funded by the iconoclast Sayyid Abdoellah Aloewi Alatas, who had been part of the group of Batavian Arabs to whom Christiaan Snouck Hurgronje had rightly attributed pan-Islamic sympathies and whose children studied in Ottoman and European schools.[47] He established the Al-Attas School in 1914 following European models and under the directorship of M. O. Hachemi, who was trained in the Zaituna Mosque in Tunis and recruited by Djamiat Cheir to teach in its school.[48] Hachemi arrived in Java initially with the batch of teachers hired by Djamiat Cheir in 1911–12. The Al-Attas School was apparently much opposed by other sayyid. In its third year, the curriculum of this school included 12 subjects ranging from grammar to chemistry, and by contrast with the modernist Islamic curricula of Djamiat Cheir or Al-Irsjad, it was not organized around religion, which constituted only one of its dozen subjects.[49] Small in comparison to Djamiat Cheir schools, the Al-Attas School had 75 students and eight teachers.

It appears that sayyid opponents of Alatas complained about the school to the Dutch authorities, and in defense of his employer, Hachemi wrote an open letter to the Turkish consul general in which he stated that

Alatas did not belong to the "Sayid Party."[50] Hachemi further stated that Alatas's support for education was all the more commendable because Arabs in Java, in general, were eager to propose establishing schools but unwilling to actually fund them. In another letter, Hachemi implied that the Al-Irsjad school, unlike his own, was not based on a sound "pedagogical" foundation.[51] He wrote to challenge a zincograph in favor of Al-Irsjad that had been distributed to some 17 newspapers in Java and Sumatra. In it, the writer of the circular presents the Al-Irsjad school as an institution based on a new system (*atoeran baroe*) set up by *kaum muda bangsa Arab* (the new generation of Arabs). He further states that in the past "we" could only send our children to Mecca and Egypt and always hoped for a school nearby. He indicated that the Al-Irsjad school had realized that hope.

Hachemi's published opinions on the proposal by the government for the establishment of a *Hollandsch-Arabische School* (Dutch Arab School, henceforth HAS) offers an insight into this man and perhaps also his benefactor Alatas. More than once, Hachemi expressed dismay that Arabs in general did not seem particularly driven toward expanding education, and that the government's proposal to set up an HAS in January 1916 was rejected by Batavian Arabs because neither religion nor Arabic was taught; the only languages offered were Dutch and Malay. He further stated the following:

> Truly the knowledge that is commanded upon to us by religion is not confined to the Arabic language and the learning of *ibadat* (devotion) only ... [Having rejected the proposal, Arab] children are left in a state of ignorance.[52]

There were signs at this time that more people than Hachemi desired better educational options.

Soerkati himself was supportive of the wider efforts to expand and improve education in the colony. As director of the Al-Irsjad school, he donated five guilders toward the establishment of a madrasa in Bandung under the guidance of A. H. Wignjadisastra, president of the SI branch there.[53] His contribution was the largest of a published list of names and their donations. In a letter from Soerkati that accompanied the above list, he stated his firm support for the establishment of Islamic schools and promised to send a guilder a month in addition. He said that he would pray for the school's progress and hoped that it would "benefit us Bumiputra Muslims and others in order to head toward the path of honor and tranquility."

Further Grounding the Notion of Equality during the Pergerakan

Besides schools, Al-Irsjad established other institutions to substantiate its drive for equality. Until the organization's efflorescence in the late 1910s, newspapers, publications, and printing presses in the Arab community were dominated by sayyid. While financial resources were available, printers and newspapers were in short supply for the Irsjadis, so they were at the mercy of sayyid-owned institutions.[54] Malay and Arabic-language publications of the Arab community in the 1910s assumed new importance when journalism developed in earnest in the pergerakan years. Before this time, the writings and publications were primarily religious works written and published by Sayyid Oesman and a few others such as Sayyid Ali Alhabsji, who had a considerable impact on local life and maintained intellectual kinship with those in the Hadramaut and Mecca.

By 1920, Al-Irsjad was publishing its very own Arabic-language periodical in Surabaya, titled *Al-Irshad*.[55] The newspaper was founded by Al-Maari in December 1919. Seven Arabic newspapers were established before 1924. However, publications were now geared toward principally Arab — if not Islamic — communities, with Arabs seen as the spiritual, intellectual, and financial leaders. Although Irsjadis and sayyid dominated in their respective camps, there was nevertheless quite a variety of opinion and publishers in circulation.

Soerkati and Al-Irsjad clearly believed that effecting change in the world meant dedication to *dunia perusahaan* (the world of industry). From the early 1900s, they had seen the fruits of commercial success and voiced it in their calls to the public. Material advancement had brought about many changes in the lives of their communities and had put them in positions of some power in colonial society *vis-à-vis* Islam, trading, and landownership. One can suggest that from after the 1910s the growth of Islamic modernism was linked as much with the new aspirations of the trading culture as to a religious transformation. As we have seen, Mobini-Kesheh attributes the organization's concern with financial accounting and well-being to its association, from the beginning, with successful traders. Arguably, the article "Inheritance and Nobility" in *Azzachiratoel Al-Islamijah* makes a powerful argument for the kind of change that Al-Irsjad stood for. Underlying Al-Irsjad's struggles over kafa'ah was a completely different material and economic worldview.[56]

It should be noted that the position of Arabs *vis-à-vis* the native world was so disparate materially and culturally that the call for an end to politico-legal separations did not necessarily mean the end of "racial" divisions. Al-Irsjad's politics and mission in the overall context of educational movements was nevertheless creating an example for, as well as being influenced and driven by, the *tijdgeest* (zeitgeist) of the pergerakan. For instance, in 1915 the pergerakan Islamic leader Agus Salim was the SI liaison to Al-Irsjad and other Muslim organizations.[57] Soerkati's publications and their radical interpretations found growing followers within and beyond Arab communities. A new ideology, Islamic modernism, began to take root. Al-Irsjad reconfigured the whole relationship with natives with a democratic interpretation of Islamic ideology that related well to the visions of pergerakan leaders.

Conclusion

An observation critical of the hierarchical social structure of Arabs in the Malay-Indonesian Archipelago was made by a writer from this region as early as the beginning of the 19th century. The Malay-Arab writer Abdullah al-Misri lived sometime from the late 18th century until the early 19th. He typically quoted from the Qur'an in his work, translating excerpts into Malay and expanding on them as he saw fit. In one of his writings, probably dated early in the 19th century, he quotes from the Qur'an an admonition against human beings exalting themselves over others. The following, however, is what appears in the Malay translation:

> [Y]ou did not want to obey My words but say that so-and-so who is the child of so-and-so is of a more noble people than the other, and that *Ba'isi* is more noble than *Bahidir* and *Baswih* is more noble than *Bagarib* and *Bahafani* is more noble than *Bahayazi* and *Bafaqih* is more noble than *Jufri* and *Jamal ala-Lail* is more noble than *Jamal an-Nahar* and *Abud* is less than *'Aidid* and *Al-Habsi* is more noble than the people of *al-Attas* and *al-Aidarus* is more noble than *as-Saqqaf* and so forth.[58]

By introducing recognizable clan names of the Hadramaut such as Al-Attas, Al-Aidarus, and others, the author lightly mocks the competing claims to superior lineage among Arabs in the archipelago.

Al-Irsjad brought to the surface and challenged inequalities among Arabs in Java, which Al-Misri observed some 100 years earlier and which developed over the course of the millennium. The organization found intellectual leadership in Soerkati, received funding from a variety of wealthy benefactors including sayyid, and was part of an Islamic debate that can be located in Java from at least as early as the 1880s, when Sayyid Oesman published his views on kafa'ah in which he supported sayyid privileges.[59] While it is easy to agree with Bujra that the internecine conflict that emerged in the 20th century was a struggle for power between a traditional elite and a movement for social change, it is harder to accept his dismissal of the controversies that arose regarding kafa'ah when he suggests that these "were merely symbols."[60] I would argue that it was these controversies that were at the crux of the struggle. More than their symbolic value, they led to an articulation and critique of the entrenched social hierarchy of Arabs in colonial Java; this had much wider ramifications as the debates generated dialogs between residents of colonial urban centers in Southeast Asia and Cairo, thus having an impact not only in Java but in the Hadramaut itself.[61]

From the manner in which the Dutch addressed their subjects and the hierarchical political culture of the colony, it is clear that notions of hierarchy, privilege, and rank pervaded all aspects of Indies society. Arabs in Java provide special insights in this context. This chapter has shown that sayyid power within the Arab hierarchy in Java was not created or sustained by careful design so much as an unquestioned tradition that had developed over time — a "usurped tradition," in Rinkes's words. This tradition was sustained through the institutionalization of ideas about sayyid privilege by influential and often Dutch-appointed scholars such as Sayyid Oesman. Within the context of the hierarchical social world of the colony, Al-Irsjad's critique raised a salient challenge to sayyid authority and found kinship with the people, language, and goals of the pergerakan era, and substantiation through its successful schools. From 1915 onward, Al-Irsjad shook the tacit and unquestioned dominance of the sayyid and brought a new sense of the world for young Arabs. The issues raised by Irsjadis reflected a striving for democracy and equal rights in the eyes of pergerakan leaders. Therefore, the critique of sayyid authority was not only, as Rinkes believed, a democratic struggle against an antiquated Hadrami social system, but also an attack on rank and privilege in colonial society.

Notes

* I would like to thank the editor and members of the workshop that resulted in this volume for their valuable comments and criticisms. Items in the notes

marked by a number preceded by "H" indicate material that may be found in the archives of the Koninlijk Institute voor Taal-, Land-, en Volkenkunde (Royal Institute of Anthropology and Linguistics), in Leiden, Netherlands.

1. "Sajid Palsoe," *Oetoesan Hindia* 2, 152 (11 August 1914).
2. Engseng Ho, "Before Parochialization: Diasporic Arabs Cast in Creole Waters," in Huub de Jonge and N. Kaptein, eds., *Transcending Borders: Arabs, Politics, Trade and Islam in Southeast Asia* (Leiden: KITLV, 2002), 185–201; "The Precious Gift of Genealogy," paper contributed to the research workshop "Creolization in the Indian Ocean," Kevorkian Center, New York University, New York, 2000, 1–21 (published as "Le don précieux de la généalogie," in P. Bonte, É. Conte, and P. Dresch, eds., *Émirs et presidents. Figures de la parenté et du politique dans le monde arabe*, Paris: CNRS editions, 2001, 79–110).
3. Sumit K. Mandal, "Natural Leaders of Native Muslims: Arab Ethnicity and Politics in Java under Dutch Rule," in U. Freitag and W. G. Clarence-Smith, eds., *Hadrami Traders, Scholars and Statesmen in the Indian Ocean, 1750s–1960s* (Leiden: Brill, 1997), 185–98.
4. The power of the person, accoutrements, and religiosity of the figure of "the Arab" is illustrated in a short story set in Sumatra about a young man who had failed at first to obtain permission to marry his true love but was embraced without much ado after he disguised himself as an Arab. See Soeman H. s., *Kasih Ta' Terlarai*, Serie no. 872 (Weltevreden: Balai Poestaka, 1929), 25–36.
5. For the *ashraf*, see Albert Hourani, *Arabic Thought in the Liberal Age, 1798–1939*, reissued with a new preface (Cambridge: Cambridge University Press, 1983), 33 (first published in 1962).
6. C. Snouck Hurgronje, *Mohammedanism: Lectures on Its Origin, Its Religious and Political Growth, and Its Present State*, American Lectures on the History of Religions, Series of 1914–1915 (New York: G. P. Putnam's Sons, 1916), 126–8. In a discussion about the authority of the caliphate in Muslim societies, the author notes the example of "petty princes in East India under Dutch sovereignty who decorate themselves with the title Khalif without suspecting that they are thereby guilty of a sort of arrogant blasphemy."
7. Bertram J. O. Schrieke, "De Strijd onder de Arabieren in Pers en Literatuur," *Notulen van de Algemeene en Directievergaderingen van het Bataviaasch Genootschap van Kunsten en Wetenschappen* 58 (1920): 189–240; Deliar Noer, *The Modernist Muslim Movement in Indonesia, 1900–1942* (Singapore and Kuala Lumpur: Oxford University Press, 1973), n. 87, pp. 62, 63.
8. Adviseur voor Inlandsche Zaken [Rinkes] aan den Directeur van Justitie, 5 February 1915, no. 22, Hazeu collection, H1083, no. 10.
9. Sumit K. Mandal, "Forging a Modern Identity in Java in the Early Twentieth Century," in de Jonge and Kaptein, *Transcending Borders*, 164–6.

10. Bertram Schrieke, the Dutch adviser to the *Kantoor voor Inlandsche en Arabische Zaken* (Office of Native and Arab Affairs), located these struggles within the overall "strivings toward emancipation in a sociological and religious sense" in this period, which he collectively termed "Aziatisch Reveil [Asian Revival]." See his "De Strijd onder de Arabieren," p. 189, and *Pergolakan Agama di Sumatra Barat: Sebuah Sumbangan Bibliografi* (Jakarta: Bhratara, 1973), 44–5, 53–5 (translated by Soegardo Poerbakawatja from the original Dutch publication dedicated to Dr. G. A. J. Hazeu on his departure from the Netherlands Indies in *Tijdschrift voor Indische Taal-, Land- en Volkenkunde* 59 [1919–21], 249–325).
11. A. S. Bujra, "Political Conflict and Stratification in Hadramaut," *Middle Eastern Studies* 3, 4 (July 1967): 357–8.
12. *Pertimbangan* 1, 12 (22 July 1916); William Ochsenwald, "Ironic Origins: Arab Nationalism in the Hijaz, 1882–1914," in Rashid Khalidi, Lisa Anderson, Muhammad Muslih, and Reeva Simon, eds., *The Origins of Arab Nationalism* (New York: Columbia University Press, 1991), 189.
13. Bujra, "Political Conflict and Stratification," 357–8.
14. Mandal, "Forging a Modern Identity," 180–1. I refer to the organization Tentara Kandjeng Nabi Mohamad [the Army of his Lordship the Prophet Muhammad].
15. *Encyclopaedie van Nederlansch-Indië*, s.v. "Priesterraden," by L. W. C. van den Berg. As an institutionalized priesthood does not exist in Islam, the term *Priesterraden* (priestly councils) as used by the Dutch in reference to *raad agama* was misleading.
16. C. Snouck Hurgronje, "Sajjid Oethman's Gids voor de Priesterraden," in *Verspreide Geschriften van C. Snouck Hurgronje*, Bibliography and registers compiled by A. J. Wensinck (Bonn and Leipzig: Kurt Schroeder; Leiden: E. J. Brill, 1923–27), vol. 4, pt. 1, 1924, pp. 69–85, 297. (The article was first published in 1894.)
17. Ibid., 299.
18. Ibid., 298. The bulk of a treatise by Sayyid Oesman was dedicated to the *fatwa* denouncing the interpretation of kafa'ah as well as four other so-called legal and procedural mishandlings of the Panghulu of Sumenep. For a description of this work, see C. Snouck Hurgronje, "Vier Geschenken van Sajjid 'Oethman bin Abdoellah bin 'Aqil bin Jahja 'Alawi beschreven," *Notulen van de Algemeene en Directievergaderingen van het Bataviaasch Genootschap van Kunsten en Wetenschappen* 30 (1892), Append. 14, 105–6.
19. For the formative influence of Sayyid Oesman's interpretation of kafa'ah on Islamic legal thinking in the colony, see Schrieke, "De Strijd onder de Arabieren," 192.
20. Mandal, "Forging a Modern Identity," 179.
21. Adviseur voor Inlandsche en Arabische Zaken aan den Directeur van Justitie, 5 February 1915, no. 22, Hazeu collection, H1083, no. 10.

22. Schrieke, "De Strijd onder de Arabieren," 191; Noer, *The Modernist Muslim Movement*, 62.
23. A. Buno Heslinga, "Said Oethman," *Weekblad voor Indië* 10, 47 (8 March 1914): 1124–5.
24. Hourani, *Arabic Thought*, 223.
25. *Qanun Jami'iyat al-Islah wa al-Irshad al-'Arabiyya: Al-Asasi wa al-Dakhili* (*Statuten dari Perkoeompoelan "Djamyat Alislahwalersjat Al Arabia" di Batavia*). Surabaya: Matba'at al-Islamiyya khassa Sulaiman Mara'i (Islam-Drukkerij), H 1337 (1919).
26. Ibid., 12–3. I have used *ummah* in its more general meaning of "people" following the usage in this Arabic text. When referring to Muslims in particular, as in Article 4, the term *al-ummat al-Islamiyya* (Islamic people) was used in the text.
27. Ibid., 5.
28. Adviseur voor Inlandsche en Arabische Zaken aan den Directeur van Justitie, 5 February 1915, no. 22, Hazeu collection, H1083, no. 10.
29. *Qanun Jami'iyat al-Islah*, 13–4.
30. Ibid., 24.
31. Natalie Mobini-Kesheh, *The Hadrami Awakening: Community and Identity in the Netherlands East Indies, 1900–1942* (Ithaca: Cornell University Southeast Asia Program, 1999), 58.
32. Ibid., 59, 60.
33. Mandal, "Forging a Modern Identity," 166–72.
34. Ibid., 166.
35. Joseph Kostiner, "The Impact of the Hadrami Emigrants in the East Indies on Islamic Modernism and Social Change in the Hadramawt during the 20th Century," in R. Israeli and A. H. Johns, eds., *Islam in Asia*, 2 vols., vol. 2: Southeast and East Asia (Jerusalem: Hebrew University Press, 1984), 215.
36. Noer, *The Modernist Muslim Movement*, n. 97, p. 64.
37. *Pertimbangan* 2, 30 (7 February 1917). See also 2, 31 (8 February 1917) for more details on the procedures of the school.
38. *Pertimbangan* 2, 33 (10 February 1917).
39. Noer, *The Modernist Muslim Movement*, 64–6.
40. *Qanun Jami'iyat al-Islah*. See also Noer, *The Modernist Muslim Movement*.
41. Mobini-Kesheh, *The Hadrami Awakening*, 82–3.
42. *Oetoesan Islam* 1, 23 (5 August 1918); "Arab Weerbaar," *Pertimbangan* 1, 65 (5 October 1917); Chantal Vuldy, "La communauté arabe de Pekalongan," *Archipel*, 30 (1985), L'Islam en Indonésie II, 114.
43. *Sinar Islam* 2, 38 (19 September 1918). The other subjects covered in the program were *tajwid*, *nahu*, *tauhid*, geography of the Indies, history, composition, *saraf*, *iman*, and *mantik*.
44. *Sinar Islam* 2, 38 (19 September 1918).

45. I owe my present understanding of the meaning of "Elmoe Perangi" — having long eluded me — to Michael Laffan.
46. *Pertimbangan* 2, 23 (30 January 1917). The other subjects introduced in the third year and after were *saraf*, geography, history, *ilmoe Alam*, *elmoe tabeat*, *elmoe gambar*, and *elmoe salin*.
47. He published a book on accounting. See Said Abdullah bin Aloeie bin Abdullah al Attas [sic], *Alkitaab pada Menjatakan Daftar (Boekoe) den di Namaken Kitaab inie Perkakas Boewat Pendjaga Harta Orang Yang Berniaga* (Batavia: Ogilvie & Co., 1890).
48. Schools carrying the names of their wealthy Sayyid sponsors, such as the al-Sagoff and the al-Junied, had been set up in Singapore earlier.
49. "Soerat terboeka kepada toean Consul-Generaal Turkye," *Pertimbangan* 1, 137 (30 December 1916). The other subjects were arithmetic, geography, history, geometry, hygiene, physiology, logic, astronomy, and physics. See also "Al Atas School [sic]," *Pertimbangan* 1, 28 (22 August 1916).
50. Ibid.
51. *Pertimbangan* 2, 36 (15 February 1917). In a comment that does not seem to relate to the rest of the article, Hachemi also issues a stern warning to Manggoesj to obey the law, as "we" can defend ourselves unlike the "Bedouin from the mountains that are well known to him." Hachemi registers his differences with Manggoesj by targeting the latter's descent.
52. "Hollandsch-Arabische School," *Pertimbangan* 2, 56 (10 March 1917). See also "Alataschool di Ambachtsschool" *Pertimbangan* 2, 52 (6 March 1917).
53. *Pertimbangan* 2, 73 (30 March 1917). Hasan Ali Soerati contributed 140 guilders earlier; see *Pertimbangan* 2, 52 (6 March 1917).
54. Schrieke, "De Strijd onder der Arabieren."
55. See "*Al-Islah wa al-Irshad*," in *Al-Irshad* 1, 27 (23 December 1920).
56. "Kemoeliaän toeroenan dan harta warisan," *Azzachirah Al-Islamijah* [Only its first issue is titled *Azzachiratoel Islamijah*] 1, 2 (1923): 61.
57. Hadji Agoes Salim, *Djedjak Langkah Hadji A. Salim: Pilihan Karangan Utjapan dan Pendapat Beliau dari dulu sampai sekarang* (Jakarta: Tintamas, 1954).
58. Zaini-Lajoubert, *Abdullah bin Muhammad al-Misri*, 154–5. For the dating of the manuscript *Hikayat Mareskalek* II, from which this excerpt is taken, see p. 17. For a discussion of Hadrami clans as well as a listing of their names, see Berg, *Le Hadhramout*, 48–61.
59. Nico Kaptein, "The Conflicts about the Income of an Arab Shrine: The Perkara Luar Batang in Batavia," in de Jonge and Kaptein, *Transcending Borders*, 195.
60. Abdalla S. Bujra, "Political Conflict and Stratification in Hadramaut," *Middle Eastern Studies* 3, 4 (July 1967): 371.
61. Ho, "The Precious Gift of Genealogy."

8

Southeast Asian Debates and Middle Eastern Inspiration: European Dress in Minangkabau at the Beginning of the 20th Century*

NICO J. G. KAPTEIN

Introduction

Dress is an important indicator of identity, revealing many different aspects of culture. Gender, age, social position, ethnic background, religion, and regional background may be made apparent through choice of dress. Present-day discussions about Muslim dress throughout the world are dominated by debates over the way women dress, in particular the wearing of the headscarf; but surprisingly, discussions about Muslim dress in the Netherlands East Indies at the beginning of the 20th century deal entirely with male dress. Interestingly, in sharp contrast to the situation in the Muslim Arab world, where — according to the authoritative expert on Islamic dress Y. Stillman — from the end of the 19th century the matter of the veil formed one of the most burning issues, in the Netherlands East Indies the head covering of women seems to have become a topic of debate only in the 1930s.[1] These debates over male dress focus on the question of whether or not a Muslim man is allowed to wear particular items of Western dress, such as trousers, a necktie, a hat, and a jacket.

The core of this paper will be a discussion of some legal opinions of Muslim scholars, called *fatwa*s, as well as other documents in Malay and Arabic that, as far as I know, have never been used previously in dealing with the issue of dress in the Netherlands East Indies. I will endeavor to show in detail how Middle Eastern ideas concerning European dress were transmitted to and received in Southeast Asia, and comment on the nature of these contacts. Before discussing these documents, I will give some background information about the views of colonial administration on dress.

The Colonial Administration and Dress

The introduction of Western dress in the Netherlands East Indies is related to the arrival of Western merchants at the beginning of the 16th century, which eventually led to the colonial domination of the Malay-Indonesian Archipelago by the Dutch. It is a well-known fact that in the Netherlands East Indies the colonial administration classified the population into three main ethnic groups on the basis of race: the Europeans; the so-called Foreign Orientals (the Arabs and the Chinese); and the indigenous population, which formed the overwhelming majority of inhabitants. Each of these three groups was subject to its own legal system, all of which were simultaneously in force. Over time, the colonial administration also developed a set of rules with regard to dress, which boiled down to the principle that each different ethnic group was obliged to wear its own distinctive type of dress. The underlying reason for this seems to have been a concern for public order: it was thought that if irregularities were to occur, it would be easier to trace the troublemakers if they were easily recognizable by their outward appearance.[2] Another reason had to do with power. In government circles, it was thought that the wearing of European dress by indigenous men was a challenge to the existing social and political hierarchy in which the Dutch colonizer occupied the apex.[3] Around the year 1900, the government stopped enforcing these dress prescriptions,[4] but as late as 1905, in Palembang, a number of Arabs had to pay a fine because they failed to adhere to their own dress codes.[5]

An interesting description of the dress conventions of the three different ethnic groups in the Netherlands East Indies is found in a small brochure, dating from 1904, written by Sayyid 'Uthmân of Batavia. This person, whose full name is Sayyid 'Uthmân ibn 'Abd Allâh ibn 'Aqîl ibn Yaḥyâ al-'Alawî, lived from 1822 until 1914 and was one of the most productive Islamic scholars in the Netherlands East Indies in his own day. As his title "sayyid" shows, he was a descendant of the Prophet Muḥammad and, as such, part of the small but influential group of persons of Arab descent who played an important role in the Netherlands East Indies. In Dutch colonial historiography, Sayyid 'Uthman is best known in his capacity as informant to the Dutch colonial administration on Muslim affairs, or as "honorary adviser for Arab affairs" (Honorair Adviseur voor Arabische zaken), in which function he cooperated closely with the well-known architect of the Dutch Islam policy, Christiaan Snouck Hurgronje (1857–1936)[6] In 1904 Sayyid 'Uthmân published a small lithographed brochure that reads on the title page: "Ini Buku Kecil Buat Menyatakan Pertegahan Hukum Adat Negeri Yang Bersamaan Pada Pertegahan Hukum Agama Islam Atas Orang Yang Menukar Pakaian Bangsanya Dengan Memakai Pakaian Lain Bangsanya Adanya" (This little book [was written] to explain the restrictions in customary law and Islamic law on those who change the dress of their own ethnic group for that of another). This booklet includes a nice passage that illustrates the different types of dress worn by various ethnic groups in the Netherlands East Indies. In the sixth section of the brochure, it reads as follows:

> It is well known that the dress of Europeans consists of a jacket for the body and a hat or a black cap. Arab dress consists of a *jubbah* (long, open gown) or a vest together with a shirt for the body, and for the head a turban, unless one remains inside the house, in which case only a small white cap is worn. Dress for the Malays or the Javanese is a shirt, called *kebaya*, to cover the body, and the head cloth (*setangan*) for the head.[7]

I will not go into the details of this little text or the different items of dress that Sayyid 'Uthmân mentions. However, it is clear that Sayyid 'Uthmân took the view that each of the three ethnic groups — the Europeans, the Arabs, and the indigenous people — had their specific type of dress and should stick to it. In short, he was completely in agreement with the colonial policy on dress.

The different types of dress used by various ethnic groups in the Netherlands East Indies were, of course, not immutable, but always open to changes emanating from outside their own cultural sphere. Examples of this can be found very early in Indonesian history, when the European colonial expansion into Southeast Asia had not yet started. For instance — and this is a relevant example in the framework of the present volume — after Muslims from the Malay-Indonesian Archipelago had completed the pilgrimage to Mecca (Hajj) and returned to their home country, they adopted particular items of dress from the Arab urban middle class in Mecca in order to distinguish themselves from their countrymen who had not been to Mecca. This always included the turban, and sometimes both the turban and the long gown; and consequently this had become the customary dress for persons who had performed the pilgrimage, as well as for the Muslim officials, known as *panghulu*, who were in charge of the management of Islam, basically related to the administration of Islamic family law and matters related to the mosques. In other words, these once-foreign items of dress had become part and parcel of indigenous customs, or *adat*.[8]

From the end of the 19th century, Snouck Hurgronje discussed the issue of dress in a number of official pieces of advice to the colonial administration.[9] In the first place, he took issue with "the government's fear of turbans," as part of his struggle to dispel the Hajji-phobia of the government. Prior to Snouck Hurgronje's appearance on the stage as the adviser to the government on native affairs in 1889, the general opinion on pilgrims returning from Mecca was that they were potential rebels and, as such, a threat to law and order in the country. For this reason, a set of rules and regulations pertaining to the pilgrimage had been developed to make it difficult for Dutch East Indian Muslims to perform it. Snouck Hurgronje was well aware of the anticolonial ideas that could be transmitted through the returning pilgrims, but he thought that as a result of these rules and regulations the government had made the Hajj more important than it really was. He considered the pilgrimage to be first and foremost a religious ceremony, which believers should be able to undertake unencumbered by too many government restrictions. In his recommendations against the hindering of the pilgrimage, Snouck Hurgronje also denied that the wearing of Hajj dress posed a problem. On the contrary, he considered the very thing that would provoke protests from the population was the prohibition of this dress. In order to illustrate this point, Snouck Hurgronje developed a — in my view — rather artificial argument. According to him, the Arab turban is wrapped around a little cap, called a *kupiyya*, which is worn on a shaven head. If they were forbidden from wearing this turban, the indigenous population would be forced to wear a local headcloth wrapped around the hair. For this reason, the prohibition on the Arab turban would imply a prohibition of the shaving of the head. Because the Shari'a recommends regular shaving of the head, the prohibition on the turban could easily be understood as a prohibition on shaving the head and hence as an anti-Islamic measure, which might lead to fanaticism. In short, Snouck Hurgronje considered the prohibition on Hajj dress to be not only useless, but also dangerous and provocative.[10]

Besides his recommendations against the prohibition on Hajj dress, Snouck Hurgronje also took a stand against the prohibition on the wearing of European clothes by indigenous civil servants. Contrary to the view upheld by many Dutch people, Snouck Hurgronje thought that this did not affect the hierarchical relationship between Dutch civil servants and their indigenous staff members. Moreover, he was convinced that this prohibition was doomed to fail because he had observed a general rapprochement toward Western dress as a result of the intensified interaction between the different ethnic groups in the archipelago. He stated: "a gradual transition has already begun, and in the long run will definitely come about." Here we see that Snouck Hurgronje predicted the globalization of Western dress. A final point he made was that as a result of this prohibition the government would play into the hands of fanatical Muslims who also prohibited the wearing of Western dress.[11] This latter point implies a difference of opinion concerning the acceptance of European dress that existed within the Muslim community itself, and this will be studied in the following sections.

Muslim Debates over European Dress

The first debate I would like to deal with is revealed in a *fatwa* from an important collection titled *Muhimmât al-nafâ'is fî bayân as'ilat al-ḥâdîth*, or "The Precious Gems Treating the Explanation of Questions about Current Topics." This work consists of a large number of Arabic *fatwa*s and Malay renderings, which were issued by the most prestigious Meccan *muftî*s in the final quarter of the 19th century; the bulk of these *fatwa*s was issued by the most important *muftî* of the Holy City, Aḥmad Dahlân (d. 1886), who belonged to the Shafi'ite school of law (*madhhab*), the prevailing school in the Netherlands East Indies. For a proper understanding of the importance of this collection, it should be borne in mind that at the end of the 19th century the intellectual center of Indonesian Islam was located in Mecca — specifically, in the group of Indonesian students and their teachers who resided there permanently, the so-called Jawah colony. In the words of Snouck Hurgronje, Mecca formed "the heart of the religious life of the East-Indian Archipelago."[12] This centrality of Mecca at times also played a role in the process of *fatwa* making, for besides the many *fatwa*s that were given in the archipelago until the end of the 19th century, many issues that could not be resolved at the local or regional level were eventually brought to the great *muftî* of the Shafi'ite school in Mecca, who was regarded as the highest religious authority by the *fatwa*-petitioners (*mustaftîn*) in question.[13] A number of these *fatwa*s have been preserved in the *Muhimmât al-nafâ'is*. What makes them so important to the purposes of this discussion is that they were given at the request of Muslims from the Malay-Indonesian Archipelago.[14]

One of the *fatwa*s from the *Muhimmât al-nafâ'is*, addressed to Aḥmad Dahlân, tackles the question of which item of dress of the unbelievers (*kâfir*) is forbidden to a Muslim. Unfortunately, the answer to this question is rather short and sparing in details. It is just mentioned in general terms that a Muslim should avoid any article of dress that is typical of unbelievers. Fortunately, in the Malay rendering of the question it is clarified that *sirwal* and *baju* are meant.[15] Looking first at *sirwal*, it is evident that in this *fatwa* it refers to tight European trousers. From ethnographical observations of this period, we know that — at least in Aceh — immensely wide trousers with a large piece of material in the crotch were regarded as typically Muslim, while tight trousers were thought typical of unbelievers.[16] Turning to the *baju*, we may infer from the fact it is mentioned that, in one way or another, it presented a problem, but it is not directly clear why. Perhaps the European style of jacket is meant.[17] Despite its paucity in detail, the Meccan *fatwa* shows at least that there were Muslim discussions about European dress, and indeed an aversion to this type of dress among Muslims from the Malay-Indonesian Archipelago, in the last quarter of the 19th century.[18]

From the beginning of the 20th century, the debates about European dress grew more heated. These debates have to be understood as part of the changes that began to take place in the world of Islam from the end of the 19th century. This period of time witnessed an awakening in the Muslim world, which was signaled in the religious domain by the Salafiyya movement. The most outstanding characteristic of this movement was its affirmation of early Islam, as had been practised by the pious ancestors (*al-salaf al-ṣâliḥ*), as true and original. In dealing with the challenges of modern life, this original Islam should be taken as the yardstick. In the study of Islamic law, including the issuing of *fatwa*s, this basic idea implied that only the Qur'an and the Prophetic tradition literature (Hadith) could be regarded as valid sources, while the entire body of legal manuals that had been developed later in the various schools of law should not occupy the central place as in traditional Islam, and according to some it should even be rejected completely. In the field of Muslim life and ritual, this new basic principle meant that many beliefs and practices that had not been observed in early Islam (which could be learned from the Qur'an and the Hadith) should be eradicated. The foremost scholars who gave shape to this new way of thinking were Muḥammad ʿAbduh (1849–1905) and his pupil Rashîd Riḍâ (1865–1935), both working in Egypt. Besides his many other publications, the latter accrued much of his fame as editor of the famous reformist journal *al-Manâr*. This journal appeared in Cairo between 1898 and 1940 (E.I.(2), vi, 360–61) and was one of the most prominent voices of the reformist movement in the whole Muslim world, including the Netherlands East Indies.[19]

In the first decade of the 20th century, these reformist ideas began to spread into the Malay-Indonesian Archipelago, making their initial appearance in Singapore and slightly later in other parts of the region. In the Netherlands East Indies, the first region where Indonesian Muslims came into contact with these new modernist ideas was Minangkabau, in West Sumatra. Shortly after the introduction of these new ideas into the area, two camps emerged in West Sumatra. The first rejected the modernist ideas and continued to embrace Islam as it had developed during the course of its history. These traditionalist Muslims came to be known in Malay as the Kaum Tua, the "Old Generation." Among the most vocal spokesmen of this group was Chatib Ali (1861–1936).[20] In their legal thinking, the Kaum Tua maintained the traditional process of legal reasoning, that is, *taqlîd*, the uncritical following of the authoritative legal manuals of the Shafiʿite school of Law (*madhhab*). Moreover, they had a positive attitude toward all kinds of matters that had not been in existence in early Islam but had developed later within the Muslim tradition, such as saint worship. Furthermore, on the whole they adopted a more flexible position on a variety of local customs. For their intellectual guidance they continued to look up to the great *ʿulamâʾ* of Mecca, as Muslims in the Netherlands East Indies had done in the past.

On the other hand, there were the Muslims in West Sumatra who had come under the influence of these new ideas; they were called the Kaum Muda, the "Young Generation" in Malay, and they started to orient themselves toward Cairo. Among the earliest persons representing the Kaum Muda were Haji Abdul Karim Amrullah alias Haji Rasoel (1879–1945) and Haji Abdullah Ahmad (1878–1933).[21] In their legal thinking they followed the principle of *ijtihâd*, that is, independent reasoning on the basis of the Qur'an and the Hadith only. In general, they were less tolerant of local customs and later innovations in Islamic thought and ritual (*bidʿa*). In contrast to the Kaum Tua, on the whole the Kaum Muda also had a much more positive attitude toward modernity, or *kemajuan*, "progress," as this was made apparent in all kinds of manifestations of Western culture in education, customs, administration, and technology.

These two camps were engaged in — often very polemical and intertwined — controversies about the future of Minangkabau society in the fields of politics, education, the preservation of traditional culture (*adat*), and Islam. Both camps had their own channels of publication, for instance, the famous Kaum Muda journal *al-Munir*, which was published in Malay by Haji Abdullah Ahmad in Padang, the principal city in Minangkabau, from 1911 to 1915.[22]

In the domain of Islam, there were many controversies between the Kaum Muda and the Kaum Tua in Minangkabau. In the biography of one of these reformers, Haji Abdul Karim Amrullah, which was written by his son, the well-known Muslim scholar and man of letters Hamka (1908–81), it is recorded that at least 16 of these controversies were fought out among themselves. Among these were the debate on the *berdiri mawlid*, or the "standing up" (Arabic *qiyâm*; Malay *berdiri*) during the ceremonial reading of a pious biography of the Prophet Muhammad, called *mawlid*, at the moment his birth is recited;[23] the issue of whether or not the intention (*niyya*; in Malay also called *usalli*) preceding the ritual prayer should be uttered aloud or inwardly;[24] the question of the visiting of graves (*menziarahi*); the custom of holding traditional ceremonial meals (*kenduri*) when a death occurs, as well as other controversies.[25]

Debates about Dress in Minangkabau

In the framework of the present paper, it is noteworthy that Hamka mentioned that the issue of European dress was heavily debated in Padang in particular. He adduced the following reason for this interest. In accordance with the racial segregation imposed in the Netherlands East Indies, in trains there was a difference in fares between the tickets for indigenous people and Europeans, the latter being cheaper than the former. At that time, the customary dress for indigenous men was a short s*arung* reaching down to the knees, wrapped over trousers. This *samping* indicated that the wearer was Muslim. Now, in order to get the cheaper tickets, certain indigenous persons were ready to discard their *samping*. Wearing just trousers, they looked similar to the Europeans. As Hamka claims, this triggered the debate about dress and eventually prompted people to ask for a *fatwa* from the Padang-based reformist journal *al-Munir*.[26]

I have this *fatwa* from the journal *al-Munir*, but before I deal with this, I will go into the objections to Western dress raised by the Kaum Tua. Compared to the views of the Kaum Muda, the Kaum Tua position on various issues was laid down in writing rather late, because these traditionalists, who had always held the monopoly in Islamic discourse, only felt obliged to publish their thinking in reaction to the publications of the Kaum Muda side.[27] Another reason why these Kaum Tua ideas appeared in print rather late might have been that printing as a feature of modernity had only recently become available, and that the Kaum Tua had underestimated the power of the printed word as a challenge to the centuries-old oral tradition. Despite their tardy arrival on the scene, these rather late publications reflect the Kaum Tua discourse from the very first debates that they had with the modernists, and so I shall consider them here before I discuss the earlier published Kaum Muda documents.

In one particular publication prepared by the Kaum Tua spokesman Chatib Ali, there is a clarification of the traditionalist position on a number of topics. This book is in Malay and was intended for those "brethren" who were not able to read the works of the great Arab ʿulamāʾ for themselves. After the introduction, the book starts with a poem that clarifies the Kaum Tua position and attacks the Kaum Muda. This poem, which is written according to the rhyming scheme of the classical Malay *syaʿir* (aa/aa; bb/bb), includes the following line:

> They (sc. the Kaum Muda, N.K.) allow the wearing of a tie // in order to look the same as the Christians; but do not want to go to church // nor venerate the idols together with the Jews.[28]

In another booklet also published as a reaction to the Kaum Muda publications, Chatib Ali tackles the issue of European dress. It appeared in Padang in 1920 and is titled *Al-khatima al-bahija*, "The Beautiful Conclusion" (sc. of the debate between Kaum Muda and Kaum Tua in Padang on 15 July 1919).[29] This text contains five *fatwa*s that were given in Arabic by Muhammad Mukhtar at the request of Chatib Ali.[30] This scholar was originally from the Indies but since 1913 had taught in Mecca, where he was hailed as one of the most competent of the Jawah scholars.[31] The original Arabic text is followed by a Malay rendering (in Arabic script) by Chatib Ali, who states that he translated it so that all people would be able to see the error of the ways of his greatest modernist opponent, Haji Abdullah Ahmad. Besides providing this translation, Chatib Ali gives his own views on the five subjects dealt with by Muhammad Muchtar, plus a number of other topics. One of these topics is European dress. The issue is dealt with under the heading "Questions about the Hat (Malay *capiu*, cf. French *chapeau*) and the Necktie (Malay *dasi*, cf. Dutch [*strop*]*das*)" and is a small *fatwa*, possibly also of Meccan origin. This *fatwa* states that both these items of dress are regarded as forbidden (*haram*) to Muslims because there is a statement of the Arabs with this purport. The background to this opinion is a *hadîth* saying: "Whosoever wears clothes which are characteristic of another religion, such a person is considered equal to them."[32] These rather weak contributions to the discussions show that the Kaum Tua completely rejected the wearing of Western clothes. Other viewpoints were adduced, which we can catch some glimpses of in the debate that took place in the Kaum Muda camp, to which I shall now turn.

The first document I would like to discuss with regard to the Kaum Muda position on the issue of dress originates from Egypt and is in Arabic. In the 1911 issue of the Egyptian journal *al-Manâr*, "Hâjj Abdullâh Ahmad from Padang, Jâwah" poses to Rashîd Ridâ ("My Lord, the Noble and Most Erudite Professor, Sir Muhammad Rashîd Ridâ") six questions, two of which deal with dress.[33] The first tackles the issue of whether Muslim law enforces the wearing of particular items of dress, and whether a person who does not wear these should be regarded as someone beyond the bounds of Islam, "as many *'ulamâ'* in our country have declared in a *fatwa*." These scholars did not specify which items of dress they regarded as compulsory nor what was forbidden, and they based their opinion on the Prophetic tradition "Whosoever imitates a group, belongs to it." Is it right to adduce this saying of the Prophet as proof of the correctness of this opinion, and, moreover, what does this tradition mean?

The second question posed by Haji Abdullah Ahmad is more specific and deals with the issue of whether someone's faith is affected simply by wearing a hat (*burnayta*), which was also known as "the European headgear" (*qalansût al-ifranjî*), or a necktie (*zunnâr*). The *'ulamâ'* of his country hold this opinion, because they regard the hat and the necktie as items of dress that are characteristic of Europeans.

In his answer Rashîd Ridâ combines these two questions, because they deal with the same issue. This answer begins as follows:

> Islam does not oblige people to wear a particular style of dress, apart from the ritually prescribed dress (*ihrâm*) for the *hajj* and *'umra*, the Greater and Minor Pilgrimage [...] No one among the forefathers and the later scholars (*salaf* and *khalaf*) has said that the Law obliges Muslims to wear particular items of dress, apart from the *ihrâm*.

The idea behind the prescribing of the *iḥrâm* is that people during the pilgrimage should refrain from luxury and should not be distinguished from each other by different styles of dress. Rashîd Riḍâ supports the opinion that Islam does not prescribe any specific Muslim type of dress by pointing out two Prophetic traditions, one of which reports that the Prophet once wore a Byzantine mantle (*jubba Rûmiyya*), while the other mentions that the Prophet once wore a *ṭaylasân*[34] of Persian origin.[35]

Interestingly, Rashîd Riḍâ showed no compunction about expressing his opinion of the Kaum Tua *'ulamâ'* in Padang in plain terms. He said the *'ulamâ'* had declared people who wore European dress to be unbelievers, although very many Turks, Tatars, Egyptians, and Syrians wore European dress. Rashîd Riḍâ went on to say, "... those people referred to, are ignorant, and the *'ulamâ'* of this group have made Islam and the Muslims an object of derision by issuing this kind of *fatwa*s." Instead of seeking their justification in Islam, they adhere too closely to their own local customs and use the Qur'an and the Hadith arbitrarily, as witnessed by their use of the Prophetic saying "whosoever imitates a group, belongs to it."[36]

After this *fatwa* from Rashîd Riḍâ had reached Abdullah Ahmad in Padang, the latter published on the issue of dress in his own journal *al-Munir;* in the issue of 1 Dhū l-ḥijja 1329/22 November 1911, two questions about dress were dealt with.[37] In his introduction to these *fatwa*s, Abdullah Ahmad mentions that many requests about these topics had reached *al-Munir* from different places, such as Bukit Tinggi and Padang Panjang (both in West Sumatra), Bengkulen (South Sumatra), Batavia, and even the Malay states of Perak and Pahang. No names of *mustaftîn* are mentioned, because the list would have become too long. Abdullah Ahmad apologizes that it took him so long to answer these questions. The reason for this was not negligence, but because he wanted to proceed very carefully, and therefore he waited for the answer from the *'ulamâ'* from Egypt and their journal."[38] The questions about dress run as follows: Does the Shari'a prescribe certain items of dress for Muslims, and if a Muslim does not comply with these, does he cease to be a Muslim? Is the wearing of a hat (*topi yang bercapiu*) or a necktie (*tali leher yang dinamakan dasi*) harmful to one's faith? The answer reads as follows:

> O readers, you should know that the religion of Islam in no way troubles the Muslims with [the prescription of] certain items of dress, nor with a particular mode of wearing it, apart from the *ihram* which should be worn during the *hajj* and the *'umra*.[39]

A person who does wear these items of dress is definitely not a *kâfir*. The people who have claimed this cannot justify this assertion on the basis of religion, and they have falsely accused hundreds of millions of Muslims in Turkey, the land of the Tatars, Egypt, and Syria of unbelief. Finally, the entire *fatwa* is supported by the same two Prophetic traditions referred to in the preceding *fatwa* in *al-Manâr*, in order to illustrate that the Prophet himself did not object to the wearing of foreign items of dress. The first one, from the Hadith collection of al-Bukhari, reports that the Prophet once wore a Byzantine mantle (*jubba Rûmiyya*), while the other (from the collection of Muslim) mentions that the Prophet once wore the *taylasân*.[40] Indubitably, Abdullah Ahmad is just putting forward the same opinion as his source of inspiration, the Egyptian journal *al-Manâr*.

A final document that sheds light on these heated debates in Minangkabau at the beginning of the 20th century is a small collection of *fatwa*s originating from Mecca. This collection is titled *al-Fatâwâ al-saniyya fî al-mazâ'im al-bad'iyya*, "The Sublime *Fatwas* Dealing with the Marvellous Allegations," and contains 20 *fatwa*s given by ʿAbd Allâh ibn Muḥammad Ṣâliḥ al-Zawâwî (1850–1924). ʿAbd Allâh al-Zawâwî was born in Mecca in 1850 and was educated there. In 1893 he was forced to flee by the tyrannical grand sharif ʿAwn al-Rafîq. Most of his exile was spent in the Netherlands East Indies, after 1896 as *muftî* of the sultan of Pontianak, in West Borneo. After he was able to return to Mecca in 1908, he became involved in education in the Masjid al-Ḥarâm, eventually attaining the most prestigious position of the *muftî* of the Shafiʿites. He held this position until he was killed in the fighting in al-Ṭâ'if in 1924, when the Saʿûdî forces were establishing their rule.[41]

This collection of *fatwa*s was published twice in quick succession, the first time in Jeddah (1 Rabîʿ al-awwal 1342 [12 October 1923]) and the second time in Padang, West Sumatra, on 14 Shawwal 1342/19 May 1924, by Chatib Ali. Both editions of the booklet include the original Arabic texts of the *fatwa*s, as well as their translation into Malay. Both booklets are interesting in themselves for various reasons, but for the purposes of the present paper, suffice it to mention that the issues dealt with are precisely the great controversies that kept the Kaum Muda and the Kaum Tua busy for so long in West Sumatra.[42] All in all, it is clear that Muslims from Minangkabau had requested *fatwa*s on these issues from the great Shafiʿite *mufti* in Mecca, ʿAbd Allâh al-Zawâwî, in order to finally settle the debates in West Sumatra. We thus owe the publication of this *fatwa* collection of this important Meccan scholar, who did not leave behind much published work, to the efforts of Indonesian scholars.

For the purpose of the present paper, I use the latter edition here, because this was the one published by Chatib Ali, who was, as we have seen, the most important spokesman of the Kaum Tua.[43] The Malay introduction to this booklet says it was translated by Chatib Ali himself "... for the benefit of all Malay Muslims and to eliminate the fifth School of Law which has strayed from the circles of the *ahl al-Sunna wa-l-jama'a.*"[44] This second edition is especially interesting because it includes a long letter in Malay, dated Mecca 24 Rabî' al-âkhir 1342/4 December 1923, which reports a speech that Sharîf Ḥusayn of Mecca gave in his palace on 2 Ṣafar 1342/ 2 October 1923 in the presence of the most important religious authorities in Mecca, all Jawi students, including those from Minangkabau, and thousands of others. In this speech, which is summarized in the letter, Sharîf Ḥusayn fully supports Chatib Ali and rejects the Kaum Muda; it contains so much detail[45] that it is undoubtedly a forgery. This letter includes some exciting polemical material, which I cannot refrain from quoting here:

> We have heard that there are Kaum Muda '*ulamâ*' in Minangkabau. After having seen their journal, *al-Munir*, it is evident that *al-Munir* has strayed from the four Schools of Law, as well as from the consensus (*ijmâ'*) of Muslims. To use it is equivalent to opening an ulcer and rashly seeking to deceive stupid people. It is necessary that the seekers of knowledge inform the Minangkabau and the Jawa that they should not be deceived by the Kaum Muda (p. 59).[46]

Among the 20 issues that are dealt with in the collection of *fatwa*s is, not surprisingly, the issue of the wearing of European items of dress. The *muftî* is asked (Number 6) whether or not the wearing of a hat (*burnayta/capiu*) and a necktie (*dasi*) in order to make oneself more attractive (*li-ajli al-zayna /bagi karena perhiasan*) is forbidden (*ḥarâm*).[47] In his answer, 'Abd Allâh al-Zawâwî makes a distinction between two situations: Should one wear these items of dress with the aim (*qasad*) of imitating the unbelievers, this is forbidden; on the other hand, should one wear a hat in order to protect one's head and the tie in order to protect one's neck and shoulders from the cold, and if one does not intend to imitate the unbelievers, this is allowed (*harus*). However, whoever says that the wearing of these items is allowed unconditionally, is wrong (*o.c.*: 9-10/28).

Summarizing the materials presented above, the following picture emerges. At the beginning of the 20th century, the traditionalist Muslims of Minangkabau still held the same opinion as that voiced by the great Shafi'ite Meccan *muftî* Aḥmad Dahlân (d. 1886) at the request of Muslims from the Netherlands East Indies, namely, that Muslims should avoid items of Western dress. However, spurred along by the sharp polemics with their reformist opponents, the Kaum Tua even went a step farther, declaring Muslims who wore Western dress to be unbelievers. These traditionalist opinions were sharply criticized, and even ridiculed, by the Egyptian reformer Rashîd Riḍâ, whose authority was called in by the Minangkabau reformist leader Haji Abdullah Ahmad. Asked about the issue of dress, Rashîd Riḍâ, and in his wake Abdullah Ahmad, took a secularist position: Apart from the ritual context of the pilgrimage, which forms an exception, Islam does not prescribe particular forms of dress in ordinary life. Consequently, dress does not constitute part of a person's religious identity and is irrelevant from a religious point of view.

Of particular interest is the last opinion dealt with in this section, that of the Meccan *muftî* 'Abd Allâh al-Zawâwî, who was the champion of the Minangkabau Kaum Tua. Not to be bested by the Kaum Muda, who mobilized their intellectual leaders in Cairo through the efforts of their main spokesman, Chatib Ali, the Kaum Tua also called upon their highest authority, in this case the Shafi'ite *muftî* in Mecca. Without having to sacrifice his traditionalist principles, al-Zawâwî found a clever compromise: The wearing of European dress was no longer regarded as strictly forbidden, but it was allowed on the condition that it was done without the *intention* of imitating the Christians. Because it is impossible to discern a person's intention from his outward appearance, this opened up the possibility for traditionalist Muslims to wear European dress without being regarded as acting against Islam. In this way al-Zawâwî created the possibility of resolving the controversy over dress between the Kaum Tua and the Kaum Muda.

Concluding Remarks

The debates about male dress in the Netherlands East Indies in the early 20th century are couched in religious terms, but in the discussions a number of underlying motives played a role, all of which are in one way or another linked to the relentless encroachment of modernity that followed the European expansion into this part of the world.

The first factor that might be mentioned here is the rise of individualism — among other incentives supported by the ongoing spread of the money economy — which enabled people who could afford it to abandon traditional dress in favor of European dress, or in other words to make an individual choice for a particular kind of dress. Second, political factors were at play. By assuming European dress, it was possible to show that colonial rule was accepted or, until the very beginnings of the 20th century, when the Dutch regulations concerning dress were still in force, that the Dutch rule was contested.[48] A third important underlying reason for the discussions about dress was the rise of secularism. The idea that type of dress was irrelevant to a person's religious identity and the notion that Islam did not regulate all aspects of human life might have been shocking at that time, and might also account for the intensity of the debates. In short, the discussions about dress took place at a time when rapid changes in social and cultural circumstances were occurring and the traditional religious worldview was under severe threat. The wearing of European dress functioned as a symbol, or as a *pars pro toto*, showing the wearer's attitude toward progress and his readiness to accept other features of Western civilization alongside dress.

When we look at the source materials presented in this paper from the perspective of the relationship between the Middle East and Southeast Asia, a number of interesting points appear. Mecca has always occupied, and will always occupy, a central place for Muslims throughout the world, including the Netherlands East Indies. I aim to underline here the circumstances under which the Holy City takes a prominent place in the sacred early history of Islam: It is the direction towards which believers orient themselves during prayer, and it forms the aim of the annual pilgrimage. Besides this, as we have seen above, before the introduction of reformist ideas in Southeast Asia, Mecca also formed the most important intellectual center for Muslims from the Netherlands East Indies. It was in Mecca where the best religious education was available, and from where the most authoritative *fatwa*s came.

After the introduction of reformist ideas from the Middle East into Southeast Asia and the formation of the Kaum Tua and the Kaum Muda, Mecca retained the same position it had always possessed for the Kaum Tua. Therefore, this persuasion within Islam remained dependent on their intellectual forerunners in Mecca, who upheld the traditionally transmitted, centuries-old type of scholarship. In real terms, the Kaum Tua scholars in Minangkabau derived their ideas on dress from Mecca and used real or forged opinions from Mecca in order to legitimate their opinions and to convince their followers. Forging a new path, the Kaum Muda no longer looked toward Mecca for their intellectual inspiration, but to the new center of Cairo, where a novel way of interpreting Islam was being propagated. As we have seen, the Kaum Muda scholars of Minangkabau directed themselves to the most prominent mouthpiece of the reform in Egypt, *al-Manâr*, and transmitted the opinions expressed in it in their own journal. In conclusion, we may therefore say that at the beginning of the 20th century the traditional hegemony of Mecca as the foremost intellectual center in Southeast Asian Islam had come to an end, and the orientation in Southeast Asia toward the Middle East had become more diverse.

Notes

* Earlier versions of this paper were presented at Leiden University, the Netherlands, and the Universität zu Köln, Germany.
1. See Yedida Kalfon Stillman, *Arab Dress: A Short History from the Dawn of Islam to Modern Times*, ed. Norman A. Stillman (Leiden: Brill [Themes in Islamic Studies vol. 2], 2000), 153; and Kees van Dijk, "Sarongs, Jubbahs, and Trousers: Appearance as a Means of Distinction and Discrimination," in Henk Schulte Nordholt, ed., *Outward Appearances: Dressing the State and Society* (Leiden: KITLV Press, 1997), 65. An exception to this is a brief *fatwa* of Sayyid 'Uthmân from Jumâdâ al-âhkira 1317/October 1899 in which he mentions that the wearing of the headscarf (*kerudung*) is obligatory for women when they leave the house; see Sayyid 'Uthmân, *Lima Su'al Didalam Perihal Memakai Kerudung* (Batavia: Self-published, 1899). This *fatwa* contains the earliest prescription from Indonesia that women should cover their heads, as far as I know, and is more in line with contemporary discussions in the Middle East. This early occurrence has to be explained by the fact that it addresses the position of Arab women, and perhaps the situation in Batavia, where the Shari'a was adhered to more strictly than in other parts of the archipelago; see G. F. Pijper, "De vrouw en de moskee," in his *Fragmenta Islamica* (Leiden: Brill, 1934), 19, 31. In the article by Sumit Mandal in this volume, we also see that at first the issue of *kafâ'a* was debated only within the Arab community, while later it became relevant to the Muslim community at large. The only other early reference to the headscarf that I have seen so far is from the Minangkabau reformer Haji Rasoel, who made a plea for a (partial) covering of the female head in 1918; see B. J. O. Schrieke, "Bijdrage tot de bibliografie van de huidige godsdienstige beweging ter Sumatra's Westkust," in *Tijdschrift van het Bataviaasch Genootschap* 59 (1919–21), 294, n. 2.
2. Van Dijk, "Sarongs, Jubbahs, and Trousers," 43–9.
3. C. Snouck Hurgronje, *Ambtelijke adviezen van C. Snouck Hurgronje, 1889–1936*, ed. E. Gobée and C. Adriaanse ('s-Gravenhage: Nijhoff, 1956–57), 1041–5.

4. Van Dijk, "Sarongs, Jubbahs, and Trousers," 40.
5. Snouck Hurgronje, *Ambtelijke adviezen van C. Snouck Hurgronje, 1889–1936*, 1589.
6. Nico Kaptein, "Sayyid 'Uthmân on the Legal Validity of Documentary Evidence," *Bijdragen tot de Taal-, Land- en Volkenkunde* 153, 1 (1997): 86–8.
7. Bermula barang yang telah diketahui bahwasanya pakaian orang Eropa yang dibadan yaitu jas dan yang dikepala yaitu topi atau peci hitam. Dan bahwasanya pakaian orang Arab yang dibadan jubbah atau sudayriyya bersama-sama qamis dan yang dikepala yaitu serban melainkan jikalau dirumah-rumah saja maka kupiah putih saja. Dan bahwasanya pakaian orang Melayu atau orang Jawa yang dibadan yaitu baju kebaya dan yang dikepala yaitu setangan adanya. Sayyid 'Uthmân, *Buku Kecil Buat Menyatakan Pertegahan Hukum Adat Negeri Yang Bersamaan Pada Pertegahan Hukum Agama Islam Atas Orang Yang Menukar Pakaian Bangsanya Dengan Memakai Pakaian Lain Bangsanya Adanya*, s.l. (1904), 6.
8. Snouck Hurgronje, *Ambtelijke adviezen van C. Snouck Hurgronje, 1889–1936*, 1328. Women might also have changed their dress after returning from the pilgrimage by starting to wear a white cloth, the *mahramah*, around the head. See G. F. Pijper, "De vrouw en de moskee," in his *Fragmenta Islamica* (Leiden: Brill, 1934), 20.
9. For a discussion of the politics of pilgrimage from a wider perspective, see the paper by Eric Tagliacozzo in this volume.
10. Snouck Hurgronje, *Ambtelijke adviezen van C. Snouck Hurgronje, 1889–1936*, 1321–2, 1326–7.
11. Snouck Hurgronje, *Ambtelijke adviezen van C. Snouck Hurgronje, 1889–1936*, 1041–5; 1589–90.
12. Mecca took a similar position in the 17th and 18th centuries; see Azra Azyumardi, *The Origins of Islamic Reformism in Southeast Asia: Networks of Malay-Indonesian and Middle Eastern 'ulamâ' in the Seventeenth and Eighteenth centuries* (Leiden: KITLV Press, 2004).
13. Nico Kaptein, "Sayyid 'Uthmân on the Legal Validity of Documentary Evidence," *Bijdragen tot de Taal-, Land- en Volkenkunde* 153, 1 (1997): 86–8.
14. Nico Kaptein, *The Muhimmât al-nafâ'is: A Bilingual Meccan Fatwa Collection for Indonesian Muslims from the End of the Nineteenth Century* (Jakarta: INIS Materials #32, 1997).
15. Ibid., 70–1, 160–1, 199.
16. Snouck Hurgronje, *De Atjèhers*, Deel I (Leiden: Brill, 1893), 27.
17. In a slightly later *fatwa*, originating from West Sumatra, it is asked whether it was permissible for a person to be buried in a *baju;* see *al-Munir* 1, 11 (1911): 136.
18. In Java the issue of dress also became more important as an identity marker in this period; see the article by Merle Ricklefs in this volume.

19. B. J. O. Schrieke, "Bijdrage tot de bibliografie van de huidige godsdienstige beweging ter Sumatra's Westkust," *Tijdschrift van het Bataviaasch Genootschap* 59 (1919–21), 289, 305; Jutta E. Bluhm, "A Preliminary Statement on the Dialogue Established between the Reform Magazine *al-Manâr* and the Malayo-Indonesian World," *Indonesia Circle* 32 (1983): 35–42.
20. M. Sanusi Latief, ed., *Riwayat Hidup dan Perjuangan 20 Ulama Besar Sumatera Barat* (Islamic Centre Sumatera Barat, 1981), 21–54.
21. Deliar Noer, *The Modernist Muslim Movement in Indonesia, 1900–1942* (London: Oxford University Press, 1973), 33–9.
22. Schrieke, "Bijdrage tot de bibliografie van de huidige godsdienstige beweging ter Sumatra's Westkust," 312–22.
23. Nico Kaptein, "The *Berdiri Mawlid* Issue among Indonesian Muslims in the Period from circa 1875 to 1930," *Bijdragen tot de Taal-, Land- en Volkenkunde* 149, 1 (1993): 124–53.
24. John R. Bowen, "Modern Intentions: Reshaping Subjectivities in an Indonesian Muslim Society," in Robert W. Hefner and Patricia Horvatich, *Islam in an Era of Nation States: Politics and Religious Renewal in Muslim Southeast Asia* (Honolulu: University of Hawai'i Press, 1997), 157–81.
25. Hamka, *Ajahku: Riwajat hidup Dr. H. Abd. Karim Amrullah dan perdjuangan kaum agama di Sumatera, cetakan keempat* (Jakarta: Umminda, 1982), 102–4.
26. See Hamka, *Ajahku: Riwajat hidup Dr. H. Abd. Karim Amrullah dan perdjuangan kaum agama di Sumatera, cetakan keempat*, 103; Sayyid 'Uthmân, in his *Buku Kecil Buat Menyatakan Pertegahan Hukum Adat Negeri Yang Bersamaan Pada Pertegahan Hukum Agama Islam Atas Orang Yang Menukar Pakaian Bangsanya Dengan Memakai Pakaian Lain Bangsanya Adanya*, s.l. (1904), p. 5, also mentions that people changed their native dress for European dress in order to enjoy the cheaper fares on trains and steamships.
27. The same phenomenon can be seen in the rise of organizations among Muslims in Indonesia: The traditionalists began to organize themselves only after the modernists had started to do so, and the traditionalists could not stay behind; see Deliar Noer, *The Modernist Muslim movement in Indonesia, 1900–1942* (London: Oxford University Press, 1973).
28. Ali Chatib, *Burhan al-haqq*, Padang: [s.n.]: 1919. "Diharuskan pula memakai dasi // supaya serupa dengan agama Nasrani; tetapi kegereja tak mau pergi // menyembah berhala bersama-sama Yahudi." This reference to the Jews here is awkward, because there is no anti-Jewish discourse in the Kaum Tua–Kaum Muda debates.
29. Nico Kaptein, "The *Berdiri Mawlid* Issue among Indonesian Muslims in the Period from circa 1875 to 1930," 143–8.
30. These issues were the *berdiri mawlid*, the *usalli*, the use of Malay in the Friday sermon, the Naqshabandiyya brotherhood, and the depiction of living creatures.

31. Michael Francis Laffan, *Islamic Nationhood and Colonial Indonesia: The Umma below the Winds* (London and New York: RoutledgeCurzon, 2003), 175.
32. Chatib Ali, ed., *Al-khatima [al-]bahija* (Padang: De Volharding, 1920), 22. [karena kata hadith] Barangsiapa memakai pakaian kebesaran atas agama lain pada agama Islam maka dihukum menyerupai.
33. *Al-Manâr* 14 (1911): 669–71. The other four deal with pictures of living creatures, the phonograph, the use of musical instruments (Rashîd Ridâ did not regard any one of these as being problematic), and some technicalities of Muslim law.
34. According to Stillman, this is a shawl-like garment worn over the head and shoulders; see Yedida Kalfon Stillman, *Arab Dress: A Short History from the Dawn of Islam to Modern Times*, ed. Norman A. Stillman (Leiden: Brill [Themes in Islamic Studies vol. 2]), 2000), 18.
35. In a footnote Ridâ refers to *al-Manâr* 13 (1910): 61, where in a reaction to a piece by Sayyid ʿUthmân he also stressed that if Muslims imitated expressions of Western culture in education, warfare, customs, administration, technology, and certain items of dress, this had no implications for their religiosity. For this reason the *hadîth* about imitating is not regarded as relevant to the discussion. (It is noteworthy that the work by the Sayyid was apparently available to Rashîd Ridâ.) Second, Ridâ refers to *al-Manâr* 13 (1910): 113, where he gives a *fatwa* at the request of a certain al-Ramzî from Sambas in West Borneo, stating that an item of dress, such as a necktie, is not a badge of a particular religion.
36. *Al-Manâr* 14 (1911): 669–71, published 3 Ramadân 1329/23 September 1911.
37. Together with three other questions: one about pictures, one about photography, and one about listening to songs.
38. It is interesting to note that since the publication of the relevant *fatwa* in *al-Manâr* in Cairo (which came out on 3 Ramadân 1329/23 September 1911), it took only two months before it was being discussed in this Southeast Asian journal.
39. "Ketahuilah oleh tuan-tuan pembaca bahwa agama Islam tiadalah sekali-kali memberati akan orang-orang Muslimin dengan pakaian yang tertentu dan dengan kayfiat yang tertentu, melainkan pada waktu ihram dengan hajj dan umrah."
40. *Al-Munir* 1, 17: 231–3, published on 1 Dhū l-ḥijja 1329/22 November 1911.
41. C. Snouck Hurgronje, *Ambtelijke adviezen van C. Snouck Hurgronje, 1889–1936*, ed. E. Gobée and C. Adriaanse ('s-Gravenhage: Nijhoff, 1956–57), 1600–11; Laffan, *Islamic Nationhood and Colonial Indonesia*, 223.
42. *Ajahku Hamka: Riwajat hidup Dr. H. Abd. Karim Amrullah dan perdjuangan kaum agama di Sumatera, cetakan keempat* (Jakarta: Umminda, 1982), 102–4.
43. The other one was published by a certain al-Ramzî. This might be the same al-Ramzî from West Borneo who requested a *fatwa* from Rashîd Ridâ.

44. "... supaya memberi manfa'at bagi umum segala orang Melayu min al-muslimin dan memadamkan akan madhhab yang kelima yang keluar dari da'irah Ahl al-Sunna wa l-Jama'a."
45. 'Abdallâh al-Zawâwî, *al-Fatâwâ al-Saniyya fî al-mazâ'im al-bad'iyya* (Padang: Electrische Snelpers Drukkerij Liem Eng Tjiang, 1924), 59. For instance, the name of the Dutch colonial civil servant B. J. O. Schrieke (1890–1945) is mentioned (p. 61), which would not have been known to the sharif.
46. "Kami sudah dengar di-Minangkabau ada 'ulama' qaum muda. Sudah dilihat karangannya al-Munir sudah terang al-Munir itu diluar madhhab yang empat dan dliluar ijma' al-muslimin. Gunanya pembuka puru pemudah-mudah buat cari orang pengicu orang bodoh-bodoh. Wajiblah oleh talib al-'ilm memberitahu ke-Minangkabau dan ke-Jawa supaya merekaitu jangan terkicu oleh kaum muda itu."
47. 'Abdallâh Zawâwî, *al-Fatâwâ al-Saniyya fî al-mazâ'im al-bad'iyya* (Padang: Electrische Snelpers Drukkerij Liem Eng Tjiang, 1924), 3/18.
48. Later the dress issue, this time of a more distinct anticolonial character, flared up again. For instance, it is interesting to see that in 1930 Rashîd Ridâ again gave a *fatwa* about European dress in *al-Manâr* (vol. 31, 736–9) at the request of a person from Netherlands East Indies — 'Aydit ibn Ahmad al-Bahri al-Sadafi, from Solo in Central Java. In this *fatwa*, Rashîd Ridâ adopted a more negative view of European dress, declaring it to be reprehensible (*makrûh*) from the point of view of the Shari'a for political and patriotic reasons. We thus see that in a later phase of his career, Rashîd Ridâ, in addition to the purely religious dimension, added a much stronger element of anticolonialism to his reasoning, resulting in his preference for non-European types of dress. It would be beyond the scope of this paper to deal with this shift in Ridâ's thinking.

III

The First Half of the 20th Century

Traditional Daggers, Aden (Yemen) (Photograph E. Tagliacozzo)

9

Topics and Queries for a History of Arab Families and Inheritance in Southeast Asia: Some Preliminary Thoughts*

MICHAEL GILSENAN

Wills and trusts made by Muslims are therefore construed according to the principles of English law and not according to Muslim law. This is not wholly satisfactory from the Muslim point of view. [1]

Personal laws are sometimes called hybrid laws, and so they are in the sense that they are offspring of quite different parents. ... The source of a personal law, whether it is by mistake or invention, does not really matter; it is the process of its growth and development which is important. [2]

Migrants and Settlers

"Property distribution and transmission within families are in fact intimately connected to the policies of states."[3] From the early 19th century, new forms of law and property were institutionalized to varying degrees by different state authorities as foundational processes in the appropriation of powers over persons and territories in the Middle East, Africa, India, and Southeast Asia. Whether Ottoman, French, British, or Dutch, imperial rule sought — through reforming the legal regulation of properties and persons — to consolidate or transform patterns of economic and social control. In trade diasporas, themselves existing in the expanding colonial and imperial spheres of power of the 19th and early 20th centuries, the movement of persons, groups, goods, ideas, laws, and legal practices across spaces and times are obviously central topics for investigation.

Using material derived from two case reports from the courts of 19th-century colonial Singapore, I shall offer an introductory outline of what I consider to be some of the analytical problems in the study of the complex interactions between the state, law, property, and reproduction of family forms among Arabs who moved between Arabia and Southeast Asia. My attention is not on trade and commerce, but rather on the constitution of "landed property," *real* estate, and its transmission through inheritance and succession practices in which Islamic and English practices were brought into complex relations. Migrants, sojourners, and settlers became settlors, with sometimes major implications for "family" over generations and multiple spaces.

Anthropologists have often studied disputes and conflicts of many kinds in colonial contexts, disputes involving different institutions, agents, hierarchies, ritual performances, and discourses. Relations, distinctions, and amalgamations between "customary law," "Islamic law," and "English law" have similarly been pondered, by colonial lawyers themselves as much as by historians or anthropologists. They have also been the subject of dispute, strategizing, manipulation, and confusion among the settlors and beneficiaries who engage in legal devices, the implications of which may only reveal themselves over many years and in different places. Migrants and settlers make legal settlements, employ professional specialists, dispose of properties, establish trusts, direct executors to distribute goods to different persons for different purposes and according to different criteria, then go to court to fight over the results. They do so in terms of English or of "Mohammedan" law, sometimes a hybrid of both. At every point, they can be challenged.

I begin with an introduction to the Hadrami migrations to Southeast Asia and then sketch out the broader analytical questions that particularly interest me concerning law, family, and colonial rule. In the main body of the chapter, I refer to two early legal cases over wills in Singapore in order to draw out some of the main themes of family legal disputing, whether in English or Mohammedan terms, or both. Succession issues in families that quickly invested in landed property in the Straits Settlements and elsewhere equally quickly focused minds wonderfully upon the control of inheritance, shares, and rights by different persons seeking differential advantage. I shall refer in the briefer final section of the chapter to the importance of the English forms of charitable endowment or trusts for family fortunes over time — for endowment is, of course, an instrument to control time — and the problems that would-be founders or their heirs might encounter.

Arabs in Southeast Asia

The Hadramis came, in the large majority, from an area called the Hadramaut in the southeast of what is now Yemen.[4] The period of their major migrations in larger numbers begins in the later middle 19th century. Here, I focus on the elite or once-elite families of the Hadrami diaspora in Southeast Asia, and specifically those much of whose capital, property, and economic base was for more than 100 years mainly, but by no means entirely, in Singapore and Java. The port city was part of a rapidly expanding and intensifying space of movements and of flows, of encounters, mixings and differentiations, of persons, of goods, of cultural practices and forms that had their origins in those routes that passed from Europe to China and many points between. British, Dutch, and French colonial projects were as central to the modern political economy of the Malay Archipelago as British and French interventions were in the Eastern Mediterranean and India.

I follow the eastward flows of specific Arab families, households, and networks, questioning these terms, across succeeding generations and multiple spaces linked in multiple ways. These links might be fragile for reasons beyond the fluctuations of personal or familial fortune or control. The most meticulous or expert calculations of risks and investments in trade or partnership, or marriage, or testamentary disposition, or education, or migratory movement might prove in vain; once-reasonable and approved decisions or strategies might devastate the family enterprise and the enterprise of family in a crisis or almost imperceptibly over time or through the very costs, social as well as economic, of those English legal instruments of properties, inheritance, and trusts adopted to guarantee family fortunes over time.

"Shirtsleeves to shirtsleeves in three generations," an Asian as much as an American piece of popular wisdom, speaks of an internally driven rise and fall of family. But world and regional economic swings and cycles, of course, played their part. Local and transnational crises in politics, war, or commodity prices played their part, disrupting carefully constructed networks and expectations. British, Dutch, Japanese, and other interventions might have enabled or destroyed diasporic strategies. Nationalist revolutions and independence might have led to the confiscation of properties so carefully acquired, of capital so cunningly accumulated and managed. Finally, land acquisition and that phrase so crucial to state power, "public benefit," might have proved the cruelest blow of all.

In Southeast Asia, the Hadramis distributed family members across spaces in the many islands of the Malay Archipelago, as peddlers, traders, agents of land and goods, moneylenders, sailors and ship owners, batik distributors or manufacturers, shop owners, religious specialists, *rentiers*, teachers, and preachers. A certain instrumental sense of what a recent collection of papers has called the "dividends of kinship," characteristic of a major dimension of so many migrations, marks their tactical and strategic thinking as much as it structures family narratives.[5] Calculation and miscalculation across legal, cultural, and familial spaces become part of the lived routines of certain families.

The sense of Arab *family* networks across the region, in competition sometimes with European traders and sailors, marked the experiences of a Polish seaman who had for a time in the 1880s sailed under a seyyid's flag. In Joseph Conrad's *Outcast of the Islands*, the Arabs are represented as omnipresent outsider-insider figures, "innumerable" and assuring linkages across the whole sea-space of the archipelago: "An uncle here — a brother there; a father-in-law in Batavia, another in Palembang; husbands of numerous sisters; cousins innumerable scattered north, south, east and west — in every place where there was trade: a great family lay like a network over the islands."[6] This image, which has its own seduction in the fantasy of the power of "the Arab," inscrutable, implacable, scheming as is Conrad's Abdullah, is of a kind of unique capacity to create and sustain multi-stranded relations through marriage across all the zones of interaction and relation, whether on sea or land, of the Indies.

Robert Hampson's use of Deleuze and Guattari's concept of the rhizome to correspond structurally and organizationally to the Arab network seems to me very helpful here: "The rhizome with its transversal communication, its acentred multiplicity, its shifting directions, provides a model of alliance and flexibility" that subverts individualism as much as political agency.[7] That the concept of the rhizome was proposed "as an alternative to arborescent command systems" has its own additional relevance, given the significance of arborescent genealogy in these settings. It counters the powerful imaginary of the linear, the patrilinear, line of descent, that iconographic form of genealogy so significant in one major form of claiming authority and authorizing claims in certain Hadrami discourses.

The Reproduction of the Family across Space

In such multiple contexts and processes of movement, the consolidation and distribution of different forms of wealth and property over time and space presented opportunities and problems to the Hadramis, not least because the nature of "property," as relations between persons over things, was changing.[8] In Southeast Asia, they were part of the growth and attempted systematizations of colonial powers and regulations (especially from the 1870s on), imperial rivalries on a global scale, developments and fluctuations in international commerce and trade, the growth of plantation economies, and the importance of Chinese migrations and growing control of capital. What were "family," "relatedness," and "descent" in such migratory worlds to the actors concerned throughout the period? How were they apprehended and practiced, and how might they, did they, change? How could migrants who might spend most of their lives in the region, returning only later to Hadramaut, or who might make journeys back and forth to Arabia, to different points of the archipelago, and maintain different families, legal or otherwise, in different places with women of different linguistic, regional, and cultural groups, transmit their goods to their descendants in such a way as to attempt to ensure the family's reproduction and prosperity?

The socioeconomic reproduction of all family and kindred relations in their varied local and historical constructions refers, of course, not only to the biological but also to the acquisition, transmission, transformation, and expending of different kinds of capital, goods, and properties in the widest sense: forms of socialization, of what is "proper" and "appropriate," of knowledge, religious practice and belief, taste, dress, cuisine, profession, material resources, and social honor. Insofar as the families made up, or were part of, what Max Weber called "communities of shared memory," that memory itself may be a precious good to be worked and handed on in varying circumstances and media: rites, languages, genealogies, books, documents, photographs, narratives, anecdotes and characteristic idioms or figures of speech, culinary practices, pieces of furniture, heirlooms, and much besides. Memory itself is perceived as a resource of fluctuating value and significance, differentially possessed, deployed, and invested in by persons and groups.

For families of Arab descent in Southeast Asia, as for so many, these are transnational as well as intensely local processes. They require a great deal of sociocultural as much as economic and, in the cases with which I deal here, legal work. People had to negotiate and establish legally who and what they were in different emergent legal spaces, to whom they were related, and in what precise or possible ways they should seek to establish particular rights or claims as well as to fulfill certain obligations laid down by the state or states. The documentation and the degrees of the "bureaucratization of relatedness" became part of the collective and individual archive of the family, another resource in what might be struggles over property and over family itself.

To talk about the reproduction and transmission of family and rights in property is to talk about gender. Though she is referring to the world of English landed society, Eileen Spring points to the perspectives that such a concentration can open up: "No right of inheritance was more significant than the right to succeed to a landed estate; no right was more symbolic of the status of women."[9] On a more specific point, Beshara Doumani's work on Greater Syria has shown not only that women's endowments of *waqf*, religious endowments of different forms, might be almost equal to that of men in some contexts but that women might be "disproportionately represented as litigants in lawsuits between kin" in the 19th century.[10] And in the same volume, Martha Mundy and Richard Saumarez Smith in their study of property and family suggest that "to women the denial of women's legal personality as ungendered owners of property — as heirs in the registers of the state — and even more so of *mahr* (dowry) remains illegitimate."[11] Though such studies are centered on later Ottoman history in Syria, we should remember that state attempts to "reform," in what were seen as transformative, modern regulatory ways using new technologies of power, were crucial across the world, colonial or not. Registration, title deeds, degrees of state control over *waqf* properties, surveys, however partial and incomplete their institution, were part of a transnational discourse of changing state legal power with immense implications for gender and property.

Changes in land law and in personal law were thus intimately related at this period of "the rise of a system of capitalist nation-states — mutually suspicious and grossly unequal in power and prosperity,"[12] the times of Empire.

In terms of the predominantly male Hadrami migrants in the earlier years, many of whom, as I have mentioned, married local women of different cultural and linguistic backgrounds, gender also linked intimately with forms of household, residence, conceptions of rights and properties, and a sometimes far greater role of the matriline and affines in relatedness in the archipelago. Idioms and practices of kindred, descent, family, and household, not to mention rites of birth, marriage, and death, also over time became more polysemous and polyglot. Children grew up with a mother's tongue, not a father's (though sons might have spoken Arabic to their fathers in the first generation, and in some cases the second), looking "Malay," "Javanese," "Chinese," "mixed," and all the other possibilities of family comment, street joking, readings of "blood(s)" and "race" in the face, the hair, the limbs, and all those appetites, desires, and traits taken stereotypically to be their "nature."

Legalizing Families

One of the many dangers the researcher faces in such a conceptually and methodologically complicated field is that of slipping into what Pierre Bourdieu called the "fallacies of legalistic thinking," a flaw he saw as characteristic of too much anthropological analysis of marriage and family. I am mindful of his constant warning against producing a set of cultural "rules" as explanation. Working on law and family can easily draw one into such analysis. Bourdieu's concern was to draw out rather the habitus generating the strategies and practices of inheritance, family, and property that seemed part of the taken-for-granted world of the Béarn or Kabylia.[13] But here I understand habitus in the contexts of which I speak to be, so to say, brought to the surface in encounters with radically other modes of reproduction, strategizing, constituting relatedness and power in the diasporic setting. The "just is," "the way things are done" that is not expressed in reflected-upon or conventionally codified statements, cannot continue to be unquestioned life assumptions. This is certainly true where persons introduce, for example, the English law of trusts or English courts' adjudications on Muslim wills or of Muslims writing English wills into the heart of family and descent group as strategies of controlling the distribution of properties. Wills become key terms, a crucial dialect of "family talk" for talking about "family," a vehicle and expression, too, of forms of modernity.

The categories of landed property that came into being in Singapore in the first 50 or more years of its existence were new, hybrid, and loosely regulated, rather like what grew into "law" in Singapore, law derived from multiple sources.[14] For some Arab merchants, the land grants, long leases (the 999-year term being common), and other devices of relative indeterminacy of regulation in the early decades, seem to have been identified as presenting enormous opportunities. There were also new devices of succession and transmission for such new forms of accumulation, not least in English wills, in appeals to English courts for justice under Islamic principles of distribution, and in English forms of the trust that began to be used from the 1860s. Such moves necessarily obliged or gave the chance/risk to persons to engage the radically different structures and discourses of law and property developed in quite different historical contexts. This latter fact is something that later judges themselves comment on in judgments where they explicitly say that the property regime has no organic origin in Singapore history, is the product of England, and in fact misrepresents local property practices and forms. Nonetheless, they insist that the property regime and its classifications are to be followed, given that the case law constituting it has built up and chaos would follow were attempts to be made to reconstitute it in a more "organic" fashion (whatever that might be taken to mean or entail). Some judges, in other words, recognized key aspects of the contradictions at the heart of property and law while at the same time furnishing the pragmatic legitimation for arbitrary colonial practices.

To engage in the law meant to use the paid services of increasingly professionalized specialists. The lawyers became indispensable quasi-members of "the family," crucial mediators with legal institutions of which they were themselves agents. In the increasingly significant processes of managing the transmission, division, and issues of succession in family fortunes, they became the guardians and motivators of the legalized and bureaucratized genealogies in the language of which claims were made. They structured and framed the legal kindred and family relations and narratives over time in a potent, often obscure and contradictory legal language, which in fragments, phrases, and fractured understandings became part of family histories, family talk, and talking about "family."

When a member of one family that has a major trust in contemporary Singapore said to me, in a phrase that is quite typical, "It's only property that makes us family," he was expressing what many years after the trust's foundation has become a kind of proverbial cynicism: a wry reflection, an ironizing that in willing the future of the family through the trust, the founder has in fact willed the degradation of that which he sought to maintain and its reduction to "property." The deeply divided family members, expending their collective as much as individual resources on legal challenges between one group or person and others, become property's dependents. *They* are *its* instruments.[15] They express a sense of being "forced" into litigation, that litigation generates family relations. "Legalistic thinking" becomes for them inseparable from the forms of calculation and strategy of interested parties that go uneasily with other discursive constructions and taken-for-granted facts of being kin, being family, keeping up relations, giving and receiving, inheriting and transmitting wealth and goods within a moral as well as an economic frame.

Personal Law and Property Law in Colonial Modernity

It seems to me critical that we take "personal law" as having the same historical and analytical significance that we accord to criminal and other forms of law, regulation, and governance in understandings of modernity. My concern is particularly with the intersections of personal and property laws in social practices over time, those practices of which they are both a constitutive part and over which they appear to be a regulatory set of instruments "transcending" the social.

Timothy Mitchell has argued in a recent book that in Egypt "the history of private property is rather silent on the conditions that produced it and the precedents incorporated into it." This "silence" is crucial, in his view, to what Bourdieu would call a misrecognition of law and power and its ideological effects; little is said about the "actual constitution" of private property. Mitchell goes on: "The break in history caused by the colonial occupation of Egypt (in 1882) helped to establish the universal character of law. The *ad hoc*, violent, and exceptional character of the law of property was entirely hidden by presentation of law as something abstract, as a universal rule."[16] It is my view that in the very different colonial site and history of Singapore between 1819, when it was treated, for all practical purposes, as "empty space," and the 1880s, when it had grown into a city of migrants, mostly from China, and a major trading port of "the East," it was the *ad hoc*, ungeneralized regime of colonial government that was for a long period the relatively unconcealed determining element in the nature of the "thin" imperial power the British exercised. The arbitrariness of law, in such a context, was only partially masked. But the opportunities offered by a relatively unsystematized and unregulated set of ordnances, acts, and precedents were quickly grasped by some members of an Indian

Ocean trading network, the Hadramis, as they were by members of other communities.

The institutional, political, and economic dimensions with which law is articulated need to be complemented by understandings of its cultural significance. It is not only that emerging legal regimes may change the basis of the state in a relatively short time by changing the nature of land law and property. Sally Engle Merry has shown in the case of Hawaii that land went from chiefly control to individual ownership "in a regime of fee simple" (an interest in land that continues until the death of the last inheritor who dies without heirs).[17] It is that law becomes critical to the construction of persons as well as subjects and citizens. The objective of the law becomes "the creation of a self charged with making itself through discipline and self-control rather than defending the order of distinction and rank or maintaining connections with local communities."[18] (Engle is discussing a specific moment in Hawaiian history, but there is a general point there too.) Law is partly constitutive of social selves and of idioms of relatedness between those selves. Bill Maurer's focus on the role of law in defining "family" and "land," both of which are powerfully reified categories, in relation to the construction of "family" and "genealogy" in the British Virgin Islands is one that I share: "Changes in the laws encouraged people to think of kinship as an objective genealogical grid of bio-genetic relatedness, and not as a system of relationships and obligations among persons. This shift accompanied a change in legal and popular notions of land ownership."[19] With this change, people have come to relate to landed property increasingly as a *thing*, yet as a thing in which they as persons are crucially vested. In the narratives of personhood as of family and relatedness, legal cases, language, and assumptions become far more important both in anecdote, small talk, jokes, and accounts of conflict as well as in the framing of family narratives as a whole.

For the purpose of my (unsystematic) treatment of colonial law and the nexus of personal and "real" property law, I want also to draw attention to two closely linked arguments that Martin Chanock makes in his general thesis on law in the context of colonial Africa. The first is that colonial government was not infrequently "predominantly extra-legal," depending on administrative "discretion" with all its personalized, pragmatic implications rather than "the promotion of legal rights."[20] The second, and more germane to the case of Singapore, is his comment on the "overall failure of the colonial states ... to survey land and introduce land registries." The effort was, despite some exceptions, simply "too costly."²¹ I assume that Chanock means "costly" here in terms of colonial judgments of benefits and purposes attained against budget outlays and human investment, judgments that might change. But his first point throws a different light on the word "failure": "a land registry, registered titles, and a definition of ownership raised a specter of legality that ran quite contrary to the reign of colonial administration. Colonial government had been predominantly extra-legal; administrative discretion, not the promotion of legal rights had been its modus operandi."²²

Despite the force of these arguments, they need some refinement. The role of the "personal" is crucial but can itself take several forms. Regimes become more bureaucratic, recruitment policies and promotion more bound to examination, reports, supervision, the development of filing and administration, to professionalization in which the figure of the district officer ruling as king of his patch of "country" would become, in most instances, anachronistic. The policies of states might be fundamentally incoherent, or unclear, or shift according to the official in charge on the ground or to political changes in the metropole or to newly influential interest groups. States' interests in defining property ownership or inheritance rights might indeed be limited, at least until a particular moment. For migrants and locals of all kinds, conflicts and negotiations over status, rights, and claims were bedeviled or enabled, or both at once depending on the point of view of litigants and colonial officials, by official "failure" with its functional advantages that might benefit not only the rulers. In changing circumstances, however, legally established "property" itself, that *real estate* so central to English family fortunes and to conceptions of what constituted status, estate, and personhood, might come to be seen as fundamental to rule even if, to the new rulers themselves, it was often a source of uncertainty and contradiction that was more than a matter of the "extra-legal" nature of colonial governance.

An important article of 1884 will illustrate the point. Malay "customs" in the tenure of land were newly significant. Understanding them presented problems created by the officials themselves. W. E. Maxwell, a senior official, intervened to point to the sources of confusion and what underlay the need for "understanding." In India, always the point of reference, officials had wisely used "the native revenue system as the ground work" for the land-revenue administration and employed their "technical terms in the vernacular."²³ In Larut as early as 1876, by contrast, "land was being transferred and mortgaged with all English legal technicalities by the aid of two or three ignorant scribes who brought printed forms from the nearest British Settlement—Penang!" In the Malay states, alas, one faced endlessly unresolved land questions that had "derived from the joint forces of ignorance and neglect an extraordinary vitality ... a great deal of well-meant labor has been employed in trying to bring Asiatic customs and English law into harmony without the aid of legislation, and it need hardly be said that the task is an endless one."[24] Maxwell trenchantly observed the following: "Nothing so fatal to the prosperity of the country and so unsuited to the native mind as the introduction of English real-property law has been dreamt of."[25]

Maxwell's lament had an immediate, practical cause that was full of consequence. Writing in 1884, he was most concerned with the officials and "independent class of British settlers, planters, miners and others" who might find it important to know what "rights in contiguous land their native neighbors may have, and how far they are at liberty to alienate them."[26] It was the moment of that increased economic exploitation in tin and rubber that would have an enormous impact on some of the Malay states in a very short period of time. The "liberty to alienate" had a new urgency that was not disguised by Maxwell's all too ostentatiously pious hope that he would be amply repaid for his trouble if "increased recognition and respect for the rights of native land-holders should be obtained thereby." Here, the need to "understand" and to legislate is explicitly bound to a more complex and far-reaching form of domination of Malay society.

In Singapore and Penang, by contrast, where plantations and mining were of only minor significance, the administrator could rely on the convenience of the fiction that these islands "had no population prior to their acquisition by the East India Company," a reliance that opened up minimally regulated spaces for the growth of "real property," to Hadrami, Indian, Jewish, and Chinese advantage.

Such were the contexts in which Hadrami migrants used their "discretion" as well as their understandings of the colonial modus operandi in ways to which I now turn.

Contesting Wills[27]

In order to pursue my argument about the ways in which over different times and spaces, state, legal, family, and property forms were articulated and inflected one another, as they still do, I shall give a necessarily limited account of two cases. They appear to be among the earliest suits in Singapore and the Straits Settlements in which Arabs went to the colonial courts to contest what they asserted were their rights concerning central issues in family succession and inheritance in terms of both English and Muslim law against other family members.

We should note that both involved heiresses as well as heirs. Both cases concern migratory and legal spaces and jurisdictions. Both unfold over something like 20 years in actual legal action as well as, in the second, having long-term implications and leaving social residues over many decades. One challenged the validity of a will made in Arabia but in terms of English law. The other involved a complex set of claims and counterclaims in the administration of several estates of a family of great importance in both Hadramaut and Singapore. After giving the outline of the suits, I shall also sketch their multiple contexts and the different levels of articulation between family, law, and property. The suits in turn became part of the context of other conflicts and modes of relatedness as well as becoming part of the family narratives of rights, goods, belonging, and relationship. In the rapidly growing Hadrami diaspora of the later 19th century, legal cases also moved across spaces and times; they, too, became rhizomic, had complex forms, and generated experiences of time in which property, persons, and law were shaped and to which they gave shape. Cases took on and generated their own temporalities and rhythms, their own configurations and constellations of relationships and interests.

In the first example, a sheriffa took a seyd to court, and though we do not know the nature of any kin relations between them or between them and the testator, it seems obvious that there were such links. In the second, an immensely wealthy man died, leaving a will.[28] The death of one of his sons and the remarriage of his widow led to multiple claims within the family, claims that were addressed by Islamic mediators and an "umpire" as well as by the court.

Sheriffa (or Sharifah) Fatimah Binte Aboobakar bin Mahomed Al Mashoor brought a case against one Syed Allowee before Justices Ford and Wood of the Court of Appeal of the Straits Settlements sitting in Singapore in 1883.[29] Probate on the will in question had been granted some 14 years earlier, around 1868. We do not know when the testator acquired the property(-ies), when he made the will and in what language, or when and where he died. Executors, attorneys, or administrators must have been appointed, though they are not named in the appeal report. Syed (or Sayyid) Allowee was probably either an original executor or one appointed on the death or departure of the first. In any case, the date of probate is no guide to date of death. After all, as Braddell notes, "In

Chia Keng Siew v. Chia Ann Siew and ors., the testator died on August 18th, 1828. Letters of Administration with the will annexed were granted on October 17th, 1887."[30]

Executors or those holding powers of attorney might have taken no action, been in or returned to Arabia or Sumatra or Java or Penang, or died and in any of these cases not yet been legally replaced. It may be that there had been no action to dispose of the property, or that the sheriffa or one of her relatives had only recently been made aware of the issues by an attempt to convey the leasehold through sale or auction. The news of a person's death, never mind the existence of a will in English forms, might have taken a considerable time during that period to travel. "Proving" the death with a document or documents, properly witnessed and signed by various persons, was a new and lengthy process in several languages—English, Arabic, and Malay. The number, as well as the nature and complexity, of the documents that were necessary to authenticate and *prove* modern identities and legal personhood expanded apace.

The unfamiliar came in obscure and entangling forms. People "forgot" property; did not know of a relative's purchase of land in a distant country; were not clear about who had bought what or when in Singapore, Palembang, Surabaya, Cirebon, Semarang, or Pekalongan; or could not prove it even if they were certain. Persons with an "interest" may never have realized that they in fact had such an interest, especially if they were dispersed across different spaces and jurisdictions. Different members of families have very different knowledge and cultural competencies in situations that may demand a great deal of both and a new kind of social/cultural virtuosity. All of these possibilities in varying combinations are quite common, and most occur repeatedly in documents of much later periods when means of communication offered far greater likelihood of timely communication that was not necessarily utilized. The courts themselves followed procedures, rituals, and forms vastly different from those of the Qadis of Yemen and Hadramaut.

The sheriffa had made her challenge. She could hardly have chosen a more significant matter. As plaintiff, she "sought to set aside a will devising certain leasehold property in this Colony, and properly executed according to English law, on the ground that it had been executed in Arabia, and that its provisions were contrary to Mohamedan law."

She claimed that the fact that the will was made in Arabia meant that "the law of Arabia" should rule, whether or not the properties at issue were in Singapore: that is, *domicile* should prevail over the *place* of the "real" property. Second, she argued that the provisions of the will were contrary to "Mohamedan law." In an obvious irony, the claims were, perforce, made to a colonial court using arguments based on the very law to whose use by the deceased the sharifah was objecting. The articulation and the hierarchy of the two legal "systems" was at stake, in a highly unequal world of power. Sheriffa Fatimah did not argue either that Muslims should not make a will according to English law, or that they were not permitted to do so. The shocking cultural transgressions in the testator's act were no doubt obvious to those Muslims who knew of it. But that was not the point in court. Forty-three years earlier a crucial decision had already been made on this very point. The sharifah's counsel would certainly have been aware of *In the Goods of Abdullah*, 1835.[31] There, it was "held that a Mohammedan might by will alienate the whole of his property and that such alienation will be good *pro tanto* although contrary to Mohammedan Law." The issue had thus arisen in law only some 16 years after the "founding" of Singapore by Raffles. Whatever Muslims had done in practice in terms of inheritance and property disposition, there was already one potentially crucial decision in existence.

Whatever had happened in the interim between death and probate, in the lower court to which the sharifah brought her suit against the defendant, the acting chief justice had found against her. "The validity of a Will disposing of immoveable property, must be decided by the law of the country where the land is situated ... the validity of the Will must be determined by the law of this Colony and not by the law of Arabia, and the Will, was therefore valid." The will stood. The appeal court endorsed the lower court's decision, though it did give permission to appeal to the highest authority, the queen in council, provided that the sheriffa gave a security of S$1,500 for the costs of the appeal and prosecuted it within 12 months. This permission presumably reflects the importance in the judges' minds of the issue at stake. But no further appeal was made.

In bringing the action before the appeal court, the sheriffa was represented by a legal specialist, a relatively new figure in the region and in an increasingly professionalized legal world.[32] (Who advised the testator in the correct drawing up of a will in English terms in Arabia we do not know, assuming that that was, in fact, where he drew it up, but such advice he must have had.)

J. D. Vaughan was a classic transitional figure of the changing colonial world of his times. A midshipman in the Bengal Marine in 1842, he served in the China War in many operations. In the Straits he eventually became chief officer of an East India Company war steamer. In the early 1850s he held the position of superintendent of police at Penang before becoming master attendant at Singapore. On his retirement in 1869, he had been assistant magistrate and resident councilor at Singapore for eight years. As the pages from which I draw this brief account put it, "He was called to the Bar at the Middle Temple in 1869 while home on leave, and on his return was admitted in Singapore." The description indicates something of the relative ease of the procedure at the time.[33]

Midshipman, "pirate hunter," policeman, newspaper editor on a short-term basis, briefly a puisne judge, legal eminence, and participant in those amateur theatricals (as "Mr. Jingle" and "a fine singer and the best amateur actor of his day") that seem so obscurely central to the wider colonial performance, he excited the admiration of the compilers of *One Hundred Years of Singapore* writing in 1921, 30 years after his death: "His practice was chiefly a criminal one, for which his experience in the police and as a magistrate peculiarly fitted him, as did his great knowledge of the native ways and customs." This is a biography that would rapidly become almost unimaginable though it had all the iconographically familiar traits of its period. Even its ending was of its time: "His death was sad and mysterious." One night he vanished from a ship returning to Singapore from Perak.

In Vaughan, Fatimah binte Aboobakar certainly had a major local figure to plead her case. She must have had the legal advice of Vaughan or a colleague that she should or could press her suit with some hope of success. She may have been in fact as well as name the person initiating the action against the syed; she must have paid for that advice, or at least been billed; discussions must have taken place, either directly (though I think it would be unusual for an Arab woman of the time to speak English) or through translators or intermediaries. Questions as to who were the beneficiaries under the will and who would have been the beneficiaries and with what shares under "Mahomedan law" must have been urgently debated, together with speculation, uncertainty in the face of the unfamiliar, and the mobilization of supporters and opponents.

The defendant, however, was not represented by counsel, we do not know why. Yet it is a not unimportant fact, since it indicates that the sheriffa and/or those members of her kindred who also had an interest in the will had the means as well as the determination to pursue her case on what was an important point of law that had considerable implications for Muslims with various forms of property in Singapore, as well as for Muslims in general.

The testator's decision to make colonial law the instrument of succession and the disposition of property had strategic implications of great consequence. It suggested a new reading of the possibilities and choices with major significance for the nature of "family," rights, claims, and expectations that a Muslim landholder could make, one that was indeed counter to profound social, cultural, and economic forces in Muslim societies. It challenged a key distinction, that between *shari'a* and English law, that has, in various and often highly ambiguous forms, run through the debates and practices of law in many areas of what was the British Empire, from India to Singapore, since the late 18th century.

The testator, whose name we are not given nor his relation to Sheriffa Fatima, had thus made his will in Arabia in what Justice Wood called "a manner repugnant to the law of Arabia." Many died intestate, and later wills by Muslims up to the present often simply repeat that the testator wishes her or his estate to be distributed according to Muslim law, after an introductory section giving brief or more lengthy instructions for burial, the preparation of the body, and the execution of various practices and duties as well as certain rituals and the distribution of customary gifts to servants, the poor, and others. This will, however, clearly made disposition of immovable property on leasehold in Singapore in the terms and forms of appropriate English legal formulation and practice.

I have not seen the documents brought before the judges to which they allude. It seems safe to assume—from those bundles of papers in other cases through which I have trawled—that they must have included, first and not too simply, "the will" or "a copy of the will." This in itself needed to be "proved" to be "the will." Probate had indeed been granted. Since the testator had made it, it was said, "in Arabia" and in the English forms, one question is how he came to make that crucial decision and what understanding he had of its implications. The apprehension of those implications and choices would have required professional "translation" of a high order. "The original" must have been drafted by an English-trained lawyer in the appropriate jargon of technical language. In terms of translations from one language to another, problems could easily arise over disputed words, clauses, or interpretations. Moreover, I have seen cases where it was not at all clear whether an Arabic or an English (or a Malay) document was "the original," assuming that "the original" was still thought to be in existence rather than only "authenticated" copies, nor was it clear which was translated from which. The will must have been written out in copperplate hand on proper legal paper of the proper legal paper bond, signed and witnessed by the proper persons whose identities were properly attested by a sequence of higher authorities. The criteria of propriety and what made a witness a witness, a fit and proper person known to the registering authority, had to be clear. The well-known phrase "signed, sealed, and delivered" required considerable technical work. The document had to be *constituted* as "a document" for legal purposes and in the correct ways, a multileveled process.[34]

The bundle of documents before the appeal court would also have included in its new colonial forms some certification of death, probably with the statement of witnesses who signed or thumb-printed their names in front of a person who knew them both and who occupied an official position, affixing his signature and seal. There might have been a translator's signed and registered statement of his position and credentials, as well as documents appointing executors, perhaps powers of attorney and letters of administration, all again authenticated by authorities, step by step.

A crucial focus of interest was the indentures and deeds of conveyancing together with survey measurements of the lots in question. Wills dealt in families and descent. Conveyancing, too, had its genealogy, what is called the "roots of title."[35] Given the dating and from research on indentures of the 1880s as well as the laws relatively recently come into force, I would expect that the genealogy had to be traced back through successive owners to its first constitution as "property" in, to take one possibility, a government land grant in the 1820s, just after Raffles's treaty acquiring Singapore for the Crown.[36] Such a genealogy was a required element in the "proof" and delimitations of ownership. Moreover, by the 1880s, there was much emphasis on the need to define, regularize, and above all re-survey and establish registries for lands in the rapidly growing colony, part of those wider processes to which I have already referred. All these documents would have had to meet criteria of validity and form, from their material substance, paper, size, ink, and seals to their formulations and formulae, lexicon, grammar and punctuation, signatures, and so on.

The sheriffa's case was thus of great importance. The key questions of the significance of domicile and the "Mohammedan" or English nature of the will continued to trouble the courts, as a 1950 report in which the case was again cited makes clear.[37] The case was not, however, the first one to resort to the Singapore courts in matters of Islamic laws of inheritance and the disposition of properties of different kinds. A perhaps more significant and enormously complex case (which I am treating elsewhere) had come to court only five years previously, in 1878: *Syed Awal bin Omar Shatrie v. Syed Ali bin Omar Al Junied & Ors.*[38] Since the Al Junieds (the standard Singapore spelling of the name) were at the time perhaps the wealthiest Arab family and one of the earliest in Singapore with a fortune based on land and houses as well as trade, the suit has a particular interest.[39] Its traces and the ways in which it has structured and sedimented in personal and family histories mark the present moment.

The suit referred back to the will made in September 1852 by Syed Omar bin Ali Al Junied. Syed Omar, a famous figure and one of the first Arabs to come to Singapore, died only two months later, in November of that year. In January of the following year, 1853, the will was proved by the three executors he had appointed: two of his sons, Abdullah (d. 1865 in Arabia) and Ali, and a paternal first cousin, Ali bin Mohamed Al Junied (d. 1858). English legal formulations of the duties, responsibilities, and liabilities of executors appointed by the testator and, on the other hand, of administrators appointed by a court, sometimes to displace executors who were judged to have failed in their duties, were to feature centrally in the unfolding of this and other cases. Muslim families came to see the legal possibilities of challenge available in the new language, positions of responsibility, and practices of managing inheritances over time. The personnel and administration of "family" increased exponentially.

The first named plaintiff in the case, Syed Awal bin Omar Shatrie, was the administrator of the estate of a deceased son of the testator, Haroon bin Omar al Junied, who died without issue in 1860. Awal brought suit against another son, Ali bin Omar, the remaining executor of his late father at the time of the action. Since Shatrie — whose father was not an Al Junied, as the name shows, though it would be interesting to know whether his mother was — had married the Sheriffa Fatimah binte Alley bin Mohamed Al Junied, the widow of Haroon bin Omar and daughter of that first paternal cousin, Ali bin Mohamed Al Junied, who had originally been appointed one of the executors, he had an interest in claiming the share of that son's widow in the estate. The "outside" affine and his new "insider" wife, in her relatively weak position as young widow without children, brought the action.

There were allegations of "conversion": that following the death of the executor paternal cousin, the executor sons of Syed Omar, Ali and Abdullah, had misappropriated for personal use a large proportion of "divers large sums of money" relating to the testator's immovable estate that should have gone to the estate of Haroon bin Omar, or his legal representatives. They had then "absconded," so it was claimed, by moving out of the jurisdiction of the colony. The plaintiffs wanted the court to administer the estate, not those persons appointed by Omar Al Junied himself, the (literally) errant sons, to ensure that proper Islamic partition was carried out.

Those sons admitted to having left Singapore but denied that their departure could "appropriately" be described as "absconding" as it was in the plaintiff's petition. In their perspective, one may easily imagine, they were Hadrami merchants and traders for whom traveling was an integral part of life as much as business. They were, moreover, the elder sons of the deceased patriarch, his executors, the now senior males of the family, exercising the kinds of decisions and powers that must often in practice have been exercised: to move, to administer and/or take over the funds and properties of the father with lesser or greater accounting, orally as much as in any documentary form and according to the particular dynamics of the relations between the siblings and between the siblings and their paternal cousins. They were, so to say, "running" the multisited family or a major part of it and its material resources. Furthermore, the judge tells us later in the report that at the time of the testator's death, "all or many" of the heirs were minors. Just as it is common today in Singapore, in conversations about family trusts, to be told, for example, that "X was always the brother who looked after everything" or "Y was the one his father trusted" or "it was my grandmother who was the businesswoman and ran the family," so one can construct Syed Abdullah and Syed Ali's actions in the light in which they presented them, given the cultural expectations and practices that would have been appropriate to one set of relationships. But those cultural expectations and practices, not to mention the legitimation of authority and decision-making and what was "right and proper," were challenged in another arena according to a discourse in which what they had done was "to abscond."

At stake were land, houses, and buildings, "and the surplus rents and profits thereof," new forms of investment in a new property regime as much as new, rapidly developing social and political spaces and the equally new articulations between them. Since the petition charged, as one of its 25 clauses, that "the surplus of the one third of the testator's moveable estate amounted to dollars one hundred and twenty-eight thousand five hundred and fifty-one, and cents sixty-three and a half," a wonderfully fine accounting precision if ever there was one and almost a parody of that exactitude held to be the mark of modern, scientific practice, we can see that the monetary, as much as the social and spatial, scale of the case was considerable.

As so often occurs in such reports, in order to make and justify his ruling, the judge constructed a history and a genealogy for the current purposes at hand, what I would call a compound narrative of events and procedures that is itself constitutive of the force of his judgment. In constructing that narrative, the judge related "certain matters that took place in 1864." On 29 June of that year, the administrator of the will of Syed Haroon bin Omar al Junied, Syed Awal bin Omar Shatrie,[40] our plaintiff of 1878, who had married the young widow of Syed Haroon, Sheriffa Fatimah binte Alley bin Mohamed al Junied, brought a suit with her against Syed Abdullah bin Omar al Junied in the Court of Judicature of Prince of Wales Island, Singapore, and Malacca. Sheriffa Fatimah was 17 when her first husband died in 1860 and thus an "infant" in law at that moment. Since she was a young widow with no children, she was in a very precarious position to press any claims, though she was the daughter of the important testator's cousin. Her marriage to Shatrie gave her a slightly greater social leverage, depending on his social standing and buttressed by his stressing the claims of the next-of-kin as a whole.

Matters turned on the intestacy of Haroon; the distribution of his and his father, Omar's, estates; and complex accounting of monies as well as for actions, "curious omissions," and a very great deal else besides. The petition argued that Haroon's next of kin according to the Statutes for the Distribution of the Estate of Intestates, English Statutes, should benefit from the distribution: his widow, his mother, four brothers, and three sisters.[41] The claim was thus a collective one drawing together a wide range of legally defined persons. What was crucial in that argument was that under those statutes, the widow "is entitled to one-half of his [i.e., Haroon's] personal estate and effects." This is a higher fraction than she would have been entitled to under Islamic law, where she would have received one-quarter as a widow without children. The judge's account, read in court by him and/or published in the report, includes the full petition of 1864.

The account also shows what I would call the incorporative as well as the hybrid nature of the processes in which the various actors engaged. In December 1864 there was an order of court requiring that all the differences between the parties be referred "to the award, arbitrament and final end and determination" of two distinguished syeds of the Al Hadad and Al Sree families respectively. Both were appointed by order of court. And in the event that they were unable to agree in making an award, then the case should go "to the umpirage and final end and determination of Syed Hassan bin Alwee bah Rekman as umpire."[42] The arbitrators agreed on what Syed Haroon's estate was worth and what his widow's share should be ("five thousand nine hundred and ninety-seven reals and forty-six cents"). But they disagreed on her share from her late husband's share in the "rents of houses and land that are remaining" and other matters. They further disagreed as to the costs of the suit and over whether the "request" by Syed Abdullah bin Omar, his father's executor, that trustees should be appointed over the estate of the litigious Sheriffa Fatimah, should be granted. The arbitrators' signed declaration of 13 January 1865 is incorporated, probably in full and in English translation from the Arabic, in the judge's narrative. Next is included the declaration of the umpire, similarly translated, who, "to cut this matter in two," as the translation has it, decided on 14 January, the very next day, to end the disputes by a calculation of all that was owed to the sheriffa, which he computed as a total of 20,052 reals and 52 reals and 24 cents.

Notwithstanding the fact that the initial award seems to have been acted upon, the judge says, the plaintiffs presented their suit in June 1877. The parties appealed to "the direction of this Honorable Court" for justice. In other words, they sought the colonial court's authoritative ruling on matters of conflict at the heart of a Muslim Arab family, specifically, the rights of the widow in the distribution of her husband's estate. They did so at a moment when the rights of Muslim married women were receiving particular judicial attention.[43]

Let me make a few simple points. First, already by the 1860s at least, there was a readiness to initiate legal action in the courts of the Straits Settlements concerning inheritance, executors' actions, and, indeed, the possibility of a Muslim using English law to make a will. Such actions, as they unfolded unpredictably over time, had great importance for different Hadrami persons, families, and communities in terms of succession and the disposition of goods. Second, we have seen that women might have been among the initiators of those actions as well as being interested parties. Third, such actions would become part of what was emerging as Singapore case law, and in some cases would be cited for decades afterward in the courts. Those actions were strategic choices increasingly regularly made by Arabs in a complex mix of practices, laws, and constructions of "family." But they were also choices that required the paid specialized services of an emerging class of English professional guardians, interpreters, and mediators of legal practice and points of law that were themselves frequently obscure, contradictory, or ambiguous.[44] Finally, to make a somewhat different point, such cases would become fundamental to family narratives and the experience of the intimate relationship between property, law, and the person. They would leave traces and residues in memory and also in the testamentary and gift-giving practices of succeeding generations. And they might be the beginning of conflicts over rights, properties, norms, and kinship that once entered into proved extraordinarily difficult to end, structuring notions of "family" for the participants. If one may speak of a family *longue durée*, then the forces that come together in such suits find in them key punctuating moments and times that give that *durée* its characteristics, rhythm, and expression.

Laws, Combinations, and Powers

Let us return to issues of context for this period of the 1850s to the 1880s. Sheriffa Fatimah's counsel, J. D. Vaughan, and the imposing group of advocates in the Al Junied case would have known, though in what detail and with what understanding we cannot say, of the varying decisions following on from different Indian acts and "Anglo-Muhammedan law" as developed in India, not to mention the legal tangles of the position of the "heir at law" and "estates of inheritance" as it had evolved over the years since the first settlement of Penang in 1786.[45] They would also have had some appreciation of just how problematic "the law" was on heirs, estates, and properties, just how in-the-making it seemed to judges who debated over the decades just what laws had been "accepted" and when, what the relationship was with "custom," that all-purpose and problematic term, not to mention with Mahomedan law in their understanding of "it," an understanding they not infrequently and quite rightly referred to as "partial" or "uncertain." Moreover, various Indian acts whose implications were not always agreed upon nor interpreted in the same way were crucial in the matter of the disposition of property and inheritance as in so much else in the Straits Settlements. And, finally, they must have had practical as well as legal experience of the fact that not only were boundary markings supposedly the responsibility of landowners who did or did not act in the matter in any systematic way, there was no enforcement of this provision anyway. As Lo Wai Ping and Lim Jen Hui further point out, the Indian Act Registers from April 1830 to June 1887 show only a total of 27,837 deeds: "*Many thousands had obviously remained unregistered*"[46] (my emphasis).

More broadly, both cases were brought in the rapidly shifting context of imperial expansion in the late 19th century. They played their own part in changing relations between space, property rights, and the cartographies and geographies of power, as well as in the circulation of knowledge about the strategies, tactics, and (unpredictable) outcomes of cases whose shifting temporal aspects were also difficult to judge. Those rights and geographies were being argued and mapped in ever greater detail, often in conflict with colonial subjects or among members of the colonial services themselves. Colonial legal establishments, Singapore's included, were being expanded as law, ordinances, and regulations were multiplied in new regimes of rule. It was part of the variable but increasing emphasis on, acceleration of, and changes in the nature of the bureaucratization and rationalization of the colonial order as well as of its militarization to which I have alluded above. The cases were a very small part of a longer period, too, of constant shifts in the movements of political and religious reform among Muslim populations and states from West Africa to Southeast Asia that were, at least in part, in a dialectical and/or contestatory relationship to colonial hegemony.

The sheriffa's attempt to overturn an English will made by a Muslim and Al Shatrie's move to challenge the testator's son's actions were, therefore, part of emerging processes and combinations of laws and customs, discourses and practices, institutions and symbols that were transnational and transterritorial in their very nature and combined from many sources.

The narrower context of the cases is that of movements and migrations in a world increasingly colonial and imperial. The sheriffa and (I assume) the syed, like the Al Junieds, came from a family of Hadramis, in her case the Al Mashoor (of some significance in Penang, among other places; the Junieds had previously been established in Palembang).[47] But the particular historical moment of the suits is important for two distinct, if linked, reasons. The first is that it was one of markedly increased Hadrami emigration to Southeast Asia.[48] The Hadramis voyaged to and between many places in the Malay Archipelago, as far as the eastern islands of Timor and all along the coast of Java. The second reason is that, as suggested by the documentary evidence I have so far seen, it was also a period in which land ownership (and housing and rents) in Singapore, Java, and elsewhere was increasingly central to the investments and the foundations, whether modest or grand, of many immigrant families' material, social, and cultural standing in Hadramaut, the Hejaz, and Southeast Asia. In some cases this was to remain so more or less until the end of the colonial period around the Indian Ocean.

Charity Begins Abroad

The standing, the social honor, of such families depended as much on the moral and cultural economy as it did on "real" estate. Other closely related orders of reality were also profoundly affected by the partial and uneven combinations and articulations of colonial law with diasporic family. By way of a short coda to this chapter, I shall use two citations to indicate briefly the significance of the field of charity in the disposition of goods by Arab families and how such charity, pious works, and religious injunctions have been framed, or excluded, in the colonial context. The citations are drawn from what, as far as I can tell, is one of the most important early cases concerning the stipulations made by a rich Arab landowner concerning charitable gifts and endowments in an English legal document: *Re. Syed Sheik Alkaff, decd.: Alkaff and Anor. v. Attorney-General, S.S.*[49] Again, I shall present only a sketch of the complex matters at stake.

The year is 1923. The testator concerned, "an enormously rich Arab" named Sheik bin Abd Ar-Rahman AlKaff who had built up a fortune in land and properties in Singapore as well as interests in Jakarta, Surabaya, and elsewhere, had died in 1910 back in the Hadramaut. Between 1888 and 1906 he had set up under English law the six AlKaff Settlements, of some fame in legal circles in Singapore in the succeeding 80 years or more and of some importance in later Hadrami history until the independence in 1967 of what had been the Crown Colony of Aden and the Protectorates, Hadramaut having been in the East Aden Protectorate. He had made a separate charitable trust, the provisions of which were being tested and challenged in this suit.

The first opinion, that of Judge Barrett-Lennard, concerns a specific provision in the deed. The second, that of Acting Supreme Court Justice Whitley, offers a sweeping perspective on the wider field of charity and religion as a whole. Both demonstrate a striking certainty and an imperial confidence in the truth of their observations.[50]

"I must confess that the imputation to an Arab of the wish to assist all poor Muslims in Singapore strikes me as not within the bounds of probability. Singapore is the meeting place of members of many Oriental races or nations of whom a proportion professes Mohammedanism. But the link between Arabs and other Oriental people is of a slight enough character. I am unable to conceive any Arab resident in Arabia desiring to benefit Mohammedans in Singapore equally with, or in preference to, his own race" (Barrett-Lennard).

The flow of monies and provision to poor Muslims was thus excluded from "probability" on grounds of "racial character," the grammar and motivational structurings of which were part of the colonial judicial habitus. English rulings and underlying politico-cultural assumptions thus penetrated the heart of Muslim forms and circulations of charity and the gift. They undermined cultural conceptions and practices of piety and moral obligation in the creation and reproduction of wider relationships of persons across diasporic spaces. Meritorious giving by an Arab to "poor Muslims" could not be permitted as it defied that deeper racial logic. The accumulation and reproduction of symbolic capital through charity did not, in this form, meet the new criteria of the legitimate good.

Indeed, the whole concept and practice of "religion" was at stake in the English criterion of a "religious purpose" that might make a charitable bequest valid, as Justice Whitley's opinion made all too clear:

"[It is argued] that *amur-al-khaira* ['good works,' MG] represents to the mind of a Muslim works of a religious purpose which are therefore *prima facie* charitable ... Now it seems to me the fallacy in this argument lies in the assumption that a purpose which is religious in the eyes of a devout Muslim is for that reason religious in the sense in which that word is used in the proposition religious purposes are *prima facie* charitable ... To be religious *in the true sense* [my emphasis], a purpose must tend to the promotion of religion, not merely secure the approval of the Almighty ... Whereas in the eyes of the Muslim such approval is the only test ... For these reasons I have no hesitation in holding that a purpose is not *prima facie* charitable merely because it is regarded by a devout Mohammedan as religious."

This regulation by the introduction of a new set of criteria by which specific forms of gifts could be made to specific persons or for specific purposes, moves to the heart of the articulation in a colonial context between different legal and moral practices shaping the flow of benefit, of goods and the good. Family, state, property, and law here are brought together in ways that, at least in theory, were meant to prohibit deeply grounded cultural practices. Interestingly enough, different members of the family were on different sides of the argument and used different firms of solicitors. Most of the provisions were, in fact, rendered null;

and it was not until 1928 that the English lawyers, who themselves failed to satisfy the judges as to the validity of the settlor's wishes, were able to construct documents, framings, and provisions that met the standards demanded and excluded what to a Muslim testator — who had himself used English lawyers in the first place, since by this period he would have needed to do so to have some of the properties and incomes distributed after his death in the ways he wished — would otherwise have been taken for granted.

As in the cases of the wills, legal proceedings — with everything that fed into them and flowed from them — played a crucial role in raising to oral and written debate the unwritten cultural assumptions of diasporic communities. Since the language of *intention* is central to counsels' and judges' arguments around wills, settlements, and trusts — what did the settlor *intend*? — we can see just how far reaching the implications of colonial legal discourse and practice were. It was not only the Dead Hand of the settlor that constructed memory in advance through the problematic and contradictory outworkings of the dialectics of power and culture in these settings; not only the testator who wrote the family scripts and authored in part the family narratives, sometimes for generations after. It was also the construction of the "testator," the "will," the "trust," the "beneficiaries," and the "family" in contested legal processes over time and space that penetrated into the heart of diaspora relatedness and its histories.

Notes

* As this is the first published material of my project, detailed acknowledgments are in order. Since September 1999, I have conducted some 25 months of research in Singapore, with visits to Penang, Kuala Lumpur, and Johor and six months in Java, chiefly in Jakarta and Surabaya. I finished this chapter while a visiting research fellow at the Asia Research Institute at the National University of Singapore. To the institute, its staff, and its director, Professor Anthony Reid, my thanks for their collegiality and support.

For four months in 2002 I was a visiting fellow at the Institute for Southeast Asian Studies, whose staff, faculty, and wonderful library were of the greatest help. I cannot list all the people who have helped me in so many ways but must certainly mention the then rector of the now Islamic University of Indonesia, Dr. Azyumardi Azra, for his crucial help in sponsoring my six months' research in Java in 2000. To his and his students' contributions to the study of Islam in Southeast Asia I also owe an intellectual debt. Drs. Jeffrey Hadler and Benjamin Zimmer, then graduate students in Java, showed me vividly how students could instruct professors. They played a key part in introducing me to the complexity and richness of the archipelago.

In Singapore, Dr. Farid alAttas, who has been a generous and enthusiastic guide to many of us studying the Hadramis, has been unstinting in his assistance, introductions, and intellectual engagement. Audiences in seminars to which I have presented papers in Singapore, most often organized by the National University of Singapore Sociology Department, which kindly gave me an affiliation in 2002, have tried to stop me stumbling too blindly in these very new territories. Seminar members at New York University, the Wharton School at the University of Pennsylvania, Harvard University, and Johns Hopkins University have helped me to develop the lines of argument I trace out here.

To members of the families of Arab descent, I owe a very great debt. S. Alwi AlKaff and many members of that family have become friends as much as helpers and willing participants in interviews, conversations, lunches, and other occasions. The AlKaff office has indeed become the most familiar place to me in the whole region. The family's trust, friendship, and generosity are deeply appreciated. To have privileged access to the papers of the family is a responsibility and a debt of which I am very aware. Members of the Bin Talib, Aidid, and Bin Shahab families have similarly gone to great lengths to provide me with materials and to discuss them with me in detail. Individuals of the Abdat, Al Attas, BaIsa, Bagarib, Al Junied, Martak, Nabhan, Bin Shahab, Al Sree, and other families have spent many hours in talk, travel, and discussion with me. Dr. Jamhari, Muhamad Ali, Ebyhar, and Iqbal at various times worked with me in Java and made research possible. They were my guides. In Singapore, S. Kheirudin Al Junied and Kamaludeen have been my research assistants and have given invaluable help.

The project was entirely financed on generous paid research leave from New York University until the summer of 2003, when I was given a two-year award by the Carnegie Corporation of New York, an award crucial to enabling me to spend additional time in Southeast Asia. I am most grateful to Dr. Vartan Gregorian and the Corporation for their support. To the specialists and colleagues who have worked often for many years in the region and have been so considerate of the questions of a complete newcomer and so helpful in their responses, my thanks. Engseng Ho, whose own work on Hadramaut is a most remarkable and imaginative contribution to anthropology and history, has been more generous and a more valuable friend and interlocuter than anyone has a right to expect. His subtle comments and responses have played a key part in helping me shape my materials over the past five years.

1. Ahmad bin Mohamed Ibrahim, *The Legal Status of Muslims in Singapore* (Singapore: The Malayan Law Journal Ltd., 1965), 32. Dr. Ibrahim was at one time the state advocate-general in Singapore.

2. M. B. Hooker, "English Law and the Invention of Chinese Personal Law in Singapore and Malaysia," in M. Barry Hooker, ed., *Law and the Chinese in Southeast Asia* (Singapore: Institute of Southeast Asian Studies, 2002), 95–6.
3. C. M. Hann, "Introduction: The Embeddedness of Property," in C. M. Hann, ed., *Property Relations: Renewing the Anthropological Tradition* (Cambridge: Cambridge University Press, 1998), 4.
4. There is a growing bibliography on aspects of these migrations. For current predominantly historical research in English, see, for example, Ulrike Freitag and William G. Clarence Smith, eds., *Hadhrami Traders, Scholars and Statesmen in the Indian Ocean, 1750s–1960s* (Leiden, New York, and Koln: Brill, 1997); Huub de Jonge and Nico Kaptein, eds., *Transcending Borders: Arabs, Politics, Trade and Islam in Southeast Asia* (Leiden: KITLV, 2002); Linda Boxberger, *On the Edge of Empire: Hadhramawt, Emigration, and the Indian Ocean, 1880s–1930s* (New York: State University of New York Press, 2002); L.W.C. van den Berg, *Le Hadhramaout et les Colonies Arabes dans L'Archipel Indien* (Batavia: Imprimerie du Gouvernement, 1886). In anthropology, there is Abdullah Bujra's *The Politics of Stratification: A Study of Political Change in a South Arabian Town* (London and Oxford: Oxford University Press, 1971). Engseng Ho's *The Graves of Tarim: Genealogy and Mobility across the Indian Ocean* (Berkeley: University of California Press, 2006) is a major anthropological study.
5. Peter P. Schweitzer, ed., *Dividends of Kinship: Meanings and Uses of Social Relatedness* (London: Routledge, 2000). See also Antonia Pedroso de Lima, "Assets for Succession in Contemporary Lisbon Financial Elites," in Joao de Pina-Cabral and Antonia Pedroso de Lima, eds., *Elites: Choice, Leadership and Succession* (Oxford and New York: Berg, 2000).
6. Joseph Conrad, *An Outcast of the Islands*, 110.
7. Robert Hampson, *Cross-Cultural Encounters in Joseph Conrad's Malay Fiction* (Basingstoke: Palgrave, 2000), 109.
8. In other writing, I consider the closely related strategic questions of marriage, gifts, dowry, and the selection of those who would take responsibility for particular ventures or areas of family life.
9. Eileen Spring, "The Heiress-at-Law: English Real Property Law from a New Point of View," *Law and History Review* 8, 2 (fall 1990): 273. One should not, perhaps, have to argue the point to anthropologists or historians, but inheritance in general does seem to have attracted much less attention than it deserves. Lawrence M. Friedman, in a book review of Shammas, Salmon, and Dahlin, refers to the "woefully small" literature on the subject in the United States and quotes the opening sentence of the authors: "The bulk of household wealth in America, perhaps as much as 80 per cent of it, is derived from inheritance, not labor force participation." He adds, "estates and trusts work is

one of the staples of the profession." Lawrence M. Friedman, review of Carole Shammas, Marylynn Salmon, and Michel Dahlin, *Inheritance in America: From Colonial Times to the Present* (New Brunswick, NJ: Rutgers University Press, 1987), *Law and History Review* 6, 2 (autumn 1988): 499–504.

10. Beshara Doumani, "Adjudicating Family: The Islamic Court and Disputes between Kin in Greater Syria, 1700–1860," in Beshara Doumani, ed., *Family History in the Middle East: Household, Property and Gender* (Albany: State University of New York Press, 2003), 178. As the title indicates, Doumani is writing about the appeal to Islamic courts in the Ottoman Empire. He finds that the overwhelming majority of cases involved conflict over immovable property, *waqf* access rights, and associated issues of inheritance for at least one set of litigants. See also his "Endowing Family: *Waqf*, Property Devolution, and Gender in Greater Syria, 1800–1860," *Comparative Studies in Society and History* 40, 1 (1998): 3–41. In this article, he discusses the remarkable difference between Tripoli and Nablus in terms of the percentage of *waqf* that included female children and progeny, 98.3 per cent and 12.1 per cent respectively (p. 20).

11. Martha Mundy and Richard Saumarez Smith, "*Al-Mahr Zaituna*: Property and Family in the Hills Facing Palestine, 1880–1940," in Doumani, *Family History*, 139.

12. Talal Asad, *Formations of the Secular: Christianity, Islam, Modernity* (Stanford: Stanford University Press, 2003), 7.

13. Pierre Bourdieu, "Marriage Strategies as Strategies of Social Reproduction," in Robert Foster and Orest Ranum, eds., *Family and Society: Selections from the Annales Économies, Sociétés, Civilisations,* transl. Elborg Forster and Patricia M. Ranum (Baltimore and London: Johns Hopkins University Press, 1976), 117–44.

14. Speaking of the penal code in the Straits Settlements, Chan Wing Chong and Andrew Phang note that it "appears to be a modified version of the then English criminal law, together with influences from the French Penal Code as well as Livingston's Code of Louisiana ... when the Penal Code was ultimately enacted in 1871, it was a *local* [emphasis in text] re-enactment of the Indian Penal Code." Chan Wing Cheong and Andrew Phang, "The Development of Criminal Law and Criminal Justice in Singapore," in *Singapore: Singapore Journal of Legal Studies* (Faculty of Law, National University of Singapore, 2001), 4–5. Just to complicate matters further, R. H. Hickling notes that by 1918 the law of the Straits Settlements could be defined as comprising five major elements: the common law, equity, civil, and statute prevailing in England on 26 November 1826, insofar as they were applicable; English mercantile law as applied by the Civil Law Ordinance of 1878; those imperial acts post-26 November 1826 as applied in general to colonies or to the Straits Settlements in particular; Indian acts passed while the Straits Settlements were

under the government of India (1826–67); and Straits Settlements ordinances from 1876 on. With reference to the topics of this paper, Hickling notes that the list is "rather misleading" as it seems to ignore Malay or Chinese law and that personal law, "inheritance and succession to land, rents and goods, and all manners of contract," is likewise left out of legal history. Hickling, perhaps wisely, does not even address at this point the vexed question of just what "Muslim law" was, not to mention the endless inventive possibilities of "custom," colonially codified with all the implications with which scholars are familiar. See also the Hooker reference, note 2 above. Law was thus universal, not so much in an Enlightenment sense as in the kinds of combinations, accretions, accumulations, and "travelings" through which it was being constituted. Judges frequently comment on the problems and confusions they saw themselves as facing, a kind of metacommentary that becomes part of the legal discourse and which certainly marks the writings of legal historians on Singapore.

15. See also Bourdieu, "Marriage Strategies," for the Béarn sense of the child belonging to the estate, his/her identity tied inexorably to it.
16. Timothy Mitchell, *Rule of Experts: Egypt, Techno-Politics, Modernity* (Berkeley: University of California Press, 2002), 57. Mitchell's discussion of private property in our categories of social understanding and rooted in social practices that it helps to define is most illuminating.
17. Sally Engle Merry, *Colonizing Hawaii: The Cultural Power of Law* (Princeton: Princeton University Press, 2000), 5. See also p. 48 for a further discussion of how clientage and kinship were replaced by relations based on the market. See also Laura Benton, *Law and Colonial Cultures: Legal Regimes in World History, 1400–1900* (Cambridge: Cambridge University Press, 2002). On colonial law in India, see Bernard Cohn's well-known article "Law and the Colonial State in India," in his *Colonialism and Its Forms of Knowledge: The British in India* (Princeton: Princeton University Press, 1996), 57–75.
18. Merry, *Colonizing Hawaii*, 45.
19. Bill Maurer, *Recharting the Caribbean: Land, Law and Citizenship in the British Virgin Islands* (Ann Arbor: University of Michigan Press, 1997), 171.
20. Martin Chanock, "Paradigms, Policies and Property: A Review of the Customary Law of Land Tenure," in Kristin Mann and Richard Roberts, eds., *Law in Colonial Africa* (Portsmouth, NH: Heinemann, 1991), 79.
21. Chanock, *Paradigms, Policies and Property*, 77.
22. Ibid., 79.
23. W. E. Maxwell, "The Law and Customs of the Malays with Reference to the Tenure of Land," *Journal of the Straits Branch of the Royal Asiatic Society* (June 1884): 75.
24. Ibid., 75.
25. Ibid., 75–6.

26. Ibid., 77.
27. The cases here refer only to the reported versions in legal journals. It is obvious that the report is only one part of a cumulative social, legal, and documentary set of processes and practices. Its interpretation sociologically and historically requires much more development. I use the reports here very much as indications of some of the factors involved, with no pretension to completeness. Thanks to the generosity of certain Arab families in Singapore, I have much more developed documentary and oral sources for many wills, trusts, and disputes, some of which stretch back to roughly the period of the cases discussed here.
28. *Sheriffa* (in the court transliteration) is the word used by a woman of a family claiming descent from the Prophet Muhammad; *syed* (or, in some parts of the Arab world, *sherif*) is the male title. Hadramaut is one of the many areas in the Muslim world in which such descent may be of considerable cultural or social significance. The issue of prophetic descent became a major division among Arabs in Southeast Asia in the modern period. See especially Natalie Mobini-Kesheh, *The Hadrami Awakening: Community and Identity in the Netherlands East Indies, 1900–1942* (Ithaca: Cornell Southeast Asia Program Publications 28, 1999).
29. Sheriffa Fatimah Binte Aboobakar Bin Mahomed Al Mashoor v. Syed Allowee, in J. W. Norton-Kyshe, ed., *Cases Heard and Determined in Her Majesty's Supreme Court of the Straits Settlements, 1808–1884*, vol. 2 (Eccl.) (1883), 31–3. For the sake of consistency, I do not change the spelling of names used in case reports. Arab naming caused, and continues to cause, problems in English-language legal documents, witnessing, and the authentication of personal identity in a discourse in which notions of clarity, unambiguity, and exhaustiveness are crucial to procedure and authority, whatever the other realities. It continues to be the case not only that the spelling of, for example, Hassan (Hasan, Hason, Hasson) might be at issue, but also the spelling of the "family" name (Balfaqih, Bilfagih, Balfagih, and other variants). So the practices of naming-in-use can generate, in legal processes and texts, long lists of "also known as ... also known as ... also known as ..." A person's name might or might not include the name of the father, grandfather, and great-grandfather (A bin/binte B, A bin B bin C, ABE, etc.), or jump to the eponymous ancestor according to context. Moreover, in the Malay Archipelago, that person might also generally be known by a "nickname" or "the name we know her by" (in Malay, *gelaran*), such as *Wan Chu*, which is so generally used that the "real name" is unknown to most people familiar with the person, including family members. The very heading of this particular report illustrates typical variations: the sheriffa's name (to the gratitude of historians and anthropologists, no doubt) is given with two male ascendants, father and father's father, and the "family" name, whereas the syed is simply

"Allowee." Note that both incorporate the status titles, sheriffa and syed, which presumably were thus part of the "legal name."
30. Braddell, "Heirs," xlix. One of the obvious aspects of common law is that it brings together in reasoning and citation cases that involved persons and groups classified as being by "race," "custom," "religion," and so on as quite distinct.
31. Norton-Kyshe, "In the Goods of Abdullah," in Norton-Kyshe, *Cases Heard and Determined* (Eccl.), 8. The question of whether "goods" referred to movable or immovable property, an important distinction, can here be left on one side. For a discussion of this important case in Singapore legal history, see R. H. Hickling, "The Influence of Islam on Singapore Law," in M. B. Hooker, ed., *Malaysian Legal Essays: A Collection of Essays in Honour of Professor Emeritus Datuk Ahmad Ibrahim* (Singapore and Kuala Lumpur: Malayan Law Journal, 1986), 306–8. This ruling was not actually modified until the Muslim Ordinance of 1957, and it was formally abolished in 1966 by the Administration of Muslim Law Enactment, which established Muslim law as a determinant in the validity of dispositions by will. I should note here that when I asked a Singapore judge, himself a Muslim and someone I know quite well, whether it had ever been possible for a Muslim to alienate all of his property by will contrary to *shari'a*, he was shocked and vehemently denied that that could possibly have ever been the case.
32. In the Straits Settlements, a person could act as both solicitor and advocate in court, unlike the English tradition of separation between the two (until recently).
33. Walter Makepeace, Gilbert E. Brooke, and Roland Braddell, *One Hundred Years of Singapore*, vol. 1 (London: John Murray, 1921), 223–4, 479. When the Straits Settlements Association Singapore branch was formed on 20 March 1868, Vaughan was a founding member.
34. I am currently writing about documents and "the calligraphic family" for publication elsewhere. I owe much to the now-classic work of Brinkley Messick, *The Calligraphic State: Textual Domination and History in a Muslim Society* (Ann Arbor: University of Michigan Press, 1993).
35. Referring to a parcel of land sold in Ibb, in Yemen, Brinkley Messick tells us: "On one occasion, I was shown a series of such contracts relating to a land plot going back as far as three hundred years, all in the possession of the contemporary owner." "Literacy and the Law: Documents and Document Specialists in Yemen," in Daisy Hilse Dwyer, ed., *Law and Islam in the Middle East* (New York, Westport, and London: Bergin and Garvey, 1990), 65.
36. Ricquier points out that 40 years was substituted for 60 "as a good root of title" in the English statutes of the 1870s and 1880s that were the models for Singapore legislation of the latter decade. W. J. M. Ricquier, "Land Law and Common Law in Singapore," in A. J. Harding, ed., *The Common Law in*

Singapore and Malaysia: A Volume of Essays Marking the 25th Anniversary of the Malaya Law Review (Singapore: Butterworths, 1985), 237–8.

37. "In re Alshaikh Abdullah bin Ali bin Ahmad bin Alshaikh Ali Harharah (deceased); Shaikh Salim bin Abdullah bin Ali bin Ahmad bin Shaik Ali Harharah v Shaikah Howdash binte Salim Naser Lahmadi," *Malayan Law Journal*, 221 (1950). All parties admitted, "the testamentary powers of the Testator are governed by the *lex domicilii* (domicile, MG) (not the *lex loci situs*) (place of the goods and properties, MG), which is in this case Arabia, not Singapore. Here the will directed that the estate should be divided in accordance with "Mohammedan law" 21 years after his death. The court held that under the law of the colony (Singapore) "there was nothing to prevent immediate distribution of the estate." It stated that "postponing distribution of the estate was contrary to Mohammedan law." Nor could a Muslim "*by will* dispose of more than a third of his estate" (my emphasis). Here the court cited the Privy Council's understanding of "Mohammedan law." In other words, it seems to me that the court was saying that Sh. Abdullah had made a Muslim will but had done so in invalid terms by creating a kind of hybrid of Muslim and English law. Citing the *Sheriffa Fatimah* case, counsel for the defendant raised the separate issue of "doubt as to whether Mohammedan Law on testamentary capacity applies in the case of immoveables." He also acknowledged the existence of a *contrary* decision in *Re Syed Hassan bin Abdullah Aljofri deceased* of 1949. In both these cases, the principal defendants were women.
38. Norton-Kyshe, *Reports* (Civil Cases), 448–53.
39. On the Al Junied in Hadramaut, see Ulrike Freitag, *Indian Ocean Migrants and State Formation in Hadhramaut: Reforming the Homeland* (Leiden and Boston: Brill, 2003), 101–8. Commenting on Ahmad b.'Ali al Junayd's piety and devotion, Freitag also comments on "the circumstances which allowed him to lead such a scholarly and charitable life. This was not a cheap affair …" (Freitag, 105–6). He had large landholdings in parts of Hadramaut. Omar Al Junied, Ahmad's brother, sent him 500 reals a year (Freitag, 107). The court case gives the date of Omar's death as 1852, but Freitag suggests 1858 following Abd al-Qadir b. Abd al-Rahman b. Umar al-Junayd, *Al-'Uqud al-asjadiyya fi nashr manaqib ba'd afrad al-usra al-junaydiyya* (Singapore: Matba'at Kyudu, 1994), 167, 176–8. The court report gives the death of the cousin executor, Ali bin Mohamed, as December 1858. In the circumstances, I am inclined to follow the court's dating.
40. Later in the report, he is referred to as Awath, closer to what would now be the more conventional "Awadh" transcription of the Arabic; note that the shift in spelling goes uncorrected in the report.
41. "Next of kin" is a term, like "issue" or even "grandchildren" and "children," that could easily become the source of much dispute, especially where the

parties were mingling contested meanings in various legal and customary terminologies, not to say languages, as well as commonsense interpretations.

42. The name is an intriguing mixture of "syed," indicating descent from the Prophet, and the "ba-" prefix on the final name, indicating rather a "sheikhly" family. The usages of such titles, and whether or not "Syed" was a name or a title or part of a composite name might be slippery, as it sometimes still is in the archipelago, where naming practices and others' understandings of them may vary considerably. My assumption here is that the court took "syed" either as an equivalent of something like "Mr." or part of the name and that the umpire was not a syed. If that was the case, it is an example of an interesting choice of supposedly *final* decision-maker: the shaikh came in when the syeds disagreed. The court, and one assumes the parties concerned, found the different status of "outsider" the structurally and positionally appropriate authority. He had the (not-so-final) word.

43. Their counsel and counsel for the defendants will have been aware of growing concern in the legal community about the rights of Muslim women in marriage, divorce, and property, though judges were divided. Sir Thomas Braddell, attorney-general, who appeared in the case for certain of the defendants, was eloquent on the position of Muslim married women in Singapore at the time: "The position of these women has been so difficult, and the operation of our rules of law as to them has been so detrimental to them and their children, that most of our judges have made strong efforts to protect them, and in this way rules have been laid down, and have acquired a certain force by usage; such as … on his (a Mahomedan's) death intestate all his widows should be allowed to take among them, the share allowed by English law to a widow." *Straits Settlements Government Gazette* (21 May 1880), 416. Quoted in Hickling, "The Influence of Islam," 314. These issues also arose in somewhat different form in consideration of Chinese marriage, divorce, and inheritance.

44. In the Shatrie v. Junied case, three counsel were retained, including Thomas Braddell (1823–91), the attorney-general (1867–82), and a member of a celebrated Straits Settlements legal dynasty for several of the defendants. Given the stakes, it is not surprising that such a relatively large array of counsel were retained. For Braddell, see Wong Kok Weng and Sia Aik Kor, "A History of the Singapore Legal Service," in Kevin Y. L. Tan, ed., *Essays in Singapore Legal History* (Singapore: Marshall Cavendish Academic and Singapore Academy of Law), 80. J. D. Vaughan, Sheriffah Fatimah Al Mashoor's counsel, wrote an appreciation of Braddell in the *Straits Law Journal* of November 1891. See Andrew B. L. Phang, "The Reception of English Law," in Tan, *Essays*, 12–3.

45. See Roland Braddell, "Heirs and the Common Law of the Colony," *The Malayan Law Journal*, X: xlviii–l, for a historical survey of cases and judgments on these issues. This particular case would have come under the Indian Act XX of 1837.

46. Lo Wai Poing and Lim Jen Hui, "The Development of Land Registration in Singapore," in Tan, *Essays*, 223–4. The authors comment on the problems caused to land administrators by "the absence of a proper system of survey," the frequent boundary disputes and uncertainties, and the "extensive encroachment of Crown lands" (p. 227).
47. "That's the Burmese branch," "that's the Palembang side," "he's the Penang line," "she was really the Meccan branch," "we're the Singapore line" are examples of very common labelings, sometimes followed by the speaker's elaboration of just what the links were, or were not, between various persons or groups.
48. The *Singapore and Straits Directory* for 1883 cites the 1881 Census figures, which may be a rough guide if not much more: 551 Arab males and 285 Arab females in Singapore; 292 and 282 respectively in Penang, Port Wellesley, and the Dindings; 111 and 116 in Malacca. The 1901 Census gives 1,508 Arabs and 72 per cent of "all races" as Chinese. For detailed material, particularly from the Hadrami side, see Freitag, *Indian Ocean Migrants*.
49. 2 *Malayan Cases*, 38 (1923). The court relied on Syed Ameer Ali's *Muhammadan Law*, vol. II, 4th edition, for its understanding of *waqf*, though judges might — and did — profoundly disagree as to what to infer from Ameer Ali's codification. The Singapore courts of that period could accept as proof of "Muslim law" any "definite statement" on Muslim law made in Ameer Ali. There were other canonical texts that need not be elaborated upon here.
50. A wider treatment of the problems of charity in the Hadrami diaspora is the subject of a chapter in the book I am writing.

10

From Golden Youth in Arabia to Business Leaders in Singapore: Instructions of a Hadrami Patriarch*

ULRIKE FREITAG

Introduction

Links between the Middle East and Southeast Asia grew more extensive in the late 19th century. Steam shipping, introduced to the Indian Ocean in the 1830s, greatly accelerated travel and, by the 1870s, had contributed to a major increase in the number of travelers.[1] The majority of indigenous travelers on the route from Southeast Asia to Arabia and back were probably pilgrims performing the Hajj, although we have to imagine the boats as also having been populated by businessmen, mercenaries, politicians, scholars, and assorted fortune seekers. Thus, while the late 19th- and early 20th-century phase of globalization, complete with fears of anticolonial pan-Islamism and the spread of disease, in many ways resembles the discourses unfolding since 1989, we still know relatively little about the process of traveling and integration from the perspective of those involved.[2] This article cannot remedy the deficit, but it can at least add an interesting, if somewhat individual, perspective to the process.

The document presented here is a *tawṣiyya* or *waṣiyya* (pl. *waṣāyā*).[3] The latter originally meant "will" but also became a term to denote advice, counsel, or admonition. Contrary to the fairly widespread phenomenon of religious *waṣāyā*, frequently issued to the followers of religious authorities, such as Sufi shayhks,[4] this particular document is of a more secular, if not private, nature. It is not a will in the sense of testament, but rather a command, admonition, or, perhaps more appropriate, letter of advice.[5] It will thus be referred to in this chapter by the term *tawṣiyya*, which has less religious connotations.

The author, a Hadrami businessman named Shaykh b. ʿAbd al-Raḥmān b. Aḥmad al-Kāf, addresses his son ʿAbd al-Raḥmān and his great-nephew Abū Bakr b. Ḥusayn, both of whom were about to travel from Hadramaut to Singapore to take charge of the family business. In the *tawṣiyya*, Shaykh al-Kāf gives the two young men in their 20s some words of advice. He speaks of central issues pertaining to the process of traveling, and of the transition from protected descendant of a major Hadrami clan to leader of an internationally operated business firm in colonial Singapore. The document thus provides a rare insight into how certain knowledge and standards of behavior were transmitted from one generation to the next. Documents showing how individuals organized their trans-local existence, or even revealing family relations and expectations, are still a rarity. This is notably true for studies on historical trans-local relations, such as those developed by Hadrami Arabs who straddled the various shores of the Indian Ocean while maintaining physical and spiritual links with their homeland on the Arabian Peninsula. Therefore, the document merits being made available to a wider audience, partly in the hope that similar evidence will become accessible and allow us to ask new questions about trans-local social history.

The al-Kāf Family in Singapore

Before entering a detailed discussion of the document, a few words on the wider context are in place.[6] Hadramis have been part of the Indian Ocean trade network for many centuries. While the beginnings of this involvement, and notably of travel to Southeast Asia, are difficult to determine, there is little doubt that the 17th century saw a major expansion of Hadrami emigration to this region. A second boost of emigration in the latter half of the 19th century can be linked to the aforementioned amelioration of transport facilities in conjunction with an expanding colonial economy that presented entrepreneurial minorities with new opportunities.

By the early 19th century, Hadrami communities were well established in the port towns of the Malay Archipelago, with particular concentrations on the west coast of present-day Malaysia, the northern and northeastern coastal and interior towns of Sumatra, and the ports of northern and eastern Java. From there they conducted local, regional, and interregional trade, often at the interface of local and colonial markets. Links with the homeland seem to have consisted more of familial and religious ties than of trade, which is easily explained by the low population and poverty of Hadramaut.[7]

When Thomas Stamford Raffles established Singapore as a free port in 1819, he set up a number of quarters for ethnic minorities, among them Arabs. This was based on his insight that without Arab and Chinese traders, "trade would be reduced to less than one third of even what it is at present."[8] It took some time for the new opportunity to be accepted; the number of Arabs rose from 15 in 1824 to 465 in 1871 and reached 836 in 1881. By 1911, the figure had reached 1,226.[9] The majority of these were men, often married to local women of Malay or Chinese parentage, or, as the community grew, the offspring of such unions.

The al-Kāf family was one such immigrant family.[10] Claiming descent from the Prophet Muḥammad, the family originally came from Tarīm in Wadi Hadramaut. Not particularly prominent before the 19th century, the family can be assumed to have been involved in agriculture and learning. They had begun to establish themselves in Southeast Asia by the middle of the 19th century, and rose to prominence in Hadramaut. There are indications that the migrant history of family members is actually older. At the time, however, the extraordinary economic success of Shaykh al-Kāf, the author of the *tawṣiyya*, and his older brothers attracted widespread attention both in Hadramaut and abroad.

Initially, the al-Kāf business consisted of exporting spices, sugar, and coffee from Southeast Asia, and importing Indian and European cloth. With the rise in real estate value in the 1880s, this main investment area of many Hadrami firms gained significance. The family firm also managed a high-class hotel and engaged in a series of other ventures. One of its chief lines of business was representing Hadrami investors from Java, Aden, and the Hadramaut.[11] Alkaff & Co., the name under which the family firm was registered in Singapore, was the second-biggest taxpayer in 1907–8. Legally, its base was an endowment (*waqf*), the origins of which date back to 1888.[12]

One fascinating aspect of the al-Kāf story is their trans-local existence, which included political and charitable involvement both at home and abroad. In Hadramaut, political engagement seems to have emerged from political conflict with local sultans who sought to profit from the wealth of their subjects. After World War I, ʿAbd al-Raḥmān, one of the addressees of the *tawṣiyya* and the author's son, founded an association in Tarīm that, for all intents and purposes, took over the town by paying off the local sultan.¹³ The family later sponsored a wide variety of charitable activities either directly or through various societies. To make absolutely sure their deeds were remembered, at least within the family, they paid a leading Hadrami journalist and historian to write their history in the late 1930s.¹⁴ They had meanwhile established themselves as a leading family in Singapore, not only economically but also with regard to their lifestyle.¹⁵ Nevertheless, it would seem that the al-Kāf family remained more closely tied to Hadramaut and to promoting their interests there than did some of the other families. Indicative of this is the fact that they — like numerous Hadramis in the diaspora (*mahjar*) — preferred to send their (male) children to Arabia around the age of seven. Thus, they sought to ensure a sound religious base to their education, as well as a thorough infusion of Hadrami-Arab culture. Of 'Abd al-Raḥmān b. Shaykh we know at least that he was born in Singapore to a mother from another Arab family.¹⁶ This apparent conservatism did not contradict al-Kāf support for the modernization of social and religious forces in both Hadramaut and Java.

It is quite striking that although in a number of cases successors to Hadrami businesses with both traditional and modern training were available, Hadrami families tended to prefer those with religious training. This may have been based on the belief that such training was indispensable, while concrete business acumen could be acquired in practice, as distinct from studying it. The introduction to the document exemplifies this emphasis on religious values and religious life so clearly that no further comment is needed, except perhaps to note that the books recommended on Sufism are most likely from the tradition of the *Ṭarīqa 'Alawiyya*, the Hadrami family order. Ibn Hāshim's family history provides a splendid example: Shaykh, author of the *tawṣiyya* discussed here and the most successful of the three sons of 'Abd al-Raḥmān b. Aḥmad al-Kāf, who founded the family business, is said to have begun his career in Singapore with another Hadrami family as a mere scribe. Only after he had proved his worth by successfully opening a side trade with commissioned goods was he contacted by his brothers in Surabaya and invited to join the family business.¹⁷ Quite independent of the veracity of this somewhat hagiographic account, the cultural ideal of young men even from good families working their way up from the bottom becomes obvious. Shaykh's advice to 'Abd al-Raḥmān b. Shaykh and Abū Bakr indicates that they were to be trained by their respective cousin and uncle, 'Abd al-Raḥmān b. 'Abdallāh b. Shaykh al-Kāf. This, in addition to the suggestion to book private cabins to Singapore, indicates that the launch of these particular young men into the business world in the diaspora was to be somewhat more comfortable than that of most emigrants, including the old man himself.[18]

Shaykh did not shy away from passing on a number of his own observations on the matter of proper business conduct in the *tawṣiyya*, ranging from the counsel to avoid lawsuits to details on how to treat employees. The old man's worry about the family fortune clearly shines through, although it is obvious that he is quite generous as far as the expenses of the two young men are concerned. At the same time, he is concerned about their observance of behavior in line with the social and economic status of the family, for example when he warns them against descending to the level of clerks by joking with them.

However, it was not just the children who were put in touch with the homeland. Members of the al-Kāf family regularly traveled between Singapore and Hadramaut. This movement was not erratic. Instead, the respective head of the family ordered particular individuals to take charge of operations. The *tawṣiyya* describes one such instance. It seems that one aspect may have been the conscious rotation of control over what was more or less collective property, namely, the family firm. After all, there is a certain amount of regularity in the distribution of leadership among the offspring of ʿAbdallāh and Shaykh, the sons of ʿAbd al-Raḥmān b. Aḥmad al-Kāf.[19] Given the rather unsatisfactory state of research on the business practices of these family firms, it cannot be evaluated at present whether this was unique to the al-Kāf family, or whether a similar practice was observed in other family businesses, at least those based on *awqāf*. At any rate, the organizational pattern demonstrates the obvious reign of the family patriarch.

The general functioning of social and economic networks becomes somewhat clearer through the names mentioned in the *tawṣiyya*. At a time when Hadramaut had neither hotels nor banks, travelers stayed with relatives and acquaintances, or in semi-official guesthouses. Sayyid Ḥusayn b. Ḥāmid al-Mihḍār was not only a fellow *sayyid* with family connections in India and Eastern Java, but arguably the most influential Hadrami politician and *wazīr* to the Quʿayṭī sultans of coastal and Western Wadi Hadramaut.[20] The link between the al-Kāf, who stemmed from the territory of the rival Kathīrī sultans, and al-Mihḍār may have allowed them to negotiate their movement of peoples and goods between the two sultanates on more favorable terms.[21] In economic terms, the call on Saʿīd b. Muḥammad Abū Sabʿa was of more immediate interest. This family was one of the few local merchant families involved in organizing trade with India and East Africa.²² Similarly, Sālim al-Yazīdī was one of al-Mukallā's merchants. Muḥammad Jabar, mentioned in *the tawṣiyya* as the main facilitator in Aden, was yet another Hadrami merchant. He originated from the interior town of Shibām and had become the Adeni representative of a number of Hadrami merchants.²³

Possibly the most touching aspects of the document are the most personal. They show Shaykh very concerned about the happiness of the travelers and their families, even authorizing an early return from the intended three-year appointment if need be. The advice to the two married men to remarry soon after their arrival in Singapore must be seen in the overall context of consideration for their mental and bodily health. After all, moral corruption — often exemplified by sexual temptation — was commonly associated with emigration, and was to be prevented at all cost.²⁴ Given the well-established nature of the family, there seemed to be no need for additional considerations, i.e., the pursuit of a conscious marriage strategy, as found in numerous other migrant life-stories. While remarrying was meant to cater for the young men's needs in the *mahjar*, it was clearly not meant, in Shaykh's vision, to entail estrangement from the families in Hadramaut. This becomes apparent from the repeated requests to write and send presents, not just via the family patriarch but directly.

The kinds of presents mentioned in the *tawṣiyya* are themselves of considerable interest: Hadrami honey, usually from Wadi Daw'an, was considered a highly prized speciality both in South Arabia and in India, and presumably an absolute rarity in Singapore.²⁵ However, the other presents that were to be bought in Aden — *ḥalwa*, raisins, and almonds, probably imported from other parts of the Middle East — seem to have been of only minor value. The ostentatious consumption that had been on the rise among Hadramis since the late 19th century, notably those with links abroad, did not seem to play a huge role when it came to buying presents for the immediate family.²⁶

The Document

The *tawṣiyya* was first brought to my attention by 'Abd al-Raḥmān b. Ḥasan b. 'Abd al-Raḥmān b. 'Ubaydillāh al-Saqqāf. He showed me what he said was a copy of an original document, which he later deposited in the National Archive of Say'ūn. This copy is marked A and is the basis for the translation given below. As the document was a copy handed down in the family, it is more than likely that certain parts were omitted — such as the introductory *Basmallāh* that is routinely found on documents from that period, as in the case of the second copy included in Bin Hāshim's family history (variant B).[27] The twofold preservation of the document, both in a book as well as with the family, clearly shows that it was considered to be of some value and expressing a certain *adab* beyond its immediate purpose.

The two copies vary from each other to a certain extent, and it is difficult to establish whether one was the exact model from which the other was taken. Thus, a number of small changes seem to indicate that Bin Hāshim edited the text slightly for wider distribution — for example, the person who provides the travelers with funds in al-Mukallā remains anonymous. It is possible that certain additions can be explained likewise: their descent from the Prophet, which is made explicit by calling him *jadd* — grandfather or ancestor — would have been obvious to the family, whereas a reminder of this claim would have been particularly useful with a view to readers from rival families or those of less noble descent. One also wonders whether the upgrading of the cabins from second or third class in the family copy to first or second class in Bin Hāshim's text is due to considerations regarding status. Bin Hāshim also seems to have been concerned with establishing (or restoring?) order where the document appears somewhat repetitive (i.e., in the section on telegraphing from Aden to Singapore). On the other hand, the lack of the *Basmallāh* on variant A and certain other features indicate that it might also differ from the original. The repetitions in the section on writing from Aden to Singapore might well indicate that a copyist erroneously repeated something.

Without further comparative material, it is impossible to determine whether the original document was less ambiguous, i.e., whether the copyist might have erred, or whether it actually reveals a flow of thought, as might be the case in a fairly personal piece of advice. Obviously, Bin Hāshim's editions raise the further question of whether or not the family history was originally destined to be published.

Bin Hāshim's editions are also worthy of note from a methodological perspective. Many Middle Eastern documents are available only in published form, often without exact references to their origins. If Bin Hāshim's practice can at all be generalized, it would confirm the broad veracity of such documents but clearly point to the possibility of changes. Thus, close textual analysis will always run the risk of dealing with information adapted for the intended audience of the relevant text, rather than with the original documents.

The edition and translation are based on document A, unless marked otherwise. Important variations in B will be indicated in the footnotes.

Translation of the *tawṣiyya*[28]

"Advice given by grandfather Shaykh b. ʿAbd al-Raḥmān al-Kāf to his descendants ʿAbd al-Raḥmān b. Shaykh and Abū Bakr b. Ḥusayn al-Kāf on the occasion of their travels to Singapore on 22 Rajab 1325 (A.D. 31 August 1907):[29]

I advise them first of all to exercise *taqwā* [piety][30] as God and the Lord of the Messengers advised, that is, to avoid everything that God and his Prophet — God bless him and grant him salvation — have forbidden, and to follow the commandments of God and His Prophet Muḥammad — God bless him and grant him salvation. I further advise them to be straight in their obedience of God and His Prophet, to behave properly, and to put aside everything that does not benefit them,[31] and to avoid meddling and officiousness. They should avoid [legal] fights against other believers. I advise them to read the Koran and the *awrād*,[32] and to attend the communal prayers.[33] They should read books of jurisprudence and grammar and Sufism. God willing, they will be protected by God's eye, which never sleeps, and His impeccable protection. And I approve of them in this world and the other. God willing, they will soon return to the fatherland safe and sound, well, and in good health. I will pray for them,[34] and their siblings and children day and night. God blessed them and made them our delight, and that of the Lord of the Messengers,[35] Muḥammad — God bless him and grant him and the pious forefathers salvation.

When you reach al-Mukallā, you should stay with Sayyid Ḥusayn b. Ḥāmid al-Miḥḍār, and agree with the friend (*al-muḥibb*) Saʿīd b. Muḥammad Abū Sabʿa.[36] Ask him about the wood[37] and instigate him to buy it.[38] If you fall in line with the Quʿayṭī state, afford it satisfaction.[39] Any money you might require you will obtain from Sālim al-Yazīdī,[40] whom we have notified. Send presents and letters to your families and children and to us, and write to us from everywhere[41] so that we can rejoice at your well-being.

Once you arrive in Aden: We have notified[42] the young ʿAbd al-Raḥmān b. ʿAbdallāh;[43] he will write you a letter [of introduction]. If he asks you to join him, follow his instructions. And if he advises you to proceed to the *haramayn,* follow his instructions. We have also asked Muḥammad Jabar[44] in Aden to provide you with everything you might ask for. If there is honey available in al-Mukallā, get some as a present for the relatives in Singapore.[45] In Aden, buy some ḥalwā, raisins, and almonds as presents for your families, for us, and for the relatives in Singapore. Anything you might need of my money, whether a little or a lot, is at your disposal. You also have my permission to pay alms *ṣadaqa.*

When you travel to Singapore, reserve private cabins in the second or third class.[46] Once you arrive in Singapore, follow the advice of your uncle ʿAbd al-Raḥmān b. ʿAbdallāh, and when you get to Aden, cable Singapore announcing your travel. On the day you arrive in Aden, send a cable to ʿal-Kāf, Singapore, Abū Bakr ʿAbd al-Raḥmān,' so that he knows that you are in Aden.

Set down to work. Until the end of *shawwāl* this will be under the supervision of ʿAbd al-Raḥmān b. ʿAbdallāh, and from the beginning of *al-qaʿida* the work will be handed over to you, and he will watch you until you are firmly established, then he will leave you for three years. After that you will leave and someone else will take over.

And, by God, perform your ablutions, and take digestives for the stomach, and keep your bodies clean. It is necessary to marry immediately upon arrival, either by contract [i.e., of a regular Islamic marriage] or by ownership of the right [i.e., buying a slave], whichever pleases you best, it will be a blessing.

Agree in writing that all your profits will be divided in half. You are authorized to use my capital, and the profits are yours. Do not give anybody anything without security, and follow your *ʿamm*[47] ʿAbd al-Raḥmān, i.e., co-operate with the same people as he does. *I warn you of lawsuits and lawyers and courts, do not expose yourselves to these.*[48]

If one of you changes his mind and returns home immediately, he should not consult anyone but himself and travel immediately. Safe is safe, the past is past, one needs to be very careful. Do not burden yourself with lost chances of the past. Exercise authority over the people [i.e., the employees] and treat them well, and do not let anyone confront you even once. Check on the clerks, and do not descend to their level, and do not joke with them, so that they may fear you. Settle the accounts with them every night. By God, everything should be precise and in written form, what has been written down is established, what is [merely] remembered, escapes. Start small notebooks and always have a pencil in your pocket to note down commentaries, and avoid forgetting.

God willing you will be protected in your religious and worldly affairs. We do not want you to travel, but it will be a relief for ʿAbd al-Raḥmān b. ʿAbdallāh to get out and refresh himself a little in Ḥaḍramawt. If you find a representative who can perform the work competently, even if we lose 10,000 a year through this, you do not need to inform me. The 10,000 or more can go, so that you find somebody. We only want you to be with us. You know best, because the person on the spot sees more than the absentee. Your families and children, your siblings and parents are happy about you, and delight in you, and pray for you. We will take care of your families and children like you do yourselves, and even more so. They will be happy if they are sent special things for themselves, and we would not object to that, even if it was from our property, which is in reality yours. God willing, if you cannot find a representative with whom you are happy, your place [in Singapore] will be taken by the young Ḥasan b. ʿAbdallāh and Abū Bakr b. Shaykh or Ḥussayn b. Shaykh.

This is our advice to you. God blesses our Lord Muḥammad and his offspring and all of his followers, and thanks be to the Lord Almighty. And I say, may God bless you and lengthen your lives, and grant you pardon and well-being. We will always hope to be reunited with you in the fatherland safe and well, in happiness and joy. Amen, by God, amen.

Thus said and wrote Shaykh b. ʿAbd al-Raḥmān al-Kāf, may God grant him pardon."

Arabic Text:

توصية الجد شيخ بن عبد الرحمن الكاف لاولاده عبد الرحمن بن شيخ
وابو بكر بن حسين الكاف مع سفرهم الى سنقافورا في 22 رجب 1325

أوصيهم اولا بتقوى الله تعالى كما اوصى بها الله وسيد المرسلين وهي

اجتناب ما نهى الله عنه ورسوله صلى الله عليه وسلم وإتباع أمر الله ورسوله محمد صلى الله عليه وسلم،

، وأوصيهم بالاستقامة في طاعة الله ورسوله والسيرة الحسنة واجتناب ما لا ينفعهم وترك الفضول

وترك المخاصمة على عباد الله تعالى، وأوصيهم بقرآة القرآن الاوراد وصلاة الجماعة، ومطالعة الكتب الفقهية والنحوية والصوفية، وان شاء الله محفوظين بعين الله التي لا تنام و كنفه الذي لا يرام، وانا عنهم راض في الدنيا والآخره. وان شاء الله راجعين الى الوطن عن قريب سالمين غانمين في خير و عافيه،

واني لهما داعي آناء الليل واطراف النهار لهما ولاخوانهما واولادهم بارك الله فيهم وجعلهم قرة عين لنا

Golden Youth in Arabia to Business Leaders in Singapore 245

ولسيد المرسلين محمد صلى الله عليه وسلم ولسلفهم الصالح، فاذا وصلتما الى المكلا فانزلا عند السيد حسين بن حامد المحضار واتفقوا بالمحب سعيد بن احمد بوسبعه، واسألوه عن الحطب و حرضوا عليه في بيعه، وان اتفقتوا بالدولة القعطة خذوا بخاطرهم، وكلما تطلبونه من دراهم فقد عرفنا لسالم اليزيدي يسلم لكم ذلك، وارسلوا هديه ورد لاهلكم واولادكم ولنا واكتبوا لنا من كل محل لاجل نفرح بعافيتكم، واذا وصلتم عدن فقد عرفنا للولد عبد الرحمن بن عبد الله يكتب لكم كتاب فان عرفكم بالدخول اليه فاعتمدوا امره، وان عرفكم بالتوجه الى الحرمين فاعتمدوا امره،

وعرفنا لمحمد جبر في عدن يسلم لكم كلما تطلبونه، وان شيء عسل في المكلا خذوا هديه منه لاهل سنقافورا وخذوا هدية من عدن لاهلكم ولنا ولاهل سنقافورا حلوى وزبيب ولوز وكلما تطلبونه من مالي او 2قليل او كثير رخصة لكم، وان تصدقتم رخصة لكم، واذا سافرتم سنقافورا نولوا في مخزن (قسم) شامل 3(قسم)،

واذا وصلتم سنقافورا فاجعلوا امركم لعمكم عبد الرحمن بن عبد الله ومع سفركم من عدن اضربوا كارت الى سنقافورا اعلام بسفركم، و نهار تصلون عدن اضربوا كارت. الكاف سنقافورا ابو بكر عبد الرحمن قده مفهوم انكم في عدن،

وحطوا بالكم على الشغل، وهذه السنة الى سلخ شوال على يد عبد الرحمن بن عبد الله ومن فاتحة القعدة الشغل يسلمه لكم ويكون هو نظرا عليكم، الى رسختوا يخرج وبانخليكم ثلاث سنين وبعدها تخرجون ويقبض الشغل غيركم، والله الله في الغسل واخذ المسهلات للبطن ونظافة البدن، والزواج لازم منه حال وصولكم اما بعقد او بملك اليمين الذي تفرحون به انتم فيه البركه، واجعلوا مكاتبة بينكم في كل ما يحصل لكم من ربح بينكما على الانصاف، ودراهمي رخصة لكم في استعمالها والربح لكما، انما لا تعطون احد شيئ الا برهن، واتبعوا عمكم عبد الرحمن الذي يعاملهم عاملوهم، وانصحكما في الدعاوي والمحامين والمحاكم ولا تتعرضون لذلك، وايضا ان احد تغيّر مزاجه يسافر الى طرفنا حالا لا يقول باشاور قط غيره يخرج حالا،

السالم سالم و الفايت فايت الحذر الحذر ان شييء فات عليكم تحمّلون خاطركم به هي الاتحمل لا تحملون خواطركم بشئ، وايضا خذوا الناس بالجبر و بالخاطر الطيب لا تخلون احد يعادكم مرة واحدة، والكرانية أضبطوهم ولا تنزلون معهم ولا تصفطون معهم لاجل يهابوكم وحاسبوهم كل ليلة،

والله في الضبط، والكتابة ما كتب قر وما حفظ قر واجعلوا دشته صغيره وقلم رصاص في جيوبكم للتعليق ولاجل النسيان وان شاء الله محفوظين في دينكم و دنياكم، ولاوديناكم تسافرون انما رثوه لعبد الرحمن بن عبد الله لاجل يخرج ويتنسم له قليل في حضرموت، ولوباتحصلون وكيل يقبض الشغل ولوبا يقصر علينا في السنة عشره ألف ما عندنا خبر تفوت عشره الاف او زائد عسى تحصلون احد بغيناكم الاعندنا انما انتم اعرف، والحاضر يري ما لا يراه الغائب، واهلكم واولادكم واخوانكم ووالديكم راضين عليكم وفراحا منكم ويدعون لكم، واهلكم واولادكم با نقوم بهم المقام التام مثل ما انتم هنا او زائد، وفرحوهم بالمرسل لهم خاص ما با نقول شيئ ولو من حقنا و هو في الحقيقة الاحقكم وان شاء الله بعدكم في الدول الاولاد حسن بن عبد الله وابو بكر بن شيخ او حسين بن شيخ ان لا لحقتوا وكيل الذي تفرحون به،:

هذه وصيتي لكما، وصلى الله على سيدنا محمد وآله وصحبه اجمعين والحمد لله رب العالمين، واقول بارك الله فيكم واطال في اعماركم ورزقكم العفو والعافية و طول العمر و نجتمع بكم في الاوطان في خير وعافية وفرح وسرور آمين آمين اللهم آمين،

قال ذلك و كتبه

شيخ بن عبد الرحمن الكاف

عفى الله عنه

Notes

* This article would not have written had not ʿAbd al-Raḥmān b. Ḥasan al-Saqqāf shown me the document that is at its heart, and discussed it with me in person and in writing. The editor of this book encouraged me to write the article. I am grateful to both of them, as well as to Dalila Nadi, who helped with the Arabic.

1. William Ochsenwald, *Religion, Society and the State in Arabia* (Columbus, 1984), 60–1; Ravi Ahuja, "Lateinsegel und Dampfturbinen," in Dietmar Rothermund and Susanne Weigelin-Schwiedrzik, eds., *Der Indische Ozean* (Wien, 2004), 207–26.
2. On the fear of disease, see Suraiya Faroqhi, *Herrscher über Mekka*, München (Zürich, 1990), 234–7, 253–67 on the fear of pan-Islamism, cf. Michael Laffan, *Islamic Nationhood and Colonial Indonesia* (London, 2003), 37–9.

3. The former term is used in the copy of the document presented to me by ʿAbd al-Raḥmān al-Saqqāf, the latter in the copy by Muḥammad b. Hāshim [Ibn Hāshim], [al-Kāf family History], untitled manuscript, 65–70.
4. These religious *waṣāya* were sometimes collected and treated jointly with *ijāzāt*, for example, ʿAlī b. Muḥammad al-Ḥibshī, *Majmūʿ waṣāyā wa-ʾjāzāt* (Singapore, 1990).
5. For meanings of *waṣiyya*, see Edward Lane, *An Arabic-English Lexicon* (London, Edinburgh: 1893), book I, suppl., 3055; R. Peters, *Waṣiyya*, EI², vol. 11 (Leiden, 2002), 171ff., considers the legal meanings only.
6. The following is based on Ulrike Freitag, *Indian Ocean Migrants and State Formation in Hadhramaut* (Leiden, 2003), 46–61, where references to the relevant literature can be found.
7. For details, see J. A. E. Morley, "The Arabs and the Eastern Trade," *Journal of the Malayan Branch of the Royal Asiatic Society* 22, 1 (1949): 143–76. For concrete examples, cf. Ulrike Freitag, "Arab Merchants in Singapore," in Huub de Jonge and Nico Kaptein, eds., *Transcending Borders* (Leiden: 2002), 109–42, see pp. 115–20.
8. Stamford Raffles, *History of Java* (London, 1817), quoted after Morley, "The Arabs and the Eastern Trade," 143–76, 163.
9. All figures according to Lim Lu Sia, "The Arabs in Singapore: A Sociographic Study of Their Place in the Muslim and Malay World of Singapore," BA thesis (Department of Sociology, National University of Singapore, 1986), 21.
10. For a discussion of the family and the sources, see Freitag, *Indian Ocean Migrants*, 333–44.
11. National Archives of Singapore, A000124, Alkaff transcript, 9–16; Sumit Kumar Mandal, "Finding Their Place: A History of Arabs in Java under Dutch Rule, 1800–1924," PhD thesis, Columbia University, New York, 1994, 164.
12. Arnold Wright and H. A. Cartwright, *Twentieth Century Impressions of British Malaya* (London, 1908), 710; cf. Freitag, "Arab Merchants."
13. India Office, R/20/A/1409, Translation of secret Memorandum by Said Ali bin Ahmed Bin-Shahab, encl. in Acting Consul-General, Batavia to Foreign Secretary, London, 4 December 1920; cf. Freitag, *Indian Ocean Migrants*, 302–6, 443–9.
14. Muḥammad b. Hāshim [Ibn Hāshim], [al-Kāf family History], untitled manuscript made available to me by Sayyid Muḥammad b. Saqqāf al-Kāf, Jeddah. Although the manuscript is dated 1377/1959, Ibn Hāshim mentions the date of writing as 1358 (1939–40), 51. The non-publication of the manuscript indicates that it was not intended for public consumption, as the family did not shy away from sponsoring publications in other circumstances.
15. Freitag, "Arab Merchants," 124.
16. See the family tree in Freitag, *Indian Ocean Migrants*, 337.

17. Ibn Hāshim [al-Kāf family history], 28–30. For other cases of traditional education by future business leaders, see Kazuhiro Arai, "Arabs Who Traversed the Indian Ocean: The History of the al-'Attas Family in Hadramawt and Southeast Asia, c. 1600–c. 1960," PhD thesis, University of Michigan, 2004, 261.
18. Linda Boxberger, *On the Edge of Empire* (New York, 2002), 42–4.
19. Ibn Hāshim [al-Kāf family history], 51–4.
20. For a biography, see Ḥāmid b. Abī Bakr al-Miḥḍār, *Tarjamat al-zaʿīm al-sayyid al-ḥabīb Ḥusayn b. Ḥāmid al-Miḥḍār wa-l-salṭana al-quʿayṭiyya* (Jeddah, 1983).
21. Between 1919 and 1922, they even succeeded in renting the tax farms of a number of Hadrami ports from the Quʿayṭī sultan: Freitag, *Indian Ocean Migrants*, 346.
22. Freitag, *Indian Ocean Migrants*, 166. On the political history of the period, see Boxberger, *On the Edge of Empire,* 183–241.
23. Communication by ʿAbd al-Raḥmān b. Ḥasan al-Saqqāf.
24. Engseng Ho, "Hadhramis Abroad in Hadhramaut: The *Muwalladīn*," in Ulrike Freitag and William G. Clarence-Smith, eds., *Hadhrami Traders, Scholars and Statesmen in the Indian Ocean, 1750s–1960s*, 131–46.
25. Cf. the interesting comments by Harold Ingrams, *A Report on the Social, Economic and Political Condition of the Hadhramaut* (London, 1937), 52–4.
26. On the issue of consumption and sumptuary laws, see Ulrike Freitag and Hanne Schönig, "Wise Men Control Wasteful Women: Documents on 'Customs and Traditions' in the Kathīrī State Archive, Sayʾūn," in *New Arabian Studies* 5 (2000): 67–96.
27. Ibn Hāshim [al-Kāf family history], 65–70.
28. B: *waṣiyya*.
29. B: In the name of God, the merciful Redeemer. Thanks be to God, creator of mankind, and His prayers for our Lord Muḥammad and all his descendants and companions. This is a memorandum/*tadhkira* from Sayyid Shaykh b. ʿAbd al-Raḥmān al-Kāf to his children ʿAbd al-Raḥmān b. Shaykh and Abū Bakr b. Ḥusayn al-Kāf.
30. On this key Quranic concept, which can also be translated as "god-consciousness" or "godfearing," see Ahmad Shboul, "Taqwā," in John L. Esposito, ed., *The Oxford Encyclopedia of the Modern Islamic World*, vol. 4 (New York, Oxford: Oxford University Press, 1995), 189 ff.
31. Variant B: *mā lā yuʿnīhim* (which does not concern them).
32. Special prayers recited at night before sleeping.
33. Variant B: *wa-awṣīkum bi-kuthrat al-awrād wa-l-ḥuzūb al-qurāniyya wa-l-ṣalāt fī-l-jamāʿa wa-antum in shāʾ Allāh maḥfūẓūn ...* (and I advise you to pray many *awrād* and [to read] the sections of the Qurʾān [*ḥuzūb* is read as

a variant of *ḥizb/aḥzāb*, meaning the 60th part of the Qur'ān], and [to attend] the communal prayers, and God willing you are protected....
34. From this point, B substitutes "you" for "they," i.e., *wa-anā lakum dāʿī* ...
35. B: *jaddikum Muḥammad*: your grandfather Muḥammad.
36. B: Saʿīd b. Aḥmad Bū Sabʿa.
37. According to the annotation in Bin Hāshim [al-Kāf family history], 66, this refers to wood imported from Malaya and Java. This may have been particularly valuable tropical wood, as normal building material would have consisted of mangrove poles from East Africa: W. H. Ingrams, *A Report on the Social, Economic and Political Condition of the Hadhramaut* (London, 1937), 78.
38. B: *wa-ḥarraḍūhu ʿalā biʿ al-ḥaṭab wa-is'alūh*.
39. B: *wa-in ittafaqtum bi-aḥad min rijāl al-dawla al-quʿayṭiyya fa-khudū bi-khāṭirihim*.
40. B: *wa-qad ʿarrafnā li-fulān yusallim* ...
41. B: *maḥall taṣilūn ilayh li-ajl an nafraḥ bi-ʿāfiyyatikum*.
42. A: *ʿarrafnā*, B: *katabnā*.
43. ʿAbd al-Raḥmān b. ʿAbdallāh b. ʿAbd al-Raḥmān al-Kāf, a nephew of Shaykh.
44. B: *wa-qad katabnā li-fulān bi-ʿAdan*.
45. B: *wa-in wujid hunāk ʿasal khudhū minhu hadiyya li-ahl Sinqāfūra wa-khudhu hadiyya min ʿAdan li-ahlikum wa-lanā wa-l-ahl Sinqāfūra khdhū ayḍan ḥalwā wa-lawz wa-zabīb wa-kull ma tatlubūn min darāhim qalīl wa-kathīr lakum al-rukhṣa*.
46. The two versions begin to differ significantly here. Interestingly, Bin Hāshim claims that travel was advised in the first or second class.
47. Paternal uncle, honorific title for elderly relative or acquaintance.
48. Emphasis in the original.

11

M. Asad Shahab: A Portrait of an Indonesian Hadrami Who Bridged the Two Worlds

Mona Abaza[1]

Introduction

This paper examines the biography of a Jakarta-born intellectual of Hadhrami origin, Sayyid Mohammad Asad Allah bin Ali bin Ahmad bin Abdallah bin al-Hussayn bin Shahab al-Din (hereafter referred to as SMAS) (1910–2001), who spent 18 years in Saudi Arabia and traveled widely in the Muslim world and Europe. How can an exploration of his trajectory and writings enrich a *longue durée* perspective and lead to a deeper understanding of the networks, exchanges, and transmission of knowledge between the Middle East and Southeast Asia? By looking closely at the life of a hybrid intellectual who spent most of his life moving between the diverse worlds of Islam, I aim to make SMAS an exemplar of the "intermediary," the "go-between" or the *passeur culturel*[2] of the different cultures of the Muslim world.

This intellectual wrote in various languages — Arabic, English, and Indonesian — and addressed various publics in different spaces and times of his life. His entire life consisted of constant travel and movement between the Middle East, Southeast Asia, and Europe. The international and local events he experienced in Indonesia led him to be involved in consolidating a position that can, in our time, be viewed as being a pro-Saudi *Salafi* vision. His involvement in the Muslim World League in Saudi Arabia can be perceived as part of a larger Pax Saudi era, when Saudis attempted to extend their influence all over the Muslim world by spreading a conservative version of Islam, mainly through funding religious schools and institutes for the Arabic language in various parts of Africa and Southeast Asia. The Saudi involvement is clearly evident in the book SMAS wrote on the Muslims of the Philippines, one of the three books I will discuss in this article.

SMAS is certainly not the only Hadhrami Indonesian who lived his life shifting between the different cultures of Islam while maintaining a nostalgic feeling for a "home" that was elsewhere, and which was somehow better than the contemporary world in which he lived. Certainly, what constitutes "home" is subject to many debates. If we look at the trajectory of his father and brother, we find similarities in interests and professional careers. There was a long family tradition of maintaining contacts and links with the Middle East through family ties, politics, and economic networks. The biography presented here could be seen as typical of members of the Arab diaspora in Indonesia, for whom travel for adventure and migration, alongside a longing to return "home," constituted a "second nature."

To use a Braudelian perspective, this biography could be seen as a typical example that could feature as a "long lasting constituent[s] of a system" of the *longue durée* economic and cultural exchanges.[3] Sanjay Subrahmanyam argued that a close look at Braudel's concept of the Mediterranean reveals that he was entrapped in a Eurocentric vision, as he depended almost solely on European sources.[4] Going beyond Eurocentrism,[5] Denys Lombard believed that one could apply a Braudelian perspective to Southeast Asia, which Lombard had described as "the second Mediterranean." Lombard's idea materialized in a conference titled "La Mediterranée Asiatique."[6] Here, I would like to follow up Lombard's ideas and focus on an account that highlights the significance of South-South interactions, specifically by referring to non-Western sources. At this stage, this article can provide only a preliminary introduction to the life and Arabic works of SMAS.

Life and Family Background

Sayyid Mohammad Asad Allah bin Ali bin Ahmad bin Abdallah bin al-Hussayn bin Shahab al-Din, also known as Sayyid Mohammad Asad Shahab, or SMAS, was born in Pekojan, Jakarta, on 23 September 1910 and died on 5 May 2001. He sprang from a prominent family of anticolonialist and reformist intellectuals. He was one of eight children. SMAS first studied at the Madrasat Samail Huda in Pekalongan, and in

1932 he went to the Madrasat al-Khayaariah Aliyah in Surabaya, where he learned English and Dutch.

After studying law at the University of Indonesia, SMAS launched on a successful career in journalism. He worked for the journal *Mingguan Tidar* between 1936 and 1938. Another source states that in 1935 he became the chief editor of the weekly *Tidar*, which was censored by Dutch authorities in 1939.[7] During the period 1938–42 he was also a correspondent for an Egyptian newspaper. He worked for many other press agencies, such as the Arabian Press Board. During his work as a press correspondent, he resided in many countries in the Middle East — Iraq, Egypt, and Saudi Arabia — and traveled to Japan. He worked as a correspondent for several newspapers, including *al-Mughattam* (or *al-Mukattam*) and *Al-Ikhwan* in Cairo, *al-Amal* in Iraq, *Mimbar al-Shaab* in Morocco, *al-Irfan* in Lebanon, and *al-Saqafa* in Argentina.

During the Japanese occupation of Indonesia, SMAS dedicated his time to writing novels, and he also created a youth organization named al-Futuwa. After independence, he was appointed as attaché for public relations in the office of the High Command. He soon resigned, however, and founded the Asian Press Board (APB),[8] which was recognized by the government in 1945. In 1963 Sukarno nationalized the APB and the other agencies that were not communist, and the APB was merged with the Antara press agency.[9] During the 1950s SMAS became involved in the Turkistan movement and wrote a book about this.

SMAS also published two newspapers — the English-language National Press Digest, and the National Press, in Bahasa Indonesia. Both papers encountered a similar fate as his earlier enterprises; they were censored and shut down by Sukarno. Later, SMAS published *Pembina* magazine and ran a printing company and a bookshop called Pusaka. He became known for creating the first committee in solidarity with the Palestinian people and the first *hay'at al-buhuth al-islamiyya* (Islamic Research Council) in Jakarta. When the communist rioters attacked the offices of these enterprises, he left for Germany and settled in Munich. By the time of the turbulent events in Indonesia in 1965, he was in Rabat (Morocco). But he soon moved to Saudi Arabia, where he lived until 1984;[10] during this time he worked for the *Rabitat al-'Alam al Islami*, the Muslim World League. SMAS's deliberate "exile," or *hijra*, in Saudi Arabia[11] is the background for his writing, which betrays a strong anticommunist tone and a deep dislike for the Sukarno regime. In 1985, at the age of 75, he returned to Indonesia, where he died in 2001.

SMAS's love for journalism, and for travel, seemed to run in the Shahab family. His father, al-Habib 'Ali bin Ahmad Shahab, was a well-traveled man who had many contacts with prominent intellectuals and politicians in the Middle East. He became involved with the Jamiatul Khair movement, a reformist movement founded in 1905, which aimed to spread modern education among Arab Indonesians. Its founders invited reformist scholars from the Middle East to teach in Indonesia.

SMAS's brother, Mohammad Diya', was also a prominent journalist who started his career as an editor of the journal *Hadhramawt* in Surabaya and was a correspondent for the Cairo-based *al-Balagh* and the Singaporean *al-Salam* journals. He co-founded the APB with SMAS and was a member of the central committee of the Ministry of Information in the Bandung Conference. He taught at the police academy and was a member of the Islamic Research Council and a founder of the Palestine solidarity committee, like his brother. Diya' worked as a translator at the Saudi Arabian Embassy in Jakarta and was an employee of the Muslim World League. Equally, he wrote extensively about Indonesian history and Sukarno and translated from Arabic to Indonesian some works on Islam by the Egyptian scholar known as Bint al-Shati' ('Aisha Abdel Rahman).[12] Like his brother, Diya' was fluent in many languages and wrote extensively in the Indonesian language. He worked with his brother in founding the Palestine solidarity committee.

SMAS's obituary includes numerous pictures taken in his Jakarta residence, where he received delegations, scholars, and journalists from the Middle East. The photographs include Iranian, Arab, and European scholars. For scholars who were interested in the Arab diaspora of Indonesia, SMAS was a key figure in Jakarta. Before the 1965 events, the Arabian Press Board kept an international outlook by issuing bulletins in three languages — Indonesian, Arabic, and English — and having correspondents all over the Muslim world.[13]

The Writings of SMAS

Even before SMAS left Indonesia to live in Saudi Arabia and Europe in 1965, his work as a journalist betrayed his pan-Islamic views. In addition to his journalistic articles, SMAS wrote 32 books in Arabic and many in Indonesian. My preliminary discussion of his literary output is based on three of his Arabic books — one novel and two historical/political studies. The quality of these texts suggests that Arabic could have been his mother tongue. He was, indeed, "at home" in Arabic, using subtle Arabic expressions. His son told me that he wrote poetry in Arabic, but this was never published. In the introduction to the novel that I will discuss, *Min samim al-waqe'* (*From the Innermost Reality: An Indonesian Novel*), subtitled "A Story Without Any Female Characters," which he published in 1972 in Beirut, SMAS wrote that all his novels were based on true stories, and that he tried to transform these into narratives. *Min samim al-waqe'* was his eighth novel.

I will try to contextualize his writings within the global politics of the time and the shifting worlds of Islam. The nonfiction books I will discuss, *Pages from Contemporary Indonesian History*[14] and *A Journey to the Interior of the Moro Islands*,[15] address a wide public and inform readers about the political situation in Southeast Asia at the time.

Both books were written when SMAS was living in self-imposed exile in Saudi Arabia. SMAS stated that he had left Indonesia following the destruction of his press agency by the communists. In Saudi Arabia he worked for the Muslim World League.

The two books can be understood in the context of the turbulent events of the 1960s in the Middle East and, by extension, in Southeast Asia. In the Middle East the political atmosphere was poisoned by a ferocious rivalry between the Nasserite regime, which promoted an anticolonial "progressive" version of Islam, and the Saudi Arabian pro-American axis. Gamal Abdel Nasser's rhetoric was supporting independence movements, anti-feudalism, and socialism (although he was a staunch anticommunist and was a strong supporter of the Bandung alliance). Radio Cairo, heard all over the Muslim world, launched powerful attacks against reactionary regimes such as those of Saudi Arabia. Nasser and Sukarno tried to establish a coalition against the *Salafi*-oriented movement supported by Saudi Arabia. Many commentators believe that this Islamic internationalism served US interests well at the time, by counteracting the rising nationalist regimes.

In the 1960s, Nasser and Sukarno tried to establish a coalition against the *Salafi*-oriented movement. This led in turn to the creation of the Muslim World League in 1965 in Jakarta. During that period, 111 of the *Salafi 'ulama* politicians and intellectuals of 31 Muslim countries met to counteract the Sukarno-Nasser alliance and enforce the Wahabi version of Islam.[16] The work of Reinhard Schulze reveals that the Muslim World League was created to counteract the Bandung Nasser-Sukarno axis. It is in this context that we should read SMAS's role in propagating a fervent anticommunist ideology as fitting to the then-expanding Saudi Arabian *Salafi* axis.

Pages from Contemporary Indonesian History

SMAS wrote *Safahat min tarikh Andunisia al-mu'assira*, or *Pages from Contemporary Indonesian History*, in the late 1960s.[17] The second edition I have obtained from SMAS's son was published in Beirut. It was favorably reviewed in journals throughout the Islamic world. From the various journal reviews that are listed in the book, it is clear that SMAS must have already resided in Saudi Arabia, since he arrived in 1965. The reviews included in the book were published in the following newspapers and journals: *Al-Nadwa* in Mecca on 14 October 1969; the Journal of the *Rabitat al-'Alam al-Islami* in May 1970; and *al-Jazeera* on 29 December 1970. All the reviews were favorable and positive.

Let us recall that the book was written immediately after the author "escaped" Indonesia and his press agency underwent, according to him, a massive destruction from the communists. His writings transmitted the message that he fled the country due to both Sukarno's shattering politics and the irresponsibility of the communists.

The book displays a deep dislike of Sukarno and the communists, who were portrayed as being manipulated by external forces. SMAS describes the pervasive role of the communist movement in Indonesia, showing how international communism, in particular the China version, played an important and "negative" role in the events of 1965. The entire book is a tract demonizing both Sukarno and the communists as irresponsible and cruel.

Sukarno is portrayed as a womanizer, sexually obsessed and on the edge of being mentally disordered;[18] he is said to have continued his love affairs into old age. Gossip has it that he forced a young student to leave her fiancé, a young officer, and then married her in secret.[19] It was also believed that during his visits to Japan, he spent all his money on prostitutes. The book contains many pictures of Sukarno dancing and conversing with various women. A whole chapter is devoted to the memoirs of Sukarno's Japanese wife, Ratna Dewi, which focus on the last days of Sukarno's rule and his confinement in the Bogor residence. With regard to allegations of corruption, SMAS mentions the report of the Attorney General that Sukarno salted away $2.5 million in Bank of Tokyo and another $2 million in the Netherlands. SMAS, although he was no admirer of Sukarno, admitted that he was a great orator, that he had an appreciation for fine art, and that he was a fine composer and a skillful architect.[20] The book also includes descriptions of Sukarno's house and library.

SMAS interpreted the Bandung Conference of 1955 as a failure, as no follow-up meetings were held and it was clear by the end of the conference that no harmony existed among its participants. A movement united only by the idea of non-alignment was not strong enough to overcome the very different principles and aims of the participating countries — nationalism, communism, socialism, capitalism, and varying religious orientations. The group lacked a single common interest, such as that which bound the Commonwealth of Nations, the Warsaw Pact, the United Nations, or the Organization of the Islamic Conference.[21]

SMAS seems to subscribe to the view that "Orientalists" are to blame for all the evils of the postcolonial period, especially the spread of communism. SMAS attributed the spread of communism in Indonesia to Dutch colonialism. The Dutch Orientalist Christiaan Snouck Hurgronje[22] had predicted the growing role of the Muslim anticolonial movement and recommended dismantling the Islamic movement from the inside by importing destructive concepts that would annihilate Islamic doctrine. SMAS perceived Hurgronje as having encouraged atheistic movements, such as nationalism and Marxism, on the premise that they would weaken the Islamic movement. Communism would spread atheism and corruption, and would distract the masses from resisting the Dutch colonial power.[23]

It must be pointed out that Hurgronje remains a controversial figure. He converted to Islam, married two Indonesian women, and lived in Indonesia for many years. But his intellectual honesty (particularly concerning his conversion to Islam) has been questioned both by Dutch Orientalists[24] and by some Indonesian Muslims. Until today, there is much debate over Hurgronje's Islam policy, as in the question of whether he was purely a colonial administrator or promoting a humanitarian policy toward Indonesians. He owes this reputation partly to the fact that he lived in Arabia for a year between 1884 and 1885 and spent six months as a disguised Muslim in Mecca. His personal life became a legend, perhaps because he converted to Islam in Mecca and was renamed 'Abdel Ghaffar. In Indonesia, as in Mecca, he behaved as a Muslim. Indonesians remember him under different Muslim names and titles, such as Abdogapha, Si Gam, and later Teungkoe Hadji Blanda.[25]

In some Muslim circles, be it in the Middle East or in Southeast Asia, Hurgronje is perceived on a popular level as a Dutch "spy" and an Orientalist who conducted a policy that was antagonistic to Muslims.

Nonetheless, this view is problematic because a close look at his writings reveals that for his time he was an enlightened and concerned scholar. However, it seems to me that SMAS perpetuates a populist view by blaming "Orientalists" for all evils of the postcolonial period.

SMAS wrote that the Dutch authorities chose the architect N. J. F. M. Snevliet, a known Marxist and member of the Socialist Democratic Party, to spread Marxist principles in Indonesia. Soon after the Communist Party of Indonesia (PKI) was founded in 1920, it joined the International Komintern, while continuing to obtain support from the Dutch authorities.[26]

SMAS provides a lengthy biography of Aidit, the leader of the PKI, reproducing long passages of his speeches. Aidit stated that he read the Qur'an and that Islam did not contradict communism, as it too was against injustice and poverty. In his memoirs, Aidit stated that he was responsible for the 30 September 1965 movement, which was drawn up by the central committee of the PKI. SMAS mentions that Aidit's 60-page memoirs were serialized by a Japanese newspaper. One chapter of the memoirs is dedicated to why communism had failed for the last 50 years. Aidit was hanged by a military court on 4 December 1965.[27]

SMAS describes how China, through the Chinese Embassy in Jakarta, played a pervasive role in funding the Indonesian revolutionary movement and influenced the events of 1965. The Indonesian communists became pro-Chinese as a result of signing the Jakarta-Peking treaty, thus opening the door to Chinese influence in the country; the main argument for this view was the Indonesian government's discovery, in some parts of the country, of weapons sent from China. In 1965 the Chinese Embassy in Jakarta invited several Indonesians to attend the October Revolution ceremony, providing them with first class air tickets.[28] The Chinese ambassador was reported to have been very happy when the communists announced in 1965 that they had taken power.

Several long chapters are devoted to the events of 1965, condemning the communists for killing the army generals, and especially for the brutal torture and decapitations carried out at Halim Air Base.[29] Sukarno is portrayed as having approved of these actions, and General Nasution's version of the story is given as if it is the only authentic source. Recently published documents on the 1965 massacre point to Suharto's extensive involvement in the bloodbath, which resulted in about one million deaths.[30] Suharto used as his excuse the need to defeat the left-wing military counterinsurgency, making it necessary to use the communists as scapegoats and to eliminate them.

The army generals were portrayed as innocent victims. Not one word is mentioned of the pernicious role of the Americans, in particular the CIA, in intervening at that time all over the Third World against independent nationalist regimes. The regimes of Musaddeq, Bhutto, Sukarno, Nasser, and Nehru were clearly not much loved by the Americans. In fact, these newly independent governments had to be overturned, according to the US doctrine.

Perhaps we need to be reminded that the Cold War created mounting tensions. Southeast Asia was becoming a fierce battlefield for power and hegemony between the capitalist world and the communist bloc. These facts have been ignored in SMAS's analysis. Let us remember that the US involvement in Vietnam was turning into a bitter failure.

It was a relief when, 30 years after the 1965 massacres, it became possible to release the official publications of the US State Department.[31] The CIA was held responsible for creating networks of informants in trade unions to undermine the role of the PKI.[32] The US and British superpowers were mostly concerned about the growing workers movements and their disruption of foreign financial interests. Organized strikes were threatening English, Dutch, and US interests in the form of banks, companies, and plantations.[33] Apparently, the approval for issuing the lists came from top American officials, including the ambassador.[34]

In summary, the book can be read as a harsh condemnation of the Indonesian leaders and their policies in the postcolonial period. SMAS traces the ways in which the Dutch colonial experience contributed to the events of 1965; it is clear that he understood the extent of the political and economic manipulations of ex-colonial countries such as the Netherlands. However, at the time he wrote, he could not have known the full extent of the US role in supporting the Indonesian military in their brutal suppression of those they identified as "communists," resulting in the cold-blooded murder of at least a million people.

In the final chapters, SMAS states that he personally sent the first print of the book to Sukarno in March 1970. SMAS's tone reveals his close acquaintance with Sukarno. He writes that the book was accompanied by a warm letter. The book was translated and read daily to Sukarno while he drank his morning coffee. SMAS then reproduces a letter from Sukarno, who felt that the book was a direct insult to his person and politics. He responded by defending himself, point by point. In short, the book was a shock to Sukarno, and it mentally destroyed him. But Sukarno still praised SMAS, because the latter had the courage to express his opinions at the height of Sukarno's power as president. We have to note here that SMAS emphasizes how daring Sukarno found his stance. This is why Sukarno confesses that he censored his newspaper, nationalized the APB (the Asian Press Board), "broke his pen" (this is a literal translation), and silenced him. But SMAS resisted. Sukarno is quoted as having appreciated and respected him for his persistence and courage.[35] SMAS provides authentication of the letter by reproducing Sukarno's signature on page 290.

A Journey to the Interior of the Moro Islands

Gawla fi rubu'gujur al-muru, or *A Journey to the Interior of the Moro Islands*, was published in 1979 by the Islamic Research Council in Jakarta (the organization that SMAS founded earlier), and it was printed in Beirut. The monograph was written while SMAS was resident in Saudi Arabia and already working at the *Rabitat al-'Alam al-Islami*. It is not clear whether or not his journey to the Philippines was sponsored by the Saudis. The book may be described as a detailed and precise travel account by SMAS, who went to explore the conditions of the Muslim Moro people in the Philippines.[36] The introduction is written by the president of the *hay'at al-buhuth al-islamiyya* (Islamic Research Council) in Jakarta, and it informs the reader that this account was written by the first Asian Muslim to have traveled extensively throughout the region to report on the recent dramatic events. The book also holds the distinction of being the first book published in Arabic on the contemporary situation of the Moro people.[37] SMAS states that his motives for writing the book were to highlight the struggle of a nation that was fighting for its legitimate rights. He traveled many times to the Philippines, most recently in 1973 to report on the war launched by the Marcos regime to annihilate the Muslims. He remarks that there were secret agents everywhere who kept the population under close surveillance.[38] On his earlier trips, SMAS tried to visit the Muslim regions in the south but failed because of state terrorism and total surveillance.

He was encouraged to write this book by the writings of the American journalist Carol Molony,[39] who reported on the systematic oppression of the Muslims. Yet, during the time SMAS was writing the book, this civil war in the Philippines was rarely reported. If an American woman, who originated from an entirely different culture and spoke a different language, was able to penetrate and write with such compassion and honesty about the Muslims, SMAS felt that he surely should follow in her footsteps and carry on this pioneering work.

SMAS argues that the Moro people belonged to the wider Muslim community and their cause had become the concern of the entire Muslim world. It was a cause of justice and humanity as a whole. The Moro people do belong to the wider Muslim community, and they are part of the history of the Muslim world.[40] Globally, Muslims today are doing well. They have governments, newspapers, and international organizations. The Organization of the Islamic Conference (OIC) played an important mediating role in successful negotiations between the Marcos government and the Moro National Liberation Front. It is against this background that SMAS discusses the origin of the 5.5 million Muslims in the Philippines. It is not strange that within the framework of Islamic organizations, the Islamic countries would adopt a vital cause such as the Moro people. The issue was discussed in various Islamic conferences. Mediation in negotiations between the Marcos government and the Moro liberation front was successful. SMAS's intention is to emphasize the role of the OIC and the Saudis as mediators in the conflict.

SMAS states that the term "Moro" has its origins in the Spanish wars against the Muslims in 1565; the word comes from the Spanish word "Moor," which was used to define Muslims from the Iberian Peninsula and North Africa.[41] The regions that were inhabited by the Muslims were called the Moro Islands. SMAS provides a brief history of the introduction of Islam to Southeast Asia. Islam came to the Moro Islands via the descendants of Imam Ja'far al-Sadeq in AH 270. The descendants of Ahmad bin 'Issa, known as *al-Muhajir*, went to Yemen and continued to spread the message of Islam throughout the Indian subcontinent and farther into Asia.

The core of the book is a diary of SMAS's journey to the Philippines, which lasted five months, between 12 March 1978 and 18 Tamuz 1978.[42] It includes descriptions of the various leaders and liberation movement fighters he met, and the extent of the territories controlled by the Marcos regime and by the Moro people. The book reads like a thriller, because the author is constantly encountering danger and is in close contact with the underground guerrilla fighters.

He reports interesting information about significant guerrilla warfare battles, such as the 1977 Buluan battle, which took place between the Marcos regime and the Moro National Liberation Front. It led to the slaughter of approximately 500 Muslims.[43] SMAS reports on his visit to the sites after the bloody events and concludes that it was definitively a barbarian act. The author describes long and tiring walks in the jungle, and the many boats he took to reach the various islands; he compares his discoveries and travels to those of Marco Polo and Vasco da Gama.[44] In the introduction, he warns travelers to the islands that they should carry light luggage, practically nothing apart from a camera and many rolls of film. The book contains photographs of guerrilla fighters and victims of war, including orphaned Muslim children. Detailed descriptions of the flora and fauna are provided, as well as descriptions of roads taken through the jungle to reach the guerrilla troops and their training centers[45] and a map of the Bangsamoro (the Moro Nation). SMAS followed the guerrillas into the most remote areas of the jungle. Wherever he went, he received a royal reception from entire villages. Information about his movements traveled fast among the Moro, so that whenever he arrived in a new place he found large groups of people waiting for him. The trip was undertaken in 1978, at the height of the conflict between the regime and the Muslim Moro.

SMAS landed in Manila at the peak of the conflict. He found a city of contradictions, where there were extremely rich and extremely poor people, huts side by side with modern buildings, fancy cars running close to antique bicycles, and nuns and prostitutes existing as neighbors. Manila was not a safe city; there were high levels of theft and other crime. In Manila SMAS contacted various opposition groups. These were mainly Christian and did not seem to support the Islamic cause, as such, but recognized that Marcos's dictatorship was oppressing both Muslims and Christians and treating the opposition with violence.

SMAS then made contact with the Moro Islamic Liberation Front[46] and was taken around the southern Philippines. He visited Mindanao; Zamboangga; Sacol; Pasilan; Tuburan; Sulu and its capital, Jolo; Tapul; Tawi-Tawi; Balabak; and Palawan. For the Arab reader, this monograph is instructive since it contains information not only about Muslims in the Philippines, but also about Marcos's opposition groups and the various massacres and wars that the Marcos regime perpetrated against Muslims. The author adds images of the war, the guerrilla fighters, and the wounded population.

My concern focuses on what is left "unsaid" by this text. SMAS's agenda was to become an intermediary or "go-between" for the Moro Muslims and the Saudis. This is evident throughout the book. The author begins by noting the government's fear of the spread of communism and the danger that the Muslims as well as the opposition might turn into a Marxist threat, by asking for assistance from the communist bloc.[47] This is clear from the questions he addresses to various politicians and members of the Moro liberation movement. For instance, on Palawan island he met an ʿalim named Sayyed ʿAlwi who was of Hadhrami origin, his forefathers having arrived during the 19th century from the Sultanate of Thaffar. SMAS remarks that he hardly looked like an Arab, with the exception of his dress and the ʿimma (turban). Sayyed ʿAlwi was fluent in the Arabic language, although he had completed his learning in Palawan and the neighboring islands. Sayyed ʿAlwi's family was now spread between Indonesia and Turkey. He hosted SMAS, and while he was showing him around the island,[48] SMAS asked him why the Muslims would not turn for assistance to the communist bloc. The answer was as expected: The Muslims feared the communists even more than they did the Marcos regime.[49] Posing a similar question to a Christian opposition leader in Manila, SMAS was told that the Christian opposition party consisted of just local opposition; they were not communists, nor did they wish to have any contacts with international communism.[50]

One aspect of SMAS's intermediary role between the Middle East and Southeast Asia was to report on the state of the Arabic language and Muslim customs. Naturally, the status and socioeconomic conditions of the Arab Hadhramis were for him another important link and source of curiosity. The book contains several passages about the state of the numerous religious schools SMAS visited.[51] He was astonished by the good quality of Arabic being taught even though most of the schools were extremely poor and lacked basics such as pens and pencils. He noted that there were not enough copies of the Qurʾan, so the teachers had to make copies of passages for their students. In Jolo, for instance, he visited the religious institute of Kota Mass, run by Tuan Faquih Jolo, who is described as a genius and great scholar who was not given the chance to advance farther. The institute consisted of a simple wooden building, where students sat on the floor. Tuan Faqih Jolo complained that they were isolated and encircled by the enemy, which made learning very difficult.[52]

In Balabak, the author visited a famous shaykh named ʿAbdallah al-Mindanawi, who was more than 80 years old. He was graciously received and shown the shaykh's magnificent library. The shaykh was a knowledgeable scholar who could recite *jahili* (pre-Islamic) poetry as well as the works of the 20th-century Egyptian poet Ahmad Shawqi. Shaykh ʿAbdallah al-Mindanawi went to pilgrimage during the times of Sultan Abdel Meguid. His father had contacts with Shaykh Ali Yussef, the owner of *al-Muʾayyid* newspaper; the Egyptian nationalist leader Mustafa Kamel;

S. Mohammed Bin 'Aquil in Singapore; and *al-Imam* magazine.[53] On an isolated island the author also met a Qur'an reader who chanted in perfect Arabic, in Egyptian style; he delighted with his crystal-clear voice and performance.[54]

During his travels, SMAS received from a guerrilla officer a book by Cesar Adib Majul titled *On the Muslims in the Philippines*, published in 1973, which he read during his trip. He provides a four-page summary of the work.[55] The book has been translated into Arabic by Dr. Nabil Subhi and published in Beirut. SMAS introduces Majul's analogy between the people of Palestine and the Moros. Both had internal enemies who gave away the lands for their own profit. For the Moros, those internal enemies were the Muslim leaders who used politics for personal ends.

The final chapters of the book read as testimony to the growing Saudi interest in, and intervention on behalf of, the Moro cause. For example, the author quotes a letter signed by 'Abdel 'Aziz bin Baz, the director of the *majlis* of the Rabita, concerning the position of the Muslim World League *vis-à-vis* the Muslims of the Philippines. It states that the league publicized the cause of the Muslims in the Philippines and made it an international issue. The league was presented as supporting their autonomy, and urged Marcos to comply with the resolutions of the sixth conference of foreign ministers in Jeddah. Muslim countries had to put pressure on the government of the Philippines to comply with the resolutions, including using oil as a weapon. The league was opposed to Marcos's policy of smearing the reputation of the Muslims. They also urged the creation of a Red Cross agency to rescue war victims.

Other documents reproduced in the book include the treaty/agreement between the Marcos government and the Moro National Liberation Front with the participation of the ministerial committee of the countries of the OIC in Benghazi, Libya, in 1973. This treaty clearly defined the areas that should be given autonomy. The central authority was to be responsible for national defense, while the issue of whether to allow the Moro front to participate in the Philippine Army was to be decided later. The Muslims were given the right to create autonomous courts, where they could apply the Islamic *shari'a*. The treaty specified that Muslims should be represented in all courts, including the Supreme Court.[56] The local self-governing regions had the right to create schools, institutions, universities, a local administration system, and an autonomous economic system. They also had the right of representation in the central government, and to create special security forces.

The book includes reproductions of letters exchanged between the general secretary of the OIC and the former President Marcos. The book also includes other documents, such as statements and records about Marcos's violation of these accords and his aggression against the Muslims. There are various statements and declarations by the leader of the Moro National Liberation Front about the massacres perpetrated by the Marcos regime to eliminate the Moro people, as well as the Tripoli agreement of 1976, which was signed between the Philippine government and the Moro National Liberation Front, with the participation of the general secretary of the OIC and representatives of Saudi Arabia, Somalia, Senegal, and Libya. For SMAS, this ceasefire was only a ploy toward the further elimination of Muslims.[57] These documents are an interesting testimony of the Saudi influence, even if its intervention in the Moro cause was more symbolic than real.

An Indonesian Novel

Mim samim al-waqe', subtitled *An Indonesian Novel which Has No Female Character*, is a didactic true story that took place between 1937 and 1955. It is a short novel (94 pages) written in fairly simple classical Arabic. SMAS informs the reader that he has changed the countries and the names of the protagonists because they were still alive at the time of the novel's publication. The first part clearly takes place in Indonesia, and the main character is a Muslim. Most probably he is a Hadhrami Syed, because when he rediscovers faith, he reads the *du'a* (prayer) of 'Ali Bin Hussein al-'Abidin, which is a tradition perpetuated among Southeast Asians Hadhramis. At one point he rediscovers the beauty of the Qur'an. There are no personal names mentioned at all in the whole novel, which focuses on this single character. Nor are there any female characters; we are told that the hero marries in the end, but we know nothing of his wife.

The plot is simple. The story begins in 1937 in an Asian country (not specifically referred to as Indonesia). It concerns a good-looking and extremely wealthy young man who inherits a fortune from his father: some 20 buildings, which bring him no less than $3,000 a month. He spends his money freely and leads a carefree lifestyle, driving only Cadillac and Rolls-Royce cars. He is fawned on by friends and relatives, and by rich and poor, and always surrounded by many so-called friends. He is so beautiful that he is nicknamed "the bridegroom." He loses all his money gambling.

He also has a car accident in which he demolishes a shop, and as a result he finds himself in jail. He knocks on many doors asking for help, appealing to one "friend" after another, but nobody comes to his rescue.

The main part of the story starts in 1941. That year the author visited a businessman, and while he was in the office a hungry and destitute beggar came asking for money. The beggar was thrown out of the office. When the author enquired about the beggar, he was told that he had been a rich and handsome man who had lost his money in bars and nightclubs. The writer followed him, and he discovered that since his release from jail for the second time — he had been imprisoned for allegedly killing his servant (which was not true; the servant had actually died of hunger and sickness) — he had slept on newspaper under a bridge, surviving on the charity of a baker in a popular quarter of the town. The writer took the beggar to his house, listened to his story, invited him to stay, and provided him with money and clothes. The young man was very grateful. He decided to leave his country and start a new life. The moral of this story, so far, is how hypocritical and brutal society can be: People respect only the powerful, they love money, and they would do anything to become rich.

Years pass, and one day the writer of our story receives a letter from his friend, who now lives in Geneva, thanking him for his friendship and support and inviting him to visit. When the author arrives in Geneva, he finds that his friend has become a millionaire, after much hard work, and after having understood how irresponsible he was in his youth. He tells the author that after leaving his native country for another Asian country, he started from scratch and was determined to achieve success. He began as a house messenger and, little by little, gained the confidence of a rich businessman, eventually becoming his right-hand man. This aroused the jealousy of another business associate, who gave him a better offer. Our hero refused to collaborate with this associate, who then charged him with spying. As a result, he ended up in jail, but he was then rescued by his original benefactor. After this, our hero realized that his only hope was to leave for Europe and start over.

In Europe he continued his education, learned German and French, read extensively, and obtained a university degree. He started his private business and gradually became richer than he had ever been before. When the author visited him, he was delighted to see his friend living in a beautiful villa in the middle of a garden, overlooking a lake. The rich businessman decided to return to his home country and was well received.

He was merciful and generous to those who had harmed him. After having become reconciled with his native country he returned to Geneva, which he thought of as his true home, the center of his life. He then married a good woman, who bore him two children, and was still happily living there when the story ended in 1956.

The author makes two main points in this novel. The first is that it is only in Europe that the main character discovers how materialistic the "Oriental" countries of Asia and Africa have become. The author devotes pages to the double morality of the Orient. Money is the only authority, and only rich people are respected. Hypocrisy is everywhere, and in hard times one discovers that real friends are nonexistent. This "illness" has overwhelmed the mentality of the Orient. The counter-image to the decadent, hypocritical, and deceitful Oriental is found in Europe, where people encourage the values of hard work, honesty, and directness.

SMAS bitterly criticizes the Orient, which, according to him, has departed from true Islam. This has led to ambivalent and contradictory behavior. In contrast, the Europeans seem to maintain values that are recognized as true in Islam. The author devotes many pages of his novel to the double standards of Muslims in Asia, describing the *da'i* (preachers) who travel to the West to collect money under the pretext of assisting Muslims and end up as drunkards in nightclubs and bars. He says these preachers pretend to be religious but are not even capable of praying; they wear traditional dress while collecting money, but they change into Western outfits while frequenting nightclubs. SMAS points out that the idea that the true values of Islam are to be found in the West, while they have disappeared among Muslims, is not new. It is found in the writings of the Egyptian reformist Muhammad 'Abduh, at the turn of the 20th century. In that context, the writer asks himself, where is the Albert Schweitzer (of the Islamic world) who spent long years in a remote part of Africa helping Africans?

The second important theme of the novel is the significance of faith in times of crisis. When the protagonist is jailed, the jail supervisor takes a liking to him and lends him books. In jail, the protagonist discovers the importance of reading the Qur'an, recalling that when he was young his father often advised him to read the Qur'an and the *du'a* of Iman 'Ali bin Hussein al-'Abidin, but he never followed his advice. These are the prayers given a significant role in the novel. The main character acknowledges that because he was rich and pampered (and considered himself "modern") he thought of these prayers as nothing but reactionary incantations and old-fashioned traditions stemming from the older generation, which understood little. He confesses that he belittled his father's words and did not listen to him. When he discovers the significance of faith in jail, he reproduces long passages of the Qur'an and the verses that helped him most. This discovery makes him realize how powerful and beautiful are the words of God. Thus, even though the main character emigrates and decides to make Europe his home, in reaction to the generalized corruption of the Muslim countries, he nevertheless rediscovers the Islamic faith, which he can truly practice in exile in Europe. He decides that true spirituality is to be found in the West, while the East has turned out to be materialistic and fake. This is certainly not an original idea, but the timing of the novel suggests that SMAS's real aim was to make a social critique of the postcolonial Sukarno era.

Conclusion

I have tried to contextualize SMAS's writings within the *zeitgeist* in which he wrote. That his writings betray a strong anticommunist and anti-Sukarno stand can be seen to reflect his association and work with one of the most powerful institutions of *Salafi* Islam in Saudi Arabia, the Muslim World League. Probably, the events of 1965 in Indonesia were the major reason for his move to Saudi Arabia. His personal distaste for, and experience of, communism was saluted in Saudi Arabian circles, in particular those of the Muslim World League. His writings reflect his belief in the mission of Saudis to spread a pan-Islamic solidarity in Southeast Asia.

SMAS, as an intellectual of Hadhrami origin, as a prolific writer of books and novels, as a correspondent for various Arabic papers, and as a writer in the Indonesian language for a Southeast Asian audience, is a fascinating figure, a bridge between two cultures. For scholars who were interested in the Arab diaspora in Indonesia, he was a living encyclopedia.

It is clear that scholarship in the field of South-South relations is still in its infancy. Arabic works produced in Southeast Asia and the role of translation have attracted some attention, but there is still much work to be done.

Notes

1. I wish to thank Pak Ali (bin Abu Bakar bin Ali) Shahab from Pertamina for having introduced me to Pak Abdul Muthalib M. Asad Shahab, who gave me an initiation to his father's writings. Both were extremely hospitable, and they introduced me to the Hadhrami community in Jakarta. This paper would not have been possible without the fellowship I obtained from the International Institute for Asian Studies, Leiden, in 2002–3.
2. I borrow this term from Sanjay Subrahmanyam, "Notes on Circulation and Asymmetry in Two Mediterraneans, c. 1400–1800," in Claude Guillot, Denys Lombard, and Roderich Ptak, eds., *From the Mediterranean to the China Sea* (Wiesbaden: Harrassowitz Verlag, 1998), 33.
3. Roderich Ptak and Claude Guillot, Preface, in Guillot *et al.*, *From the Mediterranean to the China Sea*, vii.
4. I believe that this critique is much too harsh. Braudel lived for 10 years in Algiers and four in Brazil, which reveals that he was interested in the Third World. As he himself stated, his major endeavor was to *mondialiser*, or globalize, history. See Fernand Braudel, Introduction, in *Civilisation matérielle économie et capitalisme XV-XVIII siècle, les structures du quotidien*, Tome I (Paris: Armand Colin, 1979), 9.
5. Subrahmanyam, "Notes on Circulation and Asymmetry in Two Mediterraneans."
6. The conference was organized by the Ecole des Hautes Etudes en Sciences Sociales, Paris, and led to the publication of *From the Mediterranean to the China Sea*.
7. S. al-Sharif 'Abdel Rahman bin M. bin Hussayn al-Shahir, *Shams al-thahira*, vol. 1 (Jeddah, 1984), 177. Edited by M. Diya' Shahab.
8. In SMAS's obituary in *Bulletin Malja*, "APB" stands for Arabian Press Board, which was founded on 2 September 1945 (p. 9). In *Shams al-thahira* and SMAS's book *Pages from Contemporary Indonesian History*, the abbreviation stands for Asian Press Board. The brothers Diya' and M. Asad Shahab were involved in both the Arabian and the Asian press boards.
9. *Shams al-thahira*, 177.
10. Ibid.
11. *Bulletin Malja, Media Komunikasi Kelaurga al-Shahab*, no. 20. Edisi khusus, May–June 2001. Kiprah Perjuangan M. Asad Shahab, 5, 38. Note that the Malja' Shahab is mainly a family association that is concerned about spreading information about the Shahab family in Indonesia and sending money to the families in Hadhramaut.
12. *Shams al-thahira*, 179–80.
13. The Arabian Press Board had contacts and correspondents with the following papers and journals: *Al-Mukattan Muqattam (*Cairo*), al-Ikhwan* (Cairo), *al-Amal* and *al-Alam* (Iraq), *al-Manar* (Syria), *Mimbar al-Shaab* (Morocco), *al-*

Irfan (Lebanon), *Al-Saqafah* (Argentina), *Al-Salam* (Singapore), and *fatatul Jazira* (Aden). It also collaborated with the following news agencies: Agency Sharq (Tehran), AAP (Pakistan), Lebanon News, International Press Service (Pakistan), Near East Broadcasting Station (Cyprus), and Ausland Press Bureau (Germany). *Bulletin Malja,* 6–7.

14. *Dar al-tiba 'a wal nashr,* 2nd edition (Beirut, 1971), 332.
15. Published by the Islamic Research Council (Jakarta, 1979), 245.
16. Reinhard Schulze, "Der Einfluss Islamischer Organizationen auf die Laender Suedostasien," in Werner Draghun, ed., *Mitteilungen des Instituts fuer Asienkunde* (Hamburg, 1983), 35; and Reinhard Schulze, *Islamischer Internationalismus im 20. Jahrhundert.Untersuchungen zur Geschichte der Islamischen Weltliga* (Leiden: E. J. Brill), 1990.
17. *Dar al-tiba 'a wal nashr,* 332.
18. This point is stressed again in the introduction, which was written by Salim Wakim, 27.
19. Ibid., 145.
20. Ibid., 194.
21. Ibid., 87.
22. If one wants to understand the contemporary politics of Islam, it is impossible to circumvent what has already been implanted through the philosophy of *Islam-Politik,* whose inventor was Christiaan Snouck Hurgronje (1857–1936). Hurgronje wrote fascinating ethnographies of Mecca and Aceh, in North Sumatra.
23. Ibid., 44–5.
24. Professor P. S. Van Koningsveld, an Arabist from Leiden University, has put into question Hurgronje's integrity in his conversion to Islam.
25. Jean-Jacques Waardenburg, *L'Islam dans le Miroir de l' Occident* (Paris: Mouton, La Haye, 1962), troisième édition. 21.
26. *Pages from Contemporary Indonesian History,* from Indonesian, 46.
27. Ibid., 219.
28. Ibid., 120, 125.
29. Ibid., 111.
30. The number of those massacred in the next several months varied between 300,000 and 400,000, while Amnesty International thought the numbers were between 700,000 to one million. See "Indonesia: U.S. role in the 1965 Massacres — Confessions from the U.S. State Department", <http://rwor.org/a/v23/110-19/1116/indonesia.htm>.
31. Research published as a thick volume, titled *Foreign Relations of the United States, 1964–1968: Vol. 26-Indonesia; Malaysia-Singapore; Philippines,* released in 2001, clearly reveals evidence of the malicious role played by the CIA in the massacres of the communists. The document publicizes the communication between the US Embassy in Jakarta and the State Department,

whereby the Americans provided the Indonesian military with lists of names of the communists, numbering 5,000, who were then tracked down. Moreover, there was direct US financial support for the Indonesian death squads named the Kap-Gestapu. By 1965 the United States had already trained 4,000 Indonesian officers. It trained generals who were the main actors in the massacres, in addition to supplying trucks and weapons.

32. "Indonesia: US Role in 1965 Massacres, Confessions from the US State Department," in *Revolutionary Worker* #1116, 26 August 2001, posted at <http://rwor.org/a/v231110-19/1116/indonesia.htm>, 2–3.
33. The United States orchestrated Suharto's 1965–66 slaughter in Indonesia. Part 1, World Socialist Web Site <www.wsws.org — http://www.lossless-audio.com/usa/1137134801.htm>.
34. For another piece of moving and detailed research based on interviews with American officials, see Kathy Kadane, *States News Service*. Ex-agents say the CIA compiled death lists of Indonesians, <http://www/namebase.org/kadane.html. For British involvement in the massacres, see Mark Curtis, *Democratic Genocide* (from Tapol), <http://www.antenna.nl/wvi/eng/ic/pki/uk65.html>.
35. *Pages from Contemporary Indonesian History*, 286.
36. Ethnic groups in the Philippines include the following: Chinese Malay 91.5 per cent, Muslim Malay 4 per cent, Chinese 1.5 per cent, and other 3 per cent, with a population of 86,241,697 (July 2004), <http://www.cia.gov/cia/publications/factbook/goes/rp/html>, 4–5.
37. This information is questionable, because Cesar Adib Majul's book had already been translated into Arabic.
38. *A Journey to the Interior of the Moro Islands*, 19.
39. I have transliterated the name from the Arabic transcription, but I have been unable to check whether the spelling is correct.
40. *A Journey to the Interior of the Moro Islands*, 24.
41. Some historians argue that the Moro rebellion in Mindanao dates back to the arrival of the Spaniards in the Philippines. See Mehol K. Saidan, *The Historical Antecedents of the Moro Rebellion in the Southern Philippines*, <http://www.upd.eduph>.
42. Note that he uses two calendars, the European calendar and the Babylonian calendar used in Lebanon, probably because the book was printed in Lebanon.
43. *A Journey to the Interior of the Moro Islands*, 51.
44. Ibid., 106.
45. Ibid., 107.
46. The Moro Islamic Liberation Movement, founded by Nur Misuari, is based in the region of Mindanao and the neighboring islands. Membership in the 1990s was estimated to be around 15,000. In 1976 Misuari signed the Tripoli Agreement, which led to a political split in the MNLF between Misuari and

Shaykh Salamat Hashim, an Azhar-educated intellectual (1959–69) and an active member of Asian student organizations who then moved to Cairo and created a new MNLF. See *Moro Islamic Liberation Front*, <http: //www.ict.org.il/inter-ter/orgdet.cfm?orgid=92>. SMAS included a picture of Nur Misuari (p. 58), but he does not seem to have been aware of the Misuari-Hashim conflict over leadership. He mentions the Moro Liberation Front and the MNLF.
47. For instance, he was often concerned about how the guerrilla officers would get funds for their weapons, and he wondered whether external forces were helping them.
48. *A Journey to the Interior of the Moro Islands*, 161–2.
49. Ibid., 167.
50. Ibid., 43.
51. Ibid., 100–1.
52. Ibid., 102.
53. Ibid., 148.
54. Ibid., 57.
55. Ibid., 114–8.
56. Ibid., 192.
57. Ibid., 225.

IV

Into Modernity

Burmese Mosque, Sagaing, Central Burma (Photograph E. Tagliacozzo)

12

Jihad and the Specter of Transnational Islam in Contemporary Southeast Asia: A Comparative Historical Perspective[1]

JOHN T. SIDEL

Introduction: Writing Against the "Terrorism Experts"

In the years following the 11 September 2001 attacks in New York City and Washington, D.C., Southeast Asia reemerged on the global stage as an arena of conflict, not with world Communism as during the Cold War, but with "Islamic terrorism" instead. Shadowy armed groups such as Abu Sayyaf in the southern Philippines and Laskar Jihad in Indonesia were rapidly identified by the U.S. government as "terrorist organizations" and thus legitimate targets for legal and military action. U.S. Special Forces advisers were soon deployed to the island of Basilan to assist Philippine troops in operations against the Abu Sayyaf, a group linked to the 1993 bombing of the World Trade Center in New York. Pressure was likewise applied on the Indonesian government to defeat and disband the paramilitary forces of Laskar Jihad in areas of Central Sulawesi, Maluku, and Maluku Utara, which had been plagued by interreligious violence over the preceding several years.

Finally, after a series of arrests in Malaysia, the Philippines, and Singapore in 2001–2, a hitherto unknown group identified as Jemaah Islamiyah was unveiled by security officials in these countries and in Indonesia, where this Al-Qaeda-linked terrorist network was said to be based. Jemaah Islamiyah's supposed leader, Abu Bakar Ba'asyir, had co-founded a religious school in Central Java in the early 1970s, served time in Indonesian prisons for his "extremist" views in the late 1970s and early 1980s, and lived in exile in Malaysia in the late 1980s and much of the

1990s, before returning at the turn of the century to Indonesia, where he was elected the leader of the Majelis Mujahidin Indonesia, the Assembly of Indonesian Mujahidin. Allegedly linked to Al-Qaeda by shared experiences in Afghanistan in the 1980s, a common religious and political agenda, and myriad personal, financial, and logistical ties, this Jemaah Islamiyah thus appeared as a regional franchise outlet of sorts for Osama bin Laden's efforts to spread his version of jihad to Southeast Asia.

Thus, when a car bomb killed nearly 200 foreign tourists at a nightclub on the Indonesian island of Bali in October 2002, the explosion was immediately attributed to Jemaah Islamiyah and, along with similar incidents in Yemen and Kenya, perceived as evidence of a resurgence of Al-Qaeda terrorist activity around the world. In response, the Indonesian police detained alleged Jemaah Islamiyah leader Abu Bakar Ba'asyir in connection with a series of earlier alleged offenses and questioned him as to his involvement in the bombing. In a few short months, using intelligence reportedly provided by Jemaah Islamiyah members interrogated by the authorities in Singapore, and by an Al-Qaeda operative captured by the CIA in Afghanistan, the Indonesian police made rapid progress in their investigation. By the end of 2002, a series of well-publicized arrests had revealed not only the Bali bombers and their accomplices, but a longer trail of Islamic activists and schools stretching across Java, Sumatra, and the Malay Peninsula. Alongside the U.S. invasions of Afghanistan and Iraq, it appeared that a second front in the "war on terrorism" had been opened in Southeast Asia, with Al-Qaeda squaring off against the United States and its local allies. Subsequent bombings — the Marriott Hotel (August 2003) and the Australian Embassy (September 2004) in Jakarta, a ferry off Manila Bay (February 2004), and targets in Manila, Davao, and General Santos (February 2005) — punctuated the U.S.-led crackdown on Islamic terrorism in the region.

Thus a picture of extensive Al-Qaeda operations in Southeast Asia has come into focus, in journalistic reportage, government press releases, publications and leaks, and the pseudo-academic writings of self-styled "terrorism experts" with little specialist knowledge of the region. Exemplary and influential in this regard is the book *Inside Al Qaeda: Global Network of Terror* by Rohan Gunaratna of the Centre for the Study of Terrorism and Political Violence at the University of St. Andrews in Scotland. Gunaratna, a prominent fixture on the media and consultancy circuit, wrote in 2002: "As envisaged by bin Laden, Al-Qaeda's influence spread from the Philippines to the rest of South East Asia, where its network is long-standing, well-entrenched and extensive."[2] Using the Philippines as a base, Gunaratna claimed, Al-Qaeda developed a "well-coordinated regional network" in Indonesia, Malaysia, and Singapore.[3] Zachary Abuza, an American political scientist and occasional television talk-show "terrorism expert," concurred: "Al Qaeda had slowly penetrated the region for more than a decade beginning in 1991, co-opting individuals and groups, establishing independent cells, and finding common cause with local militants."[4]

These self-evidently superficial and simplistic Al-Qaeda-centered accounts have been accompanied by more detailed and more impressively documented research on Jemaah Islamiyah and other Islamic terrorist groups in Southeast Asia by regional specialists working for the Brussels-based International Crisis Group (ICG). Led by the widely respected Indonesia expert Sidney Jones, the Jakarta office of the ICG published a series of reports describing the organizational structures and activities of Jemaah Islamiyah in Indonesia and beyond, as well as additional reports on Islamic terrorist activities in the Indonesian province of Central Sulawesi and in the southern Philippines. These reports painted a highly nuanced and complex picture of the internal structures and activities of so-called jihadist networks in Southeast Asia, tracing patterns of recruitment and processes of activity with close attention to names, dates, and places. Thanks to the efforts of Jones and her collaborators, interested readers — including appreciative intelligence analysts in Washington, D.C., and Canberra — have at their fingertips a long list of Indonesian, Malaysian, and Philippine terrorists, a fine-grained map of the interlocking directorate of terrorist networks in Southeast Asia, and a blow-by-blow account of training and bombing activities in various areas of the region.[5]

Yet for all the conspiratorial coherence of Gunaratna's and Abuza's accounts, and for all the empirical richness of the ICG reports authored by Jones and her colleagues, essential questions about jihad in the narrow but popular sense of the term remain strikingly unanswered if not utterly inexplicable in the light of their works. For even if the question of "whodunit" is taken to have been answered, if not by Gunaratna and Abuza then by Jones, the timing, the location, and the forms of violence in avowed defense or promotion of Islam in Southeast Asia have yet to be convincingly explained. Why, for example, did the turn of the 21st century witness the onset of a campaign of bombings in Indonesia — and subsequently in the Philippines — after, *and only after*, many years in which other forms of violence were mobilized under the banner of Islam? If the timing of the bombings is simply attributable to Al-Qaeda's authorship or influence, why do the bombings of recent years bear such resemblance to a similar set of explosions in Indonesia in the mid-1980s? Why have the sites of the bombings shifted from Southeast Asian targets to ones associated with the United States and "the West" in Indonesia but not in the Philippines? Finally, why has jihad in Southeast Asia come to be so narrowly associated with incendiary attacks and with the conspiratorial forms of agency and mobilization described in such loving detail by Gunaratna, Abuza, and Jones? Such comparative and counterfactual questions are arguably important ones to raise, not only for social scientists concerned with methodological rigor, but also for the broader audiences interested in the political implications of terrorist activities and counterterrorism campaigns in Southeast Asia today.

In addressing these questions, this essay takes as its analytical point of departure an interest in the political, sociological, and discursive context of so-called jihad in Southeast Asia and as its analytical prism the comparative historical sociology of Islam in the region. Following scholars of religious violence in other parts of the world, the essay shows how the timing, location, and forms of agency and action associated with jihad can best be understood with reference to the broader possibilities for mobilization in defense or promotion of "Islam" at a given time and place. This contextualization of jihad places stress on the diverging national settings and trajectories for Islam in the Philippines and Indonesia, while paying close attention to the transnational dimensions of religion in both countries. Instead of viewing Southeast Asian Muslims' connections to the Middle East solely in terms of Afghanistan and Al-Qaeda, the essay stresses the historical depth and sociological breadth of transnational networks linking Muslims across the two regions of the Islamic world. Rather than depicting these networks and links as somehow external to Southeast Asia, the essay shows how the long-standing connectedness of Muslims in the region and beyond has run up against other transnational currents and circuitries — those of capitalism, Christianity, and the global system of modern nation-states.

Overall, as signaled above, the aim is to address two interrelated questions: What circumstances have enabled — and constrained — association and mobilization under the banner of Islam in Southeast Asia? Why has terrorism — or, in the narrow but now widely popular sense of the term, jihad — waged under the banner of Islam in Southeast Asia assumed certain forms at certain times in certain places but not others? On the one hand, the answers to these questions can be found only through a comparative historical and sociological analysis of Islamic institutions and practices in the Philippines and Indonesia. On the other hand, the essay reveals how jihad in Southeast Asia has been shaped not only by Islam, but also by the variegated forms and forces of Christianity, capitalism, and nationalism in the region.

The Abu Sayyaf of the Southern Philippines

In the case of the Philippines, the most recent and noteworthy manifestations of jihad have consisted of the bombing, kidnapping, and extortionary activities of the shadowy Abu Sayyaf ("Bearer of the Sword") group, whose primary base of operations appears to be located on the island of Basilan in the Sulu Archipelago. Allegedly founded by a Libya-trained Muslim Filipino veteran of the anti-Soviet resistance in Afghanistan, the Abu Sayyaf group first surfaced in the early-mid-1990s in connection with a series of killings and kidnappings of Christian missionaries, nuns, and priests in Basilan and Zamboanga City, a short ferry ride away from the island. In 1995, the group grabbed headlines in the Philippines and beyond in connection with a violent attack on the town of Ipil, Zamboanga del Sur, which emptied the town's bank vaults and store tills and left some 50 residents dead. After a hiatus of five years, the Abu Sayyaf group resurfaced in 2000–1, with a series of highly publicized kidnappings of Filipino Christians and foreign tourists in the southern Philippines and on the Malaysian resort island of Sipadan, just a brief speedboat ride from the group's hideaways in Basilan and Sulu.[6] Meanwhile, Abu Sayyaf also gained international notoriety as local hosts to Al-Qaeda operatives such as Ramzi Yousef, who bombed the World Trade Center in 1993, and Khalid Shaikh Mohammed, who allegedly masterminded first an abortive multiple commercial airliner bombing scheme in 1995 and later the successful September 11 attacks on the Twin Towers and the Pentagon in 2001.

Colonial Origins of "Moro" Marginalization in the Philippines

The context and content of the Abu Sayyaf's distinctly predatory brand of jihad have been shaped not only by the minority status of Islam in the predominantly Catholic archipelago, but also by the distinctive processes through which capitalist development and national integration began to unfold under Spanish and American colonial auspices. Crucial in this regard was the post-Reconquista zeal that animated the Spanish project to stem the spread of Islam in the archipelago, which was well under way by the time of Magellan's ill-fated arrival in Cebu in the early 16th century. Colonization meant evangelization, among both the natives of the islands and the Chinese immigrants who served as commercial intermediaries in inter-island commerce and the Spanish galleon trade with the Middle Kingdom. The assimilation of this immigrant minority, achieved through intermarriage with native women, conversion to Catholicism, and the baptism and redesignation as *mestizo* (mixed) of the children born to such unions, prefigured the emergence of a commercial class whose Chinese ancestry did not stand in the way of its capacity to rule "for itself" and in the name of the Filipino nation. It was thus a class of assimilated Catholic, Chinese *mestizos* — rather than a stigmatized, closed "foreign" minority as in Indonesia — which pioneered the expansion of market circuitries from various port cities into the hinterlands of the archipelago in the 19th century. It was also this same class of now self-assuredly Filipino moneylenders, merchants, and landowners who predominated in the national integration of the Philippines through elections in the 20th century, as municipal mayors, provincial governors, congressmen, senators, and presidents.

Against this backdrop, the marginality of those Filipinos residing in the Islamicized southern areas of the archipelago — now dubbed and demonized as "Moros" — was twofold. First of all, insofar as these areas had remained outside the orbit of Spanish colonial rule, they only belatedly experienced the processes by which the elimination of barriers to free trade in the 19th century gave rise to a Chinese *mestizo* comprador class for foreign firms in the prosperous port cities in the archipelago. Thus, with the incorporation of previously unhispanicized areas into the Philippines in the early 20th century, the path of internal colonization of Muslim Mindanao and the Sulu Archipelago was opened wide to coconut, corn, and rice millers; moneylenders and bankers; bus, electricity, and shipping companies; and colleges and universities based in Cagayan de Oro, Cebu, Davao, and Manila.

Second, inasmuch as the national integration of the archipelago was achieved through the expansion of colonial democracy "upward" from small-town mayorships to the Philippine presidency, the delayed onset of this process in the Moro Province and the deferral of its completion until the mid-late 1950s further facilitated internal colonization by non-Muslim interests. Without locally elected congressmen, and with city mayors and provincial governors appointed by Manila, the dispensation of patronage in Muslim Mindanao and the Sulu Archipelago in the first several decades of the 20th century did not allow local Muslim politicians to accumulate as much wealth and power as did their Christian counterparts elsewhere in the archipelago. Logging concessions, pasture lease agreements, transportation franchises, and titles for large tracts of "public" land fell into the hands of carpetbaggers and their allies from Christian areas of Mindanao, Cebu, Iloilo, and Manila.[7] In short, since before independence, the Muslims in the Philippines have been systematically disadvantaged and subordinated *vis-à-vis* Christians in the accumulation of cultural, financial, political, and social capital.

Transnational Islam and the Sulu Zone

At the same time, the combination of peripherality within the Philippines on the one hand, and transnational connectedness beyond its borders on the other, provided the basis for alternative modes of acquiring power and prestige in Muslim Mindanao and the Sulu Archipelago. Manila and other major cities colonized other hinterlands elsewhere in the Philippines, including the "pagan" highlands of the Gran Cordillera mountain range. The entire eastern shelf of the archipelago — stretching from Cagayan Valley in northern Luzon through Quezon Province, the Bicol Peninsula, down to Samar in the Eastern Visayas and the Agusan and Surigao provinces of eastern Mindanao — evolved into an impoverished provider of cheap labor, agricultural commodities, and mineral resources to western centers of capital in the country. It was precisely in these provinces where the Communist Party of the Philippines (CPP) and its New People's Army (NPA) was most successful in its mobilizational efforts against the Marcos regime in the 1970s and early mid-1980s.

By contrast, the possibilities and patterns of armed mobilization under the banner of Islam in Muslim Mindanao and the Sulu Archipelago were shaped by a uniquely different set of circumstances. Crucial in this regard was the long history and continued reality of the region's close connections with other parts of Southeast Asia, most notably the eastern Malaysian state of Sabah and the Indonesian province of North Sulawesi. As the historian James Warren has shown, the late 18th century saw the rise of a loosely structured port polity in the southern Philippines, centered around the Sulu Sultanate and extending as far as North Sulawesi and northeastern Borneo. This polity, which Warren memorably dubbed the "Sulu Zone," was based on trade with English merchants eager for marine and jungle products for sale in Chinese ports — and, crucially, on the mobilization of labor to obtain them. Labor for the gathering of tripang, pearl, tortoise shells, and birds' nests was accumulated through "slave-raiding" expeditions in the Hispanicized areas of the Philippine Archipelago and elsewhere in Southeast Asia that annually brought thousands of captives to Sulu to work as pearl divers and fishermen.[8] Only in the mid-late 19th century did the "Forward Movement" of the regime in Manila succeed in forcing the Sulu Sultanate — and the Muslim sultans of central Mindanao — to submit to Spanish authority.[9] Yet as elsewhere in Southeast Asia, the success of the Spanish Forward Movement and its consolidation under U.S. auspices created a new Sulu Zone across modern state boundaries, as seen in the reemergence of the dispersed slave-raiders of the Sulu Archipelago as bandits, pirates, and smugglers preying on inter-island and international trade.

Even after Philippine independence in the mid-20th century, moreover, hundreds of thousands of Filipinos found work in Sabah, on tuna fishing fleets operating off the coast of North Sulawesi, and elsewhere in Indonesia and Malaysia, while smuggling and an officially sanctioned barter trade linked southern Jolo, Zamboanga, and Cotabato City to ports such as Labuan and Manado.[10] In a frontier zone where property rights — titles to agricultural lands, pasture areas, and logging concessions — have remained highly contested and insecure, the extensive illegal flows of goods and labor across international boundaries further strengthened the economic importance of violence, whether asserted in the name of the Philippine state or otherwise.

At the same time, moreover, these linkages between the southern Philippines and the world beyond were reinforced and expanded through the transnational educational pilgrimages and networks associated with Islam. The institutions and practices associated with the Islamic faith in the southern Philippines — located at the easternmost fringes of the Muslim world — by the time of independence in 1946 appear to have been relatively weakly touched or transformed by the religious trends observed in countries where Islam has constituted not only the dominant religion but also a state-supported faith.[11] To this day, Muslim society in Mindanao and the Sulu Archipelago has remained predominantly rural, with levels of literacy and education among the lowest in the Philippines; and thus local institutions of religious learning have achieved only limited success in promoting an understanding of Islam as an abstract system of belief.[12] Yet since the 1950s, local Qur'anic schools and formal Islamic schools (*madaris*) have gradually expanded in number and in enrollment, as have Islamic colleges and other tertiary institutions of religious learning, even as mosques and numbers of pilgrims making the Hajj have grown in number.[13]

Notwithstanding their small numbers and modest credentials, such schools have had an important impact on Muslim society in the southern Philippines. Instead of preparing students for admission into Philippine public high schools or universities, these schools have linked young Muslim students in Mindanao and the Sulu Archipelago to wider Islamic educational networks beyond the archipelago. Over the years, increasing numbers of Muslim students have left the southern Philippines to enroll in Islamic schools and universities in Indonesia and Malaysia, or to avail of opportunities for study in the Middle East, whether at the prestigious Al-Azhar University in Cairo or in lesser-known institutions in Pakistan and Saudi Arabia. Not only have such foreign-educated Muslims returned to work as *ustadz* and *ulama* in Mindanao and the Sulu Archipelago, but various foreign Muslim governments, foundations, and groups have provided funding and personnel for the promotion of the faith in the southern Philippines. Thus, precisely in the same decades as the Catholic Church in the archipelago experienced a dramatic Filipinization, the institutions and practices associated with Islamic learning and worship became increasingly internationalized in the country.

Jihad

It is the combination of these transnational connections with the distinctly U.S. pattern of decentralized democracy that has shaped the possibilities — and limitations — of jihad in the southern Philippines. While the early postwar era saw the incorporation of Muslim Mindanao and the Sulu Archipelago into the circuitries of Philippine electoral politics, Marcos's declaration of martial law in 1972, the centralization of law enforcement in the hands of the Integrated National Police, Philippine Constabulary, and Armed Forces of the Philippines (AFP), and the awarding of control over the barter trade to the AFP Southern Command (Southcom) engendered considerable local resistance. In the late 1960s, Liberal Party politicians from the predominantly Muslim provinces of Cotabato and Lanao had already begun to sponsor a Muslim Independence Movement and to arm and train Muslim guerrilla fighters as a defensive strategy against "an increasingly aggressive national president who was actively strengthening (with money and arms) their Nacionalista Muslim rivals in their home provinces."[14] With the declaration of martial law, moreover, local resistance to Marcos began to coalesce around the Moro National Liberation Front (MNLF).

From its inception, the MNLF drew strength from Islamic and Southeast Asian links stretching far beyond the southern Philippines. As is well known, alongside Manila-educated activists such as MNLF Chairman Nur Misuari were dozens of Muslim Filipinos who had studied in Indonesia, Malaysia, and the Middle East; and the MNLF received considerable diplomatic, financial, and logistical backing from foreign sources, ranging from Libya's Qaddafi to Tun Mustapha, the chief minister and political boss of Sabah through the mid-1970s.[15] More generally, over the course of the 1970s and 1980s, the MNLF (and a splinter group, the Moro Islamic Liberation Front or MILF) drew sustenance from the density of remaining cultural, economic, and political linkages across the Sulu Zone. Smuggling and the government-sanctioned barter trade between southern Philippine ports and Labuan provided a regular predatory income for rebel commanders through protection rents, piracy, and shareholder profit, and the thousands of Muslim Filipinos working (illegally) in Malaysian Sabah or on fishing boats in the tuna-rich Indonesian waters off North Sulawesi served as a network for arms, training, and guerrilla recruitment. According to knowledgeable observers, many of the MNLF and MILF rank and file spent time as overseas laborers in Sabah. In terms of funding, moreover, Libyan support for the MNLF was matched by Saudi backing for the MILF.

Yet with the revival of competitive electoral politics and the re-decentralization of law enforcement in the late 1980s and early 1990s, the southern Philippines witnessed the domestication and incorporation of many such "Muslim rebels," some of whom had already been demobilized and co-opted into local government posts since the Tripoli Agreement between the MNLF and the Marcos government in 1976. Local elections in the late 1980s and 1990s saw the elevation of numerous MNLF and MILF commanders and backers to local government positions, revealing and reinforcing the close linkages between the rival guerrilla groups on the one hand, and local and national electoral politics on the other.

Local "Muslim rebel" commanders became municipal mayors, provincial governors, and congressmen and thus developed diverse — and divisive — alliances with (Christian) politicians and businessmen in Manila and elsewhere in the country. The project of unifying the Muslims of the southern Philippines tended to dissolve in the absorptive webs of the country's highly decentralized democracy.

It was thus in the context of both formal peace talks and informal political alliances that in 1996 the MNLF agreed to cease armed struggle in exchange for government backing of Nur Misuari's bid for the governorship of the Autonomous Region of Muslim Mindanao (ARMM), even as the avowedly more hard-line MILF continued to exercise influence through elected officials in its stronghold in central Mindanao. Subsequent changes of government in Manila trickled down to the ARMM through these byzantine alliances of national politicians and Muslim rebels, a pattern loosely paralleled among the two main factions of the CPP. Following the Estrada administration's "total war" against the MILF in 2000, new president Gloria Macapagal-Arroyo engineered an abrupt reversal of government policy, as seen in the junking of Misuari as ARMM governor in 2001 and subsequent efforts to forge a new deal with the much-reduced forces of the MILF. By 2004, with Misuari extradited from Malaysia and imprisoned outside Manila, and with U.S.-backed Philippine government troops occupying former MILF and MNLF strongholds in Maguidanao and Sulu, the struggle for an independent Moro nation in the southern Philippines had clearly run aground.[16]

Yet much as the Spanish Forward Movement of the mid-late 19th century saw the reemergence of the slave-raiders of the Sulu Sultanate as bandits, pirates, and smugglers, so too did the post-Marcos reincorporation of Muslim Mindanao and the Sulu Archipelago into the democratic Philippines witness new forms of predation and resistance, now under the rubric of jihad. Indeed, the shadowy Abu Sayyaf group surfaced with kidnappings, robberies, and bombings — first in 1994–96, then in 2000–1, and again in 2004–5 — precisely in the midst of shifts and squabbles over the terms of trade between Manila politicians and their local MNLF/MILF partners. Moreover, the Abu Sayyaf group emerged from among the Samal, Yakan, and Taosug areas of Basilan, Sulu, and the southern Zamboanga Peninsula, in roughly the same arc as their counterparts of the preceding century.[17]

In part, this location must be understood in terms of the decentralized structure of law enforcement in the Philippines, wherein local elected officials enjoy considerable formal and informal influence. It is in this context that market centers and trade routes can be preyed upon from an outside jurisdiction or, better yet, a base of operations spanning several jurisdictions. With such a base in Basilan and Sulu and connections beyond, an armed group can "tax" logging concessionaires, bus companies, and plantation owners on Basilan while using speedboats for kidnappings, killings, and robberies in nearby Zamboanga City, at island tourist resorts off Sabah or Palawan, and along the trade routes connecting the southern Philippines to Sabah, Sulawesi, and Singapore.

In what way should we understand the Abu Sayyaf group to be acting under the banner of Islam in the southern Philippines? Perhaps, as many knowledgeable observers have claimed, the supposedly 200-strong Abu Sayyaf group has been operating in cahoots with local politicians and policemen,[18] and under a franchise from the Zamboanga City-based Southern Command (Southcom) of the Armed Forces of the Philippines. Whether in the raid on Ipil in 1994 or in the various kidnapping episodes over the years, there have been many indications of military — and police — connivance and coordination with the Abu Sayyaf, analogous to the involvement of military intelligence in Manila with the kidnapping activities of the allegedly ex-NPA "Red Scorpion Gang" in the early 1990s.[19] In this context, the rubric of "Islamic terrorism" can be used as a flag under which to justify a continued military presence in the southern Philippines, to legitimate violence in the name of the state, and to attract U.S. military assistance, especially in today's "war on terrorism."

Yet perhaps there is more to the rubric of Islam in the southern Philippines than such cynical machinations. Islam, after all, has been a rubric under which Moros have established certain kinds of connections beyond the borders of the archipelago and enjoyed avenues for the accumulation of power and prestige not afforded them within the confines of the Philippine nation-state. Thus, the bombings of churches and missionary centers, the killings and kidnappings of nuns and priests, and the abductions conducted in Zamboanga City and in various tourist resorts — not to mention the more highly publicized bomb attacks in Manila and other Philippine cities — might well have some broader meaning beyond their role in attracting the attention and support of Osama bin Laden and his Al-Qaeda network for the activities of the Abu Sayyaf.

Whether in the form of Christian missionary efforts in Zamboanga, Basilan, and Sulu, tourist resorts catering to foreigners off nearby Sabah and Palawan, or the plantations, logging concessions, and mining operations in these areas run by companies based in Manila, Tokyo, and New York, a new "Forward Movement" is in the making in the old Sulu Zone. The U.S.-backed military campaigns in Mindanao and the Sulu Archipelago since 2000 have paved the way. Against this backdrop, as MILF and MNLF commanders compete for the favor of Manila politicians and the spoils of local state offices, what better rubric for resisting — or taxing — this Forward Movement than Abu Sayyaf, "Bearer of the Sword"? This name, it is said, was imported to the Philippines by returning Muslim Filipino *mujahidin* who had lived and fought in Afghanistan under the leadership of Abdul Rasul Sayyaf, an anti-Soviet *mujahidin* leader sponsored by Saudi Arabia, Pakistani military intelligence, and, for a time, the CIA in the 1980s.[20] Thus, the transnational Islam under whose banner the Abu Sayyaf group has been operating connotes the power of violence in an insecure border zone, especially violence licensed and subcontracted out by state authorities. Yet, as suggested above, linguistic and cultural diversity and the divisiveness, domestication, and parochialism that come with a highly electoralized and decentralized organization of state power have sharply constrained the capacity of this Islam to attract, mobilize, and unify the Muslims of the southern Philippines.

Laskar Jihad and Jemaah Islamiyah in Indonesia

Meanwhile in neighboring Indonesia, jihad has assumed both similar and different forms in recent years, as seen first with the dispatching of armed contingents to areas of interreligious violence by Laskar Jihad, and then with the bombings — of first Southeast Asian, and then Western targets — attributed to the shadowy group identified as Jemaah Islamiyah. In comparison with the Philippines, the content and context of this jihad in Indonesia at the turn of the 21st century have been shaped not only by the broader purchase of the Islamic faith in the archipelago, but also by a pattern of class and state formation that has presented very different constraints and opportunities for association and mobilization under the banner of Islam.

Colonial Rule and Islam in the Netherlands East Indies

Despite the extent of Islamization in the Indonesian Archipelago by the time of the VOC's arrival in the 17th century, the pattern of class and state formation that unfolded under Dutch colonial auspices in the

Indies constrained the possibilities for Islam in three decisive ways. First of all, the gradual creation of a modern state was achieved through the incorporation, subordination, and bureaucratization of local aristocracies in Java and elsewhere in the archipelago. Unlike in neighboring British Malaya, this process saw the various sultanates of the Indies stripped of authority over religious affairs and encouraged instead to develop local culture — and codify local custom (*adat*) — in ways that reinforced parochial particularisms and reified ethnic divisions among Muslims in the Indies.[21] As Dutch rule spread and deepened in the late 19th and early 20th centuries, moreover, these local aristocracies were retooled into bureaucrats whose entry and ascendancy within the rapidly expanding colonial state spurred the creation of a modern secular school system, out of which many leaders of the Indonesian nationalist movement would eventually emerge. For both the Dutch colonial regime in the era of the "Ethical Policy" and the Indonesian nationalist movement in its infancy, secular education and modernization thus came to supplement, if not fully supplant, a set of reinvented "traditions" as the basis for the claim to rule over the archipelago.

Second, under Dutch colonial auspices, the spread and deepening of capitalist market relations in the Indonesian Archipelago was pioneered by a comprador business class of decidedly non-Muslim complexion. Thanks to Dutch policies of segregation, the small minority of immigrants from southern China and their offspring were sharply defined as Chinese and confined to urban ghettos, with assimilation into local societies (especially on Java) and conversion to Islam strongly discouraged. Spurred on by the establishment of the Cultivation System on Java in the mid-19th century, Chinese revenue farmers and merchants expanded their commercial and credit networks deep into the rural hinterlands, firmly establishing themselves as the compradors of the Dutch colonial "plural society." With the abandonment of segregation and the abolition of the revenue farms in the early 20th century, subsequent generations of immigrants from China and their offspring developed into an Indonesia-wide Chinese business class.

Third, and finally, the Dutch colonial era saw the emergence of a privileged Christian minority within the ranks of the urban professional classes and the expanding colonial state. In various localities around the archipelago, residual Catholic influences from the early Portuguese era (especially in the eastern islands) and Protestant missionary efforts under Dutch (or occasionally English or German) auspices created pockets of Christian identity centered around missionary schools of various denominations and affiliations. Such schools not only introduced these converts to the Bible and to a distinctly modern notion of ("Great Tradition") religious faith and identity, but also served as transmission belts for the recruitment of colonial civil servants, soldiers, teachers, and professionals. This small but privileged minority of Indonesian Christians was destined to be markedly overrepresented in the ranks of the bureaucracy, the army, the university belt, and the urban middle class.[22] Thus, a close connection between Christianity, education, and access to state power was established, in a pattern strikingly reminiscent of the "pillarization" (*verzuiling*) of Dutch society along Protestant and Catholic lines back in the metropole as early as the 19th century.

Yet alongside and against the entrenchment of local aristocracies and *adat* chiefs on the one hand, and the growth of new circuitries of modern secular, Christian, and Chinese power on the other, the long centuries of Dutch colonial rule also produced new possibilities for identity, association, and mobilization under the banner of Islam. Muslims had been leaving their villages to visit religious shrines and study in religious boarding schools (*pesantren*) around the Indonesian Archipelago for centuries, with small but significant flows of pilgrims and scholars to Mecca on the one hand, and a trickle of Hadrami Arab migrants to Southeast Asia on the other, linking the "periphery" to the "center" of the Islamic world through the circulation of men, ideas, and texts as well as membership in Sufi brotherhoods (*tarekat*) such as the Naqshbandiyah.[23] A community of Southeast Asian Muslims — known collectively as the "Jawah" — was well established in Mecca, studying, playing host to Southeast Asian Hajjis, and returning home to the region to impart their wisdom to their coreligionists.[24] These linkages persisted, indeed prospered, under Dutch rule with little interference on the part of the colonial regime.

Yet by the late 19th century, economic, political, and technological conditions helped to broaden and deepen the connections between Muslims in the Indonesian Archipelago and their coreligionists in the Middle East, where social and intellectual changes were giving rise to new conceptions of Islam. With the intensification and spread of market relations and modern state circuitries on Java and elsewhere in the Indies came increasing travel — seen most dramatically in the construction of railroads — which thickened the flow and widened the arc of religious sojourns and scholarly pursuits across the landscape of Islamic shrines and schools in the Indies and neighboring colonies such as British Malaya. With the growth of inter-island trade and travel and the rise of the publishing industry, moreover, the dissemination of books and other publications written in Jawi — i.e., Malay written in Arabic script — greatly strengthened the field of shared communication and consciousness among Muslims in Southeast Asia. Finally, with the opening of the Suez Canal, the invention of the steamboat, and the establishment of Pax Brittanica, making sea travel across the Indian Ocean more affordable, rapid, and safe, more and more Muslims from the Indies came to make the Hajj or visit centers of Islamic learning elsewhere in the Middle East, even as larger numbers of migrants from the Hadramaut came to settle in the Indies.

It was against this backdrop that new conceptions of Islam came into focus in the Netherlands East Indies, circulating from Cairo and the Hejaz via Singapore, the hub of Hajj travel and Islamic publishing in Southeast Asia. Inspired by Cairene authors ranging from Jamal al-Din al-Afghani and Muhammad Abduh to Rashid Rida, and impelled by the widening scope of their own experiences and awareness of the world, some Muslims in the Indies began to think, write, and act in ways that transcended the loose sense of the *bilad al-jawa* ("land of Jawa") and the personalistic and particularistic networks of *tarekat* and *pesantren*. They bewailed the divisions and the constraints upon intellectual and social advancement among Muslims that colonial rule, feudalism, and traditional Islamic teaching methods had imposed upon the Islamic world. They embraced Islam as a project for the (re)unification and reschooling of the *ummah*.[25]

Signs of these trends were in abundant evidence by the second decade of the 20th century. The year 1912 saw the founding by Javanese Muslim merchants and scholars of Muhammadiyah, an association devoted to the development of modern schools, known as *madrasa*, which combined new forms of religious instruction with the kind of Western-style schooling that had given Christians such advantages in the Dutch East Indies.[26] Subsequent years witnessed the establishment of other such associations, most notably Al-Irshad and Persatuan Islam (Persis or Islamic Unity) by elements of the Hadrami Arab immigrant merchant community concerned with preserving and promoting both modern educational advancement along the lines pioneered by Christian and Chinese schools in the Indies, and a sense of Islamic identity transcending the borders of the island colony. By the 1920s, the inroads made among Muslims by these associations had inspired religious scholars (*kyai* or *ulama*) affiliated with the established system of rural Islamic boarding schools (*pesantren*) to form Nahdlatul Ulama (Awakening of the Religious Scholars) in defense of traditional forms of Islamic learning and worship.

Islam and Nationalism in Indonesia

It was also against this backdrop that new forms of identity and association under the rubric of Islam came to contribute some of their considerable energies and organizational resources to struggles against Dutch colonial rule. The modernist education promoted by Muhammadiyah fitted well within the rubric of the Dutch "Ethical Policy" of the early 1900s and won encouragement and support from the colonial regime, and immigrant Arab merchants served as commercial and financial intermediaries for Western firms in the Indies. But the possibility that Islam would provide a rubric for anticolonial resistance was already evident in the so-called Padri movement in West Sumatra in the early 1800s, the Banten revolt of 1888, and the long Aceh War in the final quarter of the 19th century.[27] Thus, Dutch fear of pan-Islamic movements and conspiracies emanating out of Mecca was a recurring theme in the last century of colonial rule.[28]

Indeed, the much-celebrated rise of Indonesian nationalism in the 20th century was from its inception intimately intertwined with forms of association and mobilization under the banner of Islam. The first mass movement to mobilize tens, indeed hundreds, of thousands of ordinary people around the Indies, after all, was the Sarekat Islam of the 1910s and early 1920s, whose various activities drew on the associational resources and solidarities accumulated by Islamic school networks across the archipelago and beyond.[29] While the Sarekat Islam fell prey to internal dissension and later Dutch suppression after the failed rebellions of 1926–27, Islamic networks and associations reemerged in the 1940s to play a crucial role in the Revolusi against the Dutch. Under the Japanese Occupation, a nationwide Council of Indonesian Muslim Associations (Masjumi) was created to help in the administration of occupied Indonesia, and Muslim youths from around Java and beyond were given paramilitary training and organized into armed units of the Hizbullah to confront an anticipated Allied invasion.[30] Thus, the school networks, symbols, and solidarities associated with Islam were crucial to the anti-Dutch guerrilla struggle during the Revolusi (1945–49), with some of the strongest resistance to the returning colonial regime and its aristocratic collaborators coming from self-consciously Islamic armed groups. In West Java, for example, the guerrilla leader Kartosuwirjo, a protégé of the Sarekat Islam leader H. O. S. Tjokroaminoto and a son-in-law of a prominent Sundanese *kyai*, even proclaimed the formation of the Islamic State of Indonesia (Negara Islam Indonesia) on 7 August 1949.

But this path of mobilization under the banner of Islam ran aground in the face of sociological obstacles to the unification of the Indonesian *ummah* as well as alternative political movements and currents in the archipelago. Under the rubric of a unifying Islam, after all, considerable diversity and contestation in Muslim associational life, educational networks, and religious practices continued to flourish, with little institutional basis for the centralization and standardization of Islamic authority and orthodoxy. Beyond the broad, pluralistic field of self-consciously Islamic education, association, experience, and consciousness, moreover, alternative solidarities came into being among the population of the Indonesian Archipelago. Bureaucratization and commercialization, after all, produced new secular pilgrimages, new school networks, and new publishing circuitries, with the Singapore-centered flow of *Jawi* texts eclipsed in the 1910s by newspapers, novels, and pamphlets printed in the cities of the Indies in the romanized Malay that became known as Bahasa Indonesia.

The egalitarian, anti-feudal appeal of Islam, moreover, was soon rivaled by that of the alternative rubric of Communism, with its own transnational networks, forms of schooling, language and textual production, and blueprints for a post-independence Indonesia. Thus, by the late 1910s, the "green" (Islamic) complexion of the Sarekat Islam was complemented — and contested — by the spread of "red" hues, and various stripes of Communism were likewise in much evidence in the affiliation of local guerrilla groups in the Revolusi of the late 1940s. Small wonder that the nationalist leader Soekarno, a graduate of Dutch secular schools, began using the slogan of NASAKOM — Nasionalisme, Agama (Religion), Komunisme — in the late 1920s to signal the embrace — and domestication — of these two competing transnational networks and currents under the sign of a secular Indonesian nationalism.

Thus, the energies and aspirations mobilized behind Islam in the Revolusi soon ran up against a very different kind of project, namely, the reconstitution of a modern secular state under an Indonesian national banner. The promise of an Islamic state was abandoned in favor of the monotheistic but multi-faith state ideology Pancasila, and "irregular" Islamic guerrilla leaders were left unrecognized and excluded from the formation of the Indonesian Armed Forces (Tentara Nasional Indonesia, or TNI) in favor of more "professional" (and, in some cases, Dutch-trained) officers. Groups led by Kartosuwirjo and other disappointed local guerrilla leaders in South Sulawesi, South Kalimantan, and Aceh continued the armed struggle for a Darul Islam (Islamic State), but they dwindled into small-scale insurgencies and were fully defeated by the early 1960s.[31]

Meanwhile, Masjumi, now reconstituted as a political party, competed in the 1955 elections, but only as one of the "Big Four" parties, each representing a different "current" (*aliran*) — and school network — in a society now defined by deep divisions among its population. Despite its second-place showing, Masjumi was effectively excluded from the fruits of power by an emerging pro-Soekarno coalition including the secular Partai Nasionalis Indonesia, the Partai Komunis Indonesia, and the "traditionalist" Nahdlatul Ulama, entrenched in the Ministry of Religious Affairs since its 1952 breakaway from Masyumi. Deeply disappointed and embittered by this turn of events, elements of the party supported a set of rebellions against Jakarta in the late 1950s, thus precipitating the banning of Masjumi in 1960 and clinching the defeat of Islam as a project for the remainder of the Soekarno era.

Islam under the New Order

Yet with the violent elimination of the Communist Party of Indonesia (Partai Komunis Indonesia, or PKI) and the forced retirement of Soekarno in the mid-late 1960s, the possibilities for mobilizing under the banner of Islam underwent a series of dramatic changes. University students affiliated with the modernist Himpunan Mahasiswa Islam (HMI) were prominent in anti-PKI and anti-Soekarno demonstrations in Jakarta during this period, and Nahdlatul Ulama played a key role in finessing the transfer of presidential power to Maj. Gen. Suharto and carrying out the anticommunist pogroms in East Java. But the New Order regime that crystallized under Suharto was one in which Islam was profoundly marginalized. The army, which occupied a dominant position within the regime, was led by officers schooled and socialized in a distinctly secular nationalist tradition, with Christians disproportionately well represented and suspicions of organized Islam amply established among their ranks. Indeed, Suharto himself had commanded TNI troops responsible for atrocities in the fight against the Darul Islam movement in South Sulawesi in the early 1950s.

Beyond the armed forces, moreover, the recruitment and circulation of networks of civilian elites in the New Order regime likewise excluded those associated with Islamic education, association, and aspirations. Initially, the regime incorporated remnants of the local aristocracies that had supported the colonial state under the Dutch and survived and prospered in the post-independence era as the conservative backbone of Soekarno's Indonesian National Party in many parts of the archipelago. But the exigencies of socioeconomic modernization and bureaucratic circulation dictated a pattern of recruitment into — and reproduction of — the political class based not on "blood" but on something dressed up as merit.

In this regard, the networks of educated Protestants and Catholics enjoyed a privileged position within the Suharto regime. Indeed, the first decades of the New Order saw the rise to unprecedented social and political prominence of members of Indonesia's small Christian minority. From parish schools scattered throughout the archipelago to seminaries to the Protestant and Catholic students' organizations at the most prestigious universities in the country, Indonesian Christians enjoyed a clear head start in the multitiered hierarchy of education that fed into the New Order bureaucratic elite, even as their church coffers and business connections were enhanced by the growing numbers of wealthy ethnic-Chinese Protestants and Catholics. Most notoriously, a clique of Catholic activists established a powerful think tank in Jakarta, the Center for Strategic and International Studies (CSIS). Through their positions at Indonesia's top universities, in the military establishment, and CSIS, Christians thus landed themselves and their protégés in the seats of civilian and military power in the cabinet, Golkar (the regime's electoral machine), its pseudo-parliamentary bodies, and key media outlets and other business ventures. Even in the late 1980s, the key economic and security portfolios in the cabinet were in Christian hands.

Besides these influential Christians, a somewhat broader pool of Westernized — and often Dutch-speaking — graduates of Indonesia's leading secular institutions of higher education (as well as universities in Europe and North America) exerted similar forms of influence within the regime and likewise used their patronage and protection to advance the careers and businesses of their former students and other protégés. Yet these cosmopolitan, Western-educated intellectuals, technocrats, and political operators represented a tiny privileged elite in a country where only a small fraction of the population reached the level of tertiary education. Moreover, although most members of these circles were nominally Muslim by faith, very few of them had received a religious education of any kind or participated in Islamic organizations.

Meanwhile, the process of capitalist development in Indonesia also saw the expansion of private non-Muslim wealth and power throughout the archipelago. In the first two decades of the New Order, the overwhelmingly Chinese business class was transformed from a collection of small-scale merchants and moneylenders into an interlocking directorate of commercial, financial, and industrial capital. Huge Chinese conglomerates emerged, with diverse interests ranging from automobile production to banking, food processing, electronics, household appliances, pharmaceuticals, real estate, and shipping. In the cities and major towns of the archipelago, the signs of Chinese capital loomed increasingly large on the urban landscape: bank outlets, department stores, factories, residential subdivisions, shopping malls, and supermarkets. The names of major Chinese capitalists, conglomerates, and commodities — Liem Sioe Liong, BCA, Maspion Group, Indomee — became household terms, even as the familiar neighborhood Chinese shopkeeper was transformed into a local retail outlet for this nationwide, if not properly national, business class.

Into the widening gulf between this narrow ruling class and the broad mass of the Indonesian population stepped the powerful figure of Islam, much as it had done during the late Dutch colonial era, but now without Communism as an alternative pole of ideological and organizational attraction. Islam, after all, represented a plausible idiom of protest by outsiders against a regime in which foreign and Chinese capital, Christians, and graduates of secular institutions of higher education were seen to occupy privileged positions. Signs of this insurgent Islam were already in evidence in the election campaigns of 1977 and 1982, with the strong showing by the United Development Party (Partai Persatuan Pembangunan, or PPP), the sole representative of Islamic political aspirations under the New Order's highly restricted electoral system. By the late 1980s, the regime had largely defanged PPP through a combination of co-optation and repression. But occasional reminders of the popular radical energies associated with an ostensibly unified but unjustly oppressed Islam — from the Tanjung Priok and Warsidi massacres of the 1980s to the riots and church burnings of the mid-late 1990s — still inspired considerable fear and hope.[32]

At the same time, state policies and social trends over the long decades of the Suharto era had worked gradually to propel new generations of Indonesian Muslims socially upward and to help them accumulate the forms of symbolic, cultural, and social capital that facilitated entry into the New Order ruling class. The Suharto era witnessed not only a dramatic expansion of higher education in Indonesia and a proliferation of all kinds of universities in the country, but also the implementation of numerous policies that furthered the objectification and functionalization of religion, long the project of modernist Muslim groups in the country. The anticommunist hysteria of the early Suharto years, for example, drove millions of Indonesians to seek refuge in religious identity, institutions, and faith in the late 1960s to avoid fatal charges of atheism.[33] New government regulations requiring all citizens to declare their faith, expanding religious classes in state schools, and impeding interfaith marriages strengthened the public markers and boundaries of religious identities. Thus Indonesian Muslims, in a process observed elsewhere in the Islamic world, increasingly came to understand their religion as "a coherent system of practices and beliefs, rather than merely an unexamined and unexaminable way of life," to think of "knowing Islam" as "a defined set of beliefs *such as those set down in textbook presentations*," and to put Islam "consciously to work for various types of social and political projects."[34]

Indeed, the system of Islamic education in Indonesia grew considerably over the three decades of the New Order. The network of traditional, rural Islamic boarding schools (*pesantren*) expanded dramatically, as did the self-consciously modernist *madrasa*, teachers' academies, religious training schools, college faculties, and universities associated with Muhammadiyah. At the same time, the State Islamic Institute (Institut Agama Islam Negara, or IAIN), first opened by the Ministry of Religious Affairs in 1960, had established 14 branches around the country by the 1990s, even as the branches of Universitas Islam quadrupled in number during the same period. Meanwhile, mainstream state universities throughout Indonesia saw a marked rise in the numbers of devout Muslim students and the popularity of campus mosques, prayer and religious discussion groups, and Islamic student organizations.[35] By the 1990s, the rising numbers of Indonesians schooled under a distinctly, self-consciously Islamic rubric had become a visible feature of urban society.

With the rising number of Muslim professionals, the public sphere of modern, urban middle-class life, for the very first time in Indonesian history, was now also claimed by those who defined themselves as pious Muslims. Indeed, the markers of Islamic piety were now incorporated into the habitus of mainstream Indonesian bourgeois propriety and prestige.

Wealthy Indonesian Muslims began to avail of luxury pilgrimage tour packages to Mecca[36] and to enroll in various institutes, foundations, clubs, intensive courses, and workshops in Sufi spirituality and Islamic learning in Jakarta and other major Indonesian cities.[37]

Alongside these rising numbers of self-consciously Muslim professionals were the swelling ranks of what might be termed "professional Muslims," in other words, men — and, to a considerably lesser extent, women — who made distinctly modern careers through the promotion of Islam. IAIN graduates filled the growing numbers of posts of religious instructors in state schools, *madrasa*, and *pesantren*, and joined the expanding ranks of functionaries in the vast Ministry of Religious Affairs. Books, magazines, pamphlets, and other publications on Islamic affairs proliferated, as did Muslim radio and television talk shows promoting the rise of "pop Islam" in the form of pious music stars and preachers (*daʿi*).[38] Meanwhile, HMI student leaders from elite universities were being recruited in record numbers into the bureaucracy, the business world, and Golkar.

It was to recognize, reinforce, and rechannel these trends that the Ikatan Cendekiawan Muslim Se-Indonesia (ICMI, or Association of Indonesian Muslim Intellectuals) was founded under the leadership of Minister of Research and Technology and close Suharto associate B. J. Habibie in the early 1990s. As minister of research and technology since the 1970s, Habibie controlled a sprawling empire of state-owned high-tech enterprises, an enormous state-based patronage empire outside military and technocratic control in the name of high-tech economic nationalism. Through his hold over "strategic industries" and responsibility for infrastructure projects and industrial development schemes, Habibie wielded considerable discretion over government personnel and contracts and built up an enormous clientele of university-educated Muslim *pribumi* (indigenous) businessmen, through privileged access to state loans, contracts, and regulatory breaks. With Suharto's support, Habibie was elevated to the governing body of Golkar and various Habibie protégés won key cabinet positions and other plum civilian and military posts. Meanwhile, a steady process of ICMI-*isasi* moved forward in Golkar, in the awarding of state contracts, on many university campuses, and beyond. CIDES (Center for Information and Development Studies), an ICMI-affiliated think tank, soon began to compete with the Catholic CSIS, and its daily newspaper *Republika* tried to rival the Catholic-owned *Kompas*. ICMI support and influence soon extended to Islamic publishers, preachers, and pilgrims, into *pesantren*, *madrasa*, and IAIN, and to figures within both Nahdlatul Ulama (NU) and Muhammadiyah. With Habibie at its helm, ICMI incorporated an expanding network of Muslim professionals and "professional Muslims" into the ranks of the national political class.[39]

As this network moved upward within the political class, remaining obstacles to the ascendancy of Islam became increasingly palpable. In particular, the accumulation of wealth and power by the Suharto family imposed a ceiling on any further ICMI-ish ambitions for the foreseeable future. Suharto's children, after all, had also won seats on the governing board of Golkar and begun to lobby for their own minions and allies in the parliament, the armed forces, and the cabinet; and their huge conglomerates continued to capture the juiciest state contracts and monopoly concessions. So long as Suharto was president, his children would remain entrenched at the pinnacle of power, and succession struggles could leave state control in the name of their father, rather than in the hands of those who spoke on behalf of Islam.

Viewed against this backdrop, the Reformasi campaign that led to the resignation of Suharto in the spring of 1998 was the culmination of a process of self-definition and self-promotion by an ascendant segment of the national political class claiming to represent Indonesian Islam. In the Indonesia of the 1990s, after all, the struggle of "reformist" Muslims was a struggle fought largely through and within the New Order state, as HMI alumni and other affiliates of ICMI asserted their claims to increasing shares of parliamentary seats, Golkar posts, cabinet ministries, army commands, and other positions and perks of power. In this struggle, the enemy was not so much Suharto himself but rather the aging dictator's children, whose advantages in the contest over power, wealth, and the impending presidential succession were increasingly experienced — and resented — as a glass ceiling confining the interests and aspirations of an arriviste Muslim segment of the political class. In this context, the riots that swept various provincial towns and cities in 1995–97, and the massive conflagration that hit Jakarta in May 1998, served as powerful reminders of the popular energies that could be mobilized in the name of Islam. In the end, the call for Reformasi was indeed a call by Muslims for the ouster of Suharto, precisely when members of his family were poised to seize control of the armed forces, Golkar, and the cabinet, and, not coincidentally, when ICMI chief Habibie was installed as vice-president.

Islam and Democracy in the Post-Suharto Era

Suharto's resignation and Habibie's ascendancy to the Indonesian presidency in late May 1998 thus represented an unprecedented — and long-awaited — opportunity for the assumption of state power in Indonesia by those claiming to represent Islam. During Habibie's months in office, these forces worked assiduously to assert greater control over the armed forces and to build a broad coalition of parties that would combine an HMI-dominated Golkar with PPP, Muhammadiyah chairman Amien Rais's National Mandate Party (Partai Amanat Nasional, or PAN), the Masyumi-style Crescent Moon and Stars Party (Partai Bulan Bintang, or PBB), and other allied forces. Such a coalition of parties, it was hoped, would provide a rubric for the retention of power by Habibie and the segment of the political class that claimed to speak for Islam.

But the contradictions and weaknesses of the position of those claiming to represent Islam impeded the effective consolidation of their control over the Indonesian state. After all, these Muslims still comprised only one segment of the political class, as suggested by the complex pattern of alliances and maneuvers — within the regime and in the university belt—that brought it into the driver's seat in May 1998. Whether in the armed forces, Golkar, or the cabinet, modernist Muslims found themselves constrained by the Suharto family's residual influence and by competing clusters of interests and associations variously identified with Christian and secular nationalist lineages. The New Order years, after all, had produced not only visible evidence of modernist Muslim upward mobility, but also significant growth in Indonesia's Christian population and in the number of graduates from non-Muslim and secular institutions of higher education. Among themselves, moreover, these modernist Muslims, like their multifarious Protestant counterparts in the Christian world, suffered from the fissiparous tendencies of all post-Reformation religions, and their diverse pieties and purposes were reflected in debilitating political fragmentation and factional strife.

In Indonesian society, moreover, this self-consciously Muslim segment of the political class found its claim to represent Indonesia — or Islam, for that matter — persistently challenged and hotly contested from below. Islam, after all, was destined to remain an overly ambitious, indeed presumptuous, banner in a nation boasting the largest Muslim population and the most popular nongovernmental Islamic organizations in the world. The elitist pretensions of middle-class modernist Muslims to represent Islam ran up against the reality of the millions of unschooled and underemployed ordinary Indonesians of the faith. Even in the boom years of the early mid-1990s, when ICMI was expanding its network, thousands of Muslim youth had left the nation's *pesantren, madrasa*, IAIN, and universities for the job market, only to find opportunities for state or private sector employment or upward social mobility highly limited.

Compared to the upwardly mobile, middle-class modernist Muslim professionals and political operators who traced their roots back to the *madrasa*, the social and political advancement of those hailing from the *pesantren* belt was decidedly more modest.[40] A few steps behind — or below — their *madrasa*-schooled counterparts on the ladder of educational and social hierarchy, such students flocked in record numbers to the expanded network of IAIN and provincial universities, but at elite university campuses the NU-affiliated Pergerakan Mahasiswa Islam Indonesia (PMII, or Indonesian Islamic Student Movement) was much more modest in its activities and alumni roster than HMI. With high rates of unemployment for university-educated youth persisting through the boom years of the mid-1990s, it was clear that even those *pesantren* students who made it as far as college faced an uphill struggle into the new Muslim middle class.[41] Beyond the *pesantren* belt, moreover, where state patronage had made significant inroads by the 1990s, the broad majority of Indonesian Muslims were poor and unlettered, and thus excluded from the kinds of educational experiences and networks that were so crucial for the emergence and ascendancy of the political class that claimed to speak for the *ummat*.

Against this backdrop, the June 1999 elections constituted an abrupt reversal of the trends that had led to the ascendancy of Islam, along the lines of the betrayal and disappointment following the Revolusi and the winning of Indonesian independence 50 years earlier. If for decades the path to power in Indonesia had led from schools to universities to the circuitries of the state, now control over state offices and resources was achieved not through educational networks but through electoral mobilization, in a largely poor and "under-educated" society. Small wonder, then, that the parties that proved most popular were those most inclusive with regard to the extent and form of schooling of the voting public. Most notable in this regard was the Partai Demokrasi Indonesia–Perjuangan (PDI-P, or Indonesian Democratic Party of Struggle) led by Megawati Soekarnoputri, the daughter of Indonesia's first president, which captured a plurality of votes in the elections in June 1999. Like her father before her, Megawati represented a secular nationalist tradition, with the PDI-P dominated by non-Muslims (more than one-third of its parliamentary slate) and nominal Muslims with no history of Islamic education or associational affiliation. With Megawati's rise to the vice-presidency in late 1999, her increasing influence under the administration of former NU chairman Abdurrahman Wahid, and her eventual ascendance to the presidency in mid-2001, Islam thus experienced a considerable diminution of its previously rising status in the public sphere and claim to state power.

Jihad

It is against this backdrop that the emergence of groups such as Laskar Jihad and Jemaah Islamiyah at the turn of the 21st century must be understood. Already in mid-late 1998, sudden political liberalization, widespread antigovernment protests, and the impending 1999 elections encouraged the Habibie administration and its supporters to expand and experiment with forms of violent mobilization in the name of Islam. Elements in the Habibie administration supported the formation of the thuggish Front Pembela Islam (Front for the Defenders of Islam) in Jakarta in 1998 to counter student demonstrations against the government, and various Islamic parties were provided funding and assistance in the 1999 election campaigns.

With Habibie's demise in 1999 and the diminution of modernist Muslim influence in the state, the sense of disappointment and desperation only grew. In Jakarta, Habibie's immediate successor, former NU chairman Abdurrahman Wahid, had a long history of defending his "traditionalist" constituency against "modernist" Muslim encroachment by forging alliances with Christians, secular-nationalists, liberal intellectuals, and foreign interests, which were well represented in his cabinet and entourage and his policy preferences. In various parts of the archipelago, moreover, the processes of democratization and decentralization combined with the strong electoral performance of the PDI-P to endanger those forces identified with Islam.

Nowhere was this more evident than in areas of interreligious conflict such as Maluku and Poso, where Protestants backed the PDI-P against a Muslim vote divided between Golkar and various Islamic parties, even as the PDI-P's leader, vice-president Megawati Soekarnoputri, came to enjoy increasing influence within the Indonesian Armed Forces leadership in Jakarta. Violence against Muslims in Maluku and Poso, after all, was being committed by armed groups of Christians enjoying close links with the PDI-P, financial and logistical support from fellow Christians elsewhere in Indonesia and beyond, as well as the evident protection or collusion of sympathetic elements in the security forces.[42] By mid-2001, moreover, the ascension of Megawati Soekarnoputri to the presidency brought the secular nationalist/Christian PDI-P into a dominant position in Jakarta, along with senior military officers (both active and retired) with well-established records of opposition to the promotion of Islam. Thus the champions of Islam in Jakarta were understandably keen to help their beleaguered coreligionists in Maluku and Poso, and to protect and promote a stronger sense of religious boundaries in the national arena, where political parties commanding multi-faith constituencies such as Megawati's PDI-P won millions of votes, dozens of parliamentary seats, and a dangerous level of influence at their expense.

While various Islamic political party leaders thus began to voice support for an organized response to supplement the government's feeble measures to protect Muslims in Maluku and Poso, those most visibly and vehemently committed to this struggle were associated with a group formed in early 2000 and known as Laskar Jihad. Hundreds of well-armed and trained Laskar Jihad troops — along with paramedics and other civilians — were dispatched to Maluku in the months following a series of large-scale massacres of Muslims by armed Christian groups in Maluku and Maluku Utara in late December 1999 and early January 2000.[43] Additional Laskar Jihad troops began to arrive in Poso in July 2000, several weeks after large-scale killings of Muslims in the Central Sulawesi regency of that name, including the execution of dozens of villagers in a *pesantren* outside Poso town.[44] These troops, along with those of smaller and lesser-known Islamic militias, provided protection to vulnerable Muslim towns and villages, and launched large-scale attacks on Christian localities. Thanks to previous training in camps on Java, possession of automatic weapons, and coordination with sympathetic elements in the armed forces, Laskar Jihad troops achieved considerable success in the latter half of 2000 and the first six months of 2001 in avenging Christian atrocities and consolidating Muslim gains in Maluku, Maluku Utara, and Poso.[45]

But by mid-2001, the window of opportunity for paramilitary mobilization under the banner of Islam in areas of interreligious violence had already begun to close. In Maluku, Maluku Utara, and Poso, the very "success" of pogroms had produced clear local patterns of religious segregation, elaborate arrangements for self-defense on both sides of the divide, and a stalemate of sorts, with the earlier waves of large-scale mob attacks replaced by sporadic bombings, drive-by shootings, and military-style raids. Meanwhile, the ouster of Wahid from the presidency and his long-anticipated replacement by Megawati Soekarnoputri in July 2001 installed at the pinnacle of state power in Jakarta the head of the "secular nationalist," ecumenical PDI-P, the party representing Protestants in both Maluku and Poso. Already in early 2001, military officers eager to please the ascendant vice-president Megawati had initiated a crackdown on Laskar Jihad forces, launching large-scale assaults against them in June in Maluku, and in the final months of the year in Poso. With overwhelmingly Muslim North Maluku hived off as a separate province, Christians now enjoyed a slim majority in Maluku and predominated in Ambon City, while gerrymandering produced a mostly Protestant rump Poso through the creation of two new largely Muslim regencies — Morowali and Tojo Una-Una — in Central Sulawesi. Thus, by the end of 2001, interreligious pogroms had already peaked and subsided, with little large-scale violence in subsequent years, even during the election campaign period of 2004.

Against the backdrop of Laskar Jihad's rise and fall, the early years of the 21st century also witnessed a series of terrorist attacks in the form of bomb explosions in various locations around Indonesia. Beginning, like Laskar Jihad's paramilitary campaign, in the wake of the defeat of Islam in the 1999 elections and in the aftermath of well-publicized atrocities against Muslims in Maluku, Maluku Utara, and Poso, these bombings first focused on local Christian targets.[46] Christmas Eve of 2000, for example, witnessed a wave of explosions at churches in cities around the Indonesian Archipelago, stretching from Pekanbaru and Medan in the west to Bandung, Jakarta, and other towns on Java and Mataram on the eastern island of Lombok. Timed to coincide with the most important Christian holiday of the year, and to commemorate the onset of the wave of Christian atrocities against Muslims in Maluku and Maluku Utara in late December 1999, the explosions signaled efforts to continue and escalate interfaith conflict at a time when religious pogroms were subsiding rather than spreading across the Indonesian Archipelago.[47]

With the crackdown on Laskar Jihad in the spring and summer of 2001, and the events in New York and Washington, D.C., on 11 September of the same year, the bombing campaign began to shift to identifiably foreign and specifically Western targets. This trend was first evident in the explosions at a nightclub catering to foreign — mostly Australian — tourists in Bali in October 2002, which left nearly 200 casualties in its wake.[48] Subsequent explosions in Jakarta continued along these lines, with the bombing of the U.S.-owned Marriott Hotel (reportedly a favorite hangout of U.S. Embassy personnel) in August 2003 and the Australian Embassy in September 2004.

The internationalization of jihad in Indonesia from 2002 onward coincided with a set of interrelated trends in the country and beyond. First, as already noted above, by this time, large-scale interreligious violence in Maluku, Maluku Utara, and Poso had begun to subside, with patterns of accommodation rather than violent antagonism prevailing between Muslims and non-Muslims around the archipelago. Meanwhile, as also suggested above, the inauguration of Megawati Soekarnoputri in mid-2001 had reasserted claims to state power at the national level by forces identified not with the promotion of Islam but with secular nationalism and Christianity. With Hamzah Haz, the chairman of the largest Islamic party (PPP), accepting the vice-presidency without winning any real concessions from Megawati, the resubmission of Islam to these forces in Indonesian society appeared to be complete.

These domestic trends were reinforced by developments in the international arena. The newly installed Megawati administration's efforts to defang the networks of Muslim politicians, civil servants, businessmen, gangsters, and retired and active army officers mobilized for interreligious warfare in Maluku, Maluku Utara, and Poso were further impelled by pressures from without, with the U.S. and Australian governments taking the lead in the "war on terrorism" in the region. A wave of arrests beginning in mid-2001 landed not only the head of Laskar Jihad in jail but also other Muslim cogs in the machinery of sectarian violence in various degrees of hot water.[49] At the same time, with the 11 September 2001 attacks on New York City and Washington, D.C., the U.S. invasions of Afghanistan and Iraq, and terrorist attacks attributed to Al-Qaeda occurring with some regularity in locations around the world, the attractiveness of foreign, Western targets for bombing attacks in Indonesia was greatly enhanced. Compared to soldiering on with merely local, losing, battles, the prospect of fighting in a jihad of truly global proportions carried considerably greater appeal.

Indeed, the transnational dimensions of jihad were already evident in the mobilization of Laskar Jihad in early 2000. As with other Muslim groups mobilized to help their embattled coreligionists in Maluku and Poso, Laskar Jihad viewed these small pockets of Protestantism as beachheads for Christian evangelization and influence in Indonesia, funded, organized, and, since 1999, armed by wealthy churches in North America and Western Europe. As for Laskar Jihad itself, the estimated several thousand members of this saber-wielding group clearly drew inspiration from the Middle East, as their long, flowing white robes and goatees amply suggested. The group's founder was of Hadrami Arab descent, studied in Saudi Arabia, Pakistan, and Yemen, and allegedly spent some time among the *mujahidin* in Afghanistan in the late 1980s.[50]

In fact, Laskar Jihad was a group with deep historical roots in transnational Islamic educational networks and experiences. Many of the *pesantren* and *madrasa* where its leading members had been schooled were established by Islamic associations — Al-Irshad and Persatuan Islam (Islamic Union or Persis) — which were founded in the early 20th century by Muslims of Hadrami Arab descent and others influenced by the teachings of modernist Islamic scholars in the Middle East. From their inception, these schools placed great emphasis on the study of Arabic and, far more than the more Westernized *madrasa* of Muhammadiyah, prepared their students for higher education in centers of Islamic learning far from the Indonesian Archipelago.[51] While the founders and first students were predominantly drawn from among the immigrant Hadrami Arab community in the Indies, by the 1930s the vast majority of students were, by assimilation or ancestry, Indonesians. Yet the fact that these schools fed into an overseas education network promoted a "sense of separateness" and an "outward orientation, back to the Middle East," encouraging students to understand "that their center was not 'here' in the Indies, but rather 'there' in the heartland of the Arab world."[52] Thus, Al-Irshad and Persis activists were understandably ambivalent toward Indonesian nationalism, supporting the struggle against Dutch colonial rule on the one hand, while opposing the construction of a secular nation-state in its stead on the other. Although they contributed their energies to the Revolusi that led to Indonesian independence in 1945–49, many members of these groups were understandably dissatisfied with the place of Islam in the new nation-state and its constitutional democracy and backed the Darul Islam rebellion in areas such as West Java, South Sulawesi, and Aceh in the 1950s and early 1960s.

While Al-Irshad and Persis entered the 1960s on the very fringes of Indonesian politics, their enduring transnational linkages combined with the sociological and political trends described in the pages above to allow their networks of schools — and their aspirations for Islam in Indonesia — to survive, grow, and prosper in subsequent decades. Banned for its role in supporting the regional rebellions, by the 1960s Masjumi could no longer provide an umbrella of state patronage and protection as it had in the early years after independence. Despite their contributions to the anticommunist campaigns of 1965–66, activists from these circles found themselves utterly marginalized and at times actively persecuted by the seemingly Christian-dominated New Order state. Yet the detention of alleged "Komando Jihad" members in 1977 and the wave of arrests and trials in connection with the Tanjung Priok incident and related bombings and protests in 1984 must have strengthened the faith of such activists, timed as they were to coincide with general elections in the first instance and a major PPP congress in the second. With PPP winning in Jakarta and garnering considerable popular support elsewhere in 1977 but then shedding its oppositional stance, Islamic markings, and many of its most prominent backers in 1984, the message seemed clear. Only the repressive tactics of a regime dominated by Catholic generals, Chinese financiers, and secularized, Westernized technocrats could keep at bay the popular forces of Islam.

Fortified by such hopes and by domestic and foreign sources of funding, Al-Irshad and Persis activists devoted themselves to the crucial task of religious schooling. Their efforts were nurtured by Dewan Dakwah Islamiyah Indonesia (DDII, or Indonesian Islamic Preaching Council), an umbrella group founded by former Masjumi leaders in 1967 that drew on donations from Saudi Arabian and other foreign sponsors, as well as those made by sympathetic Indonesian professionals, businessmen, and government officials. As industrialization and urbanization in the 1970s and 1980s brought millions of Muslim migrants to Jakarta and other major Indonesian cities, DDII established hundreds of *pesantren* and *madrasa* and constructed thousands of mosques. The diversity of origins, ethnicity, and language of this growing new constituency, it was hoped, could be transcended by the universalism of Islam.

DDII was also especially successful in its *dakwah* activities in the campus mosques of state universities in major Indonesian cities, including such prominent institutions as Institut Teknologi Bandung, Institut Pertanian Bogor, Universitas Gadjah Mada in Yogyakarta, Universitas Airlangga (Unair) in Surabaya, and Universitas Indonesia in Jakarta.[53] Thanks to its access to scholarships offered by Saudi-sponsored and other international

Islamic organizations, Dewan Dakwah was also able to facilitate study in the Middle East. By the 1990s, moreover, with the demise of the Catholic military intelligence czar Benny Murdani and the rise of Habibie and ICMI, well-connected Dewan Dakwah activists (including some recently released from prison) enjoyed new freedom to preach and to publish, as well as unprecedented access to state patronage and support. Through their inclusion in Habibie's vast patronage empire, such activists extended their influence among government-funded students pursuing postgraduate technological and scientific degrees in Europe and North America, and among the ranks of university lecturers, journalists, publishers, and other professional Muslims in Indonesia.

Over the years, the transnational pilgrimages of those schooled under the umbrella of the Al-Irshad, Persis, and DDII networks decisively shaped their understandings of Islam. Beyond the influence of individual Islamic reformist intellectuals from the Middle East, or that of Wahhabi sponsors in Saudi Arabia, the experience of education in countries far from Indonesian shores helped to nurture an understanding of Islam that stressed its most universal principles, its appeal as a foundation for supranational social and spiritual unity, and its potential as a basis for the exercise of power. Graduates of these schools were thus concerned with purifying (*memurnikan*) the faith of those accretions of local custom (*adat*) — promoted by the Dutch colonial regime and its successors, sustained by the parochialism and ignorance of the *ummah* and the particularism and opportunism of ill-intentioned intermediaries — standing in the way of Muslim unity.

Alongside this concern with preventing the localization and fragmentation of Islam in Indonesia, there was an abiding sense of urgency about the defense of the faith against the encroachment of rival transnational forces and forms of identity. After all, the 20th century saw a significant expansion of the Christian population in Indonesia, as well as increasing inroads by the secularizing circuitries of the capitalist market and the modern nation-state. Thus, just as the Persis journal *Pembela Islam* (Defender of Islam) bewailed the weaknesses of Muslims in the face of a dynamic Christianity in the 1930s, so did Dewan Dakwah activists rail against the closet secularism of liberal, Western-educated/affiliated Muslim intellectuals in the 1980s and early 1990s. It was thus with ample historical precedent that the spokesmen of Laskar Jihad voiced disappointment with the place of Islam in Indonesia's restored constitutional democracy at the turn of the 21st century, and tried to rally Muslims divided by partisan and parochial interests against the predations of Christians and secular nationalists affiliated with Megawati and the PDI-P. It was also in echo of the forced demobilization of irregular Islamic guerrillas at the end of the Revolusi some 50 years earlier that Laskar Jihad found itself losing backing from within the state and facing violent retribution and imprisonment at the hands of the authorities by mid-2001.

These lineages have also been amply apparent in the personage and proclamations of K. H. Abu Bakar Ba'asyir, the elected leader of the Majelis Mujahidin Indonesia and the man accused of inspiring (if not himself operating) the allegedly Al-Qaeda-linked Jemaah Islamiyah network. Ba'asyir and his followers are said to have plotted terrorist attacks against U.S. targets in the Philippines and Singapore, as well as the Christmas church bombings across the country in December 2000 and the incendiary attacks on foreign targets in Bali (October 2002) and Jakarta (August 2003 and September 2004).[54] Born in 1938 in Jombang, an East Javanese town well known for its institutions of Islamic schooling, Ba'asyir attended the famous "modern" *pesantren* in Gontor and then went on to Universitas Al-Irsyad, where he studied Islamic jurisprudence. After graduation, he worked with other young Islamic activists under DDII to set up two radio stations, whose broadcasts were soon terminated by the government because of their critical and extremist content. In the early 1970s, Ba'asyir and his colleagues founded a school, known as Pondok Pesantren Al-Mukmin Ngruki, located first in Solo and then on the outskirts of the city in the regency of Sukoharjo.

There, Ba'asyir's teachings attracted both a growing stream of Muslim students and the increasing interest and concern of the Indonesian government. Indeed, by the late 1970s Ba'asyir was in prison for his views, and after several years of imprisonment he was able to leave the country for a long period of exile — and continued *dakwah* activity — in Malaysia that ended only with the fall of Suharto.[55] Over the years, Ba'asyir, as well as his school, its students, and its alumni have been repeatedly linked by the authorities to various Islamic terrorist activities, as seen in the Komando Jihad affair in 1977, the post-Tanjung Priok trials of the mid-1980s, and the massacre of an Islamic community founded by Pesantren Ngruki graduates in Lampung in 1989.[56] Most recently, the authorities have rounded up countless members of this "Ngruki network" in Indonesia, Malaysia, the Philippines, and Singapore, accusing them of involvement in a variety of terrorist activities and of membership in a Jemaah Islamiyah network unheard of since the 1970s. As detailed in the International Crisis Group's reports, many of those convicted of involvement in the Bali bombing and accused of other terrorist activities are former Ngruki students or members of a broader and more complex network of which it forms a part.

Thus, the origins and aspirations of Ba'asyir and his followers are clearly rooted in a tradition of transnational Islam in Indonesia that dates back many decades. With his former students working as preachers and starting up small *pesantren* across the archipelago and in neighboring Malaysia and the Philippines, and his own children pursuing further Islamic education in Pakistan and Saudi Arabia, Ba'asyir has helped to continue and expand the transnational pattern of pilgrimage, education, and circulation embodied in Al-Irshad and Persis since the early 20th century. Unlike the *madrasa* founded by the mainstream modernist association Muhammadiyah, which help to prepare Muslim pupils for Indonesian state universities and government employment, Ba'asyir's *pesantren* and the broader network of Al-Irshad, Persis, and now DDII-supported schools open the eyes and minds of their students to horizons that stretch far beyond the shores of the archipelago.

To be sure, the Indonesian state exercises a highly attractive — and absorptive — power for activists such as Ba'asyir, whether through the tactical necessity of reaching an "accommodation" of some kind with its intelligence apparatus, or the strategic goal of codifying and implementing Islamic law throughout the country. Indeed, there is abundant evidence of linkages between elements in the armed forces and these activist networks over the years, from infiltration and imprisonment in the 1970s and 1980s to close cooperation against the foes of the Suharto and Habibie regimes in the mid-late 1990s, and provision of support to armed Muslim groups in Maluku and Poso at the turn of the century. At the same time, the manifold sinecures in the vast Ministry of Religious Affairs in Jakarta and the provisions of regional autonomy, especially in those regencies where Islamic parties control the local assemblies, have offered considerable opportunities for the promotion of Islam within the rubric of the Indonesian nation-state. Yet the means and ends of this dream transcend the borders of Indonesia, with the nation-state and nationalists viewed as — inherently secular — obstacles and enemies dividing Muslims and thwarting the spread and deepening of a universalist Islam. As Ba'asyir commented acerbically with reference to Soekarno and one of his great heroes: "For me, Kemal Ataturk is not the Father of Turkey, but a traitor to the Islamic community in Turkey."[57]

Conclusion: The Making and Unmaking of Jihad in Southeast Asia

In short, as suggested above, jihad in the Philippines and Indonesia today must be understood against a broader historical and sociological canvas, one depicting national and transnational institutions, networks, experiences, and horizons. Overall, the location, timing, and form of the activities of Abu Sayyaf, Laskar Jihad, and Jemaah Islamiyah reflect the very different *national* constraints, opportunities, and imperatives presented by national politics, on the one hand, and the widely varying possibilities of mobilizing armed followers under the banner of Islam, on the other. In the Philippines, where local elections reemerged after the fall of Marcos as the primary path of access to state power, the potential attraction of jihad has been weakened by parochialism, partisanship, and competition for patronage among the small, poor, and largely unlettered Muslim minority in the southern periphery of the archipelago. Thus, jihad has manifested itself through shadowy armed groups engaged in criminal rackets, rather than rallying cries for mass mobilization. Even the bombings of — Filipino rather than foreign — targets in Manila and other cities in recent years serve as acts of retribution and deterrence in the face of the Philippine government's continuing push to assert control of the remote Sulu Zone.

In Indonesia, by contrast, where educational institutions long served as key transmission belts for both social mobilization and access to state power, and where Islamic school networks have grown and prospered in recent decades, the call for jihad has been issued in the face of a sudden, sharp decline for Islam under conditions of democratization. The call for armed mobilization under the banner of Islam in early-mid 2000 came precisely when and where Muslim communities in Maluku and Central Sulawesi found themselves in violent conflict with well-connected and protected armed Christian groups. The bombings around the country at Christmas 2000, in a nightclub in the predominantly Hindu PDI-P stronghold of Bali nearly two years later, and again in sites of foreign, Western influence in Jakarta in 2003 and 2004, reasserted the ubiquitous spectral power of Islam, just when its strength and integrity in the parliamentary arena in Indonesia had reached new lows with the co-optation of PPP Chairman Hamzah Haz as Megawati's vice-president. The timing of the bombings was strikingly reminiscent of the series of explosions — at malls, banks, and the Buddhist temple complex of Borobodur — that unfolded in the pre-Al-Qaeda Indonesia of the mid-1980s, during a similar period of dashed hopes for forces promoting Islam and reconsolidation of secularist and Christian influence in the New Order state.

Yet, as suggested above, the content and context of the Islam in whose name such forms of jihad are waged in the Philippines and Indonesia have also been profoundly *transnational* in nature. This transnational dimension of jihad in Southeast Asia is best understood not in terms of an international "Islamic terrorism" conspiracy under the leadership of Osama bin Laden, nor merely as "blowback"[58] or default option[59] in the wake of the Cold War, nor simply as "sanctified rage"[60] against what has been pithily described as McWorld.[61] In both the Philippines and Indonesia, after all, Islam has long been understood — and experienced — not only as an underlying basis for achieving social unity that transcends national boundaries, but also as a project, inherently incomplete, for unifying Muslims divided by political conspiracies, particularistic practices, and parochial interests and understandings, a project whose further advancement can be experienced firsthand elsewhere in the Islamic world, even in neighboring Malaysia.[62]

From its inception, this project has been defined in no small measure by religious orthodoxy. As scholars have suggested, orthodoxy is best understood not as a disembodied system of belief, but as a relationship of power: "the power to regulate, uphold, require, or adjust *correct* practices, and to condemn, exclude, undermine, or replace *incorrect* ones."[63] But relations of orthodoxy, it has been noted, are "a peculiar form of property relation — a relation between people with regard to texts and intellectual technologies — that are potentially more fluid than other sorts of class relations."[64] These relations are contingent both on the sociology of education, and on the politics of competition between other claimants to knowledge and power. Thus, even — indeed, especially — for those Muslim Filipinos and Indonesians who have spent many years in schools closely connected through language, scholarship, and circulation to centers of Islamic learning beyond their national borders, Islam has remained a horizon of sorts, one that now appears to be rapidly receding.

Measured in terms of disappointment with the present or imperative for the future, this horizon has been shaped by other transnational forces as well, most notably those associated with Christianity and the supposedly secular(izing) circuitries of the capitalist market and the modern nation-state. As noted above, it was the impact of first Spanish Catholicism and then U.S. liberalism that condemned Muslims in the Philippine Archipelago to minority status, internal colonization, and sociopolitical fragmentation within a nation-state dominated by Christians. In a similar vein, it was the promotion of *adat* and aristocratic localisms by the Dutch, and the head start enjoyed by Christian missionary school graduates and Chinese businessmen that made graduates of Islamic schools feel like such outsiders and latecomers, even in predominantly Muslim Indonesia. The past decade of triumphs for global liberalism in economic, political, and cultural terms has thus been experienced not as the extensions of inclusive, universalistic freedoms, but rather as the intrusions of colonizing, particularistic interests at the expense of Islam.[65] Small wonder that Osama bin Laden and Al-Qaeda inspire a measure of enthrallment, adulation, and emulation among some of their fellow coreligionists in Southeast Asia, and serve as signs of a truly great struggle rather than simply sources of support and instructions for identifying targets of terrorist activity in the region.

Thus today, as U.S.-backed Philippine troops besiege Abu Sayyaf camps in Basilan and Sulu and as alleged Jemaah Islamiyah activists face interrogation in jail cells in Jakarta, Manila, and Singapore, it is important to remember that jihad in Southeast Asia is, as elsewhere in the Muslim world, overwhelmingly reactive and defensive in nature. The floundering struggle for a Moro homeland in the southern Philippines and the precipitous decline of Islamist forces in Indonesia since the turn of the century resemble other contexts around the world where terrorist bombings serve, as Michele Wieviorka has argued, "not [as] a faltering movement's last best hope or final act of desperation but rather a substitute for a movement which has either become imaginary or has fallen out of sync with the hopes pinned on it."[66] Thus, the internationalization of jihad most apparent in the Bali and Jakarta bombings of recent years represents an extrusion of the problems encountered in mobilizing Muslims behind an Islamist agenda within the national confines of Indonesia.[67]

Playing late catch-up in the profane world of modern politics, the purveyors of jihad in both the Philippines and Indonesia are in fact waging a rear-guard, losing battle under the banner of Islam, making desperate, last-gasp efforts to rally — or reawaken — the faithful. With Madonna on the radio in Basilan and Santa Clauses roaming the shopping malls of Jakarta, bin Laden on the run and bin Bush on the warpath, K. H. Abu Bakar Ba'asyir is surely right to describe jihad as a "defensive concept."[68]

Notes

1. This essay is a revised version of an earlier piece, "Other Schools, Other Pilgrimages, Other Dreams: The Making and Unmaking of 'Jihad' in Southeast Asia," in James T. Siegel and Audrey R. Kahin, eds., *Southeast Asia over Three Generations: Essays Presented to Benedict R. O'G. Anderson* (Ithaca: Cornell University Southeast Asia Program, 2003), 347–82. The revised and updated version is published here with the kind permission of the Cornell University Southeast Asia Program.
2. Rohan Gunaratna, *Inside Al Qaeda: Global Network of Terror* (London: C. Hurst, 2002), 175.
3. Ibid., 185–6. See also Rohan Gunaratna, "Al-Qaeda's Operational Ties with Allied Groups," *Jane's Intelligence Review* (1 February 2003).
4. Zachary Abuza, "Tentacles of Terror: Al Qaeda's Southeast Asian Network," *Contemporary Southeast Asia* 24, 3 (December 2002): 427–65. See also Zachary Abuza, *Militant Islam in Southeast Asia: Crucible of Terror* (Boulder: Lynne Rienner, 2003); and Zachary Abuza, *Muslims, Politics, and Violence in Indonesia: An Emerging Jihadist-Islamist Nexus?* (Seattle: National Bureau of Asian Research, September 2004).
5. See *Al-Qaeda in Southeast Asia: The Case of the "Ngruki Network" in Indonesia* (Jakarta and Brussels: International Crisis Group, August 2002); *Indonesia Backgrounder: How the Jemaah Islamiyah Terrorist Network Operates* (Jakarta and Brussels: International Crisis Group, December 2002); *Jemaah Islamiyah in South East Asia: Damaged but Still Dangerous* (Jakarta and Brussels: International Crisis Group, August 2003); *Indonesia Backgrounder: Jihad in Central Sulawesi* (Jakarta and Brussels: International Crisis Group, February 2004); *Southern Philippines Backgrounder: Terrorism and the Peace Process* (Jakarta and Brussels: International Crisis Group, July 2004); *Indonesia Backgrounder: Why Salafism and Terrorism Mostly Don't Mix* (Jakarta and Brussels: International Crisis Group, September 2004); *Recycling Militants in Indonesia: Darul Islam and the Australian Embassy Bombing* (Jakarta and Brussels: International Crisis Group, February 2005).
6. Mark Turner, "Terrorism and Secession in the Southern Philippines: The Rise of the Abu Sayaff," *Contemporary Southeast Asia* 17, 1 (June 1995): 1–19; Marites Danguilan Vitug and Glenda Gloria, *Under the Crescent Moon: Rebellion in Mindanao* (Quezon City: Ateneo Center for Social Policy and Public Affairs, 2000), 192–245.
7. Patricio N. Abinales, *Making Mindanao: Cotabato and Davao in the Formation of the Philippine Nation-State* (Quezon City: Ateneo de Manila University Press, 2000).
8. James Francis Warren, *The Sulu Zone 1768–1898: The Dynamics of External Trade, Slavery, and Ethnicity in the Transformation of a Southeast Asian Maritime State* (Quezon City: New Day Publishers, 1985), 53.

9. Warren, *The Sulu Zone*, 104–25; Reynaldo C. Ileto, *Magindanao 1860–1888: The Career of Datu Uto of Buayan* (Ithaca: Cornell University Southeast Asia Program, 1971); James Francis Warren, *Iranun and Balangingi: Globalization, Maritime Raiding and the Birth of Ethnicity* (Singapore: Singapore University Press, 2002), 343–417.
10. By one 1995 estimate, some 300,000 undocumented Filipinos were working in Sabah and Sarawak. See Zeus A. Salazar, "The Malay World: Bahasa Melayu in the Philippines," in *The Malayan Connection: Ang Pilipinas sa Dunia Melayu* (Quezon City: Palimbagan ng Lahi, 1998), 99.
11. See Howard M. Federspiel, "Islam and Muslims in the Southern Territories of the Philippine Islands During the American Colonial Period (1898 to 1946)," *Journal of Southeast Asian Studies* 29, 2 (September 1998): 340–56, see pp. 347–55.
12. Patricia Horvatich, "Ways of Knowing Islam," *American Ethnologist* 21, 4 (1994): 811–26.
13. For impressions and estimates of these trends, compare: Luis Q. Lacar, Gabino T. Puno, and Nagamura T. Moner, eds., *Madrasah Education in the Philippines and Its Role in National Integration* (Iligan City: MSU-IIT Coordination Center for Research and Development, 1986); "Estimated Number of Madaris (Arabic Schools) as of July 31, 1993," Bureau of Muslim Cultural Affairs, Office on Muslim Affairs, Quezon City, 1993; and Richard Martin, "Resurgent Islam," *Far Eastern Economic Review* (17 February 1994): 36–7.
14. Thomas M. McKenna, "The Sources of Muslim Separatism in Cotabato," *Pilipinas*, 21 (Fall 1993): 11. At the same time, (Christian) Liberal politicians in Central Luzon such as Senator Benigno S. Aquino Jr. were similarly engaged in collaboration with the revived Communist Party of the Philippines and its New People's Army.
15. T. J. S. George, *Revolt in Mindanao: The Rise of Islam in Philippine Politics* (Kuala Lumpur: Oxford University Press, 1980); Thomas McKenna, *Muslim Rulers and Rebels: Everyday Politics and Armed Separatism in the Southern Philippines* (Berkeley: University of California Press, 1998), 138–69; Lela G. Noble, "The Moro National Liberation Front in the Philippines," *Pacific Affairs* 49, 3 (1976): 405–24; Samuel K. Tan, *The Internationalization of the Bangsa Moro Struggle* (Quezon City: University of the Philippines Press, 1993).
16. For background, see Arnold Molina Azurin, *Beyond the Cult of Dissidence in Southern Philippines and Wartorn Zones in the Global Village* (Quezon City: University of the Philippines Press, 1996); and Kristin Gaerlan and Mara Stankovitch, eds., *Rebels, Warlords and Ulama: A Reader on Muslim Separatism and the War in Southern Philippines* (Quezon City: Institute for Popular Democracy, 2000).

17. Jim Warren, "Who Were the Balangingi Samal? Slave Raiding and Ethnogenesis in Nineteenth-Century Sulu," *Journal of Asian Studies* 37, 3 (May 1978): 477–90.
18. For example, Wahab Akbar, who has served as provincial governor of Basilan, was not only a former MNLF commander and Islamic preacher, but also allegedly one of the founders of the group identified today as Abu Sayyaf.
19. See, for example, Jose Torres Jr., *Into the Mountain: Hostaged by the Abu Sayyaf* (Quezon City: Claretian Publications, 2001), 145–8.
20. On Sayyaf, see Barnett R. Rubin, *The Fragmentation of Afghanistan: State Formation and Collapse in the International System* (New Haven: Yale University Press, 1995).
21. See, for example, John Pemberton, *On the Subject of "Java"* (Ithaca: Cornell University Press, 1994).
22. Gavin W. Jones, "Religion and Education in Indonesia," *Indonesia* 22 (October 1976): 19–56.
23. Azyumardi Azra, "The Transmission of Islamic Reformism to Indonesia: Networks of Middle Eastern and Malay-Indonesian 'Ulama' in the Seventeenth and Eighteenth Centuries," PhD dissertation, Columbia University, New York, 1992.
24. See C. Snouck Hurgronje, *Mekka in the Latter Part of the 19th Century* (Leiden: E. J. Brill, 1970), 215–92.
25. Michael Francis Laffan, *Islamic Nationhood and Colonial Indonesia: The Umma below the Winds* (London: RoutledgeCurzon, 2003).
26. Deliar Noer, *The Modernist Muslim Movement in Indonesia 1900–1942* (Kuala Lumpur: Oxford University Press, 1973).
27. See, for example, Sartono Kartdirdjo, *The Peasants' Revolt of Banten in 1888* (The Hague: Martinus Nijhoff, 1966); and James T. Siegel, *The Rope of God* (Ann Arbor: University of Michigan Press, 2000).
28. See Anthony Reid, "Nineteenth Century Pan-Islam in Indonesia and Malaysia," *Journal of Asian Studies*, 6, 2 (1967): 267–83; and C. van Dijk, "Colonial fears, 1890–1918: Pan-Islamism and the Germano-Indian Plot," in Huub de Jonge and Nico Kaptein, eds., *Transcending Borders: Arabs, Politics, Trade and Islam in Southeast Asia* (Leiden: KITLV Press, 2002), 53–89.
29. Takashi Shiraishi, *An Age in Motion: Popular Radicalism in Java, 1912–1926* (Ithaca: Cornell University Press, 1990).
30. Harry J. Benda, *The Crescent and the Rising Sun: Indonesian Islam Under the Japanese Occupation 1942–1945* (The Hague: W. van Hoeve, 1958).
31. C. van Dijk, *Rebellion Under the Banner of Islam: The Darul Islam in Indonesia* (The Hague: Martinus Nijhoff, 1981).
32. See John T. Sidel, "*Islam Fanatik?* PPP and the Limitations of Islamic Populism in Indonesia," in Eva-Lotta E. Hedman and John T. Sidel, eds.,

Populism and Reformism in Southeast Asia: The Threat and Promise of New Politics (New Haven: Yale University Southeast Asia Monograph Series, forthcoming).

33. Avery Willis Jr., *Indonesian Revival: Why Two Million Came to Christ* (South Pasadena: William Carey Library, 1977); Robert W. Hefner, "Islamizing Java? Religion and Politics in Rural East Java," *Journal of Asian Studies* 46, 3 (August 1987): 533–54.
34. Gregory Starrett, *Putting Islam to Work: Education, Politics, and Religious Transformation in Egypt* (Berkeley: University of California Press, 1998), 9–10. Emphasis added.
35. See "Islam Sebagai Baju Zirah di Kalangan Muda," *Tempo*, 13 May 1989: 74–8; and Nurhayati Djamas, "Gerakan Kebangkitan Islam Kaum Muda," in Abdul Aziz, ed., *Gerakan Islam Kontemporer di Indonesia* (Jakarta: Pustaka Firdaus, 1989), 207–87.
36. Moeslim Abdurrahman, "On Hajj Tourism: In Search of Piety and Identity in the New Order Indonesia," PhD dissertation, University of Illinois at Urbana-Champaign, 2000.
37. Julia Day Howell, "Sufism and the Indonesian Islamic Revival," *Journal of Asian Studies* 60, 3 (August 2001): 718–22.
38. See "Satria Berdakwah, Raja dari Bawah," *Tempo* (20 June 1984): 27–30; "Saya Ustad, Bukan Artis," *Tempo* (28 April 1990): 74–8; "Dai-Dai baru Bak Matahari Terbit," *Tempo* (11 April 1992): 14–20; and Francois Raillon, "L'Ordre Nouveau et l'Islam ou l'imbroglio de la foi et de la politique," *Archipel* 30 (1985): 229–61.
39. Darul Aqsha, Dick van der Meij, and Johan Hendrik Meuleman, *Islam in Indonesia: A Survey of Events and Developments from 1988 to March 1993* (Jakarta: Indonesia-Netherlands Cooperation in Islamic Studies, 1995), 263–76.
40. See Andree Feillard, *Islam et Armee Dans L'Indonesie Contemporaine: Les Pionniers de la Tradition* (Paris: Editions L'Harmattan, 1995), chap. 12.
41. Chris Manning, *Indonesian Labour in Transition: An East Asian Success Story?* (Cambridge: Cambridge University Press, 1998), 177–88.
42. Gerry van Klinken, "The Maluku Wars: Bringing Society Back In," *Indonesia* 71 (April 2001): 1–26; Lorraine V. Aragon, "Communal Violence in Poso, Central Sulawesi: Where People Eat Fish and Fish Eat People," *Indonesia* 72 (October 2001): 45–79.
43. See, for example, "Pertikaian Masih Terjadi di Maluku; Bupati, Dandim, dan Kapolres Diduga Terlibat Penyerangan," *Republika* (13 January 2000); "Kepolisian Benarkan 216 Transmigran Dibantai di Masjid Maluku Utara," *Republika* (17 January 2000).
44. "Poso Menangis, Ratusan Nyawa Melayang di Pesantren Wali Songo," *Kompas* (13 June 2000).

45. On Poso, for example, see Human Rights Watch, *Breakdown: Four Years of Communal Violence in Central Sulawesi* (New York: Human Rights Watch, December 2002), 21–9.
46. On the bombing of the Istiqlal Mosque in Jakarta in 1999 and several other earlier small-scale explosions, however, see the series of articles published in the special report "Siapa Sebenarnya Pembom Istiqlal?" *Tempo* (3 May 1999): 22–9.
47. On the Christmas Eve 2000 bombings, see the series of articles published in the special investigative report "Cerita dari Mosaik Bom Natal," *Tempo* (25 February 2001): 60–80.
48. See the series of articles published under the rubric of the special issue "Setahun Bom Bali," *Tempo* (12 October 2003), especially pp. 32–83.
49. See the series of articles published under the rubric of the cover story "Untuk Apa Dia Ditangkap?" *Tempo* (19 May 2002): 24–33; as well as the collection of materials in *Manilagate: Kontroversi Penangkapan Tamsil Linrung* (Jakarta: Merah Putih, 2003).
50. See Noorhaidi Hasan, "Faith and Politics: The Rise of the Laskar Jihad in the Era of Transition in Indonesia," *Indonesia* 73 (April 2002): 145–69.
51. Howard M. Federspiel, *Islam and Ideology in the Emerging Indonesian State: The Persatuan Islam (PERSIS), 1923 to 1957* (Leiden: Brill, 2001).
52. Natalie Mobini-Kesheh, *The Hadrami Awakening: Community and Identity in the Netherlands East Indies, 1900–1942* (Ithaca: Cornell University Southeast Asia Program, 1999), 83.
53. Asna Husin, "Philosophical and Sociological Aspects of Da'wah: A Study of Dewan Dakwah Islamiyah Indonesia," PhD dissertation, Columbia University, New York, 1998, 147–76; "Bermula dari Masjid Salman," *Tempo* (13 May 1989), 79–81; Abdul Aziz, Imam Tholkhah, and Soetarman, eds., *Gerakan Islam Kontemporer di Indonesia* (Jakarta: Pustaka Firdaus, 1989).
54. On the Christmas 2000 bombings, see "Cerita dari Mosaik Bom Natal," *Tempo* (25 February 2001), 59–80.
55. See K. H. Abu Bakar Ba'asyir, *Saya Teroris? (Sebuah "Pledoi")* (Jakarta: Penerbit Republika, 2002), 35–40.
56. Al Chaidar, *Lampung Bersimbah Darah: Menulusuir Kejahatan "Negara Intelijen" Orde Baru Dalam Peristiwa Jama'ah Warsidi* (Jakarta: Madani Press, 2000); Irfa S. Awwas, *Trauma Lampung Berdarah: DiBalik Manuver Hendropriyono* (Yogyakarta: Wihdah Press, 2000); Abdul Syukur, *Gerakan Usroh di Lampung: Peristiwa Lampung 1989* (Yogyakarta: Ombak, 2003).
57. "KH Abu Bakar Ba'asyir: 'Hadapi Kaum Sekuler dengan Tegas'," *Suara Hidayatullah* (February 2001).
58. Chalmers Johnson, *Blowback: The Costs and Consequences of American Empire* (New York: Metropolitan Books, 2000).

59. Robert Malley, *The Call From Algeria: Third Worldism, Revolution, and the Turn to Islam* (Berkeley: University of California Press, 1996).
60. V. S. Naipaul, *Among the Believers: An Islamic Journey* (London: Picador, 2001), 354.
61. Benjamin Barber, *Jihad Vs. McWorld: How Globalism and Tribalism Are Reshaping the World* (New York: Ballantine Books, 1996).
62. Michael G. Peletz, *Islamic Modern: Religious Courts and Cultural Politics in Malaysia* (Princeton: Princeton University Press, 2002).
63. Talal Asad, *The Idea of an Anthropology of Islam* (Washington, D.C.: Georgetown University Center for Contemporary Arab Studies Occasional Paper Series, 1986), 15.
64. Starrett, *Putting Islam to Work*, 13.
65. In terms of "secularism," moreover, see Talal Asad, *Formations of the Secular: Christianity, Islam, Modernity* (Stanford: Stanford University Press, 2003).
66. Michel Wieviorka, *The Making of Terrorism* (Chicago: University of Chicago Press, 2004), 291.
67. See Olivier Roy, *The Failure of Political Islam* (Cambridge: Harvard University Press, 1998); Gilles Kepel, *Jihad: The Trail of Political Islam* (Cambridge: Harvard University Press, 2000); and Olivier Roy, *Globalised Islam: The Search for a New Ummah* (London: C. Hurst, 2004).
68. "Jihad Konsep Defensif," *Suara Karya* (6 June 2002).

13

Some Comparative Notes on Three Muslim Rebellion Movements in Southeast Asia (Burma, Thailand, and the Philippines)

MOSHE YEGAR

Since the end of World War II, insurrections and disturbances have occurred in many Muslim countries. Muslim communities in Southeast Asia have also been involved in such acts of violence. The increasing number of Islamic countries that attained independence intensified the sense of Islamic solidarity and the feeling of belonging to a united Muslim world community (*ummah*) among the huge Muslim populations of Asia, including countries with Muslim minorities. This happened in spite of confrontations between sister Muslim countries, such as the Indonesia-Malaysia conflict of the 1960s, the Pakistan-Bangladesh conflict of 1971, and other cases that demonstrated that the Muslim world is, in fact, not united.

Despite this, one should not underestimate the tremendous power of inspiration and influences emanating from Arab countries (often termed "the heart of Islam"), which have spread throughout Muslim countries and which have served as a great unifying religious and spiritual force. This is in spite of the political differences that may cause conflicts, and even wars, among sister Muslim countries. Such unifying influences find their expression in the pilgrimage to Mecca (Hajj); the increasing number of students from Muslim countries who pursue religious studies at the Al-Azhar University in Cairo or in Mecca, Medina, or other centers of religious learning in Arab countries; the growing number of Arab religious personnel (*ulama*) and religious teachers who go to Muslim countries where they exert great political influence, and where they sometimes indulge in subversive activities. Their prestige derives from the fact that they speak, read, and write Arabic, the holy language of Islam and the Koran.[1]

In recent decades, radical Islamic movements emerging from the Middle East have found their adherents in many Muslim countries, including in Southeast Asia. Violent and terrorist Muslim organizations have found material, financial, and even political support in some Arab countries. The relationship between three Muslim minority insurrection movements in Southeast Asia and some Arab countries will be referred to in the following pages.

This survey will try to make some comparisons and find similarities and differences between these three Muslim insurrection movements in Southeast Asia. These movements are among the Muslim community of the southern Philippines (Moro), The Malay-Muslim community of southern Thailand (Patani Muslims), and the Rohingya Muslims of north Arakan in west Burma/Myanmar. The history of each of these rebellions will not be reviewed here, as this has been done elsewhere in great detail.[2] However, an effort will be made to understand the motives of those rebellions and their sources of inspiration, as well as to find out to what extent the Muslim world at large, and the Arab countries in particular, showed interest in those movements.

Each of the Muslim minorities that rebelled against its majority government had its own local grievances, but all three (and similar Muslim insurrection movements elsewhere) also have their theological arguments to justify their stand that Muslims do not have to owe allegiance to a government that does not protect them and their religious life and institutions. They are, therefore, permitted to defend their faith by force if it is threatened.

Numerous points of similarity exist between the Muslim communities of the Philippines, Muslim communities in the Patani region of Thailand, and those of Arakan in Burma/Myanmar. It is useful to compare these three minority communities, each of which rebelled against non-Muslim majority regimes. In two of the countries, Thailand and Burma/Myanmar, the majority of the population is Buddhist; in the Philippines, it is Christian. It is not an accident, then, that in the pervasive atmosphere of heightened nationalism following World War II, rebellions by Muslim minorities broke out in several places. In Thailand and the Philippines, these conflagrations were the continuation of an ongoing tradition of resistance to a central regime that long antedated World War II. In all three countries, the rebelling Muslim minorities lived in well-defined territorial concentrations, adjacent to neighboring Muslim states. (In two cases, Thailand and Burma/Myanmar, there are Muslim communities that differ in their ethnic composition and did not revolt against the central authority; these groups remain outside the scope of this study.) According to population estimates, in all three cases Muslims comprise 4 per cent to 6 per cent of the general population.[3]

Some basic elements differentiate the communities. From ethnic and religious standpoints, the Muslims of Patani in southern Thailand and the Moro of the southern Philippines belong to the Malay World, while the Rohingya of Arakan are closer to the Muslims of Bengal. There are also significant differences in the rebel movements of each of the communities with regard to historical background, aspirations and goals, and operational effectiveness. Goals or aspirations, however, were invariably neither clearly nor unambiguously expressed. In general, the rebel groups can all be classed as separatist movements that sought independence, or at least varying degrees of autonomy. In each of the three cases, the rebel movements employed the tactics of guerilla warfare to achieve their goals. In presenting their positions, the separatist movements could give an impression of lacking both sophistication and consistency, although there is the possibility that at times the fuzziness and ambiguity were intentional. At times, it was also unclear whether the Muslim communities aspired only to independence, or whether they would have been satisfied with an improved standard of living and the acceptance of some of their demands in the religious, social, educational, and economic spheres, as well as the co-option of Muslims into governmental networks. This lack of clarity was more characteristic of the Muslims of Thailand and those of the southern Philippines; it was less true for the Rohingya of Arakan. In the Philippines, and even more in Thailand, the distinction between fighting for Muslim interests and outright banditry was often blurred, a situation that was costly to the rebel movements in terms of a tarnished image. It did nothing for their popularity, not even among members of their own community. In fact, it weakened their position.

A comparison of the three separatist movements shows distinct differences in the quality of leadership that developed in each of them. For example, the Muslims of Arakan were not able to produce a leadership from among themselves whose stature was such that it could unite the entire Rohingya people, or, for that matter, even most of the Rohingya.

Neither were they able to build a network linking them to international Muslim bodies and Islamic countries, as the Patani Muslims — and even more the Moro — were able to do. Once the leadership of the *mujahideen* leader Cassim came to an end, and that was as early as 1961, the Rohingya had no one of stature at their head. In contrast, there was a broad group of talented and able people among the Moro whose educational background and ability were such that they could function within the emergency situation in which they found themselves.

Many of the founders of the Moro National Liberation Front (MNLF) and other rebel movements in the southern Philippines were students and academics who — particularly in the early years of the rebellion — were able to work in concert with the traditional leadership elites and the *ulama*. Among the Patani Muslims, too, there were students who had acquired an education in institutions of higher learning in Thailand itself or abroad in Arab countries. In theory, they were able to develop patterns of activity similar to those of the Moro students: to mobilize members for underground organizations; to establish a network of political and propaganda work; to forge international links; and to solicit military, financial, and political aid in support of their separatist struggle. However, the Patani Muslims did not make either significant or serious efforts in this direction to equal the achievements of Nur Misuari, Hashim Salamat, and many others from the Philippines who preceded them. The only exception was Major Mayhiddin of Thailand, and even this high point in the Patani Muslim struggle was limited to the early period soon after the end of World War II.

Another reason for the weakness of the separatist movements can be found in their lack of consensus about the goals they wanted to achieve, a reflection of the personal struggles between leaders of the various factions. The schisms that characterized the separatist movements, particularly in the Philippines and Thailand, hampered the projection of a unified cause and were an obstacle to political or military decisive action. It is conceivable that if all the diverse factions in the rebel movements could have united in their struggle, their situation would have appreciably improved and their accomplishments would have been more telling.

In general, it can be said that the majority of Muslim rebels in the Philippines wanted to secede and to establish an independent Muslim state. Even the most moderate among them sought, at a minimum, full autonomy for their people. There were even some Moro who wished to unite with neighboring Malaysia. The Muslims of the Patani region, too, were striving for either independence or to become a part of Malaysia. The Muslims of

Arakan wanted an autonomy that would, essentially, guarantee freedom of religion and their civil rights as part of the Union of Burma. Only a small faction hoped for unification with neighboring East Pakistan/Bangladesh.

The diverse expectations of the three communities impacted qualitatively on the nature of their liberation movements. In the Philippines, the Muslim rebellion took on the dimensions of a full-fledged war, particularly severe during the regime of President Ferdinand Marcos. There were times when governmental control of a number of areas in the south was in serious question. In order to curb the revolt, the government had to commit heavy resources to the conflict. For internal, political, and geographic reasons, as well as because of external pressures exerted by international Islamic bodies, outright victory was unachievable. The vehemence and burning Islamic religious fervor of the Moro rebellion is attested to by the rise of the martyr phenomenon, the personal jihad, particularly true during the periods of Spanish and U.S. rule. There were no equivalent manifestations among the Muslims of Patani or the Rohingya. While the Muslims of Patani did resemble the Philippine Moro in seeing their identity as different from the Buddhist majority against which they violently rebelled, their war was less all-encompassing and certainly less effective than the one the MNLF managed to mount. The Muslims of Patani were never able to threaten the government's hold in the southern provinces or to put it in question. They simply could not withstand the military might of the Thai government.

In Burma, by comparison, after the *mujahideen* rebellion was put down and the army had reestablished its hold on Muslim areas of Arakan, resistance was more often channeled into the occasional diplomatic protest and appeal to Muslim countries or international Muslim bodies for aid, but primarily it took the form of flight across the border to Bangladesh. Ultimately, when compared to that of the other rebel movements, the Rohingya rebellion was relatively minor. Apparently, the number of fighting men whom the Arakan Muslim community was able to enlist was never more than a few hundred, not even when the fighting was at its peak during the 1950s. From those who surrendered in 1961, 500 in all, one can deduce that the *mujahideen* never exceeded several hundred fighters. This is true even if one takes into account the possibility that some men did not participate in surrender ceremonies but simply left for their homes forfeiting the financial grants, promises of land, and copies of the Koran that were being offered. Another fact that should be taken into account regarding this rebel movement is the confusion about any practical difference between indigenous Rohingya and other Muslims who had infiltrated from Chittagong. Apparently, all sides chose to de-emphasize these differences: the British during their regime, the government of independent Burma, and the Pakistani and Muslim populations of Arakan itself. From Burma's point of view, all the Muslims in Arakan were foreigners and the distinctions between Rohingya and other Muslims in the area did not present either civilian or military functions.

Any attempt to understand Muslim rebellions in Southeast Asia must take into account more than an analysis of the local factors in each country, or a description of relations between the Muslim minority and the majority government against which it struggled. It is essential to examine these phenomena against the broader background of Islamic theological concepts, originally from the Middle East, which are a part of the outlook and the ideology of Philippine, Thai, and Burmese Muslims. One also needs to view the rebellions against the background of similar occurrences in other parts of the Muslim world in the 60 years since the end of World War II.[4]

Muslims aspire to live in a Muslim state; serious problems of identity can confront those who are not able to do so, and this occasionally results in crisis. Muslims everywhere perceive themselves as belonging to the integral, undivided community of Islam, the *ummah*, a concept that is a core tenet in the political-religious thought of Islam. It is the basis for the growth of the pan-Islamic movement that arose at the end of the 19th century, calling for Islamic solidarity as a response to the challenge of Western imperialism. Muslims who live as a minority in a non-Muslim environment often have the sense that they are denied the right of sovereign expression. Many of them have opted to conduct their lives in isolation from their surroundings, which, at times, gives rise to mistrust by and confrontations with the majority society. The problem can be exacerbated in places where Muslim minorities constitute a majority within some districts of a larger non-Muslim country, a situation that causes an illusion that may obscure the fact that the Muslims are, in fact, a minority. Local concentrations can give rise to rebellious trends, separatist tendencies, and reliance on violence directed against the regime of "unbelievers." The conflict is then defined as a jihad, a holy war. In such circumstances, the non-Islamic state — that is, the society of the majority — is also confronted with a dilemma.

One course of action can be an attempt to assimilate and acculturate the minority that the regime regards as a threat to the territorial integrity and sovereignty of the country. Another option can be an attempt to minimize the extent of the minority's exclusive hold on a district by encouraging the immigration of non-Muslims into those very areas. The government can also, where circumstances are propitious, expel or weaken the presence of the minority by various means — and there are examples of such policies in all three of the countries under study here. For its part, the Muslim minority can accept life in the framework of a pluralistic, tolerant state if the majority government will permit this. *Vis-à-vis* a policy of enforced assimilation, the Muslim minority can respond by some adaptation while maintaining, as far as possible, the foundations of its faith and communal unity. Yet another option is resisting all compromise, isolation, or violent opposition that takes the form of military struggle to secede or at least achieve maximal autonomy. Indeed, when the majority society rejects the limitations of coexistence and attempts to subdue the minority, the outcome is usually violent. It is reasonable to assume that a Muslim minority will resort to violence when the prevailing dynamic within the society becomes religiously militant. Usually this takes place under the influence of external Islamic elements or when the Muslims believe that the central regime is weak and the time opportune for them to free themselves from the rule of the majority society and acquire political and cultural-religious independence. Similar phenomena have occurred throughout human history and are not limited to Muslim societies. It is this behavior which is characteristic of the three Muslim minorities in the countries studied here, particularly since the end of World War II.

In theory, Islam must ultimately strive to express itself through a political regime because its way of life is all-inclusive; there is no separation between religion and state. In essence, the origins of such a separation arose only in Western society and this separation is unknown in Islamic thought. From a tactical perspective and in certain circumstances of peace, a Muslim community can adapt to a non-Muslim policy, cultivating hopes for the realization of its political aspirations sometime in the future. Should the appropriate historical circumstances arise, it is almost certain that an effort will be made to declare a separate Muslim presence that goes as far as political independence because the rule of non-Muslims over Muslims is considered an affront to Islam and to the proper order of the world. Generally, members of a Muslim minority community living in a non-Muslim state are outsiders in many respects and cultivate separatist notions, either moderate or radical, depending on the historical circumstances.

In recent decades, there has been a radicalization of some Muslim communities throughout the world. This trend takes several forms — from the unwillingness of a Muslim minority to adapt to the majority culture among which it lives to expressions of intolerance, even persecution, by some Muslim states toward their own non-Muslim minorities. The rebel movements of the Moro and of the Muslims of Patani were certainly affected by the postwar Islamic renaissance and the spread of the pan-Islam movement. Such processes widened the gap between the Moro and the majority Christian society in the Philippines, and between the Patani Muslims and the majority Buddhist-Thai population in Patani. At the same time, the link between these Muslim communities and the international Muslim world grew stronger. From the 1970s on, this affinity was reinforced in the wake of the growing strength and increasing wealth of the oil-producing Muslim states. The three Muslim rebellions of Southeast Asia must be examined against this background as well.

This study raises the question as to whether, in principle, Muslim minorities can live within the framework of a state whose majority population is not Muslim, or whether, inexorably, the Muslim community will strive to secede whenever there appears to be the opportunity to do so. The history of the rebellions in the three countries under review indicates that there is no definitive answer. Consequently, these rebellions should also be viewed in a broader historical context as well as in the discrete circumstances that apply to each of the communities under review. Ultimately, the rebellions are not entirely the result of events that began after World War II, but each is a direct historical continuity of the relationship of the specific ethnic Muslim community to its non-Muslim surroundings over an extended period of time and in the tradition of a persistent struggle. This is particularly true with regard to the Moro in the Philippines and the Muslims of Patani.

Islam has historic precedents of Muslims living under non-Muslim rule, especially after the 19th century, when Europe's colonial expansion brought large Muslim communities under foreign domination. On a general level, Muslim thinkers and *ulama* have dealt extensively with this issue. Yet, there is no evidence that the theoretical-ideological dimension of the problem has been examined by the local *ulama* of Southeast Asia, where, it appears, the entire philosophy was dependent on import, particularly from Arab countries. Indeed, most observers and scholars make no mention of such a domestic literature. The historian W. K. Che Man is almost alone as a scholar who bases his work on the documents of Moro rebels in the Philippines that make extensive use of Arabic verses from the Koran and other Islamic expressions. There is nothing in the literature regarding the Patani Muslims or the Muslims of Arakan. If such documents exist, it would appear that they have not found their way into the hands of scholars. Many of the studies that deal with the rebellions are not useful for an understanding of the theoretical Islamic aspect of the issue. Some of the material extant can be faulted for tendentiousness. There are even publications and studies that cross the border into propagandistic and selective writing as they chronicle the rebellions or their interpretation. This is true primarily of publications that deal with the Muslim rebellion in the Philippines, which have been the subject of much attention. In Thailand, there were even fewer Muslim thinkers, historians, and observers of the scene than in the Philippines. Among the Rohingya, they were almost nonexistent.

In this respect, what emerges from the differing historical developments is the clear difference between the situation of the Patani Muslims on the one hand and that of the Moro in the Philippines and the Rohingya in Burma on the other. The turning point for the Muslims of southern Thailand came with the signing of the Anglo-Siamese Treaty of 1910, which left Patani in Siamese hands. From this point on, the Muslims lost their independence and came under non-Islamic rule. The family of the Patani sultan, along with some of the traditional elites, moved to nearby Kelantan and other places; but the majority of the Muslim population remained in place. It is doubtful whether theological considerations about leaving an area of Dar al-Harb played a part in the emigration. It was the new political reality rather than religious considerations that impelled the people to emigrate. Arakan had never had a similar history of Muslim sovereignty. There the Muslims experienced deep disappointment after World War II, when the area of Arakan was annexed to independent Burma without granting the Muslims the autonomy that they had expected. For the Moro, other elements were at work. The Moro were inspired by a sense of pride in their successful military exploits against the Spaniards during a major part of Spanish rule in the Philippines, by their courageous stand against the Americans, and by the fact that their inclusion in an independent Philippines meant the imposition of a foreign regime in which they had no interest in participating. The flight of Rohingya refugees to Bengal, or of Moro to Sabah, was not motivated by theological considerations of abandoning territory that had become Dar al-Harb but stemmed from the suffering that accompanied the fighting and a desire to avoid the hardships that it imposed.

The Muslim resistance movements in the countries covered by this study can be classed as nationalist movements. At base, these movements were an Islamic reaction by an ethnic-religious minority against foreign governments seen as representing nationalities different from those with which the Muslim communities would choose to affiliate. As a result, the national movements took on a combined political and religious aspect. In the rebellions with which we deal here, and in several other cases in the Muslim world, Islam and nationalism reinforce each other in rejecting foreign rule, which explains the tendency of the *ulama* to support such rebel groups, sometimes playing a direct leadership role in them alongside political nonreligious leaders, at times even without them.

In the case of the Malay Muslims of Patani, the fact of their being Muslim had two important outcomes. First, Islam became a focus for their separate communal, national identity differentiating them from the Thai Buddhist majority population, whose identity was centered on the Buddhist king and in all the symbolic paraphernalia of a Buddhist state. Second, their Islamic identity forged strong links with the Malays of the Malay Peninsula, and it was this that fired their irredentist aspirations. And this identity also served as the basis for the support and sympathy that many circles in Malaysia extended to the Patani separatists. For the Muslims of the southern Philippines, the Islamic religion provided a unifying cement that defined ethnic identity, which was able to overcome, in part, the ethnic and linguistic differences between the various communities: Tausug, Maguindanao, Maranao, and others. Despite the common goal, however, the tendency to break up into factions existed among these rebel movements because of personal, tribal-ethnic, and even ideological differences. It appears that even the religion of Islam could not totally overcome the fractiousness occasioned by personal ambitions or group aspirations. Indeed, this internal bickering was one of the main reasons for the weakness of the rebel groups. In Burma, religion was the major factor that motivated the Muslims of Arakan, who saw themselves as a separate community. Their separatist demands were directed not only at the central Buddhist government but also toward Arakanese Buddhists, who had their own separatist demands stemming from an ethnic-national background, but not a religious one. The religion of Islam was the one element that linked the minority populations with the larger *ummah*. On another level, it was this element that provided external moral and logistic support to the rebel movements — to a different degree in each case — in their opposition to national governments. Such assistance influenced the nature of the Muslim struggle and its effectiveness. As noted, this was particularly true in the case of the Moro rebellion, less so in the case of the Muslims of Patani, and of minimal importance in the struggle of the Rohingya.

This aspect is perhaps made more clear if stated as follows: Muslim rebellions in the Philippines, Thailand, and Burma were not simply the uprisings of ethnic minorities against national governments. They were also wars between different religious communities — between Muslims and Buddhists in Thailand and Burma, and between Muslims and Christians in the Philippines. Muslims have invariably been prepared to take violent actions that they perceived as a holy war, a jihad, in order to fight for the achievement of their goals. They did not regard themselves as part of the majority population, which they saw as alien to their religion, nationality, language, and culture. Particularly in the case of the Muslims of the southern Philippines and southern Thailand, the rule of the central government over the territory in which they had been living for generations was perceived as illegitimate. They regarded these areas as Muslim lands that had been conquered by foreign elements from which they must be liberated. They did not regard themselves as minorities; therefore, they did not believe that they had an obligation to obey the commands of a non-Muslim, illegitimate regime. From their standpoint, it was a religious duty to liberate lands that had become Dar al-Harb and to return them to the compass of Dar al-Islam. This approach does not hold true for the Muslim communities of Bangkok and its surroundings, or for Rangoon and other places in Burma/Myanmar. In these cases, Muslims do not claim to be a majority in the areas in which they live. Muslims in these communities have attempted to identify themselves as Thai or Burmese while retaining the religion of Islam. Nonetheless, despite their having undergone a certain process of integration, such Islamic groups face a not inconsiderable difficulty (which does not appear to apply to the Malay Muslims of Patani or the Rohingya); for them, too, religion will continue to be an obstacle to full identity. To be a Thai in Thailand or a Burman in Burma means to be a Buddhist, exactly as in Malaysia, being Malay means being a Muslim. These urban Muslim communities are composed of various heterogeneous groups that were uprooted from their natural historic locales. They do not enjoy the benefits of a geographic proximity to Malaysia or to Muslim Bangladesh, they do not live in significant geographic concentrations, and they do not make up the majority in their districts. Although they have a separate religious identity, they are devoid of the element that stresses national identity. Consequently, there are no separatist tendencies among them, they do not rebel against the central authority, nor do they belong to the topic under discussion here.

While it is clear that the religious factor, the sense of Islamic identity, and the commitment to jihad all have a salient importance for understanding Muslim opposition movements in the Philippines, Thailand, and Burma/Myanmar, these were not the only factors. The direct, immediate, and most blatant causes for the outbreak of the rebellions were the social and economic grievances and the feelings of bitterness that went beyond the religious sphere. Present in everyday life, these conditions served to turn the Muslim populations of the countries in question against their central governments. While it was true that on the one hand the Muslims sought independence or a broad-spectrum autonomy — a limitation to the necessity for contact with or dependence on the central governments — on the other hand, there were complaints by the Muslims that their need for economic and social development programs was not getting sufficient attention, and that members of their community had no part in senior administration roles in the governments. More important, they complained that their lands were being expropriated for the benefit of settlers (Christian or Buddhist). Indeed, in order to underpin government control in geographic areas where Muslims were a majority, the governments of the three countries each settled non-Muslim populations in Muslim areas, a potent means for restricting the Muslim communities and turning them into minorities. In the Philippines, Christians from the north were massively and systematically settled in the southern Muslim islands as early as the period of U.S. rule, and even more intensively after independence, so that the extent of Muslim majority in the south was greatly reduced. Nor is there any doubt that the settlement policy of successive Philippine governments was highly successful; in fact, only five districts of the south — Maguindanao, Lanao del Sur, Basilan, Sulu, and Tawi-Tawi — still have a Muslim majority. Indeed, this was one of the prime causes for the outbreak of the rebellion and the bitter fighting by Muslims. In Thailand, there was a similar settlement drive of a Buddhist population but in much smaller and less significant numbers. Buddhist settlements in the Muslim south did not bring about substantive demographic changes. In Arakan, Buddhists took over Muslim lands and drove out the inhabitants, but it is difficult to say whether this was the work of the government or a local initiative by Arakan Buddhists.

Another sore grievance of the Muslim population, which stood out in Thailand particularly, was that Thai leaders and government officials in the southern districts generally displayed a haughty and arrogant attitude toward the Muslims of Patani. They were disinclined to consider Muslim demands, which they invariably regarded as constituting a threat to the territorial integrity and sovereignty of the state and which were, therefore, not negotiable or amenable to compromise. It was Philippine governments that exhibited a greater readiness to search for avenues of dialogue with the Muslims, to be receptive to some of their demands, to consider reforms, and to compromise so long as there was no fear that these steps would undermine basic national principles of sovereignty and territorial integrity. In Burma/Myanmar there were simply no negotiations between the Muslim population of Arakan and the central government, particularly after the military coup of 1962.

Muslims in the southern Philippines complained of another kind of injustice: namely, that most of the natural resources and wealth in their regions were concentrated in the hands of Christians and foreign investors. Whatever economic development there was contributed little to improving conditions of the Muslim population. The situation was similar in Patani, where most of the wealth was controlled by the Chinese community or by Thai Buddhists. Consequently, the Muslims in both these countries rejected government plans for economic development, along with reforms in the educational sphere, as threatening their communal, religious, and cultural identity and endangering their way of life. They had neither the interest nor the desire to cooperate with plans meant to integrate them into the majority population, plans that they perceived as hostile, eager to take their lands, disinherit them from their traditional rights, and infringe on their way of life, turning them into a minority in their own territories.

There is another grievance at whose core lies an unexpected coincidence. It has to do with what can be seen as the "British connection" claimed by both the Rohingya of Arakan and the Muslims of Patani. A question yet to be answered is, did these Muslim groups get some kind of British promises of support during the course of World War II? Although there is no documented proof that the British did, in fact, promise the Muslims or either of these communities anything concrete, there is a surprising similarity in this unresolved issue. Conceivably, British officers gave oral promises in the field; if so, did they or did they not act on the instructions of their superiors? Perhaps some day the truth will emerge. Meanwhile, it is certainly reasonable to assume that the Muslims in Arakan as well as in the Patani region believed that in consideration for their loyalty and services during the war, they would be properly rewarded and aided in the pursuit of their aspirations. Against the background of these high hopes, one can better understand their disappointment after the war, which inevitably led them to armed resistance.

International Islamic awakening, which began in the second half of the 20th century — demonstratively marked by the establishment of the Organization of Islamic Conference (OIC) in 1969, the annual meetings of Muslim Foreign Ministers (ICFM) sponsored by OIC, and wide-ranging activity of other Islamic organizations affiliated with OIC — gave new impetus to feelings of a political and popular pan-Islam in the Muslim world. Among the declared goals of the OIC was action in support of the struggles of all Islamic peoples and communities to ensure their honor, independence, and national rights. This new international Muslim impetus affected all the Islamic nations and buttressed the self-image of Muslim minorities everywhere, including the Muslim communities in the southern Philippines, southern Thailand, and Arakan. The minorities now became aware of the growing political might of Islamic countries and the enormous wealth that was generated by their oil reserves. Radical Islamic countries, predominantly Libya but others as well, began supplying arms and funds and providing diplomatic support to separatist Muslim movements from 1972, thus investing these struggles with an international dimension. Saudi Arabia exhibited a growing interest in Muslim minorities, especially by sending religious teachers and financial gifts to Muslim institutions. To a lesser extent, such countries as Syria, Sudan, and Egypt became involved in the issue, as well as the Palestine Liberation Organization. After Khomeini's Shiite revolution, Iran also became an active player in support of separatist Muslim organizations, carrying on terrorist activities and propaganda. The annual conferences of Muslim foreign ministers whose primary interest was in the Palestinian issue and the Arab-Israeli conflict devoted a certain part of their energies and time to dealing with the problem of minorities. Thus, they became players in the diplomatic efforts to resolve these confrontations and in pressures exerted on the countries involved. Delegations were sent and resolutions adopted at the conferences of OIC and ICFM. Such diplomatic activity stood out particularly with regard to the Philippines. The Muslim states were very selective in their support of Muslim revolts in Southeast Asia. They dealt extensively with the Philippines, less so with Thailand, and only in small measure with Burma/Myanmar. And these external international Islamic factors had a great impact on the outcome of the conflict in the Philippines. In 1973–74, battles in the southern Philippines elicited a lively interest in all Islamic countries, prompted the dispatch of Libyan and other support to the rebels, and served to raise the Moro issue at international Muslim forums.

Because of connections with the Muslim world during several stages of their struggle, the Philippine Muslims experienced heightened expectations that their separatist goals would be realized. At its very outset, the MNLF rebellion received considerable aid from Colonel Mu'amar Qadhafi, the Libyan ruler, without which it is doubtful that the rebellion would have progressed as far as it did. Later, Qadhafi changed the emphasis of his policy, preferring a compromise solution — autonomy rather than separation — and moved from direct military aid to diplomatic support for the rebels. In the absence of outside pressure from Islamic states, particularly Libya, President Ferdinand Marcos might have continued, or even stepped up, his military campaign against the MNLF. Paradoxically, it was precisely the external Muslim involvement, which Marcos had encouraged in the hope that it would be instrumental in proving the justice of his government's policy, that enabled international Islamic pressure to be brought to bear on him, crippling his military campaign and forcing him to accept negotiations with the rebels. Marcos discovered that international involvement is generally partial rather than altruistic and objective, and it has a price. In many cases, such involvement means one-sided pressure rather than neutral arbitration.

Particularly during the presidency of Ferdinand Marcos, the Philippine government realized that only if it refrained from escalating the fighting and using extreme military measures would it be able to minimize a growing external involvement in support of the Muslims, and avoid the threat of an Arab oil embargo. The government knew that the issue of autonomy — and what such autonomy would include — was open to negotiation because the OIC had agreed that there would be no infringement of Philippine territorial integrity or national sovereignty. The Islamic states would be satisfied with the granting of some kind of autonomy to the Moro; that is, they did not support the MNLF demand for the establishment of a separate, independent Islamic state in the southern Philippines. In fact, the Tripoli Agreement of 1976 and subsequent agreements signed with the governments of Corazon Aquino and Fidel Ramos echoed this same understanding. Nonetheless, it was pressure by Islamic states that undoubtedly helped the MNLF extract certain concessions from the Philippine governments, which, initially, were disinclined to grant them.[5] International Muslim involvement enabled the separatist struggle in the Philippines to reap greater results than did the struggle of the Patani Muslims. The Muslims of Patani did not achieve any measure of autonomy, nor were there negotiations between the Thai government and the rebel movements. The separatist movement in the Philippines, in contrast, was more all-encompassing in its organization, pursued a more aggressive military campaign, and was certainly more successful in mobilizing foreign aid. It succeeded in unleashing a war of attrition that became one of the severest problems faced by the regime, particularly during Marcos's administration. All of this came with a price. As a result of the heavy fighting, loss of life and property were greater in the southern Philippines than in southern Thailand, where the Muslims did not mount as violent a struggle.

In the case of the Muslims of southern Thailand, external Islamic elements also contributed to the heightening of Islamic consciousness and sharpened demands for autonomy and separation. But as distinguished from the Moro, the Muslims of Patani made less headway at the OIC and the ICFM in garnering international concern for their plight, and even the extent of interest they did manage to raise at these international Muslim conferences was limited. The international Muslim community paid but scant attention to their issues and applied almost no pressure on the government of Thailand. Nor were there dramatic military events in Thailand that could equal the drama of events in the southern Philippines and so mobilize the same degree of attention. It was in neighboring Malaysia that the issue of the Patani Muslims took on importance. Even if one accepts the assumption that the aid the Patani rebels received from Malaysia was not official, but rather the outcome of local and "private" initiatives, Malaysia's involvement helped to restrain the actions of the Thai government, preventing both the intensification of Thai military activity and the Thai policy of forced assimilation, which the government imposed at various times. The presence of a Muslim state whose population was Malay on the other side of the frontier was a catalyst for Muslims of Patani in reinforcing their Islamic-Malay consciousness. In reality, the government of Malaysia could not overlook its ethnic-religious links with the Patani Muslims or act indifferently toward them without running the risk of alienating public opinion at home.

The possibility of a sharp reaction by the government of Malaysia to an overly aggressive policy by Thailand toward the Muslims of the south did go a long way toward moderating Thai policy. However, Thailand had countermeasures available that lessened the likelihood of Malaysian intervention on behalf of the Patani Muslims. In practice, a situation was created that obliged both governments to cooperate. Thailand could refrain from cooperating with the Malaysian government in its fight against the Malay Communist Party (MCP) underground. Although only remnants of MCP forces found refuge in the frontier area between the two countries, Malaysia still regarded them as a potential threat. Consequently, Malaysia wanted to avoid straining its relations with Thailand. The Malaysian government had to balance three considerations when assessing the Patani rebellion: first, Malaysia's desire to maintain correct, even good, relations with the Thai government; second, the quid pro quo policy by which the Thai government helped in suppressing the Communist rebellion in return for Malaysia's assistance in restraining Patani separatist actions; third, the Muslims of the Patani region were considered to be brothers, Malay-Muslims, with the same ethnic and religious identity as the majority of Malays in Malaysia. The government of Malaysia was, therefore, unable to agree to overt suppression but could not, on the other hand, support Patani separatist demands. Neither could the former encourage the latter without jeopardizing the advantages to be gained from the maintenance of good relations with Thailand. Only limited, highly radicalized factions in Malaysia, particularly the sultanates of the northern Malay Peninsula, could allow themselves such a "brotherly" course of action.

Yet even among the sultanates, no champion appeared who could assist the Patani Muslims as much as Tun Mustafa, the chief minister of Sabah, had when he came to the aid of his neighbors, the Moro of the Philippines. Eventually, the Malaysian government embarked on a policy of nonintervention, the outcome of which was a halt to support for Patani Muslims, even from nonofficial sources. The mutual interests of Thailand and Malaysia were certainly an important factor in limiting the separatist movement in southern Thailand and preventing its growth. Not so in the southern Philippines. There, a situation arose which was precisely the opposite, because of the Philippine-Malaysia conflict over Sabah, which served as the impetus for Malaysia's support of the Moro. Since the only effort to cultivate links to international Muslim bodies that the Patani Muslims made was directed at neighboring Malaysia, the Thai government felt no need to initiate diplomatic activity in Arab and Muslim countries to the extent that the Philippine government did in order to halt, or at least rein in, the activity of the separatist organizations.

International Islamic bodies were even less involved with the Rohingya rebellion in Arakan; there was almost no international Islamic concern or even interest in their fate. In 1983, when Rohingya leaders petitioned the ICFM to obtain observer status, which could have helped them in their struggle, they were refused. The Muslims of Arakan were simply unable to arouse the same kind of sympathetic resonance that the MNLF of the Philippines, or even the Muslim organizations of southern Thailand, had succeeded in doing. Most of the Rohingya lived in remote villages that were difficult to get to, and their economic backwardness and isolation were obstacles to the creation of a strong political movement that could effectively act against the repressive measures of their government. Furthermore, insofar as is known, there were no dramatic events, such as major battles, that could galvanize an international response. The media did not go to the Rohingya in order to report about them. With the exception of a small amount of humanitarian help offered by Muslim and other aid organizations to Rohingya refugees who crossed the border into Bangladesh, there is no evidence of significant interest by Arab states or international Islamic bodies in their plight. The major source of their help was the government of Bangladesh, which worked on their behalf because of its own interest in their repatriation. Itself a poor state, Bangladesh wanted the refugees to return to their homes so that the government would be relieved of the burden of caring for them. Had they known how to generate world pressure in their favor on the internationally isolated government of Burma/Myanmar, it is possible that the Rohingya could have mobilized international Muslim support.

From the standpoint of intervention by external forces, it is necessary to distinguish between a passive, moderate model as in the case of Indonesia, and the more active Malaysian model. Indonesia granted neither moral nor material support to the separatist Islamic organizations in southern Thailand and the southern Philippines. Apparently the only attempt was made by the Indonesian Communist Party at the end of World War II, when it tried to infiltrate men and arms into Patani from Sumatra. Indonesia itself acted only at the diplomatic level, primarily at international Islamic conferences. And this was in order to weaken the involvement of Arab countries in the affairs of Southeast Asia. Indonesia was concerned over the negative impact that ethnic rebel movements could have on its own stability, as well as the effect of foreign involvement on the stability of the entire region. Indonesia was wary because of the presence of radical Islamic groups and non-Muslim ethnic minorities such as the Christians in East Timor, the Hindus in Bali, and other communities in various places along the Indonesian Archipelago. This anxiety was a factor both in Indonesia's reservations about the MNLF's aspiration to independence, and in the position it shared with Malaysia that the Association of South East Asian

Nations rather than the Conference of Muslim Foreign Ministers was the appropriate forum for dealing with such problems.

Indonesia did not want to set a precedent in which international Muslim bodies could intervene in the internal affairs of any state in Southeast Asia. Although Indonesia kept its distance from the Moro and Patani rebel movements, it did make mediation efforts toward the achievement of a political solution. Again, its limited involvement in the struggle of Muslim minorities stemmed from its basic position that there should be no support for struggles of self-determination of ethnic or religious minorities because of its own potential vulnerability in this sphere, and because of its unwillingness to countenance foreign intervention, particularly Arab, in the affairs of the region. Despite differences in each of the three cases, international Islamic involvement needs to be viewed in perspective. International concern for the plight of the Rohingya of Arakan, the Muslims of Patani, and the Moro of the Philippines was limited to Arab and Muslim countries but did not go beyond international Islamic bodies. No attempt was made to turn the UN into a diplomatic arena in which to arraign the governments of Burma/Myanmar, Thailand, or the Philippines, as was the case, for example, with the Palestinian Arabs who mounted a systematic campaign against Israel at the UN over a period of many years. In the case of Southeast Asia, the Arab and Muslim countries did not use their great power in the UN to this end. Neither the United States nor European countries intervened directly nor offered their good offices as negotiators, as they did in the Arab-Israeli conflict.

A somewhat strange fact bears noting. Although it might have been expected, there was no cooperation between the three Muslim rebel movements. This was despite the fact that the three separatist movements obtained their aid — admittedly of vastly different proportions — from the selfsame outside sources. What information there is about this indicates that contacts between rebel movements were limited to visits by their representatives to overseas offices, where ideas and information were exchanged. No leader went to the battle areas of the others, nor was there mutual aid between them. Each movement concentrated on its own problems. It can be assumed that cooperation between them would have raised the extent of the international Islamic community's involvement to a much higher level. Perhaps it would have escalated tensions in Southeast Asia as a whole, and so increased the pressure on the three governments concerned. It is possible that another reason for the lack of cooperation between the rebel movements was precisely the absence of an external element to encourage, cultivate, and support it.

A theological aspect to the involvement of outside Islamic elements in the Muslim rebel organizations of Southeast Asia originated in radical movements within Arab countries that supported terrorism and, following the Khomeini revolution, in Iran. The theological influence was felt primarily in the Philippines but only minimally in Thailand and Burma. The Muslims of the Philippines had a history of several hundred years of war against the Spaniards, and that struggle had a marked religious dimension. It was fired by the fight against the militant efforts of the Catholic Church to convert the Filipinos, and their struggle in support of Islam. This dimension was not present in either of the other two Muslim minorities in the Buddhist countries of Thailand and Burma. For this reason, the phenomenon of religious suicide, or ritual personal self-sacrifice — the personal jihad — or, as it was called among the Moro, the *juramentado*, was not known among Patani Muslims or the Rohingya. Islamic religious devotion played a far more vivid role among the Moro. The literature of the Moro — books, pamphlets, leaflets, and speeches — was prolific compared to the paucity of publications in the Muslim movements in Patani and Arakan. And the Moro made use of highly charged religious terminology and style. Another factor that must be given its proper weight relates to behavioral differences between the separatist movements in the southern Philippines and Patani: the Muslims of Patani were subject to direct, or indirect, Thai rule from the 18th century on, whereas Christians began ruling in the administration of the southern districts of the Philippines only toward the end of U.S. rule, more so after independence in 1946. Thailand's control over its Muslim population went on for a much longer period, which, to some degree, may have inured the Patani Muslims to it. For the Moro, Christian rule was a new and aggravating burden.

The governments of the Philippines and Thailand responded to the threats of their separatist organizations by embarking on a number of economic and social programs that were implemented in parallel to military and police actions. By contrast, Burma employed almost exclusively administrative-military means. The governments of both the Philippines and Thailand attempted to integrate their Muslim populations, by force if need be, out of an aspiration to forge a national unity in the face of the centrifugal forces of traditional, communal regionalism. Efforts were directed at teaching the national language, improving the quality of the educational system, training non-Muslim officials to act with sensitivity toward Muslims in their jurisdiction, preparing Muslims for government service, offering concessions and various economic development programs, and even instituting certain reforms — particularly in the Philippines — that permitted the application of a measure of Islamic law for Muslims. Both governments took such measures not only because of a desire for pacification, but also in response to the pressures exerted by Muslim governments and other international Islamic organizations, which, at the same time, aided the rebel movements and demanded that the situation of the Muslim communities be ameliorated through political means. Both Muslim communities opposed the policies of assimilation; however, the resistance of the Patani Muslims was neither as vigorous nor as violent as that of the Moro. It would appear that the assimilatory policy of the Thai government had a greater degree of success, and from the government's standpoint, some of the measures on which it had embarked reaped positive results. This was particularly true in the area of establishing new schools, which resulted in weakening the status of the Muslim religious *pondok* and limiting their number, as well as greater fluency in the Thai language among groups of Malay Muslims in the south.

In the Philippines — even in Thailand — the central governments were hesitant to bring the full weight of their military force to bear on suppressing the rebellion. The hesitancy was caused by a fear of how neighboring Muslim countries — Malaysia and, to a lesser extent, Indonesia — would react, and by the threat of an Arab oil embargo. This was also the reason that in the 1970s and 1980s these two countries increasingly acceded to demands by Arab countries to criticize Israel. At the same time, there was a difference in the extent of the military operation, in the number of men committed to it, and in the very nature of the military activity engaged in by each of the countries. The extent of destruction, number of casualties, and level of involvement by external Islamic elements, particularly Arab, also varied from one country to the other. Still, there is no doubt that the importance of the military, material, moral, and political support that the Moro received from foreign Islamic and Arab sources made the salient difference between the achievements of the Moro in the Philippines and the other Muslim movements in Thailand and Burma. It should be added that, for the most part, the Thai government showed greater determination in the deployment of its army and police against the Muslims of Patani than the Philippine government did against its separatist movement. This may have been due to logistic and other difficulties, such as corruption and inefficiency, which the Philippine Army suffered from.

The dimensions of the problem, the size of the Muslim population, and the territorial expanse in which military activity took place were much smaller in southern Thailand than in the Philippines. The determination to fight exhibited by the Muslims of the southern Philippines far exceeded that of the Muslims of southern Thailand.

The situation was considerably different in Burma. Burma was not interested in integrating the Muslim population of Arakan, which it perceived as a foreign population over which it had no control. Administrative measures instituted for purposes of census taking caused recurrent flight by sizable numbers of Muslims to neighboring Bangladesh, whether through choice or because the army and Burmese police engaged in a planned expulsion. Beginning in 1961, the Burmese army did not encounter any meaningful armed opposition in Arakan. Nor did it seem that in the foreseeable future there would be a significant Rohingya military threat to the central government's ability to rule in the Arakan region. The marginality of Arakan Muslims in the international Islamic world can perhaps be seen in the piquant fact that the very few written reports about what was happening among them lacked even the ritual condemnation of Israel such as could be found in MNLF documents. Apparently, representatives of Arab countries who overlooked the plight of the Rohingya were equally unenthusiastic about expressions of solidarity with the Patani Muslims, whose documents also contained only meager references to Israel. All three rebel movements were equally distant from the Arab-Israeli conflict in the Middle East, about which their leadership knew little. The artificiality with which a number of the leaders of separatist movements, particularly Nur Misuari (MNLF), responded to Arab demands that they condemn Israel, both in documents and in speeches, was all the more blatant in light of the fact that in such expressions of solidarity with the Palestinians there is no mention of other Islamic issues.

In any case, Muslim populations in the Philippines and Thailand were not ready to respond affirmatively to or cooperate with government efforts at integration even if the implementation of the programs had not been tainted by corruption and inefficiency, as indeed it was. Attempts to embark on integration programs of one sort or another only served to aggravate political and religious antagonisms, to exacerbate the uprisings, and to add fuel to the demands for separatism and independence of the Muslim communities. The cruelty of the military campaigns undercut whatever advantages could possibly have been gleaned by means of economic and cultural reforms. The campaigns had precisely the effect of reinforcing feelings of Muslim identity and motivated many young people to join the rebel organizations.

Unlike Thailand or Burma/Myanmar, the Philippine government was sensitive to criticism expressed in Islamic countries about events concerning the Muslim minority, and the government attempted to refute the accusations against it. Conceivably this sensitivity stemmed from Philippine dependence on Arab oil. The Philippine government invited foreign Muslim representatives to visit the south, creating an opening for greater Arab-Islamic involvement and an implicit invitation for pressure on itself to make concessions to the rebels. Presidents Marcos, Aquino, and Ramos displayed an eagerness for peace negotiations and consequently had to compromise and grant concessions. Events in Thailand and Burma took a different turn. Their governments did not exhibit the same enthusiasm for negotiations. Insofar as they could, they rejected external involvement and bent all their efforts toward dealing with the Muslim revolts as an internal matter. They had a fair measure of success both because of objective circumstances and because of differences in the nature of the fighting. Due to diplomatic considerations, Malaysia preferred good relations with neighboring Thailand and cooperation along their common border to participation in the struggle of the Patani Muslims who were their brothers in ethnic origin and Islam. The same held true for East Pakistan/Bangladesh, which did not want the issue of the *mujahideen* in Arakan to become a stumbling block in relations with neighboring Burma/Myanmar, a position substantiated by the Pakistan-Burma Treaty of December 1961, which established procedures for cooperation along the common frontier. Perhaps OIC countries were acting according to a double standard *vis-à-vis* the Muslim rebellions for exactly the same reason. The Philippine government did want external involvement and, in fact, received it. Thailand and Burma opposed such intervention. Consequently, the OIC showed only slight interest in becoming involved, a possible explanation for the fact that neither the rebellion of the Patani Muslims nor that of the Rohingya generated serious Muslim international support. Indeed, these rebellions waned long before the Moro rebellion without having achieved their goals, unlike the Moro. It should be remembered that in the case of the Philippines, although the outcome of international Islamic involvement did not coincide with the Philippine government's desires and intentions, OIC countries did not support secession but accepted only autonomy. The important contributions of Indonesia and Malaysia to this matter have already been mentioned above.

From the end of World War II, Muslims of the southern Philippines, Thailand, and Arakan demanded independence or, alternately, wide-ranging autonomy. Toward this end, they engaged in guerilla warfare. After a half century of struggle, it appears that the Muslims of Patani failed in their goal. The Rohingya, whose distress only grew during the fighting, also failed. The Moro, however, were able to achieve autonomy, albeit limited and partial and a far cry from their original aspirations; still, a noteworthy success. What were the reasons for this partial and limited success, which nonetheless stands out against the failure of the Patani Muslims and the Rohingya?[6] One factor is the relatively weak sense of discrimination that the Patani Muslims felt as compared to the outraged sense of discrimination among the Moro. The Thai government was more interested in maintaining its sovereignty and control in the Patani region than it was in repressing its Muslim population. The transfer of Buddhist settlers from the north was very moderate when compared to the intensive settlement by Christians in the Muslim districts of the southern Philippines, a salient cause of the aggressive response by the Moro. In fact, Christians became the majority in almost all the districts of the Muslim south, which was not the case in Patani.

We have already dealt with the important issue of leadership. Particularly with the establishment of MNLF, the Moro movement was led by an educated cadre that had a sense for politics. Their organizational ability was far superior to that of the Patani Muslim leadership, most of whom were clerics and belonged to the traditional aristocracy. Despite the fact that all the members of the rebel organizations in Patani belonged to the same ethnic community — Malay Muslims — they were more divided than the Moro, though the Moro were heterogeneous and came from various ethnic communities. For most of the years of fighting in the southern Philippines, the MNLF was the foremost rebel organization on the scene, gaining political recognition by Islamic countries. This was achieved despite the serious blows the organization suffered on the field of battle, and despite splits in its leadership. Another element working for the Moro was the relative weakness of the Philippine government, which clearly felt pressured by Muslim states as it attempted to negotiate a peace agreement in the south for which it was prepared to compromise. The Thai government had no tendency to compromise or to suffer any infringement of its absolute sovereignty in the south, the only exceptions being a number of marginal concessions it made to the Patani Muslims in social and economic matters. Moreover, the separatist organizations of the Patani Muslims were unable to marshal wide support either within their own public or from Islamic countries and the OIC. This was in sharp contrast to the Moro, who were able to mobilize such wide support both at home and abroad.

The fortunes of war changed and changed again in each of the three countries in which the separatists fought. The fiercest battles were in the southern Philippines, where costly losses brought on by long periods of fighting, fatigue, and attrition resulted in frequent breaks in the fighting and in cease-fires. Although there were some military successes by government forces in the war against the separatists, the rebels — particularly in the Philippines, to a lesser extent in Thailand, and even less in Arakan — were able to maintain their strength through additional recruitment from within the Muslim community. The problem was that basic conditions remained as they had been. Most of the Muslims of the southern Philippines, southern Thailand, and Arakan still wished to live their lives in accordance with the traditions and religious precepts of their religion without outside interference from the central governments of the regions in which they lived. Linguistic and religious differences, as well as historic hostilities, between Muslim minorities and the Buddhist majority among whom they lived in Thailand and Burma, and the Christian majority in the Philippines, were not — and are not — easily bridged. For this reason, there is no chance that various development programs in the areas of education, or in economic and social spheres, will be crowned with the results that the governments of the Philippines and Thailand would like. Myanmar has no such programs.

The history of Muslim rebellions in Southeast Asia indicates that attempts to seek a solution to the problems of the Muslim minorities through economic or social instrumentalities did not succeed. The failure of those who believed in the possibility of integrating the minorities into the society of the national majority among whom they dwelled was due to a misunderstanding of the basic, deep-seated ethnic and religious dimension of the Muslim rebellions. There was an insufficient understanding of the fundamentally religious aspect of the Muslim communities. Nor was there an awareness of Muslim suspicion that the aim of the integration policies, particularly in the Philippines and Thailand, was not to improve their lot, but rather to accelerate their assimilation into the general non-Muslim society, and to undermine their religion and political identity. Members of Muslim minorities in all three countries dealt with in this survey saw the conflict in more than socioeconomic terms. They viewed it primarily as religious, ethnic, and national; and, indeed, the rebel movements were decidedly nationalist, ethnic, and religious movements. At times, the violent outbreaks were spurred precisely by stepped-up integration efforts coupled with shabby behavior on the part of the government and its officials. The Muslims accused central governments of being insensitive to their demands and their needs. At base, the rebelling Muslims in these countries called for more than freedom of religion in the narrow meaning of the term; they wanted recognition as representing a separate religion and culture and a different national grouping. (A comparison could be made here with the Muslims of India, who fought for an independent Pakistan under the banner of a separate national grouping by virtue of their unique Muslim identity.) The roots of the rebellions by the Moro and the Muslims of Patani are embedded in a long history of ethnic-religious isolation, of memories of self-rule or extended and bitter struggles to maintain it. To a large extent, this is true for the Rohingya as well. Resistance to assimilation and a striving for autonomy or independence — which means separation from the environing non-Islamic society — are the profound aims of these Muslim minority societies. The connection to religion is the primary element in their lives and in their consciousness.

The position of all three governments is no less resolute or decisive, and there is a notable similarity in the official stance of all three. The majority population regards the territories settled by Muslims as integral to the national territory; under no circumstances will they agree to grant greater autonomy to their Muslim citizens. The governments certainly will not agree to secession nor to any action that compromises the integrity of the countries as they are now constituted. Neither will they countenance a weakening of national sovereignty, a matter on which they are not prepared to negotiate, even at the cost of a protracted war. The views of the Muslim minorities are seen as a national threat. Under a great deal of pressure, the Philippines agreed to grant the Moro a measure of autonomy. Thailand avoided increased concession and halted its policy of forced assimilation. The Muslims of Arakan managed only to gain permission for their refugees, or at least some of them, to be repatriated. There is no indication that either the principles of religious belief among Muslims, or the prevailing stand by the governments of Burma/Myanmar, Thailand, or the Philippines will change in the foreseeable future.[7]

This does not necessarily mean renewed outbreaks of violence. There may be extended periods of truce, quiet, or cease-fire. There may be terrorist attacks of varying degrees of destruction depending on internal developments or influences from abroad, or the impact of external forces may have the opposite effect, pacification. Apparently, the relation of governments and majority populations to Muslim minorities will remain tense and colored by hostility. Core problems will continue as they have been — unresolved — despite the fact that in recent years there has been a sharp decline in the scope of violence. The partial autonomy that Muslims were granted in the southern Philippines, and the status quo or stalemate that has emerged in southern Thailand and in the Arakan districts, are not true solutions because they do not penetrate to the roots of problematic relationships between Muslim minorities and non-Muslim majority societies.

Questions may be posed as well about the autonomy agreement signed in the Philippines with the MNLF, which was ostensibly the solution to the long-standing crisis there. Has Nur Misuari been convinced that he cannot force a significant change in the government's position by resorting to force, as became clear during the long years of fighting, and that therefore it is preferable to make do with the autonomy he was proffered? Or, for that matter, was the autonomy agreement achieved because the Muslims suffered from attrition, exhausted by their heavy losses, destruction, flight of refugees, and because of a realization that their goals could not be gained, and therefore it was in their best interest to make do with the partial autonomy they were offered, more than which even international aid was unable to secure for them? And perhaps even Nur Misuari, after so many years of fighting, wanted to enjoy the pleasures of governing? It is a fact that there are other rebel movements — the Moro Islamic Liberation Front (MILF) and the Abu-Sayyaf militant organization — that did not accept the autonomy proposal and continued the struggle. As for President Ramos — did the autonomy he proposed to Misuari stem from an assumption that it was a temporary solution and that the reality of a Christian majority population in the south would occasion a gradual erosion of the limited Muslim autonomy that was agreed upon? Only the future can answer these questions. In any event, the autonomy plan failed. In August 2001, President Gloria Macapagal-Arroyo accused Nur Misuari of corruption. He decided to return to arms and in November fled to Malaysia, but he was extradited back to the Philippines in January 2002 and detained.

The problem of the Muslim minorities in the three countries dealt with in this article appears to be insoluble. There is no bridging the chasm between Muslim minorities that aspire to independence and are, in principle, unwilling to live under non-Islamic rule, and the majority governments that are unwilling to relinquish their sovereignty over these same areas. It is doubtful whether a change in the policy of the central government that would grant economic, social, and religio-cultural improvements will suffice, unless the Muslim populations can regard these measures as a step toward autonomy that will ultimately lead to independence or annexation to a neighboring Muslim state, if and when international circumstances permit. Information that has appeared in the past several years from the region indicates that there is no basic change in the situation of the three Muslim communities under discussion as compared to what is known about events that took place there 20 or more years ago. The problems are endemic, while the solutions — as, for example, autonomy in the Philippines — have managed to bring only partial and relative pacification. Perhaps the current situation should be regarded as a cease-fire until a change in circumstances occurs, because solutions were not properly implemented, or because there are really no substantive solutions to the problems of these regions. Because of their ideological outlook and because they will not adapt to non-Muslim rule, Muslim populations in Southeast Asia are unable to be absorbed into the majority culture. The central government, for its part, is unwilling to forgo any sovereignty. In the case of the Philippines, only a partial and limited autonomy was granted. This is not to say that it is impossible to continue living with insoluble problems without unavoidable recourse to violence, particularly in a period of fatigue and weakness. The cease-fire can persist for many years, even when it is accompanied by limited guerilla activity; the latter only serves to keep the problem on the agenda.

But what alternatives are available to the Muslim minorities? There are a few. First, acquiescence to being ruled by the majority, along with a certain measure of integration. This seems neither reasonable nor possible. From a religious and ethnic standpoint, Muslims are inherently unable to accept the degree of assimilation that the Philippines and Thailand would like. Myanmar is not at all interested in integration. The second alternative is continuation of the armed struggle for independence, or for a wide-ranging, broad autonomy to the extent that political or military circumstances will permit. The long years of fighting since the end of World War II have enfeebled and fatigued all sides so that much time will have to pass until the armed struggle can be renewed. The third option is annexation of the Moro and of the Patani Muslims to Malaysia or to Indonesia, and of the Rohingya to Bangladesh. Such an option seems utterly unrealistic at present for reasons that have been noted in the previous pages. And finally, the fourth option is acceptance of the present situation, and an end to the struggle, in each of the countries. For now, it appears that the three separatist movements have opted for this alternative, each for their own reasons.

What options exist for the governments? Here there seem to be two courses of action. The first possibility is relinquishing sovereignty in those areas in which Muslims constitute a majority. This seems completely unlikely from the standpoint of each of the governments discussed. Not a single government will agree to limit its sovereignty in any part of its national territory. The second possibility is granting certain concessions to Muslims in the sphere of religio-cultural autonomy, programs for economic welfare, etc. This appears to be the most that can be expected, in varying degrees, from the Philippine and Thai governments. It is doubtful whether the Myanmar government would be willing to initiate such a policy. What can be concluded, then, is that the present situation in all three countries will continue, with various permutations, and highs and lows of violence. One cannot really expect a transformation unless there is a drastic and dramatic change of circumstances brought on by either internal or external factors in a way that cannot now be foretold.

Notes

1. For a thorough study on the subject, see Fred R. von der Mehden, *Two Worlds of Islam: Interaction between Southeast Asia and the Middle East* (Gainesville: University Press of Florida, 1993).
2. Moshe Yegar, *Between Integration and Secession: The Muslim Communities of the Southern Philippines, Southern Thailand, and Western Burma/Myanmar* (Lanham, Boulder, New York, Oxford: Lexington Books, 2002). I am grateful to Lexington Books for permission to use the material.
3. Certain comparisons can also be made with Muslim minorities in other countries. See, for example, an attempted comparison between the Muslims of Patani and the Arab minority in Israel: Erik Cohen, "Citizenship, Nationality and Religion in Israel and Thailand," *Thai Society in Comparative Perspective, Studies in Contemporary Thailand*, vol. 1, chap. 6 (Bangkok: White Lotus, 1991), 105–27. For a general review of ethnic separatism in Indonesia (Molucca, Aceh, and West Papua), the Philippines (Muslims of the south), Thailand (Muslims of the south), Myanmar (Karen, Shan, Kachin, and Muslims), see R. J. May, "Ethnic Separatism in Southeast Asia," *Pacific Viewpoint* 31, 2 (October 1990): 28–59.

4. For a systematic and authoritative discussion of this issue, see Raphael Israeli, "Muslim Minorities under Non-Islamic Rule," *Current History* 78, 456 (April 1980): 159–64, 184–5. W. K. Che Man also deals extensively with the religious aspects of Muslim rebellions being a part in the processes that the entire Muslim world has been undergoing since the end of World War II. See Che Man, *Muslim Separatism: The Moros of the Southern Philippines and the Malays of Southern Thailand* (Quezon City: Alteneo de Manila University Press, 1990), 12–7, 24, 70–4, 113–4, 136–7, 162, 173–9.
5. For an analysis of the impact of involvement by external Muslim forces on the rebellions in the Philippines and Thailand, see Astri Suhrke and Lela Garner Noble, "Muslims in the Philippines and Thailand," in Suhrke and Noble, eds., *Ethnic Conflict in International Relations* (New York: Praeger, 1977), 195, 208–10; R. J. May, "The Religious Factor in Three Minority Movements: The Moro of the Philippines, the Malays of Thailand and Indonesia's West Papuans," *Journal of the Institute of Muslim Minority Affairs* 12, 2 (July 1991): 319. This article also appeared in *Contemporary Southeast Asia* 13, 4 (March 1992).
6. For an attempt to explain the relative success of the Moro, see Syed Serajul Islam, "The Islamic Independence Movements in Patani of Thailand and Mindanao of the Philippines," *Asian Survey* 38, 5 (May 1998): 441–56.
7. On this issue, see Clive J. Christie, *A Modern History of Southeast Asia: Decolonization, Nationalism and Separation*, Tauris Academic Studies (New York: I. B. Tauris, 1996), 162–3. See also Howard M. Federspiel, "Islam and Development in the Nations of ASEAN," *Asian Survey* 25, 8 (August 1985): 813. A Muslim view is given in Hussain Haqqani, "The Roots of Rebellion," *Far Eastern Economic Review* 118, 45 (5 November 1982): 26–7.

14

Political Islam in Post-Soeharto Indonesia: The Contest Between "Radical-Conservative Islam" and "Progressive-Liberal Islam"*

M. Syafi'i Anwar

> In a society such as Indonesia, with weak rule of law, widespread crime, low levels of administrative competence, endemic corruption, and a significant presence of extremist, terrorist groups, Islam (and enhancing religiosity in general) may be the principal "social glue" that keeps society together, peaceful, and governable, and perhaps makes it more moral, more honest, and more just. There remain significant voices of unreason and intolerance in Indonesia. But the forces of tolerant, liberal, pluralistic Islam are strongly institutionalized, well led, the source of some of the most progressive thinking in the Islamic world, able to operate free of official repression, and widely supported by the populace. These forces have been strengthened by the extremists' use of violence, which has driven the populace at large, and especially the middle class, away from extremist views.
>
> — M. C. Ricklefs[1]

Soon after the collapse of the Soeharto regime and the beginning of Habibie's presidency in May 1998, there was a new political phenomenon in Indonesia that shocked many observers: the rise of radical-conservative Islam (RCI) groups. Amidst the ongoing economic crisis, uncertain political conditions, and lawless society, the emergence of RCI groups took on a political momentum. In an attempt to resolve Indonesia's multidimensional crisis, some RCI groups undoubtedly offer radical solutions: a move back to Islamic *salafism* and the implementation of *shari'a* (Islamic law). Such a solution, however, not only worries non-Muslim citizens, but also upsets the majority of Indonesian Muslims.

Interestingly enough, the spirit and demand of RCI groups in the post-Soeharto era to return to Islamic *salafism* and uphold the *shari'a* seems to have a genealogy within previous Islamic militant movements in Indonesia. The RCI groups are also inspired by similar activities of militant Islamic groups in the Middle East.[2] There is a tendency for radical-conservative Islam groups in Indonesia to associate themselves with various radical movements in the Middle East. Although they might use different methods in implementing their religio-political agenda, the names they use for their organizations are mostly similar to the radical movements in the Middle East — for instance, Majelis Mujahiddin, Lasykar Jihad, Ikhwanul Muslimin, Hizbut Tahrir, Lasykar Hizbullah, Lasykar Jundullah, Darul Islam, Hamas. There is also evidence for a process of ideological transmission from the radical movements in the Middle East to Indonesia.

More important, certain groups of radical Islamists working with unidentified movements have also carried out violence similar to that occurring in the Middle East. This includes acts such as sweeping foreigners from buildings, bombing churches, raiding shops selling alcohol, as well as suicide bombings that kill many innocent people. This violence is accompanied by the government's incapacity to solve economic and political crises in the post-Soeharto era. Yet some perpetrators claim that their actions are inspired by the spirit of *jihadist* movements in the Middle East, especially in fighting against the "conspiracies of Islamic enemies." These include Israel, Jews, Christians, and the United States and its Western allies. It is obvious that violent acts such as suicide bombings would not previously have taken place in Indonesia, considering that Indonesian Islam has been widely regarded as Islam with a smiling face. However, only one year after the 11 September 2001 tragedy in Washington and New York, Indonesia faced a new reality in which terrorists carried out the brutal act of suicide bombings in Bali (October 2002). This atrocity killed more than 200 and wounded hundreds of innocent people, mostly tourists from Australia. Yet, this was not the end of the story. In October 2003 the terrorists again carried out a suicide bombing, at the Jakarta Marriott Hotel, and killed several more people. The most recent brutal bombing was perpetrated in August 2004 against the Australian Embassy in Jakarta, but the victims were mostly ordinary Indonesian Muslims.

Based on the above incidents, observers and media often argue that Indonesia has become a seedbed of Islamic radicalism and a center of terrorist operations in Southeast Asia. It is also believed that the radical Islam movements in Indonesia have a strong connection with international terrorist organizations such as Al Qaeda and Jamaah Islamiyah.[3] Nonetheless, most RCI groups in Indonesia have denied such suspicions, claiming that their organizations do not have any linkages with either of these organizations. Certain figures from RCI groups have also publicly declared that they fully reject the ways of Osama bin Laden and his Al Qaeda movement. However, they also state that such suspicions are only part of the US propaganda for destroying Islam, hiding under the banner of President Bush's global campaign on a "war against terrorism."[4]

Indeed, the emergence of RCI groups in post-Soeharto Indonesia and their political implications have raised questions relating to their social origin, intellectual roots, and religio-political agenda. The problem lies in the fact that certain RCI groups justify the use of hostility as a way of forcing "truth claims" based on their subjective interpretation, and also implement violence using physical action. It is also obvious that membership in RCI groups is extremely limited. However, the media often tends to give them special coverage or even magnify their actions. This kind of coverage has created the public image that the RCI groups are large, vocal, and well-organized.

Believing that the emergence of RCI groups and their actions have created serious problems within Indonesian society, a group of young Muslim intellectuals established the Jaringan Islam Liberal (the Liberal Islam Network, or JIL) in early 2001. The reason for the establishment of JIL was not only the conservative ideas of RCI, but also the violent way in which the RCI groups realized their radical aims. The JIL is basically a loose intellectual forum for discussing the ideas of Islamic liberalism and providing books, syndicated columns, and radio talk shows. The members of JIL are mostly young, urban, well-educated, liberal Muslims who believe that the entire corpus of Islamic teachings needs to be contextually reinterpreted.[5]

At first glance, the establishment of JIL was a counterbalance to the spread of RCI ideas and movements, which tend to promote a strict legal-exclusive approach on Islamic underpinnings. Unlike RCI, the JIL is committed to developing a liberal-inclusive approach, also on a bedrock of Islamic underpinning. In this context, the emergence of JIL should be considered as a revival of the generation of Muslim intellectuals dedicated to Islamic renewal thinking in the post-1970s decades. It would be a mistake to regard the emergence of progressive-liberal Islam (PLI) groups as a new phenomenon. In the 1960s, there were limited groups in Yogyakarta that carried out discussions on Islamic theology using liberal approaches. By the 1970s, Indonesian Muslims were shocked with the ideas of Gerakan Pembaruan Pemikiran Islam (the Renewal of Islamic Thought Movement, or GPPI) initiated by Nurcholish Madjid. However, it should be noted here that JIL is more liberal, provocative, and well-organized in disseminating its ideas to the public compared with the GPPI.[6]

This article attempts to map problems relating to the historical background, social origins, and continuing rivalry between RCI and PLI groups in the post-Soeharto era. It focuses mainly on the religious thinking, sociopolitical agenda, and strategies of the two conflicting groups as they respond to current political affairs and try to gain public support. The essay discusses ideological and intellectual transmissions from the Middle East to Indonesia and their implications on contemporary Indonesian politics.

Two Normative Approaches on Political Islam

Before elaborating further on the contest between RCI and PLI in the post-Soeharto era, it would be useful to discuss a theoretical framework related to political Islam. In general, I shall formulate two normative approaches on political Islam: (1) the legal-exclusive approach and (2) the substantive-inclusive approach. The legal-exclusive approach to political Islam refers to the idea that Islam is not only a religion, but also a complete legal system, a universal ideology, and a perfect system of guidance that can provide solutions to all problems in life. Proponents of the legal-exclusive approach to political Islam strongly believe that Islam is an integrated totality of the three famous "Ds": *din* (religion), *dunya* (life), and *dawla* (state). Consequently, as Nazih Ayubi suggests, this paradigm is designed for application to every aspect of life, from the family to the economy and politics. In the political realm, this paradigm obliges all Muslims to establish an Islamic state.[7] Obviously, the fundamental tenet of this paradigm lies in the interpretation of *shari'a*, which, as its proponents argue, should be the legal underpinning of the three integrated institutions mentioned above. Those who believe in this paradigm argue that the state and its functioning is part of Islamic teachings. *Shari'a* is interpreted as Divine Law and has to form the basis of the state and its constitution, as the constitution formalizes all the processes of governing, including the political behavior of the ruler.

This paradigm implies that political sovereignty is not vested in the people, but in the hands of God. There is no people's sovereignty, only God's sovereignty. Consequently, this exclusive paradigm results in the strict obligation for every Muslim to uphold the *shari'a* by whatever means available. Muslims who plead for the separation of religion and politics or for the suspension of the *shari'a* are judged to be against the spirit of Islam. Moreover, modern political concepts derived from Western sources are considered to be paradoxical to Islamic teachings. This paradigm appeals to Muslims to refer to the "ideal state" established by the Prophet Muhammad and his four successor caliphates (*khulafa ar rasyidun*), and urges Muslims not to implement Western political systems. Therefore, Muslims are strongly advised to join the political struggle to implement Islam as the basis of the state and *shari'a* as the basis of the constitution.[8] In the political realm, such a paradigm often encourages Muslims to strengthen their ideological and political identities as a form of protection against temporal, ideological, and political alternatives.

The substantive-inclusive approach to political Islam refers to the notion that Islam as a religion does not stipulate any theoretical concepts related to politics. The proponents of this paradigm believe that the Qur'an contains information about aspects of ethical or moral guidance for human life, but does not provide details on every object in creation. They argue that there is no single text in the Qur'an that insists that Muslims establish an Islamic state. Rather, they argue that the Qur'an contains ethical or moral guidance for governing a polity, including how to achieve ethical justice, freedom, equality, democracy, and other injunctions. According to them, Islam is a religion that aspires to create the most refined and ethical civilization on earth.

A key assumption of this paradigm is that the mission of the Prophet Muhammad was not to establish a kingdom or a state. Rather, it was similar to that of other prophets in that preaching Islamic values and its virtues was the main task of his mission. Thus, the mission of the Prophet Muhammad should not be understood in terms of establishing or ruling any worldly state. The Prophet Muhammad and his successors, however, governed in the spirit and ethical framework of Islam. This is not to deny that the historical circumstances imposed on the Prophet and his four successors necessitated that they act politically and assume political functions in a hitherto stateless society. However, as Husain Fawzi al Najjar argues, this does not mean that Islam as a religion is bound to the state. The concern of the Prophet Muhammad when he spread Islam was to achieve unity among followers of Islam (*al-wihda al-ijtima'i*) rather than create a state.[9]

Substantive-inclusive notions of Islam assert that the *shari'a* does not need to be bound to the state. The *shari'a* does not deal with any specific ideas related to government or political systems. Because Islam is seen as a religion and not a state order, *shari'a* should not fall under the domain of the state, but should remain in the realm of belief. According to Al-Ashmawi, an Egyptian Muslim legal scholar, even the Qur'an itself stipulates that the *shari'a* is the source of ethical orientation and does not provide an underpinning for any sort of state.[10] The Qur'anic precepts on *shari'a* were always related to historical situations dealing with traditions and customs. Ashmawi points out the following:

> ... the shari'a neither was revealed at once nor has existed as an abstract issue. It was always related to existing realities ... it drew on prevailing traditions and customs and derived its own rules from them. It also adjusted itself to further developments of those traditions and customs in keeping up with the change ... without taking into consideration these reality-related origins of the shari'a while (nonetheless) pleading that it be implemented, we will be dealing with theoretical and logical concerns contradictory to the spirit of Islam.[11]

Proponents of the substantive-inclusive paradigm argue that Islam provides opportunities and freedom to its adherents to set up or develop a political system based on their own choice. Any political concepts and systems, regardless of where these are derived from, are basically welcomed as long as they are in accordance with the ethical spirit of Islam.

Noticeably, proponents of the two paradigms above have existed in the entire Muslim world, including in Indonesia. To defend their ideas, the two groups have engaged in political debates, sometimes followed by tension and conflict. History shows that the proponents of those two paradigms debated these concepts prior to independence and also in the post-independence period. Such political debates, however, also materialized under Soeharto's New Order authoritarian regime (1966–98).

A Brief Political Context

From the mid-1960s until the early 1970s, Soeharto was widely known for his repressive approach against political Islam. Himself a Javanese Muslim,

Soeharto considered that political Islam was a serious threat and hazardous to his power, both ideologically and politically. Consequently, Islam was seen as "political enemy number two" (after communism) and was often termed the *ekstrim kanan* (the right extreme). This was a deliberate ploy to equate Islam with communism as *ekstrim kiri* (the left extreme). This situation led to mutual distrust and hostility between the Islamic groups and the New Order regime. Although the various Islamic groups had contributed to the fight against communism and the establishment of the New Order regime, these groups were then marginalized in the political arena. In the words of M. Natsir, former prime minister and former chairman of the modernist Muslim party, Masyumi, the New Order regime "treated us like a cat with ringworm."[12]

There is no doubt that Soeharto's approach to Islam was too coercive in the early years of his administration. Yet despite his coercive approach, Soeharto accommodated some Muslim religio-cultural aspirations in the late 1970s. This shift appeared to be part of a "political balancing act" that aimed to better his political image and the support of Indonesian Muslims. This balancing act led to further shifts in the late 1980s, when Soeharto began to fully develop the politics of accommodation, beginning his embrace of political Islam. After cautiously starting with the accommodation of cultural Islam, Soeharto later also formally institutionalized political Islam. One of the most important forms of institutionalizing political Islam was the establishment of Ikatan Cendekiawan Muslim Indonesia (the Association of Indonesian Muslim Intellectuals, or ICMI), which was to play a significant role in the discourse on political Islam in the late New Order regime. Having succeeded in incorporating political Islam into state politics, Soeharto moved on to implement the politics of co-optation in the mid-1990s. Soeharto's politics of co-optation led to the conversion of a state-sponsored political Islam in the late years of his regime. Consequently, the state did not favor the spirit of either the legal-exclusive model or the substantive-inclusive model. Rather, it fully accommodated political Islam based on the logic of Soeharto's power interests and state hegemony.[13]

Nevertheless, the conversion to state-sponsored political Islam occurred because of the support and pragmatic alliance between the state and "regimist" Muslim leaders. These latter individuals came especially from the "militant-scripturalist" of certain modernist Muslim schools associated with Komite Indonesia untuk Solidaritas Dunia Islam (the Indonesian Committee for Muslim World Solidarity, or KISDI), Dewan Dakwah Islamiyah Indonesia (the Indonesian Council for Islamic Propagation, or DDII), Muhammadiyah, ICMI, and others. Because of the downturn caused by the economic crisis, bureaucratic corruption, state violence, and the withdrawal of critical Muslim support to the New Order authoritarian regime, Soeharto's administration finally collapsed on 21 May 1998.[14]

Under Habibie's presidency and the euphoria of the *reformasi* (reform) movement, political Islam gathered momentum. Along with the wave of the *reformasi* movement, Habibie's administration gave greater freedoms and political openness to the people. Many people utilized this opportunity to establish new political parties, associations, media companies, and the like. As a result, more than 100 political parties were established, and more than 40 associations were grouped as Islamic parties. Under these political circumstances, certain groups rode this momentum by restoring the power of political Islam. They built new associations, including hard-line and radical Islamic groups. Under the New Order authoritarian regime, it had been impossible to do so. In addition, under Habibie's presidency press freedom and civil rights grew remarkably, contributing significantly to the strengthening of civil society.[15] Unfortunately, Habibie's administration was unable to set up good governance and control the corrupt bureaucracy, both legacies of the New Order regime. Worse, his administration was even accused for its involvement in a corrupt bank scandal. As a result, Habibie failed to gain a real political legitimacy from the people. This situation led to uncertain political conditions in which the state was weak. Civil society was comparatively strong, but it was not buttressed by serious law enforcement. Rather, what was created was a lawless society: a state of affairs in which people preferred to use the law of the jungle rather than solving problems using the rule of law.

Some Islamic political parties used this sociopolitical crisis to campaign for an "Islamic solution" to what they saw as "Indonesia's multidimensional crisis." What was meant by an Islamic solution was the demand for inclusion of the Jakarta Charter into the state constitution and the implementation of *shari'a* as an alternative to existing laws and state regulation. During the 1999 general election campaign and parliamentary session, several Islamic parties, such as Partai Persatuan Pembangunan (United Development Party, or PPP), Partai Bulan Bintang (Crescent and Star Party, or PBB), Partai Keadilan (Justice Party, or PK), and others actively campaigned for the necessity of implementing the *shari'a*, including the demand for re-inclusion of the Jakarta Charter. However, they were unable to gain significant support from the people. In total, all Islamic parties were able to gain only 17.8 per cent of the vote. They also failed to gain support when demanding the inclusion of the Jakarta Charter during the General Assembly of Majelis Permusyawaratan Rakyat (People's Consultative Assembly, or MPR). The result of the 1999 general election shows that the power of political Islam was only a myth and that it lacked support from the majority of the Muslim populace.[16]

Despite the Islamic parties' failure to gain public support and their failure in the inclusion of the Jakarta Charter and implementation of *shari'a*, the RCI groups continued their struggle for these political agendas and demanded a platform. In so doing, they often carried out political rallies, street demonstrations, and the dissemination of propaganda and pamphlets touting the necessity of implementing *shari'a*. Faced with this reality, Habibie's administration had no choice but to allow the RCI groups to exist and let them express their aspirations in any manner they chose.

This situation changed when Abdurrahman Wahid replaced Habibie as president in late 1999. At the beginning of his presidency, people had high hopes of his leadership, because Wahid was the first democratically elected president. He was expected to usher in a new era in Indonesian politics. Wahid was widely known as a noted Muslim intellectual and a charismatic leader, and he was never viewed as a "guardian of Indonesian civil society." Before becoming president, Wahid had been an NGO activist who had tirelessly struggled for empowering civil society. Most importantly for our purposes here, many scholars have regarded Wahid as one of the most prominent Muslim intellectuals representing "liberal Islamic thought," despite the fact that his social base was traditionalist NU (Nahdatul Ulama, the largest Muslim organization in Indonesia).[17]

Ironically, under Wahid's presidency the radical conservative Islam movements increased their actions and pressures aimed not only toward the government, but also toward the Indonesian public at large. The situation was worsened by bloody religious and communal conflicts in several Indonesian provinces, especially between Muslims and Christians in the Indonesian east, such as in Ambon, Palu, and Ternate. Wahid seemed to use a moderate approach in solving the problem, meaning that he tried to focus on an effort to calm the conflict by promoting a peaceful dialogue between the two groups. In so doing, Wahid asked the two sides not to send paramilitary troops into the conflict area. Yet in his public statements, Wahid condemned Lasykar Jihad as troublesome for its policy of sending thousands of paramilitary troops to Ambon. Wahid said that Lasykar Jihad had exacerbated the conflict between the two religions. He seemed to neglect the actions taken by Lasykar Kristus (Jesus Troops), who were also operating their own campaigns in Ambon and killing Muslims on the battlefield.[18]

The RCI groups united to oppose Wahid's administration policies. They considered Wahid's statements to be unfair. Therefore, despite Wahid's appeal to not send paramilitary groups, Ja'afar Umar Talib, the leader of Jama'ah Ahlu Sunnah wal Jama'ah, continuously sent Lasykar Jihad personnel to fight against Christians in Ambon. Talib claimed that this action was due to the ineffective policies of Wahid's administration in settling the bloody conflict. Talib also strongly criticized Wahid for not having a clear policy to end the slaughter of Muslims in Maluku.

Leaders of other RCI groups, such as Habib Rizieq of Front Pembela Islam (Islamic Defenders' Front, or FPI) and Habib Al Habsyi of Ikhwanul Muslimin, joined Talib in opposing Wahid's policies concerning the Ambon conflict. They felt that Wahid was unjust and that he sided with the Christians rather than his fellow Muslims who had become victims. These two RCI leaders also declared that Wahid's policies were ineffective in solving the multidimensional crisis in Indonesian society. To these two leaders, the main cause of the deepening Indonesian crisis was the degradation of moral conduct. Facing this reality, the FPI committed actions that they claimed "cleaned Indonesian society from the influences of a *haram* environment." The FPI declared that Indonesian society had been poisoned by *kehidupan yang haram dan penuh dengan kemaksiatan* ("the forbidden life fully created by violating God's law"). Under this pretext, the FPI raided shops selling alcohol, attacked brothels and gambling houses, and swept foreigners suspected of "spreading wickedness" from hotels. In doing so, they portrayed themselves as an "army of God and moral police for society." The FPI also organized street demonstrations involving thousands of its followers to demand the implementation of *shari'a* and urged the government and people to fight against immoral deeds.[19]

When Wahid's presidency ended due to the impeachment of parliament, Megawati became the strongest candidate for president. The RCI groups again united, to oppose Megawati's candidacy. Their reason for opposing her candidacy was based on their legal-textual interpretation of the Qur'an and *shari'a*, that a woman is not allowed to lead a nation. They publicly campaigned this idea to society, despite having very limited support from the people. Their campaign failed totally, because the general assembly of MPR elected her as president, replacing Wahid.

Nonetheless, the agenda to impose *shari'a* law continued under Megawati's presidency and is still alive. Such an agenda is related to a mindset or paradigm in the hearts and minds of RCI leaders and activists. In other words, the reason behind the agenda of imposing *shari'a* was related to the strong belief that the long and multidimensional crisis in Indonesian society was a product of not upholding "the law of God." Indeed, the RCI groups can be defined as having a *"shari'a*-minded" orientation due to their strong commitment to uphold *shari'a* as an ideological or practical solution for any problems facing human beings. Obviously, what they mean by *shari'a* law is the interpretation of *fiqh* (Islamic jurisprudence) based on strict, legal, and formal approaches. The problem lies in the fact that such approaches tend to neglect the nature and flexibility of *fiqh* itself. More important, such approaches tend to promote the notion that *fiqh* is a state law. As a result, they often invite manipulation of *fiqh* for the sake of political interest, hegemony of meaning, and monopoly of the religious truth.[20]

Transmission of Ideology and Religio-Political Thoughts: The Middle Eastern Connection

The emergence of RCI in the post-Soeharto era is correlated with the transmission of ideology and religio-political thought from the Middle East. In general, the victory of the Iranian Revolution in 1979 under the leadership of Ayatullah Khomeini contributed significantly to the spread of Islamic radicalism and the New Order's political anxiety. Many Indonesian Muslims, especially the young generation, were very proud of the success of the Iranian Revolution. To them, the Iranian Revolution had shown that Islamic people's power could prevail against a regime as hegemonic and despotic as the regime of Shah Reza Pahlevi. Following media coverage of the Iranian Revolution, many young Muslims were proud and respectful of Ayatullah Khomeini and, surprisingly, even regarded Khomeini as a role model. Alongside the victory of the Iranian Revolution, there was a general sense of a global Islamic resurgence. Most Muslims around the world, except in certain Islamic countries in the Middle East, welcomed the Iranian Revolution. The victory of the revolution gave a new spirit to Muslims. It also encouraged an Islamic resurgence by way of building Muslim unity and self-confidence against Western hegemony around the world.[21]

The outcome of the revolution encouraged Muslims to promote unity and self-confidence in challenging the hegemony of Western civilization.

Although the form and substance of the Islamic resurgence varied from country to country, the main theme was always the same, namely, disenchantment with Western civilization. Furthermore, as John Esposito suggests, the Islamic resurgence appeared as a form of searching for an Islamic identity and greater religious authenticity. This led to the conviction that Islam provides a self-sufficient ideology for state and society, a valid alternative to secular nationalism, socialism, and capitalism.[22]

To some extent, the influence of the global Islamic resurgence in Indonesia seemed to feature similar characteristics. It emerged in the widespread campaigns of urban-educated Muslims to revive the notions of Islamic "piety" and "authenticity," although it was manifested in a form of activism rather than intellectualism. Therefore, understandably, in the late 1970s and 1980s there were many activities expressing the "back to Islamic identity" movement of religious revivalism. In a cultural form, for example, such activities appeared as an attempt to reinvigorate public conviction that wearing the *jilbab* should be mandatory for Muslim women. Moreover, there was a series of religious lectures based on studying the basic values of Islam (*Nilai-Nilai Dasar Islam*) presented at various religious study clubs, which were very popular among university and high school students at general education institutions.[23]

Besides the ideological transformation of the Iranian Revolution and global Islamic resurgence in the late 1970s and 1980s, there were three important factors driving the transmission of militancy: (1) education, (2) publication, and (3) networks. Education played a significant role in transmitting the ideology and religio-political thought of RCI in Indonesia. Mona Abaza suggests that, based on her field research in the 1970s and 1980s, there was a shift in orientation among the Indonesian students at Middle Eastern universities. Abaza points out that during these two decades, Indonesian students shifted their ideological orientation from liberal to fundamentalist. At that time, they were interested in the ideas of militant Muslim thinkers, such as Hassan Al Banna, Sayyid Qutb, Abul A'la Al Maududi, Ali Shariati, and Imam Khomeini. They were also interested in the writings of Egyptian thinkers such as Muhammad Al Bahi and Ahmad Shalabi. According to Abaza, this orientation was different from that of the previous generation of Indonesian students, who were more interested in the ideas of Western thinkers such as Albert Camus and Jean Paul Sartre than the ideas of Islamic renewal. Moreover, the Indonesian students in Middle Eastern universities were able to have access to and interaction with Ikhwanul Muslimin activists, who were then spreading in some Middle Eastern countries. Thus, they were not only studying the religio-political thoughts of Ikhwanul Muslimin leaders such as Al Banna and Qutb, but they were also developing networks and relationships with Ikhwanul Muslimin activists.[24]

Having studied Ikhwanul Muslimin ideas and developed relationships with activists of this organization, the Indonesian students who had finished their study disseminated the ideas of Ikhwanul Muslimin when they returned to Indonesia. They got involved in social and *dakwah* activities such as teaching at schools and universities, delivering sermons at mosques, and presenting speeches or lectures at religious gatherings (*pengajian*). Some of them also developed the *dakwah* method and strategy adopted from Ikhwanul Muslimin, called *usroh*.[25] However, the dissemination of Ikhwanul Muslimin in the 1970s was still limited and had not reached a wider public. In the early 1980s, the transmission of Ikhwanul Muslimin ideas and ideas of other revivalist Muslim movements took on a political momentum along with the victory of the Iranian Revolution and the global Islamic resurgence. During this period, the alumni of Middle Eastern universities were very active in disseminating Ikhwanul Muslimin and revivalist Muslim movements' ideas to Indonesia. This was the "second phase" of transmission of the ideology and religio-political thought of Muslim revivalist groups into a more comprehensive blueprint and strategic action. The second phase of transmission was marked by the spread of leadership training models using *usroh* methods and other sources promoting Islamic revivalism.[26]

The other vehicle for transmission of the ideology and religio-political thought of Ikhwanul Muslimin was publication. This can be seen from the translation and publication of books written by Ikhwanul Muslimin ideologues and other revivalist Muslim thinkers. The radical mindset in Indonesia has been strongly influenced by the spread of references from doctrinal resources of radical groups, such as the works of Ibn Taimiyah (*Iqtidha Sirath al-Mustaqim, al-Jawab al-Bahir fi Maqabir, Majmu' Fatawa*), Ibnu al-Qayyim al-Jauziyah (*Miftah Dar al-Sa'adah, Zad al-Ma'ad*), and Muhammad Ibnu Abdil Wahhab (*Ma'a 'Aqidat al-Salafi Kitab al-Tauhid alladzi Huwa Haqullah 'ala al-'Abid*). The position of these authors is very influential in explaining the state of the Islamic faith and the need for change toward a more Islamic system (*nizham al-Islam*). These authors are also considered to be carrying on the pioneer work of Islamic contemporary radical movements from the 20th century. Radicalism in Indonesia has been influenced by prominent figures of contemporary Islamic movements in the Middle East such as Ikhwanul Muslimin, Hizbut Tahrir, Salafi, Tarbiyah, and other Islamic movements such as Hasan al-Banna, Sayyid Qutb, Taqiyuddin al-Nabhani, Abul A'la al-Mawdudi, and Hasan Turabi. Ikhwanul Muslimin is firmly established as an Islamic organization and has had a strong influence in propagating religious understanding in Muslim countries, including Indonesia.[27]

One of the books by prominent figures of Ikhwanul Muslimin, which has been translated by an alumnus of the Middle East, is *Ma'alim fi al-Thariq* (published in 1964) by Sayyid Qutb. It has become the guide for this movement. This book is "the scripture" for activists of propagation. It is even considered as the main obligatory text for alumni of Latihan Mujahid Dakwah, in the Salman Mosque, Bandung Institute of Technology. After that, a number of books from other prominent figures of Ikhwanul Muslimin were also translated, such as *Fi Afaq al-Ta'lim* by Said Hawwa, which was translated as *Membina Angkatan Mujahid* (Constructing *Mujahid's* Generation). The trilogy of Said Hawwa — *Allah, Al-Rasul,* and *Al-Islam* — has also been translated into Indonesian. These books are considered to be the core of *tarbawi*'s propagation movement in Indonesia.[28] In addition, books by Hassan Al-Banna, Muhammad Quthb, Musthafa Masyhur, Muhammad Al-Ghazali, and Yusuf Al-Qardlawi, among others, have been translated into Indonesian.

Books of Hizbut Tahrir that spread in Indonesia include the following: *Nidzamul Islam* (Life's System in Islam), *Nidzamul Hukmi fil Islam* (The System of Government in Islam), *Nidzamul Iqtishadi fil Islam* (The System of Economy in Islam), *Nidzamul Ijtimaiy fil Islam* (The System of Social in Islam), *At-Takatul al-Hizbi* (The Formation of Political Party), *Mafahim Hizbut Tahrir* (Fundamental Thought of *Hizbut Tahrir*), *Daulatul Islamiyah* (Islamic State), *Al-Khilafah* (The System of *Khilafah*), *Syakhsiyyah Islamiyah* (The Establishment of Islamic Identity Volumes I, II, and III), *Mafahim Siyasah li Hizbut Tahrir* (The Political Fundamental Thought of Hizbut Tahrir), and others. Many books from the *Salafi* movement are also found in Indonesia, particularly the works of Muhammad Ibn Abd al-Wahhab (*Ma'a 'Aqidat al-Salafi Kitab al-Tauhid alladzi Huwa Haqullah 'ala al-'Abid*), Nashirudin al-Bani (*Tahdzirus Sajid, Sifat Shalat Nabi*), Syeikh Ali Hasan Abdul Hamid (*Tashfiyah wa Tarbiyah*), Syeikh Zaid bin Hadi al-Madkhali (*al-Irhab*), Syeikh Abul Hasan (*Intima' ila Da'wat al-Salafiyah* dan *al-Hiwal ma'a al-jihadi*) in the field of *aqidah* and *ibadah*, *hadiths/hadiths* science, and *fiqh*. Books from the *Salafi* movement are mainly from the Arabian Peninsula. These

Salafi books have been brought back mainly by Indonesian students at universities in Medina, such as Ummul Qura'.²⁹

The other important path of transmission of RCI thought is international networking. To strengthen education and publication, the RCI has developed international networking with individuals and institutions in the Middle East. In this regard, the role of Indonesian students is quite significant, especially in developing networks with revivalist movements in the Middle East. Those Indonesian students were able to network with their fellow activists of the revivalist movement in some Middle Eastern countries, such as Egypt, Saudi Arabia, Syria, Jordan, Iraq, and Tunisia. Through this networking, they were able to join activities of the revivalist movements such as seminars, discussions, and training programs. These activities were transferred to junior Indonesian students, who later became the newcomers in academic communities in Middle Eastern universities.

Abdurrahman Kasdi, a former chairman of the Association of Indonesian Students in Egypt, who graduated in 2000, argued that the above transmission was effective in recruiting new members and developing networking. In so doing, senior students even made intensive contacts with potential students prior to the latters' coming to Egypt and other countries. The senior students also helped their juniors look for accommodation, process campus administration papers, and direct worldview and ideological orientation when studying at university. Senior students directed their juniors to join Ikhwanul Muslimin forums such as "Information Studies for Muslims Worlds," participate in leadership training, and read Ikhwanul Muslimin's publications. Junior students were also discouraged from joining secular and liberal groups and communities.³⁰ In this manner, Indonesian students in the Middle East and Indonesia were able to develop a solid network. This kind of network, however, had a significant impact on the transmission of ideology and religio-political thoughts of Ikhwanul Muslimin and other revivalist movements in the Middle East.

Besides Ikhwanul Muslimin, another revivalist movement connected to the global political momentum in the 1980s was Hizbur Tahrir. As in the case of Ikhwanul Muslimin, the transmission of ideology and religio-political thought of Hizbut Tahrir in Indonesia was mostly through education, publication, and networking. Studies on the transmission of Hizbur Tahrir ideas and the establishment of this revivalist movement in Indonesia show that it began to spread in 1982–83. It is said that two prominent figures were active in disseminating Hizbut Tahrir ideas in Indonesia: M. Mustafa and Abdurrahman Al-Baghdadi. Mustafa was an Indonesian student in Jordan who was interested in Taqiyuddin's ideas and then became an activist of Hizbut Tahrir. Mustafa spread Hizbut Tahrir's ideas through lectures and religious gatherings in Bogor, especially to students of the Bogor Agriculture Institute (IPB). Baghdadi was a Hizbut Tahrir activist from Lebanon who came to Indonesia in 1981 and served as a lecturer at Pesantren Al-Ghazali. Along with Mustafa, he introduced Hizbut Tahrir's ideas to the activists of Al-Ghifari mosque, in the IPB complex. Having succeeded in disseminating Hizbut Tahrir's ideas in Bogor, the two activists then established Hizbut Tahrir and developed a network throughout universities in Indonesia.[31]

It is important to note that prior to the transmission process, there was a new development of Islamic *dakwah* in Indonesia. Along with the strict political regulation of the New Order authoritarian regime, some Muslim activists tried to focus their concerns by empowering *dakwah* activities. This was a strategy of securing Islam away from government political control. The result was important, because these activists were able to increase *dakwah* activities at mosques and universities and in other public spheres. Through such activities, those activists strengthened "cultural Islam" as an alternative to government control over "political Islam." Thus, during the 1980s, "cultural Islam" actually dominated many Muslim activities.[32]

"Shari'a Minded" and Textual Interpretation

One of the most important efforts toward formalizing *shari'a* law was to revive the attempt to have *Piagam Jakarta* (the Jakarta Charter) included in the state constitution during the general assembly of the People's Consultative Assembly (MPR) in 2001. The RCI's struggle to revive the Jakarta Charter was supported by two Islamic parties, the PPP (United Development Party) and the PBB (Crescent and Star Party). However, their attempt to revive the Jakarta Charter totally failed. They did not get support either from the majority of MPR members or from the Muslim community. The two leading Islamic organizations, Nahdlatul Ulama and Muhammadiyah, formally declared that they would reject any attempt to revive the Jakarta Charter. The two leaders of NU and Muhammadiyah, KH Hasyim Muzadi and Professor Dr. A. Syafi'i Maarif respectively, openly released a joint public statement rejecting the agenda of demanding the Jakarta Charter. Both leaders declared that any attempt to revive the Jakarta Charter was counterproductive and unrealistic.[33]

The RCI groups harbor a strong disrespect for pluralism, believing that such an idea is an offense against Islam as the only truth; other ideas are regarded as "untruth" and devised by groups of "deviated people" or even "infidels." The RCI groups also claim that God has made a clear distinction between Muslims and *kafir*. Based on their literal and textual interpretation of the Qur'an, the RCI groups also believe that God has declared that the Jews and Christians are judged as "accursed groups" and will always have an agenda to proselytize amongst Muslims to make them their followers. This belief in a conspiracy was partly legitimized by literal and ideologically driven interpretations of certain verses of the Holy Qur'an, including the following:

> Never will the Jews or Christians be satisfied with thee unless thou follow their form of religion. Say: "The Guidance of God, that is the (only) Guidance". Wert thou to follow their desires after the knowledge which hath reached thee, then wouldst thou find neither Protector nor Helper against God Q.S. II (*Al Baqarah*): 120).[34]

Muslims who use legal-exclusive and textual-scriptural interpretations of this Qur'anic verse argue that Jews, Christians, and other non-Muslim groups have always employed strategies to proselytize to or compete with Muslims. As a result, they tend to bring about a serious distinction in defining who is friend and who is foe, making a very strict demarcation between "us" (*minna*, in-groups) and "them" (*minhum*, out-groups). The RCI groups also claim that there are certain *hadiths* declaring that Jews and Christians will be inhabitants of hell in the hereafter. Consequently, Muslims who are concerned with the idea of pluralism are considered to be against the spirit of Qur'an and Sunna and can therefore be categorized as *shirk*.[35]

RCI groups revitalize the binary concepts of *Muslim* and *kafir, Dar al-Islam* (house of Islam) and *Dar al-Harb* (house of the enemy). This is due to their claim of absolute truth that negates not only non-Muslim beliefs but also the beliefs of Muslims who have religious perceptions different from theirs. In the extreme spectrum, their exclusion of others is usually parallel with their call for jihad to correct the latter. Adian Husaini, Secretary General of KISDI, argued as follows:

> It becomes a true belief in the Muslim community that the path of truth and salvation is only through Islam. It means that outside the path of

Islam is a digression. Christians who believe in the Trinity concept claiming Isa as God of Son or Son of God are infidels (Al- Maidah: 72–75). It also includes the Jews, which reject the prophetic existence of Muhammad. They are also infidels. They are judged as infidels of the People of the Book (ahl al kitab). Other religions are also included as infidels.[36]

The RCI groups also condemn Muslim leaders who promote pluralism. According to the RCI groups, those who promote pluralism are agents of Christian missionaries and Zionism. They strongly believe that both Christians and Jews have agendas and conspiracies for destroying the Islamic faith. Husaini, for instance, insists, "the spread of pluralism ideology done by certain Islamic leaders, intellectuals, ulamas, and activists of Islamic organizations can be categorized as a dangerous action for destroying the Islamic faith ... they have destroyed the fundamental tenets of Islamic faith by giving misleading perceptions of the Qur'an."[37] To Husaini, such action is part of a hidden agenda for destroying Islam, and this program has been widely campaigned by Free Masonry Jews and Christian missionaries in Indonesia.

With regard to gender issues, the RCI groups hold a conservative view. They take a patriarchal perspective of Islamic law and subordinate the role of women to taking care of domestic matters (*al wilayah al-khashshah*). Women are prohibited from maintaining a presence in the public area (*al-wilayah al-ammah*). For this perspective, the RCI groups mostly refer to their literal and textual interpretation of Qur'anic verses that declare that men are determined to be leaders of women. The position of men and women is not equal. Men are determined to have better capacity compared to women (Q.S. An Nisa 4: 34 and Q.S. Al Baqarah 2:228). The RCI groups also refer to the Bukhari *hadith*, which declares that if a community gives its authority to a woman, it will never succeed. The RCI groups also quote the opinion of Ibn Katsir, a noted commentator of Qur'an (*mufassir*), and the views of Islamic legal experts (*fuqaha*) such as Abdurrahman Al Jazini, Wahbah al Zuhaili, and Yusuf Qardhawi in defending their stand on gender issues. Those leading *ulama* are quoted as saying that women are prohibited from being imams (leaders) of prayer (*al-imamah al shugra*). Thus, they are also prohibited from leading the state (*al imamah al-kubra*).[38]

The implications of such a point of view are far-reaching. The RCI groups strongly believe that Islamic teaching insists that women have to be kept within the domestic arena. Thus, their main role is limited to being housewives, educating children, and reproducing. The public sphere is believed to belong only to men, and women are prohibited from trying for public positions. Given this ideological view, it is no surprise that the RCI groups fully reject the notion that women can be elected as leaders of the nation. Therefore, RCI groups such as FPI, Lasykar Jihad, Indonesian Mujahidin Council (MMI), and KISDI totally opposed the nomination of Megawati Sukarnoputri as a presidential candidate in 2001.

It is correct to argue that the RCI groups reject the mainstream Indonesian view on women and that they offer an alternative vision of women's roles in society. The salient features of their vision are their proscriptions on the physical appearance of women and the limitations they impose on women's roles in the public sphere. In fact, their distinctive view on women has a chance to be accommodated in the new era of democratization within regional areas. Decentralization has opened up the possibility for such groups to pressure local governments to implement *shari'a* law in their own municipalities. However, their efforts to implement *shari'a* law usually put more emphasis on the formal application of these laws, and these laws lack efficacy in tackling the substance of women's problems. The formal application of *shari'a* law has limited women's roles and mobility in public life. In other words, women become the first victim of the implementation of *shari'a*. The RCI groups, for example, designate women's primary role as being in the family. They must serve both as wives, who are obliged to obey their husbands, and as mothers, who nurture and educate their children at home. Although RCI groups allow women to have a social role in public, this role is only secondary and may not harm family life. They perceive the primary role of women as being in the private sphere, but this dimension also has a significant role in the public sphere, as this particular function of women is part of the attempt to prepare for the next generation.[39]

On the other hand, Majlis Mujahidin, another RCI group, defines women as *mujahidah*, women fighters who serve a secondary role supportive to men. They take over their husbands' responsibility of *jihad* (fighting) in case the latter are caught and imprisoned. Another implication of this division is enforcement of segregation between men and women in public spaces. RCI groups usually conduct their organizational activities separately between women and men. Therefore, in some municipalities where the institution of *shari'a* law is being considered, there have been proposals to segregate public schools and public swimming pools.

Furthermore, these groups use the institution of marriage, as in the old days of sultans and kingdoms, to build political alliances and broaden the political support base. Closely related to this, early marriage is strongly encouraged (to avoid premarital sex, according to one publication).[40]

The function of women is of great importance to the development of communities. Groups are expanded through two means: recruitment and procreation. Traditionally, recruitment is conducted by way of marital networks and by biological reproduction. Females become the core in both fields of reproduction. In other words, in the hands and uteruses of women is a group of people at risk. Hence, polygamy is often practiced, and some even consider it as an obligation. This has led the noted Muslim intellectual Moeslim Abdurrahman and feminist activist Lies Marcoes-Natsir to declare, "women are the most serious victims of the sharia'ization agenda."[41]

Liberal Islam and Deconstruction of Shari'a

It is important to note here that the JIL is not the only group that has developed a liberal-progressive approach to religio-political thought. There are other groups that have promoted Islamic liberalism, such as Paramadina, LkiS (Lembaga Kajian Islam dan Sosial), Institute for Islamic and Social Studies, P3M (Perhimpunan Pengembangan Pesantren dan Masyarakat, or the Indonesian Society for Pesantren and Community Development), Lakpesdam, Lembaga Kajian dan Pengembangan Sumberdaya Manusia (Human Resource Development and Study Institute), Jaringan Intelektual Muda Muhammadiyah (Young Muhammadiyah Intellectuals Network, or JIMM), and International Center for Islam and Pluralism (ICIP). Indeed, these are generally non-government organization (NGO) groups committed to the idea of strengthening civil society by promoting the compatibility of Islam with democracy, human rights, pluralism, and gender equality values. In this regard, they have developed a collaboration with several funding agencies from the United States and other Western countries.[42] They can be grouped as the proponents of progressive-liberal Islam (PLI).

Interestingly enough, liberal Muslim scholars and activists in the Middle East have influenced the proponents of PLI, although they often use Western social science approaches in disseminating their ideas. Since its establishment in 1993, the LKiS has been very active in promoting Islamic liberalism, interfaith dialogue, and peaceful resolution to conflict.

Interestingly, this new generation of young Muslim intellectuals, especially those who have a background from the NU community, are mostly educated in *pesantren* (Islamic boarding schools) and have mastered Arabic. As a result, they are familiar with references or sources in Arabic as well. Several of them have also graduated from universities in the Middle East, such as Al-Azhar (Cairo), Jordan University, and others. This can be seen from book references, articles, and intellectual resources quoted by activists of liberal Islam. Accordingly, there is a process of intellectual transmission from the Middle East to Indonesia relating to the emergence and development of PLI in Indonesia as well.

On this last issue and others that have political significance, however, JIL stands as the most outspoken group. This aggressive stance of JIL activists has to be understood in the context of their reasonable dissatisfaction, if not outrage, over the perceived domination of discourse about Islam by the RCI groups. In its manifesto, the JIL declares the necessity for implementing *ijtihad* (the rational thinking of Islamic texts) in all aspects of human life. JIL believes that *ijtihad* is the main tenet that enables Islam to hold out through any season. JIL is an endeavor of Islam's interpretation based on the ethical-religious spirit of the Qur'an and the Sunnah. Consequently, JIL rejects interpretation of Islam based on the literal and textual meaning of the text. By using the ethical-religious spirit based on interpretation, JIL believes that Islam will live and grow creatively, in association with the universal "humanistic civilization." JIL is based on the notion *vis-à-vis* "truth" (in religious interpretation) as a *relative* thing, since an interpretation is "human activity" that is shackled in a certain context; *open*, since each form of interpretation contains a possibility of error, instead of being necessarily correct; and *plural*, since each religious interpretation, in one way or another, is a reflection of the interpreter's needs in incessantly changing times and places.[43]

From the above theological underpinning, the proponents of PLI groups would like to promote the liberal perspective concerning current religio-political issues. One of the most important issues raised by the RCI is to end the dualism of Muslims in response to religion and politics. In this regard, Luthfi Assyaukani points out the following facts:

> Since Muslims took their independence from colonialism at the end of first half of the 20th century, the problem of the relationship between religion and the state has become an unresolved puzzle. Liberal Islam, such as other renewal movements in Egypt and Turkey, tries to solve the dualism attitude by socializing a theology for the basis of the

modern state. This theology firmly declares the existing separation between religion and politics. Liberal Islam is convinced that the state is merely a profane creation of human beings. There is no specific regulation or obligation of Islamic teaching related to people's government.[44]

Such a liberal perspective on the issue of religion and politics is not something new in the arena of religious renewal movements in the Middle East. And Luthfi undoubtedly states that his concern with the idea of Islamic liberalism is strongly inspired by his personal experience when studying in Jordan. He saw Muslim activities and performances as well as read critically the works of ideologues such as Al Banna, Qutb, Said Hawwa, and others. He suggests that the ideas of Ikhwanul Muslimin and its ideologues are utopian. "It is easy to be heard, but it does not work in reality," he insists.[45] From this experience, Luthfi then studied critically the ideas of Middle Eastern Muslim thinkers such as Mahmud Thaha, Nasr Hamid Abu Zayd, Mohammad Arkoun, and others. He was impressed with their ideas.

Contrary to the RCI groups, which are greatly concerned with *shari'a* by promoting it expansively, proponents of PLI seriously maintain the agenda of deconstructing *shari'a*. To the proponents of PLI, the agenda of imposing *shari'a* is a form of Muslims' weakness in facing problems that have wedged them and a failure in solving them using rational methods. JIL coordinator Ulil Abshar Abdalla strongly argues that proposing *shari'a* as a means of solving any worldly problems is a form of laziness of thinking, and an escape from the problem. Ulil points out:

> The view that shari'a is a "complete package" and ready to use; a formula of God for solving problems in all millennium, is a form of the unknown and the inability to understand the sunnah of God itself. Proposing shari'a as a solution to all problems is a laziness of thinking, or worse is a way of escaping from the problems. It is a form of escapism using the law of God. Such escapism has become a source of Muslims' backwardness everywhere. I cannot receive this kind of "laziness", especially if it is covered by a reason that everything is to upholding the law of God. Don't forget: there is no law of God. The fact is that there is only the Sunnah of God, and the universal values belonging to all human beings.[46]

Interestingly, similar groups in Middle Eastern countries also influenced liberal Islam activists. These activists are also familiar with the ideas of liberal Muslim scholars who have been living overseas, especially in Europe and the United States. Therefore, they are familiar with the ideas of Ali Abdur Razik, Thaha Husin, Muhammad Said Al Asymawi, Muhammad Abid Al Jabiri, Hassan Hanafi, Nasr Hamid Abu Zaid, Mahmud Muhammad Thaha, Abdullahi Ahmed an Naim, Mohammad Arkoun, Bassam Tibi, and other liberal thinkers. They are also familiar with the ideas of feminist Muslims such as Fatima Mernissi, Nawal Al-Saadawi, Amina Wadud, and others. It is important to note that some works by these liberal Muslim thinkers have been translated into the Indonesian language as well.[47]

Contrary to the RCI demand for upholding the *shari'a*, the proponents of PLI strongly advocate the necessity of deconstructing the *shari'a* based on historical study. This is to counter the perception that the *shari'a* text is immutable. Zuhairi Misrawi, an activist of P3M, an NU-based Muslim NGO and alumnus of Al-Azhar University, Cairo, suggests that *shari'a* as a text is in fact a cultural product. It is historically constructed; hence, it cannot be entangled from the social-cultural background that constructed its nature in terms of cognition and psychology. During its inception, *shari'a* was entwined with the character of early Islam, which faced the political *tauhid* (oneness of Allah) culture. The first three centuries of Islam (seventh to ninth centuries) was a period of *shari'a* formation. Therefore, *shari'a* was connected with the territorial, geographical, and social-political culture in which it was established. Thus there emerges an idea to deconstruct the historicity of *shari'a*, and to find the inclusive and plural dimensions of Islam.[48]

To support the above notion, Misrawi quotes Naim's argument concerning the distinction between Qur'anic verses revealed during the Mecca and Medina periods. Naim argues that the first message of Islam, in Mecca, is more universal than the second message of Islam, in Medina. During the Mecca period the doctrines seemed to be egalitarian, pluralistic, and democratic. The Prophet existed as a common person. Qur'anic verses addressed "all human beings," reflecting a universal view that did not differentiate religions, ethnicities, and races. In contrast, during the Medina period, the doctrines seemed to be exclusive and homogeneous. The verses revealed address "the believers" as distinguished from "the non-believers." Hence, the text revealed during the Medina period was discriminative, exclusive, and fundamentalistic. This period is often quoted as a basis to justify the concept of the "Islamic state." Therefore, the Medina verses become the main target for deconstruction and are treated as exclusive and ambiguous in nature.[49]

In terms of Qur'anic knowledge, Misrawi supports Nasr Hamid Abu Zaid's views as derived from his famous book, *Mahfum al-Nash, Dirasah fi Ulum al Qur'an*. Zaid argued that the causes of revelation of Qur'anic verses (*asbab al-nuzul*) justify the historical dimension of the Qur'an. This proves that all religious products are related to their cultural context. Therefore, Nasr Hamid proposes that the *shari'a* law depends on a special cause, not on a general wording of the text (*al-'ibrah bi khusush al-sabab la bi 'umum al-lafzh*). This is in contrast with the majority of classical Islamic scholars, who perceive that the wording of the text is a given message from God; according to them, the wording of the text is immutable. The wording of the text for Islamic fundamentalists is the *shari'a* that has to be implemented comprehensively without any interpretations.[50]

In terms of respecting pluralism, Budhy Munawar Rahman of the Paramadina subscribes to a liberal interpretation of the Qur'anic verses. According to him, the notion of inter-religious tolerance and pluralism invokes the concept of "equality of believers before Allah."

> The notion of inter-religious tolerance and pluralism invokes the concept of "equality of believers before Allah". Even though we have different religions, the faith before Allah is equal since that faith involves our full and total comprehension of Allah, something which is deeper than formal religious practice and which can be termed *spiritual intelligence*. What is needed currently is an understanding that inter-religious pluralism is a notion that everyone who believes in God is *equal* before Allah because our God is the One God. From the Islamic theological aspect, it should not matter, for the Qur'an affirms that salvation in the hereafter *only* depends on whether someone believes in Allah, believes in the judgment day and performs good deeds. This is the core of the three "great" religious teachings — Judaism, Christianity and Islam. It is conveyed in Al Qur'an in surah al-Baqarah and surah al-Maidah (Q.S. 2:62 and 5:69).[51]

On the issue of gender equality, the proponent of PLI demonstrates that the gender relation concept is one of the objectives of *shari'a* (*maqashid al-syari'ah*).

Nasaruddin Umar is another proponent of liberal Islam.

> Islam introduces the gender relation concept as part of the objective of shari'a (*maqashid al-syari'ah*): that is in manifesting justice and righteousness (Q.S. al-Nahl, 16:90), security and peace (Q.S.Q.S.al-Nisa', 4:58), and in the call to righteousness and the prevention of evil (Q.S.Ali 'Imran, 3:104). These verses can be used as a framework for

analyzing gender relations in the Qur'an. Men and women have equal rights and duties in performing the role as caliph and slave. Regarding the professional role of women, there are no Qur'anic verses or hadiths, which are forbidden for women. On the contrary, Al Qur'an and hadiths mostly indicate that women are permitted to be professionals.[52]

Another young liberal Muslim intellectual and expert on gender issues, Syafiq Hasyim, urged Muslims to critically study conservative *fiqh* (Islamic law). In his important work, *Hal-Hal yang Terpikirkan tentang Isu-Isu Keperempuanan Dalam Islam* (The Unthought of Things about Women in Islam), Hasyim strongly criticizes the gender bias and patriarchal tendency of conventional *fiqh*. He offers a new analysis and methodology of *fiqh* related to women from an Islamic perspective. Furthermore, Hasyim insists on the necessity to deconstruct patriarchal *fiqh* related to polygamy, divorce, inheritance, and other issues. To Hasyim, the patriarchal *fiqh* formulated by traditional Muslim scholars is rife with gender bias and unfair treatment to women, which are definitely against the spirit of Islam that promotes equality and justice. Thus, he promotes the necessity to deconstruct patriarchal *fiqh*. Hasyim insists that the aim of Islam is to uphold justice in the world. Equality and balance as the principles of justice must be set up for developing a new *fiqh* using a perspective of gender fairness. What is meant by gender fairness is placing men and women in positions of equality, despite their biological differences.[53]

From the above discussion, there is no doubt that the young proponents of PLI are greatly concerned with the agenda of deconstructing *shari'a*, and arguing that the conventional interpretation of *shari'a* is no longer applicable in response to modern life and global phenomena. In this regard, it is fair to argue that their liberal approach to the *shari'a* and Islamic theological underpinnings is controversial and sometimes shocking to the majority of Muslim society. It is definitely against the mainstream opinion of *ulama*, the Muslim scholars and leaders who are mostly concerned with conventional or moderate perspectives.[54] In addition, those young PLI activists are, on a certain level, braver and sharper in disseminating their liberal ideas compared to their seniors in the 1970s. Therefore, the ideas of PLI often create polemics and debates that lead to tension, especially with the RCI groups, which tend to find greater support from the public. Interestingly enough, the proponents of PLI groups also use the roots of Islamic liberalism ideas from the Middle East, as can be seen from their references and intellectual role models.

Tension and the Future of the Contest

For the past four years, the contest between RCI and PLI has been in full swing. This contest has emerged as a religio-political discourse covered by print or electronic media affiliated either with the RCI or PLI, or through other public media. In this regard, the voice of RCI groups is usually published in *Sabili*, a radical Islamic magazine that has become a mouthpiece of RCI groups. According to surveys conducted by AC Nielsen, *Sabili* has the second largest circulation in Indonesia, after the women's magazine *Femina*. It reveals that *Sabili* publishes more than 100,000 copies of each edition. Other hard-line Islamic magazines — less radical than *Sabili* — are *Hidayatullah* (50,000 copies) and the Islamic women's magazine *Ummi* (75,000 copies). *Sabili* is often used as a reference by *da'i* or *mubaligh* (preachers) for disseminating their sermons in mosques and at religious gatherings. Beside these hard-line Islamic magazines, RCI groups have been publishing and selling books at cheap prices as well as distributing pamphlets and brochures to the public. Such publications are meant to widen their ideological underpinning and to counter PLI. By so doing, the RCI groups want to garner wide public support.[55]

Obviously, such discourse between the two conflicting groups is positive, provided that each group is able to set up a healthy discourse that enables an enrichment of public knowledge on religio-political issues. The problem lies in the fact that the RCI groups often use provocative language and tend to make claims of absolute truth concerning their ideas and actions, unlike the PLI groups. Consequently, people often misunderstand or receive misleading information on the ideas of PLI. Worse still, the RCI groups often use threats, which is dangerous for developing a healthy public discourse and freedom of thought and expression. This happened last year, when certain West Java clerics, on behalf of the Forum Ulama Ummat Indonesia (Indonesian Muslims Forum of Ulama, or FUUI), declared a death *fatwa* to Ulil Abshor Abdalla, coordinator of JIL. To critical Muslim intellectuals, such death *fatwas* are absurd. Therefore, most moderate Muslims were contemptuous of the death *fatwa* pronounced by the FUUI. Although some might not have been in favor of Ulil's ideas, they considered such a death *fatwa* to be against freedom of expression. Moderate Muslim leaders such as Syafi'i Maarif, the chairman of Muhamadiyah, also strongly criticized the death *fatwa*. "Muhammadiyah will never be stupid like those who declare the death *fatwa*," said M. Dawam Rahardjo, a Muslim intellectual of ICMI, to Maarif concerning the death *fatwa* on Ulil. Dawam reminds us that the *fatwa* was dangerous and could encourage someone to kill Ulil.[56]

The other case was the charge of MMI against JIL concerning advertisement of *"Islam Warna-Warni"* (The Multicolor Islam), broadcast by two leading Indonesian television stations, Rajawali Citra Televisi Indonesia (RCTI) and Surya Citra Televisi (SCTV). This advertisement was related to a one-minute message informing the public that there are various sects and groups within Islam. These groups have been growing rapidly since Indonesian politics became more open after 1998. The advertisement contained pictures showing the pluralism of Indonesian Muslims, indicating that there was no single Islam. The message was clear: a call for the necessity to respect religious plurality on the basis of mutual admiration. Thus, an attitude of tolerance toward other interpretations of Islam was asked to be honored. However, the MMI judged that such an advertisement was totally wrong and dangerous to the *ummah* (Muslim community). The MMI claimed that there was only one interpretation of Islam, and that plurality existed only within the *ummah* and was not linked to Islam itself as a religion. More important, the MMI put strong pressure on RCTI and SCTV to withdraw the advertisement, threatening that if they did not do so, they would face demonstrations. Faced with this reality, RCTI and SCTV decided to withdraw the "multicolor Islam" advertisement.[57]

Another issue relates to the strong protest and denunciation of the publication of the book *Fiqh Lintas Agama: Membangun Masyarakat Inklusif-Pluralis* (The Interfaith *Fiqh*: Building a Pluralist-Inclusive Society). This book, published by the Paramadina Foundation in collaboration with the Asia Foundation, is designed to radically change the old paradigm of *fiqh* and promote a new paradigm that enables Muslims to liberate themselves from the fetters of traditional *fiqh*.[58] It contains several controversial ideas related to interfaith marriage, interfaith inheritance, the rights and position of Jews and Christians, interfaith prayer, and other issues. The most controversial idea of the book is related to interfaith marriage, in which Muslim women are allowed to marry non-Muslim men. The authors argue that the prohibition against Muslim women marrying non-Muslim men is related to *ijtihad* (the process of interpreting Islamic ideas based on independent thought), and is committed within a certain context. It is specifically linked to Islamic *dakwah* during the early period of Islam. According to the authors, at that time the number of Muslims was small and insignificant compared to present times. Therefore, interfaith marriage was prohibited. The authors consider that it is now time to have a new *ijtihad* concerning this issue.

> Due to its position as a law based on ijtihad, it is possible to create a new opinion that Muslim women are allowed to marry with the non-Muslim men, or that inter-marriage is widely allowed, whatever a person's religion and beliefs. This is derived from the spirit of Qur'an itself.[59]

According to the authors, the spirit of marriage is related to the following: (1) the mission of the Qur'an that recognizes religious plurality as *sunatullah* (law of nature) that cannot be avoided, (2) the recognition that the aim of marriage is to develop love (*al-mawaddah*) and mercy (*al-rahmah*), and (3) the spirit of Islam is liberation, not oppression. The authors also suggest that the stages of what has been done in the Qur'an began with its prohibition against marrying apostate people. This then opens the path of marriage with *ahl al-kitab* (people of the book) as opening a stage of evolutionary liberation. "It is time for us to consider that other religious adherents are not to be regarded as second-class. They have to be treated as citizens."[60]

Having judged the above notions, the RCI groups strongly condemned the authors as infidels who had poisoned Muslims with secular and liberal ideas. The RCI groups also asked the Indonesian Ulama Council (MUI) to issue a *fatwa* prohibiting circulation of the book among Muslim society. The MUI did not release a statement banning the book; instead, it released a judgment that the book was against true Islamic teachings, and dangerous to the Muslim faith.

The latest tension was related to the idea of producing a recompilation of Islamic law. This was the job of *Tim Pengarusutamaan Gender* (the Gender Mainstreaming Team), established by the Department of Religious Affairs in 2002. Members of the team are Muslim scholars and experts on gender issues. Led by the noted female Muslim intellectual Dr. Musdah Mulia, the team worked for two years drafting a concept, namely, the Counter Legal Draft Compilation of Islamic Law. The draft contains a new approach to Islamic law based on the spirit of gender equality, pluralism, human rights, and democracy. Among the controversial issues raised in this draft are a ban on polygamy, and the allowance of interfaith marriage.[61]

Soon after the team publicly released the above draft, it received a strong reaction from the RCI groups. The latter judged the draft to be misleading and harassing of the *shari'a*. To oppose the draft, the RCI groups published books, articles, and pamphlets condemning the initiators and carried out public campaigns demanding the withdrawal of the draft.[62] Considering the dangerous implications, the Department of Religious Affairs finally decided to withdraw the draft, saying that it was counterproductive and not in accordance with the spirit of Indonesian Muslims.

From the above discussion, it is clear that the failure of the RCI's effort to revive the Jakarta Charter does not end the agenda of formalizing the *shari'a* on other levels of strategy. Instead of pressuring the government to incorporate the *shari'a* into the state constitution, the RCI groups are now using a "back-door strategy." This is a course of promoting the adoption of *shari'a* into positive law through hidden efforts, but it is often shocking to the public. This back-door strategy is aimed mainly at the inclusion of *shari'a* into law via certain proposed regulations. In this regard, there were two notable cases last year. The first was the planned amendments to criminal regulation drafted by the Department of Justice and Human Rights, which inserted the spirit of Islamic criminal law. The second was the regulations of inter-faith relations drafted by certain people from the Research and Development Sector, Ministry of Religious Affairs. After provoking a public debate, these two agendas failed to receive support from the public.[63]

It is important to note that in certain Indonesian provinces, local administration already has been incorporating *shari'a* into district regulations. This is the case in several regions and cities: Pamekasan; Madura (East Java); Maros, Sinjai, and Gowa (South Sulawesi); Cianjur, Garut, and Indramayu (West Java); and Padang (West Sumatra). It seems that these local administrations utilize the decisions of the central government in Jakarta, which exempt them from national directives and give them greater regional autonomy (*Otonomi Daerah*). These local administrations seem to believe that this autonomy translates into an opportunity to implement certain aspects of Islamic law, or *shari'a*. In addition, the central government has granted regions autonomy since 2000, even while officially administering Islamic jurisprudence.[64]

The inclusion of *shari'a* within local administrations is mainly related to regulations concerning Muslims' obligations in their daily lives, such as the wearing of Islamic dress; the regulation, collection, and distribution of *zakat* (tithe); performing prayers and reciting the Qur'an; and the allocation of more time for religious education in schools. However, there are also certain strict regulations that limit women's activities, such as requiring them to use the veil, and prohibiting them from going out after 9 p.m. unless accompanied by their *muhrim* (close relatives of the opposite sex). These restrictions caused several problems in Aceh and Padang after local RCI groups raided the homes of women who were considered to have violated the regulations. Although such regulations are not officially included by local administrations, some conservative *ulama* and Muslim puritan activists tend to endorse, or at least allow, these RCI groups to commit such acts.

From the above, it is clear that the RCI groups have changed their strategy. Previously, they advocated imposing *shari'a* within state constitutions. Currently, they maintain an agenda of "creeping shari'aization" in Indonesia. This means that the agenda for the formalization of the *shari'a* is to be gradual, but it is supported in sophisticated ways. The problem lies in the fact that the "shari'aization" agenda often manipulates religious sentiments or politicizes issues so that they will appeal to ordinary Muslims. Most important, such tendencies neglect the existence of Indonesia as a pluralistic society. Although Muslims form the majority of the Indonesian populace, Indonesia is *de facto* a pluralistic society, with religious, ethnic, and cultural diversity. Therefore, any laws and regulations should be based on the recognition of pluralism, human rights, democracy, and respect for non-Muslim groups.

Interestingly, in the arena of national politics the issue of *shari'a* seems to have declined. This can be seen from the 2004 legislative general election and the first stage of the presidential race. It seems that the issue of *shari'a*, at least on the national level, is not popular anymore. There was no public response or support for Islamic parties campaigning on *shari'a* issues, such as the PPP and PBB. They did not receive support, and their votes declined significantly. In the 2004 general election, PPP gained only 8.2 per cent of the votes, and PBB 2.6 per cent. The only Islamic party that was able to increase its vote was PKS (Justice and Welfare Party), gaining 7.2 per cent. Many observers were not only surprised with the performance of PKS, but also worried about PKS and its political agenda concerning shari'aization. However, one should note that the occasional wins of PKS during the 2004 general election were totally unrelated to *shari'a*. During the 2004 general election campaign, the PKS never campaigned about *shari'a*. Rather, it campaigned about a "clean and concerned" society, promoting anti-corruption, good governance, and the necessity for concern with needy people. All of these issues had nothing to do with *shari'a*; they were related to common and "secular" issues. It is also important to note that during the second term of the presidential election in July 2004, there was not a single issue dealing with *shari'a*. No candidate for president or vice-president raised issues of religion, let alone talked about *shari'a*. Their campaigns were mostly related to economic recovery, maintaining political stability, upholding the rule of law, and the like.[65] In this respect, Indonesian Muslims seemed to be realistic, realizing that the Susilo Bambang Yudhoyono-M. Jusuf Kalla team was more promising than other candidates in dealing with these crucial problems. As a result, this team was able to gain more than 60 per cent of the votes in the September 2004 presidential election.

Conclusion

From the above discussion, it is safe to argue that political Islam in post-Soeharto Indonesia is colored by the competition between the RCI and PLI in trying to win people's support. It seems that the contest between the two will continue into the future, considering that the two groups both have the capacity to accomplish much in the public sphere. It is clear that the main agenda of RCI groups — imposing *shari'a* — will have little prospect in the future. Indonesian Muslims are realistic in solving their problems and seem to have disregarded the *shari'a* imposed by the RCI groups. Contrary to the dream of RCI groups that the *shari'a* is a panacea, Indonesian Muslims consider that *shari'a* would not be able to solve Indonesia's multidimensional crisis. More importantly, Indonesian Muslims admit that the extreme views of RCI groups have led to justifications for the use of violence. In this regard, Ricklefs rightly argues that radical Islamic movements have no real prospect of winning political power in Indonesia.[66]

The big question is whether Susilo Bambang Yudhoyono will be able to overcome Indonesia's ongoing multidimensional crisis during his presidency. If he fails to lead Indonesia toward becoming a just, democratic, and prosperous nation, the demand for the implementation of *shari'a* will be much more vocal and extremely dangerous in the future. History has shown that social injustice, political uncertainty, and lawlessness make a society vulnerable to the rise of religious bigotry and militancy — in Indonesia or elsewhere.

Notes

* An earlier version of this essay has already appeared in T. N. Srinivasan, ed., The Future of Secularism (Delhi: Oxford University Press, 2007). Part of this article is derived from the report of ICIP's research project titled "Islam and Peace Building in Indonesia: An Analysis of Radical Movements and Their Implication for Security Development Prospects," funded by the Japan International Cooperation Agency. I thank our researchers (Ahmad Najib Burhani, Kamami Zada, Noor Hidayah, Agus Muhammad, and Edy Sudarjat) for their assistance in providing valuable information and material related to this article. However, I alone bear responsibility for any errors or imperfections.
1. Cited from M. C. Ricklefs, "Islamizing Indonesia: Religion and Politics in Singapore's Giant Neighbour," public lecture organized by Asia Research Institute, National University of Singapore, Asian Civilisations Museum, 23 September 2004, 8–9.
2. For a fuller account on the genealogies of radical Islam in Indonesia, see Martin van Bruinessen, "Genealogies of Islamic Radicalism in Indonesia," *South Asia Research* 10 (2) (2002).
3. See, for instance, ICG Asia Briefing *Al Qaeda in Southeast Asia: The Case of the "Ngruki Network" in Indonesia*, 8 August 2002; ICG Asia Report *Jamaah Islamiyah in Southeast Asia: Damaged but Still Dangerous*, 26 August 2003; Maria Ressa, *Seeds of Terror: An Eyewitness Acccount of al Qaeda's Newest Center of Operations in Southeast Asia* (New York: Free Press, 2003); Greg Barton, *Indonesia's Struggle: Jamaah Islamiyah and the Soul of Islam* (Sydney: University of New South Wales Press, 2004).
4. See "Abu Bakar Basyir," *Tempo Interaktif*, 17 April 2004; "*Diperiksa dalam Kasus Terorisme, Basyir Bungkam*," *Kompas*, 29 April 2004; "*Ustadz Abu Bakar Ba'asyir: Kezhaliman Akan terus Saya Lawan*," <www.hidayatullah.com>, 16 June 2004; Fauzan Al-Anshari, "*Riba Politik*," <www.majelis.mujahidin.or.id/kolom/siyasah/riba_politik>, 11 February 2004.
5. Ihsan Ali Fauzi, "Political Islam and Democracy in Indonesia: A Closer Look at Liberal Islam," *ICIP's Electronic Journal* (<www.icipglobal.org>) 1, 2 (August–December 2004): 2–3.
6. See Ahmad Gaus, "How Liberal Can You Go?" *Kompas*, 13 December 2002, republished in Dzulmanni, ed., *Islam Liberal dan Fundamental: Sebuah Pertarungan Wacana* (Yogyakarta: Elsaq Press), 79–84. For a comparison, see M. Kamal Hassan, *Muslim Intellectual Responses to "New Order" Modernization in Indonesia* (Kuala Lumpur: Dewan Bahasa dan Pustaka, 1980).
7. See Nazih Ayubi, *Political Islam: Religion and Politics in the Arab World* (London and New York: Routledge, 1993), 63–4; Muslim scholars who are concerned with this first paradigm are Sayyid Qutb (Egypt), Abu A'la al-

Maududi (Pakistan), and Abu Hasan Ali al-Nadvi (India). For a comparative study on this paradigm, see James Piscatory, *Islam in a World of Nation States* (London: Cambridge University Press, 1986); John L. Esposito, *Voice of Resurgent Islam* (New York: Oxford University Press, 1983); Munawir Sjadzali, *Islam dan Tata Negara: Ajaran, Sejarah, dan Pemikiran* (Jakarta: UI Press, 1990).

8. Muhammad Salim al'Awwa, *Fi al-nizam al siyasi li al-dawla al-Islamiyya* (Cairo: al-Maktab al-Misri al Hadith, 1983), 22, cited from Bassam Tibi, "The Idea of an Islamic State and the Call for the Implementation of the Shari'a," partially republished by Middle East Information Center from *The Challenge of Fundamentalism: Political Islam and the New World Disord*er. Available at <http://middleeastinfo.org/article4480.html>, 1–16 [accessed 9 June 2004].

9. Husain Fawzi al-Najjar, *al_Islam wa al-Siyasa: Bahth fi Usul al-Nazariyya al-Siyasiyya wa Nizam al-hukm fi al-Islam* (Cairo: Dar al-Sha'b, 1977), 74, cited from Tibi, "The Idea of an Islamic State," 6. For a fuller concept of this paradigm, see, for instance, Qamaruddin Khan, *Political Concepts in the Qur'an* (Lahore: Islamic Book Foundation, 1982), 75–6; Fazlur Rahman, *Islam* (New York, Chicago, and San Francisco: Holt, Rinehart, and Winston, 1966), 101; Mohammed Arkoun, "The Concept of Authority in Islamic Thought," in Klauss and Mehdi Mozaffari, eds., *Islam: State and Society* (London: Curzon Press, 1988), 70–1; M. Din Syamsuddin, "Islamic Political Thought and Cultural Revival in Modern Indonesia," *Studia Islamika* 2, 4 (1995): 51–68.

10. Al-Ashmawi, *Usul al-Shari'a* (Cairo: Maktabat Madbuli, 1983), 53, 93, cited from Tibi, "The Idea of an Islamic State."

11. Al-Ashmawi, *Usul al-Shari'a*, 89, cited from Tibi, "The Idea of an Islamic State," 8.

12. See Ruth McVey, "Faith as the Outsider: Islam in Indonesian Politics," in James Piscatori (ed.), *Islam in the Political Process* (Cambridge: Cambridge University Press, 1983), 199.

13. M. Syafi'i Anwar, *Pemikiran dan Aksi Islam Indonesia: Studi tentang Cendekiawan Muslims Orde Baru, 1966–1993* (Jakarta: Paramadina, 1995). I have discussed the political history of Soeharto's New Order Islamic Politics in my dissertation, which was submitted to the University of Melbourne (December 2004) with the title "The State and Political Islam in Indonesia: A Study of the State Politics and Modernist Muslim Leaders' Political Behavior, 1966–1998."

14. Ibid. For a useful account of "regimists Islam," see Robert W. Hefner's thoughtful work, *Civil Islam: Muslims and Democratization in Indonesia* (Princeton and Oxford: Princeton University Press, 2000), 149–50.

15. See Bahtiar Effendy, *Islam and the State in Indonesia* (Singapore: ISEAS, 2003), 202–22; Arskal Salim, *Partai Islam dan Relasi Agama-Negara* (Jakarta: Pusat Penelitian IAIN Jakarta, 1999), 7–12.

16. The Islamic parties that gained seats in the 1999 general election were PPP (58 seats), PBB (13 seats), PK (7 seats), PNU (5 seats), PP (1 seat), PPII Masyumi (1 seat), and PKU (1 seat). There are two parties often grouped by observers as "Islamic parties" that gained significant votes — PKB (51 seats) and PAN (34 seats). If these two parties are included, the total number of seats gained by Islamic parties is 173, or 37.5 per cent of the vote. However, both PKB and PAN are reluctant to be grouped as Islamic parties. Without these two, Islamic parties gained only 88 seats, or 17.8 per cent of the votes. See Effendy, *Islam and the State in Indonesia*, 214.
17. For a more detailed account of Abdurrahman Wahid's thoughts, see Greg Barton, *Gagasan Islam Liberal di Indonesia: Pemikiran Neo-Modernisme Nurcholish Madjid, Djohan Effendi, Ahmad Wahib*, dan *Abdurahman Wahid* (Jakarta: Paramadina, 1999), 325–429, 488–501.
18. The best account of the conflict and religious violence in Ambon is given in Sukidi Mulyadi, "Violence under the Banner of Religion: The Case of Laskar Jihad and Laskar Kristus," *Studia Islamika*, 75–109.
19. Suzaina Abdul Kadir, "Indonesia's 'Democratization Dilemma': Political Islam and the Prospects for Democratic Consolidation," paper presented to the conference on "Consolidating Indonesia's Democracy," Ohio State University, 11–13 May, 15–8. See also Jamhari, "Mapping Radical Islam in Indonesia," *Studia Islamika* 10, 3 (2003): 10–2.
20. See M. Syafi'i Anwar, "Developing Social Fiqh: An Alternative to Counter 'Creeping Shariahization'?" Words from the Editor, *ICIP's Electronic Journal* (<www.icipglobal.org>) 1, 1 (January–April 2004).
21. M. Amien Rais, "*Gerakan-gerakan Islam International dan Pengaruhnya bagi Gerakan Islam di Indonesia*," *Prisma*, No. Extra, year XIII (1984): 23–39.
22. See John Esposito, *Islamic Revivalism* (Washington, D.C.: American Institute for Islamic Affairs, School of International Service, The American University, 1985), 1.
23. Effendi, *Islam and the State in Indonesia*, 162–3.
24. Mona Abaza, *Pendidikan Islam Dan Pergeseran Orientasi Studi Kasus Alumni Al-azhar*, translated by S. Harlinah (Jakarta: LP3ES, 1999), 97.
25. *Usroh* is a *dakwah* system derived from Ikhwanul Muslimin for improving the faith, integrity, and total commitment of its cadres and members. The implementation of *usroh* was based on the decision released by the Congress of Ikhwanul Muslimin in 1943. The purpose of implementing *usroh* was to fulfill the needs of a system that would be able to respond to the *imtidad ufuqy* (the horizontal development) and the *numuw tarbawy* (educative development) of Ikhwanul Muslimin members when faced with political pressure.
26. The result of this second phase of transmission was more effective, as can be seen from the paradigm and activities of Muslim student activists in some universities. There was a strong tendency for the *dakwah* activities of Muslim

students on some campuses to be dominated in spirit and orientation by the promotion of Muslim unity and self-confidence to challenge the hegemony of Western civilization. Although the form and substance of the Islamic resurgence varied from country to country, the main theme was always the same, namely, disenchantment with and rejection of Western civilization.

27. "Islam, Radicalism, and Peace Building ...," 94–6.
28. Ibid.
29. Ibid.
30. Muhammad Imdadun, *"Transmisi Gerakan Revivalisme Islam Timur Tengah Ke Indonesia 1980–2002: Studi tentang Gerakan Tarbiyah dan Hizbut Tahrir Indonesia*," master's thesis, University of Indonesia (2003), 115.
31. Ibid., 115–8.
32. Anwar, *Pemikiran dan Aksi Islam Indonesia*, 121–42.
33. Maarif argued that history shows the Jakarta Charter was able to survive only 52 days during the independence period. "It will waste time and energy to debate the Jakarta Charter. We have to be realistic that Indonesia as a nation-state contains a pluralist society. It is almost impossible to impose the Jakarta Charter," he said. Muzadi shares Maarif's view, insisting that the demand to revive the Jakarta Charter was also a negation of the spirit of *shari'a* for upholding justice and respecting Indonesia's pluralist society. See *Republika* (7 September 2001); see also *"Menawarkan Substansi Syariat Islam,"* interview with A. Syafi'i Maarif, *Tashwirul Afkar*, no. 12 (2002): 105–6.
34. See A. Yusuf Ali, *The Holy Qur'an: Translation and Commentary* (Durban: Islamic Propagation Center International, 1934), 1st edition, 50–1.
35. See "Islam and Peace Building in Indonesia ...," 36–44. Based on an interview with Irfan S. Awwas (chairman of MMI), Yogyakarta, 28 July 2004; Habib Rizieq (chairman of FPI), Jakarta, 5 August 2004. See also Hartono Ahmad Jaiz, *Bahaya Islam Liberal* (Jakarta: Pustaka Al Kaustar, 2002), 82–6.
36. Adian Husaini and Nuim Hidayat, *Islam Liberal: Sejarah, Konsepsi, Penyimpangan dan Jawabannya* (Jakarta: Gema Insani Press, 2002), 82–3.
37. Ibid., 96–106.
38. Khamami Zada, *Islam Radikal: Pergulatan Ormas-Ormas Islam Garis Keras di Indonesia* (Bandung: Teraju, 2002), 136–44. See also Adian Husaini, *Presiden Wanita: Pertaruhan Sebuah Negeri Muslim* (Jakarta: Darul Falah, 2001), 77–85.
39. Kamala Chandrakirana and Yuniyanti Chuzaifah, "The Battle Over a 'New' Indonesia: Religious Extremism, Democratization and Women's Agency in a Plural Society," *ICIP's Electronic Journal* (<www.icipglobal.org>) 1, 2 (August–December 2004): 16.
40. Ibid.
41. See Lies Marcoes-Natsir, "The Brittleness of a Woman's Womb in Shari'ah," *ICIP's Electronic Journal* (<www.icipglobal.org>) 1, 1 (January–April 2004):

1–5. See also interview with Moeslim Abdurrahman, "*Korban Pertama Penerapan Syariat Islam adalah Perempuan*," in Luthfi Assyaukanie, ed., *Wajah Liberal Islam di Indonesia* (Jakarta: Jaringan Islam Liberal, 2002), 109–13.

42. Most NGOs associated with the PLI groups receive partial or significant financial support from funding institutions such as the Asia Foundation, the Ford Foundation, the European Commission, the United Nations Development Program, and others.
43. See the website of Liberal Islam Network, "About Us," <www.islamlib.com/en/aboutus.php>.
44. Luthfi Assyaukanie, "Islam Liberal: Pandangan Partisipan," in Assyaukanie, *Wajah Liberal Islam di Indonesia*, xxv.
45. Ibid., xxiii.
46. Ulil Abshar Abdalla, "*Menyegarkan Kembali Pemahaman Islam*," *Kompas*, 18 November 2002. This article created lengthy polemics and public debates between proponents and opponents of liberal Islam ideas. It was republished as a book titled *Islam Liberal and Fundamental: Sebuah Pertarungan Wacana*, ed. Dzulmanni (Yogyakarta: Elsaq Press, 2003), 7. Former President Wahid wrote the book's epilogue, titled "*Ulil Abshar Abdalla dengan Liberalismenya*," 257–62.
47. Works by these liberal Muslim scholars have been translated and published by LkiS, Paramadina, Lakpesdam, JIL, ICIP, and other PLI groups. The readers of liberal Islam books are mostly students and young Muslims. The number of liberal Islam books published by PLI groups is still small compared to the huge number of radical Islam books published by RCI groups.
48. Zuhairi Misrawi, "*Dekonstruksi Syariat: Jalan Menuju Desakralisasi, Reinterpretasi, dan Depolitisasi*," *Tashwirul Afkar*, Edition no. 12 (2002): 15–7.
49. Ibid.
50. Ibid.
51. See Budhy Munawar-Rahman, "The Theological Basis of Inter-Religious Brotherhood," Liberal Islam Network, English Edition Web (<www.islamlib.com>), 19 August 2001.
52. Nasaruddin Umar, "Women's Liberation Theology," Liberal Islam Network, English Edition Web (<www.islamlib.com>), 29 July 2001.
53. For Syafiq Hasyim's fuller account on the deconstruction of patriarchal *fiqh* related to women's rights, see his book *Hal-hal Yang Terpikirkan tentang Perempuan dalam Islam* (Bandung: Mizan, 2001). This book received an award from its publisher (Mizan). It will be re-published in English by the ICIP (forthcoming).
54. For a serious critical account of PLI ideas, see Haidar Bagir, "*Beberapa Pertanyaan untuk Ulil Abshar Abdalla*," *Kompas* (5 December 2002). See

also the interview with Din Syamsuddin, "*Ulil Melakukan Dekonstruksi Tanpa Merekonstruksi*," *Panjimas* (26 December 2002–8 January 2003): 36–7.
55. Agus Muhammad, "*Jihad Lewat Tulisan: Kisah Sukses Majalah* Sabili *dengan Berbagai Iron*," *Jurnal Pantau*, Yer II, no. 015 (July 2001), <www.pantau.ir.id/txt/15/06.html>. See also Chandrakirana and Chuzaifah, "The Battle Over a 'New' Indonesia," 16.
56. See *Gatra* (21 December 2002); see also "*Tokoh Baru, Pemain Baru*," Main Report of *Panjimas* magazine on JIL and the death fatwa, *Panjimas* (26 December 2002–8 January 2003): 22–7.
57. Ulil Abshar Abdalla, "*Islam Warna Warni*," <www.islamlib.com>, published 11 August 2002.
58. Mun'im A. Sirry, ed., *Fiqh Lintas Agama: Membangun Masyarakat Inklusif-Pluralis* (Jakarta: Yayasan Wakaf Paramadina, 2004). The writers of this book are: Nurcholish Madjid, Kautsar Azhari Noer, Komaruddin Hidayat, Masdar F. Mas'udi, Zainul Kamal, Zuhairi Misrawi, Budhy Munawar Rahman, Ahmad Gaus, and Mun'im A. Sirry. These Muslim intellectuals are widely regarded as proponents of PLI. This book was fist printed in October 2003. The publisher stated that the June 2004 printing of this book was its fifth edition.
59. Ibid., 164.
60. Ibid., 164–5.
61. Tim Pengkajian Kompilasi Hukum Islam, Pokja Pengarus Utamaan Gender Departemen Agama, "*Usulan Naskah Revisi Kompilasi Hukum Islam*," first draft, undated. Dr. Musdah Mulia is a lecturer at State Islamic University and senior researcher in the Research and Development Division, Department of Religious Affairs. He is also Secretary General of the Indonesian Conference on Religion and Peace.
62. For RCI's strong protest and condemnation of the draft, see "*Pikiran Sesat Kuasai Departemen Agama*," *Sabili* (5 November 2004): 16–36.
63. Anwar, "Developing Social Fiqh."
64. See "*Syari'at Islam yang Bagaimana*," *Panji Masyarakat* (27 November–12 December 2002), cited by Effendy in *Islam and the State in Indonesia*, 221.
65. M. Syafi'i Anwar, "The 2004 General Election and Presidential Race: Towards the Future of Indonesian Politics," notes for a roundtable seminar on "The 2004 General Election in Indonesia," organized by Indonesian Studies Group, National University of Singapore, 28 April 2004.
66. M. C. Ricklefs, "Islamizing Indonesia," 6–7.

Contributors

Mona Abaza is an associate professor of sociology at the American University of Cairo, Egypt.

M. Syafi'i Anwar is the executive director of ICIP (International Center for Islam and Pluralism), Jakarta, Indonesia.

Timothy P. Barnard is an associate professor in the Department of History at the National University of Singapore.

Ulrike Freitag is the director of the Zentrum Moderner Orient (Centre for Modern Oriental Studies) and professor of Islamic studies at the Free University, both in Berlin.

Michael Gilsenan is the David B. Kriser Chair in the Humanities and former chair of the Middle Eastern Studies Department at New York University (USA).

Nico J. G. Kaptein is the secretary of the Islamic Studies Program at Leiden University and research coordinator of the program "The Dissemination of Religious Authority in 20th Century Indonesia" at the International Institute for Asian Studies (IIAS), Leiden, Netherlands.

Michael Laffan is an assistant professor of history at Princeton University (USA).

Sumit K. Mandal is a senior research fellow at the Institute of Malaysian and International Studies (IKMAS), Universiti Kebangsaan Malaysia.

Mohammad Redzuan Othman is an associate professor and chair of the History Department, University of Malaya, Kuala Lumpur, Malaysia.

M. C. Ricklefs is a professor in the Department of History at the National University of Singapore. He was formerly the director of the Research School of Pacific and Asian Studies, Australian National University, and has held positions at the School of Oriental and African Studies (University of London) and Monash University.

John T. Sidel is the Sir Patrick Gillam Professor of International and Comparative Politics at the London School of Economics and Political Science (UK).

Eric Tagliacozzo is an associate professor of history and Asian studies at Cornell University (USA).

Moshe Yegar has taught the history of Southeast Asia at the Hebrew University, Jerusalem. He is a research fellow at the Harry S. Truman Research Institute, Jerusalem.

Index

'Ab al-Ra' ûf al-Sinkilî al Jâwî, 41, 63
Abdullah Munshi, 66, 70–1, 75, 77, 90
Abdurrahman Wahid, 357–8
Abu Sayyaf, 275, 279, 285–7, 310, 312, 345
Abû Zayd, 27–30
Aceh, 18, 24, 40, 43–4, 46–7, 60, 62, 71, 90–1, 110, 137, 149, 181, 269, 293, 305, 378
Africa, 19, 30–1, 33, 35, 46, 56, 199, 208, 266
  East, 240, 249
  North, 260
Akhbar al-Sin wa al-Hind, 93
al-Bîrûnî, 27, 29, 55, 56
al-Fansûrî, Hamza, 40–2, 61
al-Idrîsî, Muhammad bin Muhammad al-Sharif, 19, 29–33, 36, 42, 45–6, 56–7
Al-Irsjad, 5, 159, 162–70, 290
al-Kûrânî, Ibrâhîm b. Hasan, 41, 61, 63
Al-Qaeda, 8, 275–9, 286, 304, 308, 310, 312, 351
Arab
  community, 5, 163, 165–6, 169, 191
  diaspora, 251, 253, 267
Arabian Peninsula, 2, 93, 144, 146, 157, 236, 362
Asian Press Board (APB), 252–3, 259

Barus, 27, 40–1, 44, 54–5, 57
Batavia, 98, 113–4, 139, 142, 144–5, 149, 158, 160, 162–3, 165–6, 177, 186, 191, 202
"below the winds", 18, 45–7
Braudel, Fernand, 1, 251, 268
Buddhism, 1, 19–20, 49, 52

Cambodia, 21, 23, 28, 30–1, 35, 57, 92
Cairo, 5–6, 17, 39, 45, 63, 84, 92, 104, 159, 166, 171, 194, 253, 283, 319
Champa, 20–2, 28, 32, 57
Chaiya, 21, 25–6, 57
  inscription, 22, 52
Chatib Ali, 6, 182, 184, 187, 188–9
China, 1, 3, 11, 17–21, 24–5, 28–32, 34–8, 49, 52, 57–8, 63, 84–6, 93, 201, 207, 255, 257, 288
Cholas, 31–3, 53, 57
Christianity, 8, 112, 129, 278–9, 304, 311, 372
Cold War, 258, 275, 311
colonial
  -ism, 4, 147
  government, 12, 149, 209
  society, 5–6
  state, 4, 135, 146
Communist Party of Indonesia (PKI), 257–8, 293

decolonization, 10
Djamiat Cheir, 158, 162, 164, 166–7
Dutch East India Company, 159
Dutch East Indies, *see* Dutch Indies
Dutch Indies, 5, 139, 146, 290, *see also* Netherlands Indies

*fatwa*s, 39, 46, 61, 63, 176, 180–1, 183–8, 190–1, 194–5, 374–6
Faxian, 28

Gerakan Pembaruan Pemikiran Islam (GPPI), 352
globalization, 180, 235
Golkar, 294, 297–9, 301

Index

Habibie, B. J., 297–9, 301, 307, 309, 349, 356–7
Hadhramaut, *see* Hadramaut
Hadhrami, *see* Hadrami
Hadith, 181–2, 186–7, 194, 365, 373
Hadramaut, 3, 5–7, 35, 39, 41, 58, 76, 83, 86, 88, 93–8, 103, 105, 157, 160–1, 169–71, 201, 203, 211–2, 222–3, 226, 230, 232, 236–40, 264, 268, 290
Hadrami(s), 2, 9–10, 47–8, 83, 95–8, 106, 149, 157–9, 161, 164–5, 171, 175, 200–4, 208, 210, 218, 220, 222–3, 226, 234, 236–8, 240, 250–1, 262, 267–8, 290, 305
  community, 7, 236
  diaspora, 1, 6, 201, 211, 234
Haji Abdullah Ahmad, 6, 183–5, 187, 189
Hajj, 5, 12, 40, 65–7, 69, 72–3, 75–6, 78–80, 114–9, 123, 133, 135, 137–44, 146–9, 178–9, 186, 235, 283, 290, 319
Hajjis, 5, 10, 69, 76, 114–8, 120–2, 124–5, 137, 139, 141, 143–7, 150, 179
Hejaz, 1–2, 4, 41, 65, 67, 70–4, 76, 136–50, 160, 222, 290
Hikayat Hang Tuah, 81, 94
Hikayat Merong Mahawangsa, 90
Hikayat Raja-raja Pasai, 43, 88–9
Holy Cities, 138–9, 141–5

Iberian Peninsula, 86, 260
Ibn Battûta/Ibn Battuta, 36, 38–9, 59–60, 89, 94
Ibn Khurdâdhbih, 25–7, 31, 55, 93
India, 1, 7, 17–9, 21–2, 24–6, 28, 32–4, 38–9, 49, 52, 58, 71, 82, 84–5, 87, 89, 92–3, 199, 201, 239–40, 344
Indian Ocean, 1, 4–5, 7–8, 10–1, 19, 24, 28–31, 33–9, 44–6, 56, 58, 83, 85–6, 93–4, 100, 142, 146–9, 157, 207–8, 223, 235–6, 290
Indies, 137, 139–42, 144, 146–7, 149, 166–7, 171, 202, 288–92, 305, *see also* Dutch Indies *and* Netherlands Indies

Indonesia, 8–10, 92, 110, 112, 116, 129, 157, 161, 191, 193, 225, 251–7, 262, 264, 267–8, 270, 275–80, 282–4, 287–8, 291–300, 302–12, 315, 319, 336–7, 339, 341, 346–52, 354–7, 360–6, 369, 374–5, 378–9
Indonesian Archipelago, 2, 287–9, 292, 303, 305, 336
International Crisis Group (ICG), 277
Islam, 2–12, 38, 42, 47–9, 66–7, 69, 76, 78–9, 83–92, 94–6, 99, 103, 105, 111–4, 117, 122, 125–6, 129, 135–6, 144, 148, 157, 159, 162–3, 169, 179–83, 185–6, 189–91, 225, 250, 254, 256–7, 260, 266–7, 269, 277–83, 286–93, 295, 297–300, 302, 304–7, 309–12, 319–20, 324–6, 328, 338, 341, 349–57, 360, 364–6, 368–72, 375–6, 379, 384
Islamic
  culture, 41
  modernism, 169–70
  Research Council, 252–3, 259
  transnationalism, 8
  world, 4, 127, 129–30, 255, 266, 278, 289–90, 296, 311, 349
Islamization, 4, 38, 43, 86–8, 90, 99, 287
Isthmus of Kra, 21–2, 25, 27, 30–1, 45, 48, 54

Japanese occupation, 252, 291
Jakarta, 7, 223, 225, 250–4, 257, 259, 268–9, 276–7, 293, 297, 301–4, 306, 308–9, 312, 350, 377
  Charter, 356–7, 364–5, 377, 383
Jambi, 22, 36, 52, 63
Jaringan Islam Liberal (JIL), 351, 368–70, 374–5, 384
Java, 3–6, 17–8, 20–5, 28, 32–9, 42–3, 47, 49, 51–3, 57, 59, 98, 111–7, 119, 121, 124–7, 129–30, 132, 144, 156–61, 163, 165–8, 170–1, 192, 201, 212, 222, 225, 236–8, 249, 276, 288–9, *see also* Jawa, Jâwa, Yava, *and* Yavadvîpa

Jawa, 37, 188, *see also* Java, Jâwa, Yava, *and* Yavadvîpa
Jâwa, 3, 17–8, 20–1, 23, 34–5, 37–8, 40, 42, 46–9, 58–9, 136, *see also* Java, Jâwa, Yava, *and* Yavadvîpa
Jawah, 70, 72–3, 79, 180, 184–5
Jawi, 42, 61–2, 70–4, 90, 188, 290, 292, *see also* Jâwî
Jâwî, 3, 17, 24, 38, 40–3, 47–8, *see also* Jawi
Jeddah, 39, 70–3, 88–9, 97, 114, 116, 138–9, 142–3, 153, 187, 263
Jemaah Islamiyah, 275–7, 287, 301, 308, 310, 312
Johor, 66–9, 225

Kalâh/Kalah, 25, 27, 31, 54, 85–6, 101
Kaum
  Muda, 6, 182–5, 187–91
  Tua, 6, 182–90
Kedah, 54, 57, 84, 86–7, 90, 97, 101
Kitâb al-masâlik wa-I-mamâlik, 24, 26–7, 93
Kitab al-Qawanin as-sjarijjah, 161–2
Kitâb al-tafhim, 29
Kitab Dur al-Mazlum, 89
Koran, 242, 320, 323, 327, *see also* Qur'an
Kota Kapur inscription, 23

Laskar Jihad, 275, 287, 302–5, 308, 310, 350, 357–8, 367
Lasykar Jihad, *see* Laskar Jihad
longue durée, 1, 3, 9–10, 18, 221, 250–1

Majapahit, 36–7
Malacca, 39, 44, 67, 219, 234, *see also* Melaka
Malay
  Archipelago, 41, 201–2, 222, 230, 236
  Communist Party (MCP), 335
  community, 67, 98
  -Indonesian Archipelago, 85, 103, 136, 170, 177–8, 181–2
  Peninsula, 2–3, 20–2, 37, 50, 84, 86–7, 93, 99, 101, 276, 328, 335
  polity, 66–7, 69
  rulers, 67, 78
  society, 4, 77, 83, 92, 103, 210
  states, 96, 106, 210
  sultan(s), 66–7, 69–71, 79–80
  World, 3–4, 46, 67, 69, 76, 83–4, 86–91, 94–5, 105
Malaya, 3, 91–2, 94, 96–8, 105, 144, 249, 288, 290
Malaysia, 94, 98, 157, 236, 275, 277, 279, 282–5, 308–9, 311, 319, 322, 328–9, 334–6, 339, 341, 345–6
Malayu, 22–4, 28, 31, 36
-Jambi, 37, *see also* Melayu-Jambi
Marco Polo, 35–6, 38, 42, 89, 94, 261
Marcos regime, 260–2, 264, 281, 284
Maulana Abu Bakar, 89–90
Mecca, 5–6, 17, 40, 47, 65–7, 69–70, 72–6, 79, 89, 92, 111–2, 114–7, 122–3, 125–9, 135–6, 138, 140–5, 148–9, 153, 156, 160, 168–9, 178–80, 182, 184, 187–91, 255–6, 269, 289, 291, 297, 319, 371
Medina, 46, 74–5, 81, 117, 140, 142, 160, 319, 363, 371
Megawati Soekarnoputri, 300–4, 308, 310, 358, 367
Melaka, 24, 66–8, 71, 85–6, 89–90, 105, *see also* Malacca
Melayu, 48, 52
-Jambi, 32–3, *see also* Malayu-Jambi
Middle East, 1–6, 8–13, 17, 40, 44, 48, 76, 83–4, 86, 88, 91, 94, 99, 111–5, 129–30, 136, 140–1, 148, 190–1, 199, 235, 240, 250–4, 256, 262, 278, 283–4, 289–90, 305, 307, 320, 324, 340, 350, 352, 359, 362–3, 368–70, 373
Minangkabau, 6, 31, 36, 67, 182–3, 187–91
Moro Islamic Liberation Front (MILF), 345
Moro National Liberation Front (MNLF), 260–4, 270–1, 284, 287, 322–3, 333, 336, 340, 342, 345

Muslim
  community/communities, 4, 8, 98, 111, 146, 180, 191, 260, 310, 319–21, 325–6, 328–30, 332, 334, 339–40, 343, 346
  world, 3, 7–9, 38, 49, 67, 181–2, 230, 250, 253, 260, 282, 312, 319–21, 324, 326, 328, 332–3, 348, 354
  World League, 250, 252–4, 263, 267
Muhammad Rashid Rida, 159, 182, 185–6, 189, 194–5, 290
Muhammadiyah, 290–1, 298, 305, 309, 356, 364, 374

Nahdlatul Ulama (NU), 291, 293, 298, 300, 357, 364, 369
National Mandate Party (PAN), 299, 382
Netherlands East Indies, *see* Netherlands Indies
Netherlands Indies, 5, 106, 115, 136, 138–9, 144, 148, 159, 176–8, 180, 182–3, 187, 189–90, 195, 290, *see also* Dutch Indies
New Order, 9, 293–6, 298–9, 306, 311, 354–6, 359, 364
Nicolo Conti, 94

OIC, *see* Organization of the Islamic Conference
Old Malay, 22
Organization of the Islamic Conference (OIC), 260, 263–4, 332–4, 341, 343
Osama bin Laden, 276, 286, 311–2, 351
Ottoman Empire, 10, 74, 111, 160, 228

Padang, 6, 183–4, 185–7, 378
Padri movement/War, 112, 291
Palembang, 21–2, 36, 177, 202, 212, 222, 234
pan-Islamism, 235
Partai Demokrasi Indonesia-Perjuangan (PDI-P), 300–3, 308, 310

Partai Komunis Indonesia, *see* PKI
Pasai, 24, 39–40, 87, 89–90
pasisir, 4, 111–3, 120–1
Penang, 71, 96, 98, 210, 212, 214, 221–2, 225, 234
Penyengat, 68–9, 76–8
Philippines, 2, 8, 92, 251, 259–61, 263, 270, 275–87, 308–12, 314, 319–23, 326–48
progressive-liberal Islam (PLI), 9, 352, 368–74, 379, 384–5
Prophet Muhammad, 74, 89, 94, 97–8, 111, 113, 156–8, 161–2, 177, 183, 185–7, 230, 233, 237, 241–2, 353–4, 366
Ptolemy, Claudius, 18, 20, 24, 26, 33, 45, 50, 55

Qamar, 29–33, 35–6, 46, 48, 57, *see also* Qmâr *and* Qumr
Qmâr, 28–30, 32–3, *see also* Qamar *and* Qumr
Qumr, 33, 35, 38, 58, *see also* Qamar *and* Qmâr
Qur'an, 11, 90–2, 110, 113, 123, 128, 162, 165–7, 170, 181–2, 186, 257, 262–4, 266–7, 353–4, 358, 365–6, 369, 372–3, 376, 378, *see also* Koran

radical-conservative Islam (RCI), 9, 349–50, 352, 357–60, 363, 365–7, 369–71, 373–4, 376–9, 384
Raffles, Thomas Stamford, 42, 213, 216, 237
Raja Ahmad, 66, 69–76, 80
Raja Ali Haji, 69, 77–8
Raja Haji, 68, 77
Red Sea, 94, 137, 139, 140, 142–3
Revolusi, 291–2, 305, 308
Riau, 3, 65–6, 68–72, 75–6, 78–9, 81, 125
  -Lingga Archipelago, 66–8, 70

Śailendras, 21–2, 25, 32, 52
Salafi movement, 362

Samudra, 35, 38–40, 44, 54, 60, 89
 -Pasai, 38, 87
Sarekat Islam (SI), 160–1, 168, 170, 291–2
Sayyid Mohammad Asad Allah bin Ali bin Ahmad bin Abdallah bin al-Hussayn bin Shahab al-Din (SMAS), *see* SMAS
Sayyid Oesman, 160–2, 169, 171, 173, *see also* Sayyid 'Uthmân
Sayyid 'Uthmân, 58, 177–8, 194, *see also* Sayyid Oesman
Sejarah Melayu, 67, 88–9
shari'a, 4, 123–5, 127–8, 179, 186, 191, 195, 215, 263, 352–4, 356–9, 364, 367–8, 370–3, 377–9, 383
Shaykh Abu Bakar, 92
Shaykh Ahmad Musyafi, 74–5
Shepo, 23–4, 28, 43
SI, *see* Sarekat Islam
Singasari, 36–7
Singapore, 6–7, 66, 68, 70–1, 91, 96–8, 103, 106, 114–5, 125, 128, 137, 144, 157, 159–60, 175, 182, 200–1, 205–6, 208, 210–20, 222–6, 229–34, 236–43, 263, 275–7, 286, 290, 292, 308, 312
SMAS, 7, 250–64, 266–7, 271
Snouck Hurgronje, Christiaan, 4–5, 17, 66, 70, 72–4, 76, 87, 135–50, 153, 161, 167, 178–80, 256, 269
Soeharto, 9, 349–52, 354–6, 359, 379, *see also* Suharto
Soekarno, 292–4, 309, *see also* Sukarno
Sri Lanka, 18, 27, 30–1, 34, 39, 52, 55, 60
Sribuza, 27–30
Śrîvijaya/Srivijaya, 21–4, 27, 30, 32, 39, 48, 52–3, 56, 66, 85
Straits Settlements, 96–7, 139, 200, 210–1, 220–1, 228–9, 231, 233
Suez Canal, 3–4, 10, 65, 76, 96, 115–6, 290

Sufi
 Nakshabandiyya/Naqshabandiyya order, 76, 82, 125–8, 193, 289
 tarekats, 4, 125–6, 289–90
Suharto, 257, 270, 293–9, 308–9, *see also* Soeharto
Sukarno, 252–9, 267, *see also* Soekarno
Sulalat al-Salatin, 43
Sulayman, 93
Sumatra, 2, 21–3, 25, 27, 29, 33, 35–8, 40, 42, 44, 51–3, 82, 86, 89–90, 114–5, 168, 172, 212, 236, 276, 336
 North, 269
 West, 6, 112, 182, 186–7, 291, 377
Surakarta, 117–8, 120–2, 127–8, 133
Suvarnadvîpa, 18, 20, 22, 24, 27, 29, 49, 51–2, 55

Tambralinga, 30–1
Thailand, 8, 87, 92, 101, 320–3, 327, 329–30, 332, 334–46
Tuhfat al-Nafis, 65–6, 69–72, 75, 77

Vasco da Gama, 261

Wahabi, 254, *see also* Wahhabi
Wahhabi, 10, 69, 79, 81, 95, 111–2, 307, *see also* Wahabi
World War
 I, 10, 140, 160, 237
 II, 92, 98, 104, 319–22, 324–7, 331, 336, 342, 346, 348

Yang Dipertuan Muda, 67–9, 77
Yava, 20–1, 23, 28, 48–9, 51–3
Yavadvîpa, 20–1, 24, 26, 28–9, 45, 51
Yemen, 3, 16, 34, 40, 63, 90–1, 105, 198, 212, 231, 260, 305
Yijing, 22, 52
Yogyakarta, 118, 120–3, 127, 133, 306

Zâbaj, 3, 19, 24–30, 33–8, 40, 45–6, 48–9, 54–8, 60